D0312760

U F O s

THE
GREATEST
STORIES

EDITED BY
MARTIN GREENBERG

MJF BOOKS

NEW YORK

Published by MJF Books
Fine Communications
Two Lincoln Square
60 West 66th Street
New York, NY 10023

Library of Congress Catalog Card Number 95-82182
ISBN 1-56731-086-9

Copyright © 1996 Fine Communications, Inc.

All rights reserved. No part of this publication may be reproduced or transmitted in any
form or by any means, electronic or mechanical, including photocopy, recording, or any
information storage and retrieval system, without the prior written permission of the
publisher.

"Fear Is a Business" by Theodore Sturgeon; copyright © 1956 by Theodore Sturgeon. Reprinted by
permission of the Theodore Sturgeon Literary Trust.
"The Venus Hunters" by J.G. Ballard; copyright © 1967, 1995 by J.G. Ballard. Used by permission
of the author and the author's agent, Robin Straus Agency, Inc.
"All the Universe In a Mason Jar" by Joe Haldeman; copyright © 1977 by Joe Haldeman. First
published in Cosmos, 1977. Reprinted by permission of the author.
"Sightings At Twin Mounds" by Gene Wolfe; copyright © 1988 by Gene Wolfe. First appeared in
Storeys from the Old Hotel; reprinted by permission of the author and the author's agent, Virginia
Kidd.
"Or Else" by Henry Kuttner; copyright © 1952, renewed 1980 by C.L. Moore. Reprinted by
permission of Don Congdon Associates, Inc.
"Exposure" by Eric Frank Russell; copyright © 1950 by Eric Frank Rusell. Reprinted by permission
of the author and the author's agents, Jabberwocky Literary Agency, P.O. Box 4558, Sunnyside, NY
11104-0558
"What Is This Thing Called Love?" by Isaac Asimov; copyright © 1961 by Isaac Asimov. From The
Complete Stories of Isaac Asimov, Vol.1 by Isaac Asimov. Used by permission of Doubleday, a
division of Bantam Doubleday Dell Publishing Group, Inc.
"Shadows In the Sun" by Chad Oliver; copyright © 1954 by Chad Oliver, renewed 1982 by Chad
Oliver. Reprinted by permission of the Estate of Chad Oliver, Betty J. Oliver, Executrix.
"Seed of the Gods" by Zach Hughes; copyright © 1974 by Zach Hughes. Reprinted by permission of
the author.
"The Edge of the Sea" by Algis Budrys; copyright © 1958 by Algis Budrys. Reprinted by permission
of the author.
"The Silly Season" by C.M. Kornbluth; copyright © 1950 by C.M. Kornbluth. First published in The
Magazine of Fantasy and Science Fiction. Reprinted by permission of the agent for the author's
Estate, Richard Curtis.

Published by arrangement with Martin H. Greenberg
Manufactured in the United States of America
MJF Books and the MJF colophon are trademarks of Fine Creative Media, Inc.

10 9 8 7 6 5 4 3 2 1

Table of Contents

All the Universe In a Mason Jar

by Joe Haldeman

New Homestead, Florida: 1990.

John Taylor Taylor, retired professor of mathematics, lived just over two kilometers out of town, in a three-room efficiency module tucked in an isolated corner of a citrus grove. Books and old furniture and no neighbors, which was the way John liked it. He only had a few years left on this Earth, and he preferred to spend them with his oldest and most valued friend: himself.

But this story isn't about John Taylor Taylor. It's about his moonshiner, Lester Gilbert. And some five billion others.

This day the weather was fine, so the professor took his stick and walked into town to pick up the week's mail. A thick cylinder of journals and letters was wedged into his box; he had to ask the clerk to remove them from the other side. He tucked the mail under his arm without looking at it, and wandered next door to the bar.

"Howdy, Professor."

"Good afternoon, Leroy." He and the bartender were the only ones in the place, not unusual this late in the month. "I'll take a boilermaker today, please." He threaded his way through a maze of flypaper strips and eased himself into a booth of chipped, weathered plastic.

He sorted his mail into four piles: junk, bills, letters, and journals. Quite a bit of junk; two bills, a letter that turned out to be another bill, and three journals—*Nature, Communications* of the American Society of Mathematics, and a collection of papers delivered at an ASM symposium on topology. He scanned the contributors lists and, as usual, saw none of his old colleagues represented.

"Here y'go." Leroy sat a cold beer and a shot glass of whiskey between *Communications* and the phone bill. John paid him with a five and lit his pipe carefully before taking a sip. He folded *Nature* back at the letters column and began reading.

The screen door slapped shut loudly behind a burly man in wrinkled clean work clothes. John recognized him with a nod; he returned a left-handed V-sign and mounted a bar stool.

"How 'bout a red-eye, Leroy?" Mixture of beer and tomato juice with a dash of Louisiana, hangover cure.

Leroy mixed it. "Rough night, Isaac?"

"Shoo. You don' know." He downed half the concoction in a gulp, and shuddered. He turned to John. "Hey, Professor. What you know about them flyin' saucers?"

1

"Lot of them around a few years ago," he said tactfully. "Never saw one myself."

"Me neither. Wouldn't give you a nickel for one. Not until last night." He slurped the red-eye and wiped his mouth.

"What," the bartender said, "you saw one?"

"*Saw* one. Shoo." He slid the two-thirds-empty glass across the bar. "You wanta put some beer on top that? Thanks.

"We was down the country road seven-eight klicks. You know Eric Olsen's new place?"

"Don't think so."

"New boy, took over Jarmin's plat."

"Oh yeah. Never comes in here; know of him, though."

"You wouldn't hang around no bar neither if you had a pretty little . . . well. Point is, he was puttin' up one of them new stasis barns, you know?"

"Yeah, no bugs. Keeps stuff forever, my daddy-in-law has one."

"Well, he picked up one big enough for his whole avocado crop. Hold on to it till the price is right, up north, like January? No profit till next year, help his 'mortization."

"Yeah, but what's that got to do with the flying—"

"I'm gettin' to it." John settled back to listen. Some tall tale was on the way.

"Anyhow, we was gonna have an old-fashion barn raisin' . . . Miz Olsen got a boar and set up a pit barbecue, the other ladies they brought the trimmin's. Eric, he made two big washtubs of spiced wine, set 'em on ice till we get the barn up. Five, six hours, it turned out (the directions wasn't right), *hot* afternoon, and we just headed for that wine like you never saw.

"I guess we was all pretty loaded, finished off that wine before the pig was ready. Eric, he called in to Samson's and had 'em send out two kegs of Bud."

"Got to get to know that boy," Leroy said.

"Tell me about it. Well, we tore into that pig and had him down to bones an' gristle in twenty minutes. Best god-dern pig *I* ever had, anyhow.

"So's not to let the fire permit go to waste, we went out an' rounded up a bunch of scrap, couple of good-size logs. Finish off that beer around a bonfire. Jommy Parker went off to pick up his fiddle and he took along Midnight Jackson, pick up his banjo. Miz Olsen had this Swedish guitar, one too many strings but by God could she play it.

"We cracked that second keg 'bout sundown and Lester Gilbert—you know Lester?"

Leroy laughed. "Don't I just. He was 'fraid the beer wouldn't hold out, went to get some corn?"

John made a mental note to be home by four o'clock. It was Wednesday; Lester would be by with his weekly quart.

"We get along all right," the bartender was saying. "Figure our clientele don't overlap that much."

"Shoo," Isaac said. "Some of Lester's clientele overlaps on a regular basis.

"Anyhow, it got dark quick, you know how clear it was last night. Say, let me have another, just beer."

Leroy filled the glass and cut the foam off. "Clear enough to see a flyin' saucer, eh?"

"I'm gettin' to it. Thanks." He sipped it and concentrated for a few seconds on tapping tobacco into a cigarette paper. "Like I say, it got dark fast. We was sittin' around the fire, singin' if we knew the words, drinkin' if we didn't—"

" 'Speck you didn't know many of the songs, yourself."

"Never could keep the words in my head. Anyhow, the fire was gettin' a mite hot on me, so I turned this deck chair around and settled down lookin' east, fire to my back, watchin' the moon rise over the government forest there—"

"Hold on now. Moon ain't comin' up until after midnight."

"You-God-damn-*right* it ain't!" John felt a chill even though he'd seen it coming. Isaac had a certain fame as a storyteller. "That wan't *nobody's* moon."

"Did anybody else see it?" John asked.

"Ev'rybody. Ev'rybody who was there—and one that wasn't. I'll get to that.

"I saw that thing and spilled my beer gettin' up, damn near trip and fall in the pit. Hollered 'Lookit that goddamn thing!' and pointed, jumpin' up an' down, and like I say, they all did see it.

"It was a little bigger than the moon and not quite so round, egg-shaped. Whiter than the moon, an' if you looked close you could see little green and blue flashes around the edge. It didn't make no noise we could hear, and was movin' real slow. We saw it for at least a minute. Then it went down behind the trees."

"What could it of been?" the bartender said. "Sure you wan't all drunk and seein' things?"

"No way in hell. You know me, Leroy, I can tie one on ev'y now and again, but I just plain don't get that drunk. Sure thing I don't get that drunk on beer an' *wine!*"

"And Lester wasn't back with the 'shine yet?"

"No . . . an' that's the other part of the story." Isaac took his time lighting the cigarette and drank off some beer.

"I'm here to tell you, we was all feelin' sorta spooky over that. Hunkered up around the fire, lookin' over our shoulders. Eric went in to call the sheriff, but he didn't get no answer.

"Sat there for a long time, speculatin'. Forgot all about Lester, suppose to be back with the corn.

"Suddenly we hear this somethin' crashin' through the woods. Jommy sprints to his pickup and gets out his over-and-under. But it's just Lester. Runnin' like the hounds of Hell is right behind him.

"He's got a plywood box with a half-dozen mason jars in her, and from ten feet away he smells like Saturday night. He don't say a word; sets that box down, not too gentle, jumps over to Jommy and grabs that gun away from him and aims it at the government woods, and pulls both triggers, just *boom-crack* 20-gauge buckshot and a .30-caliber rifle slug right behind.

"Now Jommy is understandable pissed off. He takes the gun back from Lester and shoves him on the shoulder, follows him and shoves him again; all the time askin' him, just not too politely, don't he know he's too drunk to handle a firearm? and don't he know we could all get busted, him shootin' into federal land? and just in general, what the Sam Hill's goin' on, Lester?"

He paused to relight the cigarette and take a drink. "Now Lester's just takin' it and not sayin' a thing. How 'bout *that?*"

"Peculiar," Leroy admitted.

Isaac nodded. "Lester, he's a good boy but he does have one hell of a temper. Anyhow, Lester finally sits down by his box and unscrews the top off a full jar—they's one with no top but it looks to be empty—and just gulps down one whole hell of a lot. He coughs once and starts talkin'."

"Surprised he could talk at all," John agreed. He always mixed Lester's corn with a lot of something else.

"And listen—that boy is sober like a parson. And he says, talkin' real low and steady, that he seen the same thing we did. He describes it, just exactly like I tole you. But he sees it on the ground. Not in the air."

Isaac passed the glass over and Leroy filled it without a word. "He was takin' a long-cut through the government land so's to stay away from the road. Also he had a call of Nature and it always felt more satisfyin' on government land.

"He stopped to take care of that and have a little drink and then suddenly saw this light. Which was the saucer droppin' down into a clearing, but he don't know that. He figures it's the shriff's copter with its night lights on, which don't bother him much, 'cause the sheriff's one of his best customers."

"That a fact?"

"Don't let on I tole you. Anyways, he thought the sheriff might want a little some, so he walks on toward the light. It's on the other side of a little rise; no underbresh but it takes him a few minutes to get there.

"He tops the rise and there's this saucer—bigger'n a private 'copter, he says. He's stupefied. Takes a drink and studies it for a while. Thinks it's probably some secret government thing. He's leanin' against a tree, studying . . . and then it dawns on him that he ain't alone."

Isaac blew on the end of his cigarette and shook his head. "I 'spect you ain't gonna believe this—not sure I do myself—but I can't help that, it's straight from Lester's mouth.

"He hears something on the other side of the tree where he's leanin'. Peeks around the tree and—there's this *thing.*

"He says it's got eyes like a big cat, like a lion's, only bigger. And it's a big animal otherwise, about the size of a lion, but no fur, just wrinkled hide like a rhino. It's got big shiny claws that it's usin' on the tree, and a mouthful of big teeth, which it displays at Lester and growls.

"Now Lester, he got nothin' for a weapon but about a quart of Dade County's finest—so he splashes that at the monster's face, hopin' to blind it, and takes off like a bat.

"He gets back to his box of booze, and stops for a second and looks back. He can see the critter against the light from the saucer. It's on its hind legs, weavin' back and forth with its paws out, just roarin'. Looks like the booze works, so Lester picks up the box, ammunition. But just then that saucer light goes out.

"Lester knows good and God damn well that that damn thing can see in the dark, with them big eyes. But Les can see our bonfire, a klick or so west, so he starts runnin' holdin' on to that box of corn for dear life.

"So he comes in on Eric's land and grabs the gun and all that happens. We pass the corn around a while and wash it down with good cold beer. Finally we got up enough Dutch courage to go out after the thing.

"We got a bunch of flashlights, but the only guns were Jommy's over-and-under and a pair of antique flintlock pistols that Eric got from his dad. Eric loaded 'em and give one to me, one to Midnight. Midnight, he was a sergeant in the Asia war, you know, and he was gonna lead us. Eric himself didn't think he could shoot a animal. Dirt farmer (good boy, though)."

"Still couldn't get the sheriff? What about the Guard?"

"Well, no. Truth to tell, everybody—even Lester—was halfway convinced we ain't seen nothin' real. Eric had got to tellin' us what went into that punch, pretty weird, and the general theory was that he'd whipped up a kind of halla, hallo—"

"Hallucinogen," John supplied.

"That's right. Like that windowpane the old folks take. No offense, Professor."

"Never touch the stuff."

"Anyhow, we figured that we was probably seein' things, but we'd go out an' check, just in case. Got a bunch of kitchen knives and farm tools, took the ladies along too.

"Got Midnight an' Lester up in the front, the rest of us stragglin' along behind, and we followed Lester's trail back to where he seen the thing."

Isaac took a long drink and was silent for a moment, brow furrowed in thought. "Well, hell. He took us straight to that tree and I'm a blind man if there weren't big ol' gouges all along the bark. And the place did smell like Lester's corn.

"Midnight, he shined a light down to where Lester'd said the saucer was, and sure enough, the bresh was all flat there. He walked down to take a closer look—all of us gettin' a little jumpy now—and God damn if he didn't bump right into it. That saucer was there but you flat couldn't see it.

"He let out one hell of a yelp and fired that ol' flintlock down at it, point-blank. Bounced off, you could hear the ball sing away. He come back up the rise just like a cat on fire; when he was clear I took a pot shot at the damn thing, and then Jommy he shot it four, six times. Then there was this kind of wind, and it was gone."

There was a long silence. "You ain't bullshittin' me," Leroy said. "This ain't no story."

"No." John saw that the big man was pale under his heavy tan. "This ain't no story."

"Let me fix you a stiff one."

"No, I gotta stay straight. They got some newspaper boys comin' down this afternoon. How's your coffee today?"

"Cleaned the pot."

John stayed for one more beer and then started walking home. It was hot, and he stopped halfway to rest under a big willow, reading a few of the *Nature* articles. The one on the Ceres probe was fascinating; he reread it as he ambled the rest of the way home.

So his mind was a couple of hundred million miles away when he walked up the path to his door and saw that it was slightly ajar.

First it startled him, and then he remembered that it was Lester's delivery day. He always left the place unlocked (there were ridge-runners but they weren't interested in old books), and the moonshiner probably just left his wares inside.

He checked his watch as he walked through the door; it was not quite three. Funny. Lester was usually late.

No mason jar in sight. And from his library, a snuffling noise.

The year before, some kind of animal—the sheriff had said it was probably a bear—had gotten into his house and made a shambles of it. He eased open the end-table drawer and took out the Walther P-38 he had taken from a dead German officer, half a century before. And as he edged toward the library, the thought occurred to him that the 50-year-old ammunition might not fire.

It was about the size of a bear, a big bear.

Its skin was pebbly gray, with tufts of bristle. It had two arms, two legs, and a stiff tail to balance back on.

The tail had a serrated edge on top, that looked razor-sharp. The feet and hands terminated in pointed black claws. The head was vaguely saurian; too many teeth and too large.

As he watched, the creature tore a page out of Fadeeva's *Computational Methods of Linear Algebra,* stuffed it in his mouth and chewed. Spat it out. Turned to see John standing at the door.

It's probably safe to say that any other resident of New Homestead, faced with this situation, would either have started blazing away at the apparition, or would have fainted. But John Taylor Taylor was nothing if not a cool and rational man, and had besides suffered a lifelong addiction to fantastic literature. So he measured what was left of his life against the possibility that this fearsome monster might be intelligent and humane.

He laid the gun on a writing desk and presented empty hands to the creature, palms out.

The thing regarded him for a minute. It opened its mouth, teeth beyond counting, and closed it. Translucent eyelids nictated up over huge yellow eyes, and slid back. Then it replaced the Fadeeva book and duplicated John's gesture.

In several of the stories John had read, humans had communicated with alien races through the medium of mathematics, a pure and supposedly universal language. Fortunately, his library sported a blackboard.

"Allow me to demonstrate," he said with a slightly quavering voice as he crossed to the board, "the Theorem of Pythagorus." The creature's eyes followed him, blinking. "A logical starting place. Perhaps. As good as any," he trailed off apologetically.

He drew a right triangle on the board, and then drew squares out from the sides that embraced the right angle. He held the chalk out to the alien.

The creature made a huffing sound, vaguely affirmative, and swayed over to the blackboard. It retracted the claws on one hand and took the chalk from John.

It bit off one end of the chalk experimentally, and spit it out.

Then it reached over and casually sketched in the box representing the square of the hypotenuse. In the middle of the triangle it drew what was obviously an equals sign: ~

John was ecstatic. He took the chalk from the alien and repeated the curly line. He pointed at the alien and then at himself: equals.

The alien nodded enthusiastically and took the chalk. It put a slanted little line through John's equals sign.

Not equals.

It stared at the blackboard, tapping it with the chalk; one universal gesture. Then, squeaking with every line, it rapidly wrote down:

$$
\begin{array}{c}
1 \\
\sim \\
\text{---}1 \\
\sim \\
1 \sim 1 - 1 \sim 1 \\
\sim \\
1 \sim 1 - 1 \sim 1 \\
\sim \\
1
\end{array}
$$

John studied the message. Some sort of tree diagram? Perhaps a counting system. Or maybe not mathematical at all. He shrugged at the creature. It flinched at the sudden motion, and backed away growling.

"No, no." John held his palms out again. "Friends."

The alien shuffled slowly back to the blackboard and pointed to what it had just written down. Then it opened its terrible mouth and pointed at that. It repeated the pair of gestures twice.

"Oh." Eating the Fadeeva and the chalk. "Are you hungry?" It repeated the action more emphatically.

John motioned for it to follow him and walked toward the kitchen. The alien waddled slowly, its tail a swaying counterweight.

He opened the refrigerator and took out a cabbage, a package of catfish, an avocado, some cheese, an egg, and a chafing dish of leftover green beans, slightly dried out. He lined them up on the counter and demonstrated that they were food by elaborately eating a piece of cheese.

The alien sniffed at each item. When it got to the egg, it stared at John for a long time. It tasted a green bean but spat it out. It walked around the kitchen in a circle, then stopped and growled a couple of times.

It sighed and walked into the living room. John followed. It went out the front door and walked around behind the module. Sighed again and disappeared, from the feet up.

John noted that where the creature had disappeared, the grass was crushed in a large circle. That was consistent with Isaac's testimony: it had entered its invisible flying saucer.

The alien came back out with a garish medallion around its neck. It looked like it was made of rhinestones and bright magenta plastic.

It growled and a voice whispered inside his brain: "Hello? Hello? Can you hear me?"

"Uh, yes. I can hear you."

"Very well. This will cause trouble." It sighed. "One is not to use the translator with a Class 6 culture except under the most dire of emergency. But I am starve. If I do not eat soon the fires inside me will go out. Will have to fill out many forms, may they reek."

"Well . . . anything I can do to help . . ."

"Yes." It walked by him, back toward the front door. "A simple chemical is the basis for all my food. I have diagrammed it." He followed the alien back into the library.

"This is hard." He studied his diagram. "To translator is hard outside of basic words. This top mark is the number 'one.' It means a gas that burns in air."

"Hydrogen?"

"Perhaps. Yes, I think. Third mark is the number 'eight,' which means a black rock that also burns, but harder. The mark between means that in very small they are joined together."

"A hydrogen-carbon bond?"

"This is only noise to me." Faint sound of a car door slamming, out on the dirt road.

"Oh, oh," John said. "Company coming. You wait here." He opened the door a crack and watched Lester stroll up the path.

"Hey, Perfesser! You ain't gonna believe what—"

"I know, Les. Isaac told me about it down at Leroy's." He had the door open about twelve centimeters.

Lester stood on the doormat, tried to look inside. "Somethin' goin' on in there?"

"Hard to explain, uh, I've got company."

Lester closed his mouth and gave John a broad wink. "Knew you had it in you, Doc." He passed the mason jar to John. "Look, I come back later. Really do want yer 'pinion."

"Fine, we'll do that. I'll fix you a—"

A taloned hand snatched the mason jar from John.

Lester turned white and staggered back. "Don't move a muscle, Doc. I'll git my gun."

"No, wait! It's friendly!"

"Food," the creature growled. "Yes, friend." The screw-top was unfamiliar but only presented a momentary difficulty. The alien snapped it off, glass and all, with a flick of the wrist. It dashed the quart of raw 'shine down its throat.

"Ah, fine. So good. Three parts food, one part water. Strange flavor, so good." It pushed John aside and waddled out the door.

"You have more good food?"

Lester backed away. "You talkin' to me?"

"Yes, yes. You have more of this what your mind calls 'corn'?"

"I be damned." Lester shook his head in wonder. "You are the ugliest sumbitch I ever did see."

"This is humor, yes. On my world, egg-eater, you would be in cage. To frighten children to their amusement." It looked left and right and pointed at Lester's beat-up old Pinto station wagon. "More corn in that animal?"

"Sure." He squinted at the creature. "You got somethin' to pay with?"

"Pay? What is this noise?"

Lester looked up at John. "Did he say what I thought he said?"

John laughed. "I'll get my checkbook. You let him have all he wants."

When John came back out, Lester was leaning on his station wagon, sipping from a jar, talking to the alien. The creature was resting back on its tail, consuming food at a rate of about a quart every thirty seconds. Lester had showed it how to unscrew the jars.

"I do not lie," it said. "This is the best food I have ever tasted."

Lester beamed. "That's what I tell ev'ybody. You can't *git* that in no store."

"I tasted only little last night. But could tell from even that. Have been seeking you."

It was obvious that the alien was going to drink all three cases. Twenty-five dollars per jar, John calculated, thirty-six jars. "Uh, Les, I'm going to have to owe you part of the money."

"That's okay, Doc. He just tickles the hell outa me."

The alien paused in mid-jar. "Now I am to understand, I think. You own this food. The Doc gives to you a writing of equal value."

"That's right," John said.

"You, the Les, think of things you value. I must be symmetry . . . I must have a thing you value."

Lester's face wrinkled up in thought. "Ah, there is one thing, yes. I go." The alien waddled back to his ship.

"Gad," Lester said. "If this don't beat all."

(Traveling with the alien is his pet treblig. He carries it because it always emanates happiness. It is also a radioactive creature that can excrete any element. The alien gives it a telepathic command. With an effort that scrambles television reception for fifty miles, it produces a gold nugget weighing slightly less than one kilogram.)

The alien came back and handed the nugget to Lester. "I would take some of your corn back to my home world, yes? Is this sufficient?"

The alien had to wait a few days while Lester brewed up enough 'shine to fill up his auxiliary food tanks. He declined an invitation to go to Washington, but didn't mind talking to reporters.

Humankind learned that the universe was teeming with intelligent life. In this part of the Galaxy there was an organization called the Commonality—not really a government; more like a club. Club members were given such useful tools as faster-than-light travel and immortality.

All races were invited to join the Commonality once they had evolved morally above a certain level. Humankind, of course was only a Class 6. Certain individuals went as high as 5 or as low as 7 (equivalent to the moral state of an inanimate object), but it was the average that counted.

After a rather grim period of transition, the denizens of Earth settled down to concentrating on being good, trying to reach Class 3, the magic level.

It would take surprisingly few generations. Because humankind had a constant reminder of the heaven on Earth that awaited them, as ship after ship drifted down from the sky to settle by a still outside a little farm near New Homestead, Florida: for several races, the gourmet center of Sirius Sector.

The Edge of the Sea

by Algis Budrys

The Overseas Highway, two narrow white lanes on yellowed old concrete piers, lay close to the shallow water, passed over the little key, and went on.

All afternoon the sea had been rising. Long, greasy faced, green swells came in from the Atlantic Ocean and broke on the sharp rocks with a sudden upsurge of surf. At midday the water had been far down among the coral heads. But now it was in the tumbled limestone blocks and concrete prisms that had been dumped there to build up the key. In a little while it would be washing its spume over the highway itself, and it might well go farther, with the increasing wind.

It was dark with twilight, and darker with clouds thick as oil smoke covering the sun over the Gulf of Mexico. The gulf was stirring too, and bayous were flooding in Louisiana. But it was over the Atlantic that the hurricane was spinning. It was the broad, deep, deadly ocean that the tide and wind were pushing down through the gloom onto the side of the key where Dan Henry was struggling grimly, his massive back and shoulders naked and running with spray.

His pale eyes were red-rimmed with salt and his hide slashed shallowly in a dozen places where he had lost his balance on the tumbled stones and fallen. He had been lurching through the surf all afternoon, working frantically to save what he had seen, leaden and encrusted, rolling ponderously at the edge of the water. His shirt, the seat covers from his car—the fan belt too—and what few scraps of rope and wire had been in the trunk, all had gone for him to twist into an incredible rag of a hawser.

The men who built the Overseas Highway on the old railroad right-of-way had built up the little key, but it was still no more than a hundred feet in diameter. If the thing trapped on the rocks had chosen any other islet to wash against, there would have been a reasonable chance of saving it. But there was no one living here, and nothing to use for tools or anchors. The thing was rolling and grinding against the rocks, too heavy to float but too bulky to resist the push of storm-driven water. There were bright silver gouges on its thick metal flanks, and in a little while it would break up or break free, and be lost either way. The rope—the stubborn, futile rope passed around the two stubbly struts at its nose and wrapped around the great concrete block it was now butting at with brute persistence—was as much use as though Dan Henry had been a spider and tried to hold this thing in a hurriedly created web. But he had had to try, and he was trying now in another way. He jammed the soles of his feet against one concrete block and pushed his bare shoulders against another. With his belly ridged and his thighs bulging, his face contorted and his hands clenched, he was trying to push another massive

11

piece of stone into place behind the plunging metal thing, though his blood might erupt from his veins and the muscles tear open his flesh.

The thing was as thick through as a hogshead, and as long as two men. There was a thick-lipped, scarred opening a foot across at one end, where the body rounded sharply in a hemispheric compound curve. There were three stumpy fins rooted in the curve, their tips not extending beyond the bulge of the body, and two struts at the blunt nose like horns on a snail but bent forward so that the entire thing might have been fired out of a monstrous cannon or launched from the tubes of some unimaginable submarine. There were no visible openings, no boltheads, no seams. The entire thing might have been cast of a piece—might have been solid, except for the tube in the stern—and though barnacles clung to it and moss stained it, though the rocks gouged it and other blows had left their older scars on its pitted surface, still the thing was not visibly damaged.

Dan Henry strained at the rock, and sand grated minutely at its base. But the world turned red behind his eyes, and his muscles writhed into venomous knots, and his breath burned his chest with the fury of fire. The sea broke against him and ran into his nose and mouth. The wind moaned, and the water hissed through the rocks, crashing as it came and gurgling as it drew back. The thing groaned and grated with each sluggish move. The day grew steadily darker.

Dan Henry had stopped his car on the key at noon, pulling off the highway onto the one narrow space of shoulder. He had opened the glove compartment and taken out the waxed container of milk and the now stale sandwich he had bought in Hallandale, above Miami, at ten that morning. He lit a cigarette and unwrapped the sandwich, and began to eat. The milk had turned warm in the glove compartment and acquired an unpleasant taste, but Dan Henry had never cared how his food tasted. He paid no attention to it as he chewed the sandwich and drank the milk between drags on the cigarette. He had bought the food when he stopped for gas, and when he finished it he planned to go on immediately, driving until he reached Key West.

There was nothing specific waiting for him there. Nothing in his life had ever been waiting for him anywhere. But everywhere he went, he went as directly and as efficiently as possible because that was his nature. He was a physically powerful, reasonably intelligent, ugly man who drew his strength from a knowledge that nothing could quite overcome him. He asked no more of the world. He was thirty years old, and had been a construction foreman, a police officer, an MP sergeant in Germany, and a long-haul trailer-truck driver. In addition to these things he had been born into a derrick rigger's family in Oklahoma and raised in his father's nomadic, self-sufficient tradition.

When he first saw the dull color of metal down among the rocks, he got out of the car to see what it was. He was already thinking in terms of its possible usefulness when he reached the thing. Once near it, the idea of salvage rights came naturally.

Looking at it, he felt immediately that it had to be a military instrument of some kind. The Navy, he knew, was constantly firing rockets from Cape Kennedy, up in central Florida. But the longer he looked at the thing, the longer he doubted that possibility. The thing was too massive, too obviously built to take the kind of vicious punishment it was receiving at the hands of the sea, to be the light, expendable shell that was a missile prototype or a high-altitude test rocket. There were tons of metal in it, and the barnacles were thick on it. He wondered how long it had been surging along the bottom, urged and tumbled by the great hidden forces of the ocean, drifting this way and that until finally this morning the first high tide had heaved it up here to lie caught and scraping on the rocks, steaming as it dried under the early sun.

He did not know what it was, he decided finally. Rocket, torpedo, shell, bomb, or something else, whatever it was, it was valuable and important. The Navy or the Army or Air Force would need it or want it for something.

There was nothing on it to mark it as anyone's property. If anything had ever been written or engraved on that hull, it was gone now. He began to think of how he might establish his rights until he could reach a Navy installation of some kind. The only reason he had for going to Key West was that he had a friend in the sponge-diving business down there. The friend did not know he was coming, so there was no reason not to delay for as long as this business might take him.

He had begun with nothing more than that to urge him on, but as the afternoon grew, the sea and the thing between them had trapped him.

The thing lay awash with half its length over the usual high watermark, and even when he found it, at low tide, the water curled among the rocks above it. He had thought about that too, but he had not thought that a hurricane might have taken an unexpected turn during the night, while he drove his old car without a radio to tell him so. Only when the clouds turned gray and the water swirled around his knees like a pack of hounds grown hungry did he stop for a moment and look out to sea.

He had been clearing the smaller rocks away from around the thing and piling them in an open-ended square enclosing its forward sections, and had been scraping a clean patch in the barnacles with a tire iron. It had been his intention to make it obvious someone was working on the thing, so he could then leave it and report it with a clear claim. The few cars going by on the highway had not stopped or slowed down—there was no place to stop, with his car on the bit of shoulder, and no real reason to slow down—and after a while the cars had stopped coming entirely.

It was that, telling him the storm had probably caused the highway to be blocked off at either end, together with the look of the sea, that made him go up to the car and try to make a hawser. And by then he could not have left the thing. It was too obvious that a man had begun a job of work here. If he left it now, it would be too plain that someone had let himself be backed down.

If he had gotten in his car and driven away, he would not have been Dan Henry.

The water was almost completely over the thing now. He himself was working with the waves breaking over his head, trying to dislodge him. More important, the thing was rocking and slipping out of its trap.

The next nearest key was a third of a mile away, bigger than this one, but still uninhabited. The nearest inhabited place was Greyhound Key, where the rest stop was for the buses, and that was out of sight. It would be battened down, and probably evacuated. Dan Henry was all alone, with the highway empty above him and the sea upon him.

He set his back once more, and pushed against the concrete block again. If he could wedge the thing, even a storm tide might not be able to take it away from him. He could untangle his homemade rope and put the fan belt back on his car. Then he could drive away to some place until the storm died down.

The blood roared in Dan Henry's ears, and the encrusted concrete block opened the hide over his shoulders. A coughing grunt burst out of his mouth. The block teetered—not much, but it gave a little way. Dan Henry locked his knees and braced his back with his palms, pushing his elbows against the block, and when the next wave threw its pressure into the balance, he pushed once more. The block slipped suddenly away from him, and he was thrown aside by the wave, flung into the wet rocks above. But the thing was wedged. It could roll and rear as much as it wanted to, but it could not flounder back into the sea. Dan Henry lay over a rock, and wiped the back of his hand across his bloody mouth in satisfaction.

It was over. He could get out of here now, and hole up somewhere. After the storm, he would come back and make sure it was still here. Then he would make his claim, either at one of the little Navy stations along the chain of keys, or at the big base at Boca Chica. And that would be that, except for the check in the mail. The bruises and breaks in his skin would heal over, and become nothing more than scars.

He took his rope off the thing and took it apart far enough to pick out the fan belt. He let the rest of it wash away, shredded. As he got out of the surging water at last, he scowled slightly because he wondered if the car's spark plugs weren't wet.

It was dark now. Not quite pitch-black, for the hurricane sky to the west was banded by a last strip of sulfur-colored light at the horizon, but dark enough so that his car was only a looming shape as he climbed up to it. Then, suddenly, the wet finish and the rusty chrome of the front bumper were sparkling with the first pinpoint reflections of faraway lamps. He turned to look southward down the highway, and saw a car coming. As it came nearer, its headlights let him see the clouds of spray that billowed across the glistening road, and the leaping white heads of breakers piling up on the piers and rebounding vertically to the level of the highway. The storm was building up even more quickly than he'd thought. He wondered what kind of damned fool was crazy enough to drive the stretches where the highway crossed open water between keys, and had his answer when a spotlight abruptly reached out and fingered him and his car. Either the state or the county police were out looking to make sure no one was trapped away from shelter.

The police car pulled up, wet and hissing, half blocking the highway, and the driver immediately switched on his red roof-beacon, either through force of habit or force of training, even though there was no oncoming traffic to warn. The four rotating arms of red light tracked monotonously over the road, the key, and the water. By their light, Dan Henry realized for the first time that it was raining furiously. The spotlight was switched off, and the headlights pointed away, up the highway. It was the red beacon that lit the scene and isolated the two men inside its color.

The officer did not get out of the car. He waited for Dan Henry to come around to his side, and only then cranked his window down halfway.

"Trouble with the car?" he asked, hidden behind the reflection on the glass. Then he must have thought better of it, seeing Dan Henry's broken skin. He threw the door open quickly, and slid out with his hand on the bone-gripped butt of his plated revolver. He was thick-bodied, with a burly man's voice and brusqueness, and he kept his eyes narrowed. "What's the story here, Mac?"

Dan Henry shook his head. "No trouble. I was down on the rocks. Waves threw me around some."

The officer's uniform pants and leather jacket were already sodden. Water ran down his face, and he wiped it annoyedly out of his eyes. "What were you doin' down there? No brains?" He watched carefully, his hand firm on his gun.

Dan Henry had been a policeman himself. He was not surprised at the officer's attitude. A policeman was paid to be irritated by anything that didn't have a simple answer.

"I've got something down there I was salvaging," he said reasonably. "Storm caught me at it and knocked me around some before I got finished." Telling about it made him realize he was tired out. He hoped this business with the policeman would be over in a hurry, so that he could fix his car and get into its shelter. The wind was chilly, and the constant impact of driven water on his skin was beginning to make him numb.

The officer risked a quick glance down at the thrashing surf before he brought his hard eyes back to Dan Henry. "I don't see nothin'. What kind of thing was it? What're you carryin' that belt around for?"

"It's metal," Dan Henry said. "Big. Never seen anything just like it before. I was using the belt to hold it."

The officer scowled. "What's holdin it now? What d'you mean, big? How big? And how come I can't see it?"

"I pushed a rock behind it," Dan Henry said patiently. "It's damn near as big as a car. And it's under water, now."

"Buddy, that don't begin to sound like a likely story." The policeman pulled his gun out of the holster and held it down alongside his thigh. "What kind of a lookin' thing is it?"

"Kind of like a rocket, I guess."

"Now, why the hell didn't you say so!" the policeman growled, relaxing just a little bit. "That makes sense. It'll be one of those Navy jobs. They've got 'em droppin' in the ocean like flies. But you ain't goin' to get anything out of it, Buddy. That's government property. You're supposed to turn it in. It's your duty."

"I don't think so."

"What d'you mean, you don't think so?" The policeman's gun arm was tense again.

"It doesn't look like a Navy rocket. Doesn't look like anybody's rocket, that I know of. I said it was *kind* of like a rocket. Don't know what it is, for sure." Now Dan Henry was growing angry himself. He didn't like the way things were going. He kept his attention carefully on the gun.

"Know all about rockets, do you?"

"I read the papers. This thing isn't just a piece. It isn't the bottom stage or the top stage. It's one thing, and it never was part of anything bigger. And it's been in the water maybe a couple of years without getting broken up. You show me a Navy rocket that's like that."

The policeman looked at him. "Maybe you're right," he said slowly. "Tell you what—suppose you just step over here and put my spotlight on it. Reach through the window." He stepped back casually.

Dan Henry reached around and switched the spot on. He swept it down across the water, a little startled to see how far up the breakers had come. Under the light, the water was a venomous green, full of foam, rain-splotched and furiously alive. A gust of wind rocked the car sharply, and the light with it. The pale beam shot over the sea before it fell back, reaching beyond the swinging cross of red from the roof beacon, and out there the lashing waves disappeared in a mist of rain.

He found the thing, finally, after having to hunt for it. For an instant he thought it had been swept away after all, and felt a stab of sharp anger. But it was still there, heaving insensately under the waves, with only the dim, broad mottling of its back near enough to the surface to be seen at all, that and a constant stirring in the water, roiling it like an animal. "There it is." He was surprised how relieved he felt. "See it?"

"Yeah. Yeah, I seen enough of it," the officer said. "You got somethin' down there, all right." There was a sudden hardness in his voice that had been waiting all along for him to make the decision that would bring it completely out. "I got my gun on you, buddy. Just step back from that car easy. Anybody foolin' around out here in a hurricane must want somethin' awful bad. If that somethin's a Navy rocket, I guess I know what kind of a son of a bitch that would be."

"Jesus Christ," Dan Henry whispered to himself. He was angry with the fine-drawn kind of rage that is almost a pleasure. And not because the cop thought he was a Commie, either, Dan Henry suddenly realized, but because he persisted in not understanding about the rocket. Or whatever it was.

He turned around with a jump. The fan belt in his hand whipped out with all the strength in his arm and all the snap in his wrist, and snatched the cop's gun out of his hand. It skittered across the wet concrete of the highway, and Dan Henry pounced after it. He scooped it up with a scrape of his fingertips, and crouched with the muzzle pointed dead at the cop's belly.

"Back off," he said. "Back off. You're not takin' that thing away from me. I sweated blood to hang on to it, and you're not goin' to come along and throw me in jail to get it away."

The cop retreated watchfully, his hands up without his being told, and waited for his chance. Dan Henry backed him up the highway until the cop was past the cars, and opened the door of his own car. He threw the gun inside, together with the belt. He slammed the door and said, "You can get that back later. Or you can try and take it away from me now, barehanded." He was shaking with the tension in his bunched shoulders, and his arms were open wide. He was crouched, his broad chest deep as his lungs hunted for more and more oxygen to wash the rush of blood his heart was driving through his veins. The red flood of the revolving beacon on the police car swept over him in regular flashes.

"I'll wait," the cop said.

"Now," Dan Henry said, "I want to use your radio. I want you to call in and report this. Only I want you to report it to the Navy before you call your headquarters."

The cop looked at him with a puzzled scowl. "You on the level?" he asked, and Dan Henry could see him wondering if he hadn't made a mistake, somewhere, in his thinking about what was going on here. But Dan Henry had no more time for him. The wind was a steady, strong pressure that made him brace his left leg hard against it. The water flying across the highway was coming in solid chunks, instead of spray, and the two cars were rocking badly on their springs. The rain was streaming over them, leaving the officer's jacket a baggy, clinging mess and pounding on the top of Dan Henry's head. The sea was smashing violently into the highway piers, thundering to the wind's howl, and even here on solid ground the shock of the impacts was coming clearly up through Dan Henry's bones.

His throat was raw. Bit by bit, he and the officer had had to raise their voices until they had been shouting at each other without realizing it. "Get in the car and do it!" he yelled, and the officer came forward as he backed away to give him room.

The policeman got into his car, with Dan Henry standing watchfully a little behind the open door frame, and switched on his radio. "Tell them where we are," Dan Henry said. "Tell them my name—Daniel Morris Henry—tell them what I said about its not being one of their rockets—and tell them I'm claiming salvage rights. Then you tell them the rest any way you see it."

The officer grudgingly turned the dials away from their usual settings. After a minute, he picked his microphone out of the dashboard hanger and began calling Boca Chica in a stubborn voice. At intervals, he said. "Over," and threw the Receive switch. They heard the peculiar, grating crackle of radiotelephone static, trapped in the small speaker. And only that.

"Look, buddy," the policeman said at last, "we're not goin' to get any answer. Not if we ain't got one by now. Boca Chica radio may be knocked out. Or maybe my transmitter's shorted, with all this wet. Could be anything." He jerked his head toward the water. "How much longer you want us to stay out here?" Probably because he had seen so many hurricanes, he was beginning to grow nervous.

"Try it again," Dan Henry said. He watched the officer closely, and couldn't see him doing anything wrong. Dan Henry didn't know the Boca Chica frequency; that was where the trouble might be. But he'd used a police radio often enough so that any other trick wouldn't have gotten by him.

The officer called Boca Chica for another five minutes. Then he stopped again. "No dice. Look, buddy, you've had it. Maybe you're just a guy looking for some salvage money, like you say you are. Maybe not. But there's goin' to be waves coming across this road in a little while. Why don't we get out of here and straighten things out when this blows over?"

Dan Henry set his jaw. "Get the vibrator out of that radio. Do it." Now he had no choice. If he went with the cop, that was that. They'd throw him in some jail for resisting arrest and assaulting an officer, and keep him there until they were good and ready to let him out. By then, whatever happened to the thing down here, somebody would have figured out some way to get that Navy check instead of him. The only thing to do was to cripple the cop's radio and send him down the highway until he reached a phone. There was no guarantee that radio wouldn't work on the police frequency.

Maybe the cop would call the Navy right after he called his headquarters. Or maybe, even if he didn't, some higher brass at the headquarters would report to the Navy. Either way—if you believed it was a Navy rocket or if you didn't—it was government business. Then, maybe, the Navy would get here before the cops did. Or soon enough afterward so he'd still be here to talk to them. Once he got taken away from here, that chance was gone.

On that decision, he was ready to cling to a hundred-foot key in the middle of an Atlantic hurricane. "Let's have that vibrator. Right now."

The officer looked at him, and reached slowly under the dash. He fumbled in the narrow space where the radio hung, and pulled the sealed aluminum cylinder out of its socket. But he was getting ready to grab for Dan Henry if he could reach him quickly enough.

"Okay," Dan Henry said, "drop it on the road and get out of here. You can get it back along with your gun. And just in case you get some brains in your head, when you get to a phone, call the Na—"

The policeman had dropped the vibrator, and the wind had rolled it under Dan Henry's Chevrolet. Dan Henry had been in the act of letting the open police car door close, when a sharp thread of brilliant violet fire punched up from down in the green water, through the red light, up through the rain, up through the black clouds, and out to the stars beyond.

"There's something *in* that thing!" the officer blurted.

Dan Henry threw the door shut. "Get out of here, man!"

Down in the drowned rocks, an arc hissed between the two struts in the thing's nose. The water leaped and bubbled around it, but for all the breakers could do, the blaze of light still illuminated the thing and the rocks it ground against, turning the sea transparent; and from the crown of the arc the thin violet column pointed without wavering, without dispersing, straight as a line drawn from hell to heaven.

The police car's tires smoked and spun on the pavement. "I'll get help," the officer shouted dimly over the squeal and the roar of his engine. Then he had traction and the car shot away, headlights slashing, glimmering in the rain and the spray, lurching from side to side under the wind's hammer, roof beacon turning at its unvarying pace, the siren's howl lost quickly in the boom of the water. And Dan Henry was left in the violet-lanced darkness.

Without the windbreak of the police car in front of him, he was pushed violently backward until his own car's fender stopped him. Water struck his eyes, and the night blurred. He bent forward and rubbed his face until the raw ache of the salt was dulled to a steady throbbing, and then he staggered across the highway to the guard rail on the Atlantic side. The tops of the incoming waves washed over his shoes, just as the surf at noon had lapped at him, twelve feet below.

The rain and the spray streamed over him. He cupped one hand over his nose, to breathe, and hung on the rail.

There was nothing more to see. The pillar of light still shot up from the arc, and the bulk of the thing loomed, gross and black, down there in the water. It was feet below the surface now, cushioned from the first smash of the waves, and it stirred with a smooth, regular motion like a whale shark in a tank.

The radio, he thought. It had felt the radio in the police car. Nothing else had happened to bring it to life at that particular moment. It had waited a little—perhaps analyzing what it had encountered, perhaps then noticing the regular flash of the car's roof beacon for the first time. And for the first time since the day, years ago, when it entered the sea, it had found a reason for sending out a signal.

To where? Not to him or the policeman. The light was not pointed toward the highway. It went up, straight up, going out of sight through the clouds as his eyes tried to follow it before the lash of water forced his head down again.

There was no one inside the thing, Dan Henry thought. There couldn't be. He had scraped on the side with regular, purposeful strokes, clearing an exactly square patch, and gotten no response. And the thing had lain in the ocean a long time, sealed up, dragging its armored hide over the bottom as the currents pushed and pulled it, rolling, twisting, seamless, with only those two horns with which to feel the world about it.

He could be wrong, of course. Something could be alive in there, still breathing in some fantastic way from a self-contained air supply, eating tiny amounts of stored food, getting rid of its wastes somehow. But he didn't see how. It didn't seem logical that anything would trap itself like that, not knowing if it was ever going to escape.

He could be wrong about it all. It might not have been reacting to anything that happened on the highway. It might be ignoring everything outside itself, and following some purpose that had nothing to do with this world or its people. But whether it was that, or whether he was at least partly right, Dan Henry wondered what was sending things to drop down on the Earth and make signals to the stars.

The water came higher. It came up the key too quickly to split and go around it, and spilled over the highway to plunge into the rocks on the gulf side. It broke halfway up the side of his car. He remembered the policeman's vibrator. That would be far to the west of him by now, skipping at a thrown stone's velocity over waves whose tops were being cut off by the wind. Dan Henry's mouth twisted in a numb grimace. Now he'd have to buy one. They probably wouldn't let him get away that cheaply. They could make that stick for a robbery charge. And destroying public property. While on the other hand, if he was swept off this key they wouldn't even have to pay for his burial. He laughed drunkenly.

A wave broke over him. He had made a sling for himself by knotting the legs of his dungarees around one of the guardrail uprights, and when the wave was past, he lolled naked with the bunched tops of the dungarees cutting into his chest, under his arms. The wind worked at him now, with a kind of fury he had never felt by simply putting his head out through the window of a speeding car, and then the next wave came. It was warm, but the wind evaporating it as soon as he was exposed again made his skin crawl and his teeth chatter. He reached behind him with a wooden arm and felt the knot in the dungaree legs to make sure it was holding. The pressure had tightened it into a small hard lump.

That was good, at any rate. That and the blessed practicality of the engineers who built the highway. When they laid the roadway where the hurricane-smashed railroad had been, they had cut the rusted rails up with torches, set the stumps deep in the concrete, and welded the guardrails together out of T-shaped steel designed to hold a locomotive's weight.

Dan Henry grinned to himself. The rail would hold. The dungarees would hold, or the trademark was a liar. Only about Dan Henry was there any doubt. Dan Henry—hard, sure Dan Henry, with his chest being cut in half, with his torn skin being torn again as the waves beat him against the highway, with his head going silly because he was being pounded into raw meat.

Dear God, he thought, am I doing this for *money?* No, he thought as a wave filled his nostrils, no, not any more. When that thing turned its light on and I didn't jump in the car with that cop, that's when we found out I wasn't doing it for the money. For what? God knows.

He floundered half over on his side, arched his neck, and looked at the violet arrow through the clouds. Signal, you bastard! Go ahead and signal! Do anything. As long as I know you're still there. If you can stay put, so can I.

Well, what *was* he doing this for? Dan Henry fought with the sling that held him, trying to take some of the pressure off his chest. God knew, but it was up to Dan Henry to find out for himself.

It wasn't money. All right—that was decided. What was left—vanity? Big Dan Henry—big, strong, Dan Henry—take more than a hurricane to stop big, strong, wonderful Dan Henry . . . was that the way his thoughts were running?

He croaked a laugh. Big, strong Dan Henry was lying here limp as a calico doll, naked as a baby, praying his pants wouldn't rip. The storm had washed the pride out of him as surely as it had his first interest in the salvage money.

All right, *what,* then! He growled and cursed at his own stupidity. Here he was, and he didn't even know why. Here he was, being bludgeoned to death, being drowned, being torn apart by the wind. He was stuck out here now, and nobody could save him.

A wave roared over the highway and struck his car a blow that sent a hubcap careening off into the darkness. The car tilted onto the gulf-side guardrail. The rail bellied outward, and the car hung halfway over the rocks on the other side. Successive waves smashed into it, exploding in spray, and the guardrail groaned in the lull after each strike. Dan Henry watched it dully in the violet light, with the water sluicing down over his head and shoulders for a moment before the wind found it and tore it away in horizontal strings of droplets.

The car's door panels had already been pushed in, and the windows were cracked and bulged. Now the exposed floorboards were being hammered. The muffler was wrenched out.

With the next smash of solid water, the horizontal rail broke its weld at one end and the car heeled forward to the right, impaling its radiator on an upright. It hung there, gradually tearing the radiator out of its brackets, spilling rusty water for one instant before a wave washed it clean, scraping its front axle down the sharp edge of the roadway, breaking loose pieces of the concrete and raising its left rear wheel higher and higher. The radiator came free with a snap like a breaking tooth, and the car dropped suddenly, its front end caught by the edge of the left wheel, kept from falling only by the straining uprights still jammed against it farther back on the right side. The hood flew back suddenly and was gone with a twang in one gust of wind.

Am I going to have to buy that cop a new gun, too? Dan Henry thought, and in that moment the wind began to die. The water hesitated. Three waves rolled across the road slowly, much higher than when the wind was flattening them, but almost gentle. The rain slackened. And then the eye of the storm had moved over him, and he had calm.

He pushed himself to his feet at last, after he sagged out of the hold the dungarees had on his chest. He leaned against the guardrail and stared woodenly at the ocean and the thing.

The beam went up out of sight, a clean, marvelously precise line. But down at the surface, the sea was finally hiding the thing, and making a new noise that had none of a storm-sea's clean power. It filled his ears and unnerved him.

With the wind and the pressure gone, the waves were leaping upward, clashing against each other, rebounding, colliding again, peaking sharply. Dan Henry could hear the highway over the water booming faintly as the waves slammed up against its underside. But he could actually see very little. It had grown sharply darker, and what he saw were mostly the tops of the exploding waves, glimmering pale violet.

The thing was buried deep where it lay at the foot of the key, and the arc that had diffused most of the light was visible only as a fitful glow that shifted and danced. The violet beam seemed to spring into life of itself at the plunging surface, and it kept most of its light compressed within itself.

Dan Henry swayed on the guardrail. It was stifling hot. The thick mugginess filled his lungs and choked him. He lolled his head back. The clouds were patchy overhead, and the stars shone through in places.

There was a sudden high-pitched chime, and a concentric circle of coruscating ice-blue flame came hurtling down the beam from the thing. It came out of the sky and shot into the water, and when it touched the glimmer of the arc there was another chime, this time from the thing, and this time the water quivered. The violet beam flickered once, and a red halo spat up with a crackle, traveling slowly. When it was a hundred feet over Dan Henry's head it split in two, leaving one thin ring moving at the old rate, and a larger one that suddenly doubled its speed until it split again, doubled its speed and split again, accelerated again, and so blazed upward along the violet beam's axis, leaving a spaced trail of slowly moving lesser rings behind it. They hung in the air, a ladder to the stars. Then they died out slowly, and before they had stopped glowing the violet beam was switched off.

The sky was abruptly empty, and the thing lay quiescent in the water once more. Dan Henry blinked at the flashes swimming across his eyes. It was pitch dark. He could barely see the white of swirling water as it dashed itself into the rocks at his feet.

Except that far up the highway, coming toward him, were two headlights with a swinging red beacon just above them.

The police car was plastered with wet leaves and broken palm fronds. The policeman slammed it to a halt beside him, and flung the door open. He stopped long enough to turn his head and say, "Jesus Christ! He's still here! He ain't gone!" to someone in the front seat with him, and then he jumped out. "What happened?" he asked Dan Henry. "What was that business with the lights?"

Dan Henry looked at him. "You made it," he mumbled.

"Yeah, I made it. Got to this Navy skywatch station. Phone was out, so I couldn't call in to headquarters. Found this Navy professor up there. Brought him down with me when the eye came over. He figures we got maybe twenty minutes more before the other side of the hurricane comes around."

The other man had slid out of the car. He was a thin, bony-faced man with rimless glasses. He was dressed in a badly fitted tropical suit that was pleated with dampness. He looked at Dan Henry's purpled chest, and asked, "Are you all right?"

"Sure."

The man twitched an eyebrow. "I'm assigned to the satellite tracking station north of here. Where is this thing?"

Dan Henry nodded toward it. "Down there. It got an answer to its signal, acknowledged, and switched off. That's what I think, anyhow."

"You do, eh? Well, you could be right. In any case, we don't have much time. I'll notify the naval district commandant's office as soon as the telephones are working again, but I want a quick look at it now, in case we lose it."

"We're not going to lose it," Dan Henry growled.

The professor looked at him sharply. "What makes you sure?"

"I wedged it," Dan Henry said with a tight note in his voice. "I almost ruined myself and I almost drowned, but I wedged it. I took a gun away from a cop to keep it from getting left here without anybody to watch it. And I stayed here and got almost drowned, and almost cut in half, and almost beat to death against this highway here, and *we're not going to lose it now.*"

"I . . . see," the professor said. He turned to the policeman. "If you happen to have some sedatives in your first-aid kit, they might be useful now," he murmured.

"Might have something. I'll look," the policeman said.

"And put your spotlight on the thing, please," the professor added, peering over the guardrail. "Though I don't suppose we'll see much."

The yellow beam of the spotlight slid over the top of the water. If it penetrated at all, it still did not reach any part of the thing. The policeman hunted for it, sweeping back and forth until Dan Henry made an impatient sound, went over to him, and pointed it straight. "Now, leave it there. That's where it is."

"Yeah? I don't see anythin' but water."

"That's where it is," Dan Henry said. "Haven't been here all this time for nothin'." He went back to the railing, but there was still nothing to see.

"You're sure that's where it is?" the professor asked.

"Yes. It's about ten feet down."

"All right," the professor sighed. "Tell me as much as you can about its activities."

"I think it's a sounding rocket," Dan Henry said. "I think somebody from some place sent that thing down here a while ago to find out things. I don't know what those things are. I don't know who that somebody is. But I'm pretty sure he lost it somehow, and didn't know where it was until it signaled him just now. I don't know why it worked out that way. I don't know why the rocket couldn't get its signal through before this, or why it didn't go home."

"You think it's of extraterrestrial origin, then?"

Dan Henry looked at the professor. "You don't think so?"

"If I did, I would be on my way to district headquarters at this moment, hurricane or no hurricane," the professor said testily.

"You don't believe it?" Dan Henry persisted.

The professor grew uneasy. "No."

"Wouldn't you *like* to believe it?"

The professor looked quickly out to sea.

"Here," the policeman said, handing Dan Henry a flat brown half-pint bottle. "Sedative." He winked.

Dan Henry knocked the bottle out of the cop's hand. It broke on the pavement.

"Look up!" the professor whispered.

They turned their heads. Something huge, flat, and multiwinged was shadowed faintly on the stars.

"Oh, Lord," the officer said.

There was a burst of chiming from the thing down in the water, and violet pulses of light came up through the water and burst on the underside of the thing up in the sky.

Answering darts of tawny gold came raining down. The thing in the water stirred, and they could see the rocks move. "Tractor rays," the professor said in a husky voice. "Theoretically impossible."

"What's it going to do?" the policeman asked.

"Pick it up," the professor answered. "And take it back to wherever it comes from."

Dan Henry began to curse.

The thing in the sky slipped down, and they could feel the air throb. After a moment, the sound came to them—a distant, rumbling purr, and a high metallic shrieking.

The thing in the water heaved itself upward. It struggled against the rocks.

"We'd better get back," the professor said.

The distant sound grew stronger and beat upon their ears. The professor and the policeman retreated to the car.

But Dan Henry did not. He straightened his back and gathered his muscles. As the tawny fire came down, he leaped over the guardrail into the water.

He swam with grim fury, thrown and sucked by the water, sputtering for breath, his feet pounding. Even so, he would not have reached the thing. But the water humped in the grip of the force that clutched at the thing, and the waves collapsed. Dan Henry's arms bit through the water with desperate precision, and just before the thing broke free, he was upon it.

"No, sir," he grunted, closing his hand on one of the struts. "Not without me. We've been through too much together." He grinned coldly at the hovering ship as they rose to meet it.

Fear Is A Business

by Theodore Sturgeon

Josephus Macardle Phillipso is a man of destiny and he can prove it. His books prove it. The Temple of Space proves it.

A man of destiny is someone who is forced into things—big things—willy, as the saying goes, nilly. Phillipso, just for example, never meant to get into the Unidentified (except by Phillipso) Aerial Object business. This is to say, he didn't sit down like some of his less honest (according to Phillipso) contemporaries and say "I think I'll sit down and tell some lies about flying saucers and make some money." Everything that happened (Phillipso ultimately believed) just happened, and happened to happen to him. Might have been anybody. Then, what with one thing leading to another the way it does, well, you burn your forearm on an alibi and wind up with a Temple.

It was, on looking back on it (something which Phillipso never does any more), an unnecessary alibi devised for inadequate reasons. Phillipso merely calls the beginnings "inauspicious" and lets it go at that. The fact remains that it all started one night when he tied one on for no special reason except that he had just been paid his forty-eight dollars for writing advertising promotion copy for the Hincty Pincty Value Stores, and excused his absence on the following day with a story about a faulty lead on the spark coil of his car which took him most of the night to locate, and there he was stranded in the hills on the way back from a visit to his aging mother. The next night he did visit his aging mother and on the way back his car unaccountably quit and he spent most of the night fiddling with the electrical system until he discovered, just at dawn, a—well, there it was. At a time like that you just can't tell the truth. And while he was pondering various credible alternatives to veracity, the sky lit up briefly and shadows of the rocks and trees around him grew and slid away and died before he could even look up. It was a temperature inversion or a methane fireball or St. Elmo's fire or maybe even a weather balloon—actually that doesn't matter. He looked up at where it already wasn't, and succumbed to inspiration.

His car was parked on a grassy shoulder in a cut between two bluffs. Thick woods surrounded a small clearing to his right, a sloping glade sparsely studded with almost round moraine boulders, of all sizes. He quickly located three, a foot or so in diameter, equally spaced, and buried to approximately the same depth—*i.e.,* not much, Phillipso being merely an ingenious man, not an industrious one. These three he lifted out, being careful to keep his crepe-soled shoes flat on the resilient grass and to leave as few scuff-marks and indentations as possible. One by one he took the stones into the woods and dropped them into an evacuated foxhole and shoved some dead branches in on top of them. He then ran to his car and from the trunk got a blowtorch which he had borrowed to fix a leak in the sweated joint of a very old-fashioned bathtub in his mother's house, and with it thoroughly charred the three depressions in the ground where the boulders had lain.

Destiny had unquestionably been at work from the time he had beered himself into mendacity forty-eight hours before. But it became manifest at this point, for after Phillipso had licked his forearm lightly with the tongue of flame from the torch, extinguished the same and put it away, a car ground up the hill toward him. And it was not just any car. It belonged to a Sunday supplement feature writer named Penfield who was not only featureless at the moment, but who had also seen the light in the sky a half hour earlier. It may have been Phillipso's intention to drive into town with his story, and back with a reporter and cameraman, all to the end that he could show a late edition to his boss and explain this second absence. Destiny, however, made a much larger thing of it.

Phillipso stood in the graying light in the middle of the road and flapped his arms until the approaching car stopped. "They," he said hoarsely, "almost killed me."

From then on, as they say in the Sunday supplement business, it wrote itself. Phillipso offered not one blessed thing. All he did was answer questions, and the whole thing was born in the brain of this Penfield, who realized nothing except that here was the ideal interview subject. "Came down on a jet of fire, did it? Oh—*three* jets of fire." Phillipso took him into the glade and showed him the three scorched pits, still warm. "Threaten you, did they? Oh—all Earth. Threatened all Earth." Scribble scribble. He took his own pictures too. "What'd you do, speak right up to them? Hm?" Phillipso said he had, and so it went.

The story didn't make the Sunday supplements, but the late editions, just as Phillipso had planned, but much bigger. So big, as a matter of fact, that he didn't go back to his job at all; he didn't need it. He got a wire from a publisher who wanted to know if he, as a promotion writer, might be able to undertake a book.

He might and he did. He wrote with a crackling facility *(The first word in thrift, the last word in value* was his, and was posted all over the Hincty Pincty chain just as if it meant something) in a style homely as a cowlick and sincere as a banker's nameplate. *The Man Who Saved the Earth* sold two hundred and eighty thousand copies in the first seven months.

So the money started to come in. Not only the book money—the other money. This other money came from the end-of-the-world people, the humanity-is-just-too-wicked people, the save-us-from-the-spacemen folk. Clear across the spectrum, from people who believed that if God wanted us to fly through space we'd have been born with tailfins to people who didn't believe in anything but Russians but would believe anything of them, people said "Save us!" and every crack on the pot dripped gold. Hence the Temple of Space, just to regularize the thing, you know, and then the lectures, and could Phillipso help it if half the congre—uh, club members called them services?

The sequel happened the same way, just appendixes to the first book, to handle certain statements he had made which some critics said made him fall apart by his own internal evidence. *We Need Not Surrender* contradicted itself even more, was a third longer, sold three hundred and ten thousand in the first nine weeks, and brought in so much of that other money that Phillipso registered himself as an institute and put all the royalties with it. The temple itself began to show signs of elaboration, the most spectacular piece of which was the war-surplus radar basket of a battleship that went round and round all the time. It wasn't connected to a damn thing but people felt that Phillipso had his eyes open. You could see it, on a clear day, from Catalina, especially at night after the orange searchlight was installed to rotate with it. It looked like a cosmic windshield wiper.

Phillipso's office was in the dome under the radar basket, and was reachable only from the floor below by an automatic elevator. He could commune with himself in there just fine, especially when he switched the elevator off. He had a lot of communing to do, too, sometimes detail stuff, like whether he could sustain a rally at the Coliseum and where to apply the ten-thousand-dollar grant from the Astrological Union which had annoyingly announced the exact size of the gift to the press before sending him the check. But his main preoccupation was another book, or what do I do for an encore? Having said that we are under attack, and then that we can rally and beat 'em, he needed an angle. Something new, preferably born by newsbeat out of cultural terror. And soon, too; his kind of wonder could always use another nine days.

As he sat alone and isolated in the amnion of these reflections, his astonishment can hardly be described at the sound of a dry cough just behind him, and the sight of a short sandy-haired man who stood there. Phillipso might have fled, or leapt at the man's throat, or done any number of violent things besides, but he was stopped cold by a device historically guaranteed to stem all raging authors: "I have," said the man, holding up one volume in each hand, "read your stuff."

"Oh, really?" asked Phillipso.

"I find it," said the man, "logical and sincere."

Phillipso looked smilingly at the man's unforgettable bland face and his unnoticeable gray suit. The man said, "Sincerity and logic have this in common: neither need have anything to do with truth."

"Who are you?" demanded Phillipso immediately. "What do you want and how did you get in here?"

"I am not, as you put it, in here," said the man. He pointed upward suddenly, and in spite of himself Phillipso found his eyes following the commanding finger.

The sky was darkening, and Phillipso's orange searchlight slashed at it with increasing authority. Through the transparent dome, just to the north, and exactly where his visitor pointed, Phillipso saw the searchlight pick out a great silver shape which hovered perhaps fifty feet away and a hundred feet above the Temple. He saw it only momentarily, but it left an afterimage in his retinae like a flashbulb. And by the time the light had circled around again and passed the place, the thing was gone. "I'm in that," said the sandy-haired man. "Here in this room I'm a sort of projection. But then," he sighed, "aren't we all?"

"You better explain yourself," said Phillipso loudly enough to keep his voice from shaking, "or I'll throw you out of here on your ear."

"You couldn't. I'm not here to be thrown." The man approached Phillipso, who had advanced away from his desk into the room. Rather than suffer a collision, Phillipso retreated a step and another, until he felt the edge of his desk against his glutei. The sandy-haired man, impassive, kept on walking—to Phillipso, through Phillipso, Phillipso's desk, Phillipso's chair, and Phillipso's equanimity, the last-named being the only thing he touched.

"I didn't want to do that," said the man some moments later, bending solicitously over Phillipso as he opened his eyes. He put out his hand as if to assist Phillipso to his feet. Phillipso bounced up by himself and cowered away, remembering only then that, on his own terms, the man could not have touched him. He crouched there, gulping and glaring, while the man shook his head regretfully. "I *am* sorry, Phillipso."

"Who are you, anyway?"gasped Phillipso.

For the first time the man seemed at a loss. He looked in puzzlement at each of Phillipso's eyes, and then scratched his head. "I hadn't thought of that," he said musingly. "Important, of course, of course. Labeling." Focusing his gaze more presently at Phillipso, he said, "We have a name for you people that translates roughly to *'Labelers.'* Don't be insulted. It's a categorization, like *'biped'* or *'omnivorous.'* It means the mentality that verbalizes or it can't think."

"Who are you?"

"Oh, I do beg your pardon. Call me—uh, well, call me Hurensohn. I suggest that because I know you have to call me something, because it doesn't matter what you call me, and because it's the sort of thing you'll be calling me once you find out why I'm here."

"I don't know what you're talking about."

"Then by all means let's discuss the matter until you do."

"D-discuss what?"

"I don't have to show you that ship out there again?"

"Please," said Phillipso ardently, "don't."

"Now look," said Hurensohn gently, "there is nothing to fear, only a great deal to explain. Please straighten up and take the knots out of your thorax. That's better. Now sit down calmly and we'll talk the whole thing over. *There,* that's *fine!*" As Phillipso sank shakily into his desk chair, Hurensohn lowered himself into the easy chair which flanked it. Phillipso was horrified to see the half-inch gap of air which, for five seconds or so, separated the man from the chair. Then Hurensohn glanced down, murmured an apology, and floated down to contact the cushion somewhat more normally. "Careless, sometimes," he explained. "So many things to keep in mind at once. You get interested, you know, and next thing you're buzzing around without your light-warp or forgetting your hypno-field when you go in swimming, like that fool in Loch Ness."

"Are you really a—a—an extraulp?"

"Oh, yes, indeed. Extraterrestrial, extrasolar, extragalactic—all that."

"You don't, I mean, I don't see any—"

"I know I don't look like one. I don't look like this"—he gestured down his gray waistcoat with the tips of all his fingers—"either. I could show you what I really do look like, but that's inadvisable. It's been tried." He shook his head sadly, and said again, "Inadvisable."

"Wh-what do you want?"

"Ah. Now we get down to it. How would you like to tell the world about me—about us?"

"Well, I already—"

"I mean, the *truth* about us."

"From the evidence I already have—" Phillipso began with some heat. It cooled swiftly. Hurensohn's face had taken on an expression of unshakable patience; Phillipso was suddenly aware that he could rant and rave and command and explain from now until Michaelmas, and this creature would simply wait him out. He knew, too (though he kept it well below the conscious area) that the more he talked the more he would leave himself open to contradiction—the worst kind of contradiction at that: quotes from Phillipso. So he dried right up and tried the other tack. "All right," he said humbly. "Tell me."

"Ah . . ." It was a long-drawn-out sound, denoting deep satisfaction. "I think I'll begin by informing you that you have, quite without knowing it, set certain forces in motion which can profoundly affect mankind for hundreds, even thousands, of years."

"Hundreds," breathed Phillipso, his eye beginning to glow. "Even thousands."

"That is not a guess," said Hurensohn. "It's a computation. And the effect you have on your cultural matrix is—well, let me draw an analogy from your own recent history. I'll quote something: *'Long had part of the idea; McCarthy had the other part. McCarthy got nowhere, failed with his third party, because he attacked and destroyed but didn't give. He appealed to hate, but not to greed, no what's-in-it-for-me, no porkchops.'* That's from the works of a reformed murderer who now writes reviews for the New York *Herald Tribune.*"

"What has this to do with me?"

"You," said Hurensohn, "are the Joseph McCarthy of saucer-writers."

Phillipso's glow increased. "My," he sighed.

"And," said Hurensohn, "you may profit by his example. If that be—no, I've quoted enough. I see you are not getting my drift, anyway. I shall be more explicit. We came here many years ago to study your interesting little civilization. It shows great promise—so great that we have decided to help you."

"Who needs help?"

"Who needs help?" Hurensohn paused for a long time, as if he had sent away somewhere for words and was waiting for them to arrive. Finally, "I take it back. I won't be more explicit. If I explained myself in detail I would only sound corny. Any rephrasing of the Decalogue sounds corny to a human being. Every statement of every way in which you need help has been said and said. You are cursed with a sense of rejection, and your rejection begets anger and your anger begets crime and your crime begets guilt; and all your guilty reject the innocent and destroy their innocence. Riding this wheel you totter and spin, and the only basket in which you can drop your almighty insecurity is an almighty fear, and anything that makes the basket bigger is welcome to you. . . . Do you begin to see what I am talking about, and why I'm talking to you?

"Fear is your business, your stock in trade. You've gotten fat on it. With humanity trembling on the edge of the known, you've found a new unknown to breed fear in. And this one's a honey; it's infinite. Death from space . . . and every time knowledge lights a brighter light and drives the darkness back, you'll be there to show how much wider the circumference of darkness has become. . . . Were you going to say something?"

"I am *not* getting fat," said Phillipso.

"Am I saying anything?" breathed the sandy-haired man. "Am I here at all?"

In all innocence Phillipso pointed out, "You said you weren't."

Hurensohn closed his eyes and said in tones of sweet infinite patience, "Listen to me, Phillipso, because I now fear I shall never speak to you again. Whether or not you like it—and you do, and we don't—you have become the central clearinghouse for the Unidentified Aerial Object. You have accomplished this by lies and by fear, but that's now beside the point—you accomplished it. Of all countries on earth, this is the only one we can effectively deal with; the other so-called Great Powers are constitutionally vindictive, or impotent, or hidebound, or all three. Of all the people in this country we could deal with—in government, or the great foundations, or the churches—we can find no one who could overcome the frenzy and foolishness of your following. You have forced us to deal with you."

"My," said Phillipso.

"Your people listen to you. More people than you know listen to your people—frequently without knowing it themselves. You have something for everyone on earth who feels small, and afraid, and guilty. You tell them they are right to be afraid, and that makes them proud. You tell them that the forces ranged against them are beyond their understanding, and they find comfort in each other's ignorance. You say the enemy is irresistible, and they huddle together in terror and are unanimous. And at the same time you expect yourself, implying that you and you alone can protect them."

"Well," said Phillipso, "if you have to deal with me . . . isn't it so?"

"It is not," said Hurensohn flatly. "'*Protect*' presupposes '*attack.*' There is no attack. We came here to help."

"Liberate us," said Phillipso.

"Yes. *No!*" For the first time Hurensohn showed a sign of irritation. "Don't go leading me into your snide little rat-shrewd pitfalls, Phillipso! By liberate I meant make free; what you meant is what the Russians did to the Czechs."

"All right," said Phillipso guardedly. "You want to free us. Of what?"

"War. Disease. Poverty. Insecurity."

"Yes," said Phillipso. "It's corny."

"You don't believe it."

"I haven't thought about it one way or the other yet," said Phillipso candidly. "Maybe you can do all you say. What is it you want from me?"

Hurensohn held up his hands. Phillipso blinked as *The Man Who Saved the Earth* appeared in one of them and *We Need Not Surrender* in the other. He then realized that the actual volumes must be in the ship. Some of his incipient anger faded; some of his insipid pleasure returned. Hurensohn said, "These. You'll have to retract."

"What do you mean retract?"

"Not all at once. You're going to write another book, aren't you? Of course;

you'd have to." There was the slightest emphasis on *"you'd"* and Phillipso did not like it. However, he said nothing. Hurensohn went on: "You could make new discoveries. Revelations, if you like. Interpretations."

"I couldn't do that."

"You'd have all the help in the world. Or out of it."

"Well, but what for?"

"To draw the poison of those lies of yours. To give us a chance to show ourselves without getting shot on sight."

"Can't you protect yourselves against that?"

"Against the bullets, certainly. Not against what pulls the triggers."

"Suppose I go along with you."

"I told you! No poverty, no insecurity, no crime, no—"

"No Phillipso."

"Oh. You mean, what's in it for you? Can't you see? You'd make possible a new Eden, the flowering of your entire species—a world where men laughed and worked and loved and achieved, where a child could grow up unafraid and where, for the first time in your history, human beings would understand one another when they spoke. You could do this—just you."

"I can see it," said Phillipso scathingly. "All the world on the village green and me with them, leading a morris dance. I couldn't live that way."

"You're suddenly very cocky, Mister Phillipso," said Hurensohn with a quiet and frightening courtesy.

Phillipso drew a deep breath. "I can afford to be," he said harshly. "I'll level with you, bogeyman." he laughed unpleasantly. "Good, huh. Bogey. That's what they call you when they—"

"—get us on a radar screen. I know, I know. Get to the point."

"Well. All right then. You asked for it." He got to his feet. "You're a phony. You can maybe do tricks with mirrors, maybe even hide the mirrors, but that's it. If you could do a tenth of what you say, you wouldn't have to come begging. You'd just. . . . do it. You'd just walk in and take over. By God I would."

"You probably would," said Hurensohn, with something like astonishment. No, it was more like an incredulous distaste. He narrowed his eyes. For a brief moment Phillipso thought it was part of his facial expression, or the beginning of a new one, and then he realized it was something else, a concentration, a—

He shrieked. He found himself doing something proverbial, unprintable, and not quite impossible. He didn't want to do it—with all his mind and soul he did not want to, but he did it nontheless.

"If and when I want you to," said Hurensohn calmly, "you'll do that in the window of Bullock's Wilshire at high noon."

"Please . . ."

"I'm not doing anything," said Hurensohn. He laughed explosively, put his hands in his jacket pockets, and—worst of all, he watched. "Go to it, boy."

"Please!" Phillipso whimpered.

Hurensohn made not the slightest detectable move, but Phillipso was suddenly free. He fell back into his chair, sobbing with rage, fear, and humiliation.

When he could find a word at all, it came out between the fingers laced over his scarlet face, and was, "Inhuman. That was . . . inhuman."

"Uh-huh," agreed Hurensohn pleasantly. He waited until the walls of outrage expanded enough to include him, recoil from him, and return to the quivering Phillipso, who could then hear when he was spoken to. "What you've got to understand," said Hurensohn, "is that we don't do what we can do. We can, I suppose, smash a planet, explode it, drop it into the sun. You can, in that sense, eat worms. You don't, though, and wouldn't. In your idiom you *couldn't*. Well then, neither can we force humanity into anything without its reasoned consent. You can't understand that, can you? Listen: I'll tell you just how far it goes. We couldn't force even *one* human to do what we want done. You, for example."

"You-you just did, though."

Hurensohn shuddered—a very odd effect, rather like that on a screen when one thumps a slide projector with the heel of one's hand. "A demonstration, that's all. Costly, I may add. I won't get over it as soon as you will. To make a point, you might say. I had to eat a bedbug." Again the flickering shudder. "But then, people have gone farther than that to put an idea over."

"I could refuse?" Phillipso said, timidly.

"Easily."

"What would you do to me?"

"Nothing."

"But you'd go ahead and—"

Hurensohn was shaking his head as soon as Phillipso began to speak. "We'd just go. You've done too much damage. If you won't repair it, there's no way for us to do it unless we use force, and we can't do that. It seems an awful waste, though. Four hundred years of observation. . . . I wish I could tell you the trouble we've gone to, trying to watch you, *learn* you, without interfering. Of course, it's been easier since Kenneth Arnold and the noise he made about us."

"Easier?"

"Lord, yes. You people have a talent—really, a genius for making rational your unwillingness to believe your own eyes. We got along famously after the weather-balloon hypothesis was made public. It's so easy to imitate a weather balloon. Pokey, though. The greatest boon of all was that nonsense about temperature inversions. It's quite a trick to make a ship behave like automobile headlights on a distant mountain or the planet Venus, but temperature inversions?" He snapped his fingers. "Nothing to it. Nobody understands 'em so they explain everything. We thought we had a pretty complete tactical manual on concealment, but did you see the one the U.S. Air Force got out? Bless 'em! It even explains the mistakes we make. Well, most of them, anyway. That idiot in Loch Ness—"

"Wait, wait!" Phillipso wailed. "I'm trying to find out what I'm supposed to do, what will happen, and you sit there and go *on* so!"

"Yes, yes of course. You're quite right. I was just blowing words over my tongue to try to get the taste of you out of my mouth. Not that I really have a mouth, and that would make a tongue sort of frustrated, wouldn't it? Figure of speech, you know."

"Tell me again. This Paradise on earth—how long is it supposed to take? How would you go about it?"

"Through your next book, I suppose. We'd have to work out a way to counteract your other two without losing your audience. If you jump right into line and say how friendly and wise we aliens are, the way Adamski and Heard did, you'll only disappoint your followers. I know! I'll give you a weapon against these— uh—bogeymen of yours. A simple formula, a simple field generator. We'll lay it out so anyone can use it, and bait it with some of your previous nonsense—beg pardon, I might have meant some of your previous statements. Something guaranteed to defend Earth against the—uh—World Destroyers." He smiled. It was rather a pleasant sight. "It would, too."

"What do you mean?"

"Well, if we claimed that the device had an effective range of fifty feet and it actually covered, say, two thousand square miles, and it was easy and cheap to build, and the plans were in every copy of your new book . . . let's see now, we'd have to pretend to violate a little security, too, so the people who aren't afraid would think they were stealing . . . hmmm."

"Device, device—what device?"

"Oh, a—" Hurensohn came up out of his reverie. "Labeling again, dammit. I'll have to think a minute. You have no name for such a thing."

"Well, what is it supposed to do?"

"Communicate. That is, it makes complete communication possible."

"We get along pretty well."

"Nonsense! You communicate with labels—words. Your words are like a jumble of packages under a Christmas tree. You know who sent each one and you can see its size and shape, and sometimes it's soft or it rattles or ticks. But that's all. You don't know exactly what it means and you won't until you open it. That's what this device will do—open your words to complete comprehension. If every human being, regardless of language, age or background, understood exactly what every other human being wanted, and knew at the same time that he himself was understood, it would change the face of the earth. Overnight."

Phillipso sat and thought that one out. "You couldn't bargain," he said at length. "You couldn't—uh—explain a mistake, even."

"You could explain it," said Hurensohn. "It's just that you couldn't excuse it."

"You mean every husband who—ah—flirted, every child who played hooky, every manufacturer who—"

"All that."

"Chaos," whispered Phillipso. "The very structure of—"

Hurensohn laughed pleasantly. "You know what you're saying, Phillipso. You're saying that the basic structure of your whole civilization is lies and partial truths, and that without them it would fall apart. And you're quite right." He chuckled again. "Your Temple of Space, just for example. What do you think would happen to it if all your sheep knew what their shepherd was and what was in the shepherd's mind?"

"What are you trying to do—tempt me with all this?"

Most gravely Hurensohn answered him, and it shocked Phillipso to the marrow when he used his first name to do it. "I am, Joe, with all my heart I am. You're right about the chaos, but such a chaos should happen to mankind or any species like it. I will admit that it would strike civilization like a mighty wind, and that a great many structures would fall. But there would be no looters in the wreckage, Joe. No man would take advantage of the ones who fell."

"I know something about human beings," Phillipso said in a flat, hurt voice. "And I don't want 'em on the prowl when I'm down. Especially when they don't have anything. God."

Hurensohn shook his head sadly. "You don't know enough, then. You have never seen the core of a human being, a part which is not afraid, and which understands and is understood." Hurensohn searched his face with earnest eyes.

"Have you?"

"I have. I see it now. I see it in you all. But then, I see more than you do. You could see as much; you all could. Let me do it, Joe. Help me. Help me, *please.*"

"And lose everything I've worked so hard to—"

"Lose? Think of the gain! Think of what you'd do for the whole world! Or— if it means any more to you—turn the coin over. Think of what you'll carry with you if you don't help us. Every war casualty, every death from preventable disease, every minute of pain in every cancer patient, every stumbling step of a multiple sclerosis victim, will be on your conscience from the moment you refuse me.

"Ah, think, Joe—*think!*"

Phillipso slowly raised his eyes from his clenched hands to Hurensohn's plain, intense face. Higher, then, to the dome and through it. He raised his hand and pointed. "Pardon me," he said shakily, "but your ship is showing."

"Pshaw," said Hurensohn surprisingly. "Dammit, Phillipso, you've gone and made me concentrate, and I've let go the warp-matrix and fused my omicron. Take a minute or two to fix. I'll be back." And he disappeared. He didn't go anywhere, he just abruptly wasn't.

Josephus Macardle Phillipso moved like a sleepwalker across the round room and stood against the Plexiglas, staring up and out at the shining ship. It was balanced and beautiful, dusty-textured and untouchable like a moth's wing. It was lightly phosphorescent, flaring in the orange glow of the slashing searchlight, dimming rapidly almost to blackness just as the light cut at it again.

He looked past the ship to the stars, and in his mind's eye, past them to stars again, and stars, and whole systems of stars which in their remoteness looked like stars again, and stars again. He looked down then, to the ground under the Temple and down again to its steep slope, its one narrow terrace of a highway, and down and down again to the lamp-speckled black of the valley bottom. And if I fell from here to there, he thought, it would be like falling from crest to trough in the whorls of a baby's fingerprint.

And he thought, even with help from Heaven, I couldn't tell this truth and be believed. I couldn't suggest this work and be trusted. I am unfit, and I have unfit myself.

He thought bitterly, It's only the truth. The truth and I have a like polarity, and it springs away from me when I approach, by a law of nature. I prosper without the truth, and it has cost me nothing, nothing, nothing but the ability to tell the truth.

But I might try, he thought. What was it he said: *The core of a human being, a part which is not afraid, and which understands and is understood.* Who was he talking about? Anybody I know? Anyone I ever heard of? ("How are you?" you say, when you don't care how they are. "I'm sorry," you say, when you're not. "Goodby," you say, and it means God be with you, and how often is your goodby a blessing? Hypocrisy and lies, thousands a day, so easily done we forget to feel guilty for them.)

I see it now, he said, though. Did he mean me? Could he see the core of me, and say that? . . . if he can see such a marrow, he can see a strand of spider-silk at sixty yards.

He said, Phillipso recalled, that if I wouldn't help, they'd do nothing. They'd go away that's all—go away, forever, and leave us at the mercy of—what was that sardonic phrase?—the World Destroyers.

"But I never lied!" he wailed, suddenly and frighteningly loud. "I never meant to. They'd ask, don't you see, and I'd only say yes or no, whatever they wanted to hear. The only other thing I ever did was to explain the yes, or the no; they didn't start out to be lies!" No one answered him. He felt very alone. He thought again, I could try . . . and then, wistfully, could I try?

The phone rang. He looked blindly at it until it rang again. Tiredly he crossed to it and picked it up. "Phillipso."

The phone said, "Okay, Swami, you win. How did you do it?"

"Who is that? Penfield?" Penfield, whose original Phillipso spread had started his rise from Sunday feature writer; Penfield, who, as district chief of a whole newspaper chain, had of course long since forsworn Phillipso . . .

"Yeah, Penfield," drawled the pugnacious, insulting voice. "Penfield who promised you faithfully that never again would these papers run a line about you and your phony space war."

"What do you want, Penfield?"

"So you win, that's all. Whether I like it or not, you're news again. We're getting calls from all over the county. There's a flight of F-84s on the way from the Base. There's a TV mobile unit coming up the mountain to get that flying saucer of yours on network, and four queries already from INS. I don't know how you're doing it, but you're news, so what's your lousy story?"

Phillipso glanced up over his shoulder at the ship. The orange searchlight set it to flaming once, once again, while the telephone urgently bleated his name. Around came the light, and—

And nothing. It was gone. The ship was gone. "Wait!" cried Phillipso hoarsely. But it was gone.

The phone gabbled at him. Slowly he turned back to it. "Wait," he said to it too. He put down the instrument and rubbed water out of his eyes. Then he picked up the phone again.

"I saw from here," said the tinny voice. "It's gone. What was it? What'd you do?"

"Ship," said Phillipso. "It was a spaceship."

" 'It was a spaceship,' " Penfield repeated in the voice of a man writing on a pad. "So come on, Phillipso. What happened? Aliens came down and met you face to face, that it?"

"They—yes."

" 'Face . . . to . . . face.' Got it. What'd they want?" A pause, then, angrily, "Phillipso, you there? Dammit, I got a story to get out here. What'd they want? They beg for mercy, want you to lay off?"

Phillipso wet his lips. "Well, yes. Yes, they did."

"What'd they look like?"

"I—they . . . there was only one."

Penfield growled something about pulling teeth. "All right, only one. One *what?* Monster, spider, octopus—come *on,* Phillipso!"

"It . . . well, it wasn't a man, exactly."

"A girl," said Penfield excitedly. "A girl of unearthly beauty. How's that? They've threatened you before. Now they came to beguile you with, and so on. How's that?"

"Well, I—"

"I'll quote you. *'Unearthly . . .* mmm . . . *and refused . . .* mmm, *temptation.' "*

"Penfield, I—"

"Listen, Swami, that's all you get. I haven't time to listen to any more of your crap. I'll give you this in exchange, though. Just a friendly warning, and besides, I want this story to hold up through tomorrow anyhow. ATIC and the FBI are going to be all over that Temple of yours like flies on a warm marshmallow. You better hide the pieces of that balloon or whatever else the trick was. When it reaches the point of sending out a flight of jets, they don't think publicity is funny."

"Penfield, I—" But the phone was dead. Phillipso hung up and whirled to the empty room. "You *see?*" he wept. "You see what they make me do?"

He sat down heavily. The phone rang again. New York, the operator said. It was Jonathan, his publisher. "Joe! Your line's been busy. Great work, fella. Heard the bulletin on TV. How'd you do it? Never mind. Give me the main facts. I'll have a release out first thing in the morning. Hey, how soon can you get the new book done? Two weeks? Well, three—you can do it in three, fella. You have to do it in three. I'll cancel the new Heming—or the—never mind, I'll get press time for it. Now. Let's have it. I'll put you on the recorder."

Phillipso looked out at the stars. From the telephone, he heard the first sharp high *beep* of the recording machine. He bent close to it, breathed deeply, and said, "Tonight I was visited by aliens. This was no accidental contact like my first one; they planned this one. They came to stop me—not with violence, not by persuasion, but with—uh—the ultimate weapons. A girl of unearthly beauty appeared amidst the coils and busbars of my long-range radar. I—"

From behind Phillipso came a sound, soft, moist, explosive—the exact reproduction of someone too angry, too disgusted to speak, but driven irresistibly to spit.

Phillipso dropped the telephone and whirled. He thought he saw the figure of a sandy-haired man, but it vanished. He caught the barest flicker of something in the sky where the ship had been, but not enough really to identify; then it was gone too.

"I was on the phone," he whimpered. "I had too much on my mind, I thought you'd gone, I didn't know you'd just fixed your warp-what-ever-you-call-it, I didn't mean, I was going to, I—"

At last he realized he was alone. He had never been so alone. Absently he picked up the telephone and put it to his ear. Jonathan was saying excitedly, ". . . and the title. *The Ultimate Weapon.* Cheesecake pic of the girl coming out of the radar, nekkid. The one thing you haven't used yet. We'll *bomb* 'em, boy. Yeah, and you resisting, too. Do wonders for your Temple. But get busy on that book, hear? Get it to me in fifteen days and you can open your own branch of the U.S. mint."

Slowly, without speaking or waiting to see if the publisher was finished, Phillipso hung up. Once, just once, he looked out at the stars, and for a terrible instant each star was a life, a crippled limb, a faulty heart, a day of agony; and there were millions on countless millions of stars, and some of the stars were galaxies of stars; by their millions, by their flaming megatons, they were falling on him now and would fall on him forever.

He sighed and turned away, and switched on the light over his typewriter. He rolled in a sandwich of bond, carbon, second-sheet, centered the carriage, and wrote

THE ULTIMATE WEAPON
by
Josephus Macardle Phillipso.

Facile, swift, deft, and dedicated, he began to write.

Sightings at Twin Mounds

by Gene Wolfe

This puzzling case presents several unique features; because it is of more than ordinary interest, I shall quote several of the documents in full; my attention was originally attracted by the United Press Wire-Service story below.

UFOs SPOTTED OVER PARK

Residents of upstate Duke County report brilliant blue and white lights circling over Indian River State Park after midnight. On several occasions hundreds of persons from nearby Colbyville are said to have assembled outside the park to watch. According to a State Police report, a patrol car was dispatched to the scene Wednesday night. No lights were observed, but the officers who entered the park, which closes at six, discovered an incoherent man. The man has been hospitalized.

The *Guide to American Parks* supplied the following:

Indian River. Site of moderately extensive mounds *c.* A.D. 1300. Picnic and camping facilities (no showers). Boat trips on the Indian River. Apparently a cult site, there are several mounds of interest—Eagle Mound, Twin Mounds, Snake Mounds—surrounded by an earthen wall which remains nearly complete. An Algonquin legend has it that the site commemorates a raid on an Algonquin village by Iroquois, in which all the Algonquins perished with the exception of the chief's daughter, who fled into the forest pursued by the Iroquois war party. Encountering the wendigo, she begged it to defend her. It killed many Iroquois braves before both were slain. When avenging Algonquins drove off the raiding Iroquois, the chief's daughter and the wendigo were buried under the Twin Mounds. This legend may arise from the similarity of the hemispherical mounds to a woman's breasts.

That sent me to the public library, where the *Encyclopedia of Amerind Folklore* told what the wendigo was—or at least, what one was supposed to be.

wendigo, wiendigo, or windigo A giant ogre in the mythology of certain northeastern tribes. Hunters lost in the forest without food are thought to turn cannibal and, through the effects of eating human flesh, become wendigo, fearsome enemies of human beings possessing great strength and appearing and vanishing at will.

*   *   *

While I was at the library, I requested a week's copies of the *Colbyville Courier;* they arrived a few days later. Several carried half-jocular stories concerning moving lights and "giant spaceships" hovering over Indian River State Park. I quote only that which appears to me most significant.

Stanley J. Robakowski Found Unconscious

Stanley J. Robakowski of Colbyville, an employee of the Brewster Paper Company, was discovered in Indian River Park last night by troops investigating lights observed on park property. Police state that Mr. Robakowski was unable to account for his presence inside the park and allegedly appeared disoriented. After being administered a Breathometer test he was admitted to St. Joseph's Hospital. Asked whether Mr. Robakowski was thought responsible for lights observed at the park, a NYSP spokesperson stated that the police had no evidence to suggest that. Several witnesses stated emphatically that they had observed moving lights above the trees after police departed with Mr. Robakowski in custody.

After getting Stanley J. Robakowski's telephone number from Directory Assistance, I rang his apartment in Colbyville; no one answered. Saint Joseph's Hospital confirmed that he was still a patient but refused to put my call through to his room.

By this time I felt fairly sure that Stanley Robakowski was a contactee, and I was very anxious to interview him; I drove to Colbyville the following day. Saint Joseph's informed me that Robakowski had been discharged nearly twenty-four hours before. I checked into a hotel and telephoned his apartment again. He answered and, though reticent, gave me his address and agreed to speak to me in person.

Here I must confess my own shortcoming—one I regret more than any other involving UFO studies: I was unable to locate Robakowski's apartment that night. I was in an unfamiliar city, it was raining (which kept those who might have provided me with directions indoors, besides reducing visibility) and the streets of Colbyville are dark and poorly marked. After two fruitless hours, I returned to my hotel room, telephoned Robakowski again, explained my difficulty, and asked whether it would be possible for him to meet me there.

He refused, saying that he had to return to work at seven the following day and intended to go to bed. I then requested an interview next evening, to which he agreed.

With a day to kill in Colbyville, I drove to Indian River State Park, where I saw the mounds and spoke to several persons who had seen lights over the park. All agreed that no lights had been present for the past two nights. They were described as very bright, usually white or blue-white, but occasionally yellow. One informant stated that they proceeded from what she termed a "wingless airplane"—that is to say, a torpedo-shaped flying object. She drew the object for me, her sketch showing a row of lights, much like the portholes of a ship, along one side of the object (Plate VI).

At seven I drove to Robakowski's apartment, having provided myself in the meantime with a four-cell flashlight with which to read building numbers. A fresh reason for my earlier confusion was soon apparent. I had been looking for an apartment building, while Robakowski's apartment was in fact the upper story of an old house, now provided with its own entrance. I had parked in front of the house and gotten out of my car before I noticed the shadow of what appeared to be an embracing couple thrown on the curtains. Thinking it better to leave them in solitude for a time, I drove to a nearby cafe, drank a leisurely cup of coffee, then telephoned the apartment, intending to ask whether it would be convenient for Robakowski to see me. There was no response.

I drove back to the apartment. Save for the absence of the amorous silhouette, everything appeared to be as I had left it; lights were still on in the front room and the curtains remained drawn. Admission was through a ground-level door leading to a steep, straight stairway. As I rang the bell, I could not help observing that this door was ajar.

No doubt I should not have done what I did. I can only say that I was extremely eager to speak with Robakowski, and at that point I was already afraid some danger had overtaken him. After ringing and knocking several times, I entered the apartment and discovered extensive bloodstains in the kitchen, bedroom, and hall. I called the police at once; Robakowski's body has never been found, and I am told that no arrest has ever been made.

Dr. Ernest Schwartz, who treated Robakowski during the time he was a patient at Saint Joseph's Hospital, has contributed an account to *The Journal of the American Psychiatric Society*. The brief section that I quote here is used with Dr. Schwartz's kind permission.

Stan Roland [the pseudonym by which Dr. Schwartz refers to Robakowski— Author] was a white male twenty-three years of age. He had been employed as a maintenance technician at a paper mill since leaving school. He appeared alert but confused, and at no time exhibited either hostility or aggression. There was no history of psychopathic or psychoneurotic disturbance.

Asked about the episode which brought him to the attention of the police, Roland said that he had gone to Indian River Park with friends in the hope of seeing lights that were occasionally sighted in the park at that time. After a wait of approximately an hour, during which the members of his party chatted and drank beer, Roland and another saw, briefly, a dim blue light moving in the area of the Twin Mounds; this was challenged by those who had not seen it. Armed with a wrench, Roland then climbed the fence surrounding the park (which is closed after dark) in order to investigate. He said that he had visited the park frequently in his boyhood and sporadically thereafter, and was intimately familiar with its geography.

Nevertheless, by his own account he would seem to have lost his way almost at once. He insisted that trails with which he was familiar had been "taken away," but that the heavily wooded area was, paradoxically, almost free of underbrush, which is not in fact the case. He stated that he saw moving blue and white lights on several occasions but was never able to approach them closely.

At this point, Roland invariably became agitated, and the order of subjective events is unclear. "She ran into me in the dark." "I thought I heard somebody screaming off to my right—there was a lot of yelling, and all of a sudden this girl was holding onto me." "I was just walking along, trying to go fast, you know? And all of a sudden my arms were around her." There is no objective evidence for the existence of this mysterious young woman, who Roland said could not speak English and seemed terrified.

They ran through the park together, Roland said, until they were assaulted by invisible beings. Asked how he could know, in darkness, that the beings were invisible, Roland stated that it was not wholly dark and that he could dimly see the young woman beside him, but could at no time catch sight of their attackers, who were thus tactile and auditory hallucinations only.

Questioned regarding the outcome of this struggle with these invisible beings, Roland said that he had become separated from them and the young woman when he was detained by the police; but that he felt certain they and she were still searching for him. He described his attackers as making "little real quiet sounds," while the young woman called softly, something that sounded like "Where'd he go?" Reminded that he had said the young woman did not speak English, he declared that he did not think her words were in fact English, although they sounded something like the English phrase he repeated. He said that neither she nor those who had attacked them could see him now; nor could he see them.

And there the case of the sightings at Twin Mounds remains. UFO contactees have often reported being shadowed or threatened after their experiences were made public, most frequently by *men in black* (MIBs). Although I personally do not believe that Robakowski's attackers were MIBs, it cannot be denied that MIBs encountered in the woods at night might seem "invisible beings" to a frightened man. Reports of physical harm at the hands of MIBs are extremely rare, and murder almost unheard-of; and yet murder would appear to have taken place in the mysterious case of Stanley J. Robakowski.

Additional sightings in the vicinity of Indian River Park have been difficult to verify. Two years ago, an archeological excavation of the Twin Mounds was begun by a team from SUNY Brockport, although no report has been issued. All activity was suspended indefinitely when it was discovered that the site had been contaminated by "modern materials."

The Silly Season
by C.M. Kornbluth

It was a hot summer afternoon in the Omaha bureau of the World Wireless Press Service, and the control bureau in New York kept nagging me for copy. But since it was a hot summer afternoon, there was no copy. A wrapup of local baseball had cleared about an hour ago, and that was that. Nothing but baseball happens in the summer. During the dog days, politicians are in the Maine woods fishing and boozing, burglars are too tired to burgle, and wives think it over and decide not to decapitate their husbands.

I pawed through some press releases. One sloppy stencil-duplicated sheet began: "Did you know that the lemonade way to summer comfort and health has been endorsed by leading physiotherapists from Maine to California? The Federated Lemon-Growers Association revealed today that a survey of 2,500 physiotherapists in 57 cities of more than 25,000 population disclosed that 87 percent of them drink lemonade at least once a day between June and September, and that another 72 percent not only drink the cooling and healthful beverage but actually prescribe it—"

Another note tapped out on the news circuit printer from New York: "960M-HW KICKER? ND SNST-NY"

That was New York saying they needed a bright and sparkling little news item immediately—"soonest." I went to the eastbound printer and punched out: "96NY-UPCMNG FU MINS-OM"

The lemonade handout was hopeless; I dug into the stack again. The State University summer course was inviting the governor to attend its summer conference on aims and approaches in adult secondary education. The Agricultural College wanted me to warn farmers that white-skinned hogs should be kept from the direct rays of the summer sun. The manager of a fifth-rate local pug sent a writeup of his boy and a couple of working press passes to his next bout in the Omaha Arena. The Schwartz and White Bandage Company contributed a glossy eight-by-ten of a blonde in a bathing suit improvised from two S.&W. Redi-Dressings.

Accompanying text: "Pert starlet Miff McCoy is ready for any seaside emergency. That's not only a darling swimsuit she has on—it's two standard all-purpose Redi-Dressing bandages made by the Schwartz and White Bandage Company of Omaha. If a broken rib results from too-strenuous beach athletics, Miff's dress can supply the dressing." Yeah. The rest of the stack wasn't even that good. I dumped them all in the circular file, and began to wrack my brains in spite of the heat.

I'd have to fake one, I decided. Unfortunately, there had been no big running silly season story so far this summer—no flying saucers, or monsters in the Florida Everglades, or chloroform bandits terrifying the city. If there had, I could have hopped on and faked a "with." As it was, I'd have to fake a "lead," which is harder and riskier.

The flying saucers? I couldn't revive them; they'd been forgotten for years, except by newsmen. The giant turtle of Lake Huron had been quiet for years, too. If I started a chloroform bandit scare, every old maid in the state would back me up by swearing she heard the bandit trying to break in and smelled chloroform— but the cops wouldn't like it. Strange messages from space received at the State University's radar lab? That might do it. I put a sheet of copy paper in the typewriter and sat, glaring at it and hating the silly season.

There was a slight reprieve—the Western Union tie-line printer by the desk dinged at me and its sickly-yellow bulb lit up. I tapped out: "WW GA PLS," and the machine began to eject yellow, gummed tape which told me this:

"WU CO62-DPR COLLECT-FT HICKS ARK AUG 22 105P—WORLDWIRELESS OMAHA—TOWN MARSHAL PINKNEY CRAWLES DIED MYSTERIOUS CIRCUMSTANCES FISHTRIPPING OZARK HAMLET RUSH CITY TODAY. RUSHERS PHONED HICKSERS 'BURNED DEATH SHINING DOMES APPEARED YESTERWEEK.' JEEPING BODY HICKSWARD. QUERIED RUSH CONSTABLE P.C. ALLENBY LEARNING 'SEVEN GLASSY DOMES EACH HOUSESIZE CLEARING MILE SOUTH TOWN. RUSHERS UNTOUCHED, UNAPPROACHED. CRAWLES WARNED BUT TOUCHED AND DIED BURNS.' NOTE DESK—RUSH FONECALL 1.85. SHALL I UPFOLLOW?—BENSON—FISHTRIPPING RUSHERS HICKSERS YESTERWEEK JEEPING HICKSWARD HOUSESIZE 1.85 428P CLR . . ."

It was just what the doctor ordered. I typed an acknowledgment for the message and pounded out a story, fast. I punched it and started the tape wiggling through the eastbound transmitter before New York could send any more irked notes. The news circuit printer from New York clucked and began relaying my story immediately: "WW72 (KICKER)

FORT HICKS, ARKANSAS, AUG 22—(WW)—MYSTERIOUS DEATH TODAY STRUCK DOWN A LAW ENFORCEMENT OFFICER IN A TINY OZARK MOUNTAIN HAMLET. MARSHAL PINKNEY CRAWLES OF FORT HICKS, ARKANSAS, DIED OF BURNS WHILE ON A FISHING TRIP TO THE LITTLE VILLAGE OF RUSH CITY. TERRIFIED NATIVES OF RUSH CITY BLAMED THE TRAGEDY ON WHAT THEY CALLED 'SHINING DOMES.' THEY SAID THE SO-CALLED DOMES APPEARED IN A CLEARING LAST WEEK ONE MILE SOUTH OF TOWN. THERE ARE SEVEN OF THE MYSTERIOUS OBJECTS—EACH ONE THE SIZE OF A HOUSE. THE INHABITANTS OF RUSH CITY DID NOT DARE APPROACH THEM. THEY WARNED THE VISITING MARSHAL CRAWLES—BUT HE DID NOT HEED THEIR WARNING. RUSH CITY'S CONSTABLE P.C. ALLENBY WAS A WITNESS TO THE TRAGEDY. SAID HE:—"THERE ISN'T MUCH TO TELL. MARSHAL CRAWLES JUST WALKED UP TO ONE OF THE DOMES AND PUT HIS HAND ON IT. THERE WAS A BIG FLASH, AND WHEN I COULD SEE AGAIN, HE WAS BURNED TO DEATH.' CONSTABLE ALLENBY IS RETURNING THE BODY OF MARSHAL CRAWLES TO FORT HICKS. 602P220M"

That, I thought, should hold them for a while. I remembered Benson's "note desk" and put through a long distance call to Fort Hicks, person to person. The Omaha operator asked for Fort Hicks information, but there wasn't any. The Fort Hicks operator asked whom she wanted. Omaha finally admitted that we wanted to talk to Mr. Edwin C. Benson. Fort Hicks figured out loud and then decided that Ed was probably at the police station if he hadn't gone home for supper yet. She connected us with the police station, and I got Benson. He had a pleasant voice, not particularly backwoods Arkansas. I gave him some of the old oil about a fine dispatch, and a good, conscientious job, and so on. He took it with plenty of dry reserve, which was odd. Our rural stringers always ate that kind of stuff up. Where, I asked him, was he from?

"Fort Hicks," he told me, "but I've moved around. I did the courthouse beat in Little Rock—" I nearly laughed out loud at that, but the laugh died out as he went on—"rewrite for the A.P. in New Orleans, got to be bureau chief there but I didn't like wire service work. Got an opening on the Chicago Trib desk. That didn't last—they sent me to head up their Washington bureau. There I switched to the New York Times. They made me a war correspondent and I got hurt—back to Fort Hicks. I do some magazine writing now. Did you want a follow-up on the Rush City story?"

"Sure," I told him weakly. "Give it a real ride—use your own judgment. Do you think it's a fake?"

"I saw Pink's body a little while ago at the undertaker's parlor, and I had a talk with Allenby, from Rush City. Pink got burned all right, and Allenby didn't make his story up. Maybe somebody else did—he's pretty dumb—but as far as I can tell, this is the real thing. I'll keep the copy coming. Don't forget about that dollar eighty-five phone call, will you?"

I told him I wouldn't, and hung up. Mr. Edwin C. Benson had handed me quite a jolt. I wondered how badly he had been hurt, that he had been forced to abandon a brilliant news career and bury himself in the Ozarks.

Then there came a call from God, the board chairman of World Wireless. He was fishing in Canada, as all good board chairmen do during the silly season, but he had caught a news broadcast which used my Rush City story. He had a mobile phone in his trailer, and it was but the work of a moment to ring Omaha and louse up my carefully planned vacation schedules and rotation of night shifts. He wanted me to go down to Rush City and cover the story personally. I said yes and began trying to round up the rest of the staff. My night editor was sobered up by his wife and delivered to the bureau in fair shape. A telegrapher on vacation was reached at his summer resort and talked into checking out. I got a taxi company on the phone and told them to have a cross-country cab on the roof in an hour. I specified their best driver, and told them to give him maps of Arkansas.

Meanwhile, two "with domes" dispatches arrived from Benson and got moved on the wire. I monitored a couple of newscasts; the second one carried a story by another wire service on the domes—a pickup of our stuff, but they'd have their own men on the scene fast enough. I filled in the night editor, and went up to the roof for the cab.

The driver took off in the teeth of a gathering thunderstorm. We had to rise above it, and by the time we could get down to sight-pilotage altitude, we were lost. We circled most of the night until the driver picked up a beacon he had on his charts at about 3:30 A.M. We landed at Fort Hicks as day was breaking, not on speaking terms.

Fort Hicks' field clerk told me where Benson lived, and I walked there. It was a white, frame house. A quiet, middle-aged woman let me in. She was his widowed sister, Mrs. McHenry. She got me some coffee and told me she had been up all night waiting for Edwin to come back from Rush City. He had started out about 8:00 P.M., and it was only a two-hour trip by car. She was worried. I tried to pump her about her brother, but she'd only say that he was the bright one of the family. She didn't want to talk about his work as war correspondent. She did show me some of his magazine stuff—boy-and-girl stories in national weeklies. He seemed to sell one every couple of months.

We had arrived at a conversational stalemate when her brother walked in, and I discovered why his news career had been interrupted. He was blind. Aside from a long, puckered brown scar that ran from his left temple back over his ear and onto the nape of his neck, he was a pleasant-looking fellow in his mid-forties.

"Who is it, Vera?" he asked.

"It's Mr. Williams, the gentleman who called you from Omaha today—I mean yesterday."

"How do you do, Williams. Don't get up," he added—hearing, I suppose, the chair squeak as I leaned forward to rise.

"You were so *long*, Edwin," his sister said with relief and reproach.

"That young jackass Howie—my chauffeur for the night—" he added an aside to me—"got lost going there and coming back. But I did spend more time than I'd planned at Rush City." He sat down, facing me. "Williams, there is some difference of opinion about the shining domes. The Rush City people say that they exist, and I say they don't."

His sister brought him a cup of coffee.

"What happened, exactly?" I asked.

"That Allenby took me and a few other hardy citizens to see them. They told me just what they looked like. Seven hemispheres in a big clearing, glassy, looming up like houses, reflecting the gleam of the headlights. But they weren't there. Not to me, and not to any blind man. I know when I'm standing in front of a house or anything else that big. I can feel a little tension on the skin of my face. It works unconsciously, but the mechanism is thoroughly understood.

"The blind get—because they have to—an aural picture of the world. We hear a little hiss of air that means we're at the corner of a building, we hear and feel big, turbulent air currents that mean we're coming to a busy street. Some of the boys can thread their way through an obstacle course and never touch a single obstruction. I'm not that good, maybe because I haven't been blind as long as they have, but by hell, I know when there are seven objects the size of houses in front of me, and there just were no such things in the clearing at Rush City."

"Well," I shrugged, "there goes a fine piece of silly-season journalism. What kind of gag are the Rush City people trying to pull, and why?"

"No kind of gag. My driver saw the domes, too—and don't forget the late marshal. Pink not only saw them but touched them. All I know is that people see them and I don't. If they exist, they have a kind of existence like nothing else I've ever met."

"I'll go up there myself," I decided.

"Best thing," said Benson. "I don't know what to make of it. You can take our car." He gave me directions and I gave him a schedule of deadlines. We wanted the coroner's verdict, due today, an eyewitness story—his driver would do for that—some background stuff on the area and a few statements from local officials.

I took his car and got to Rush City in two hours. It was an unpainted collection of dog-trot homes, set down in the big pine forest that covers all that rolling Ozark country. There was a general store that had the place's only phone. I suspected it had been kept busy by the wire services and a few enterprising newspapers. A state trooper in a flashy uniform was lounging against a fly-specked tobacco counter when I got there.

"I'm Sam Williams, from World Wireless," I said. "You come to have a look at the domes?"

"World Wireless broke that story, didn't they?" he asked me, with a look I couldn't figure out.

"We did. Our Fort Hicks stringer wired it to us."

The phone rang, and the trooper answered it. It seemed to have been a call to the Governor's office he had placed.

"No, sir," he said over the phone. "No, sir. They're all sticking to the story, but I didn't see anything. I mean, they don't see them any more, but they say they *were* there, and now they aren't any more." A couple more "No, sirs" and he hung up.

"When did that happen?" I asked.

"About a half-hour ago. I just came from there on my bike to report."

The phone rang again, and I grabbed it. It was Benson, asking for me. I told him to phone a flash and bulletin to Omaha on the disappearance and then took off to find Constable Allenby. He was a stage reuben with a nickel-plated badge and a six-shooter. He cheerfully climbed into the car and guided me to the clearing.

There was a definite little path worn between Rush City and the clearing by now, but there was a disappointment at the end of it. The clearing was empty. A few small boys sticking carefully to its fringes told wildly contradictory stories about the disappearance of the domes, and I jotted down some kind of dispatch out of the most spectacular versions. I remember it involved flashes of blue fire and a smell like sulfur candles. That was all there was to it.

I drove Allenby back. By then a mobile unit from a TV network had arrived. I said hello, waited for an A.P. man to finish a dispatch on the phone, and then dictated my lead direct to Omaha. The hamlet was beginning to fill up with newsmen from the wire services, the big papers, the radio and TV nets and the newsreels. Much good they'd get out of it. The story was over—I thought. I had some coffee at the general store's two-table restaurant corner and drove back to Fort Hicks.

Benson was tirelessly interviewing by phone and firing off copy to Omaha.

I told him he could begin to ease off, thanked him for his fine work, paid him for his gas, said goodbye and picked up my taxi at the field. Quite a bill for waiting had been run up.

I listened to the radio as we were flying back to Omaha, and wasn't at all surprised. After baseball, the shining domes were the top news. Shining domes had been seen in twelve states. Some vibrated with a strange sound. They came in all colors and sizes. One had strange writing on it. One was transparent, and there were big green men and women inside. I caught a women's mid-morning quiz show, and the M.C. kept gagging about the domes. One crack I remember was a switch on the "pointed-head" joke. He made it "dome-shaped head," and the ladies in the audience laughed until they nearly burst.

We stopped in Little Rock for gas, and I picked up a couple of afternoon papers. The domes got banner heads on both of them. One carried the World Wireless lead, and had slapped in the bulletin on the disappearance of the domes. The other paper wasn't a World Wireless client, but between its other services and "special correspondents"—phone calls to the general store at Rush City—it had kept practically abreast of us. Both papers had shining dome cartoons on their editorial pages, hastily drawn and slapped in. One paper, anti-administration, showed the President cautiously reaching out a finger to touch the dome of the Capitol, which was rendered as a shining dome and labeled: "SHINING DOME OF CONGRESSIONAL IMMUNITY TO EXECUTIVE DICTATORSHIP." A little man labeled "Mr. and Mrs. Plain, Self-Respecting Citizens of The United States of America" was in one corner of the cartoon saying: "CAREFUL, MR. PRESIDENT! REMEMBER WHAT HAPPENED TO PINKNEY CRAWLES!!"

The other paper, pro-administration, showed a shining dome that had the President's face. A band of fat little men in Prince Albert coats, string ties, and broad-brimmed hats labeled "CONGRESSIONAL SMEAR ARTISTS AND HATCHETMEN" were creeping up on the dome with the President's face, their hands reached out as if to strangle. Above the cartoon a cutline said: "WHO'S GOING TO GET HURT?"

We landed at Omaha, and I checked into the office. Things were clicking right along. The clients were happily gobbling up our dome copy and sending wires asking for more. I dug into the morgue for the "Flying Disc" folder, and the "Huron Turtle" and the "Bayou Vampire" and a few others even further back. I spread out the old clippings and tried to shuffle and arrange them into some kind of underlying sense. I picked up the latest dispatch to come out of the tie-line printer from Western Union. It was from our man in Owosso, Michigan, and told how Mrs. Lettie Overholtzer, age 61, saw a shining dome in her own kitchen at midnight. It grew like a soap bubble until it was as big as her refrigerator, and then disappeared.

I went over to the desk man and told him: "Let's have a downhold on stuff like Lettie Overholtzer. We can move a sprinkling of it, but I don't want to run this into the ground. Those things might turn up again, and then we wouldn't have any room left to play around with them. We'll have everybody's credulity used up."

He looked mildly surprised. "You mean," he asked, "there really *was* something there?"

"I don't know. Maybe. I didn't see anything myself, and the only man down there I trust can't make up his mind. Anyhow, hold it down as far as the clients let us."

I went home to get some sleep. When I went back to work, I found the clients hadn't let us work the downhold after all. Nobody at the other wire services seemed to believe seriously that there had been anything out of the ordinary at Rush City, so they merrily pumped out solemn stories like the Lettie Overholtzer item, and wirefoto maps of locations where domes were reported, and tabulations of number of domes reported.

We had to string along. Our Washington bureau badgered the Pentagon and the A.E.C. into issuing statements, and there was a race between a Navy and an Air Force investigating mission to see who could get to Rush City first. After they got there there was a race to see who could get the first report out. The Air Force won that contest. Before the week was out, "Domies" had appeared. They were hats for juveniles—shining-dome skull caps molded from a transparent plastic. We had to ride with it. I'd started the mania, but it was out of hand and a long time dying down.

The World Series, the best in years, finally killed off the domes. By an unspoken agreement among the services, we simply stopped running stories every time a hysterical woman thought she saw a dome or wanted to get her name in the paper. And, of course, when there was no longer publicity to be had for the asking, people stopped seeing domes. There was no percentage in it. Brooklyn won the Series, international tension climbed as the thermometer dropped, burglars began burgling again, and a bulky folder labeled "DOMES, SHINING," went into our morgue. The shining domes were history, and earnest graduate students in psychology would shortly begin to bother us with requests to borrow that folder.

The only thing that had come of it, I thought, was that we had somehow got through another summer without too much idle wire time, and that Ed Benson and I had struck up a casual correspondence.

A newsman's strange and weary year wore on. Baseball gave way to football. An off-year election kept us on the run. Christmas loomed ahead, with its feature stories and its kickers about Santa Claus, Indiana. Christmas passed, and we began to clear jolly stories about New Year's day, a ghastly ratrace of covering 103 bowl games. Record snowfalls in the Great Plains and Rockies. Spring floods in Ohio and the Columbus River Valley. Twenty-one tasty Lenten menus, and Holy Week around the world. Baseball again, Daylight Saving Time, Mother's Day, Derby Day, the Preakness and the Belmont Stakes.

It was about then that a disturbing letter arrived from Benson. I was concerned not about its subject matter but because I thought no sane man would write such a thing. It seemed to me that Benson was slipping his trolley. All he said was that he expected a repeat performance of the domes, or of something like the domes. He said "they" probably found the tryout a smashing success and would continue according to plan. I replied cautiously, which amused him.

He wrote back: "I wouldn't put myself out on a limb like this if I had anything to lose by it, but you know my station in life. It was just an intelligent guess, based on a study of power politics and Aesop's fables. And if it does happen, you'll find it a trifle harder to put over, won't you?"

I guessed he was kidding me, but I wasn't certain. When people begin to talk about "them" and what "they" are doing, it's a bad sign. But, guess or not, something pretty much like the domes did turn up in late July, during a crushing heat wave.

This time it was big black spheres rolling across the countryside. The spheres were seen by a Baptist congregation in central Kansas which had met in a prairie to pray for rain. About eighty Baptists took their Bible oaths that they saw large black spheres some ten feet high, rolling along the prairie. They had passed within five yards of one man. The rest had run from them as soon as they could take in the fact that they really were there.

World Wireless didn't break that story, but we got on it fast enough as soon as we were tipped. Being now the recognized silly season authority in the W.W. Central Division, I took off for Kansas.

It was much the way it had been in Arkansas. The Baptists really thought they had seen the things—with one exception. The exception was an old gentleman with a patriarchal beard. He had been the one man who hadn't run, the man the objects passed nearest to. He was blind. He told me with a great deal of heat that he would have known all about it, blind or not, if any large spheres had rolled within five yards of him, or twenty-five for that matter.

Old Mr. Emerson didn't go into the matter of air currents and turbulence, as Benson had. With him, it was all well below the surface. He took the position that the Lord had removed his sight, and in return had given him another sense which would do for emergency use.

"You just try me out, son!" he piped angrily. "You come stand over here, wait a while and put your hand up in front of my face. I'll tell you when you do it, no matter how quiet you are!" He did it, too, three times, and then took me out into the main street of his little prairie town. There were several wagons drawn up before the grain elevator, and he put on a show for me by threading his way around and between them without touching once.

That—and Benson—seemed to prove that whatever the things were, they had some connection with the domes. I filed a thoughtful dispatch on the blind-man angle, and got back to Omaha to find that it had been cleared through our desk but killed in New York before relay.

We tried to give the black spheres the usual ride, but it didn't last as long. The political cartoonists tired of it sooner, and fewer old maids saw them. People got to jeering at them as newspaper hysteria, and a couple of highbrow magazines ran articles on "the irresponsible press." Only the radio comedians tried to milk the new mania as usual, but they were disconcerted to find their ratings fall. A network edict went out to kill all sphere gags. People were getting sick of them.

"It makes sense," Benson wrote to me. "An occasional exercise of the sense of wonder is refreshing, but it can't last forever. That plus the ingrained American cynicism toward all sources of public information has worked against the black spheres being greeted with the same naïve delight with which the domes were received. Nevertheless, I predict—and I'll thank you to remember that my predictions have been right so far 100 percent of the time—that next summer will see another mystery comparable to the domes and the black things. And I also predict that the new phenomenon will be imperceptible to any blind person in the immediate vicinity, if there should be any."

If, of course, he was wrong this time, it would only cut his average down to fifty percent. I managed to wait out the year—the same interminable round I felt I could do in my sleep. Staffers got ulcers and resigned, staffers got tired and were fired, libel suits were filed and settled, one of our desk men got a Nieman Fellowship and went to Harvard, one of our telegraphers got his working hand mashed in a car door and jumped from a bridge but lived with a broken back.

In mid-August, when the weather bureau had been correctly predicting "fair and warmer" for sixteen straight days, it turned up. It wasn't anything on whose nature a blind man could provide a negative check, but it had what I had come to think of as "their" trademark.

A summer seminar was meeting outdoors, because of the frightful heat, at our own State University. Twelve trained school teachers testified that a series of perfectly circular pits opened up in the grass before them, one directly under the education professor teaching the seminar. They testified further that the professor, with an astonished look and a heart-rending cry, plummeted down into that perfectly circular pit. They testified further that the pits remained there for some thirty seconds and then suddenly were there no longer. The scorched summer grass was back where it had been, the pits were gone, and so was the professor.

I interviewed every one of them. They weren't yokels, but grown men and women, all with Masters' degrees, working toward their doctorates during the summers. They agreed closely on their stories as I would expect trained and capable persons to do.

The police, however, did not expect agreement, being used to dealing with the lower-I.Q. brackets. They arrested the twelve on some technical charge—"obstructing peace officers in the performance of their duties," I believe—and were going to beat the living hell out of them when an attorney arrived with twelve writs of habeas corpus. The cops' unvoiced suspicion was that the teachers had conspired to murder their professor, but nobody ever tried to explain why they'd do a thing like that.

The cops' reaction was typical of the way the public took it. Newspapers—which had reveled wildly in the shining domes story and less so in the black spheres story—were cautious. Some went overboard and gave the black pits a ride, in the old style, but they didn't pick up any sales that way. People declared that the press was insulting their intelligence, and also they were bored with marvels.

The few papers who played up the pits were soundly spanked in very dignified editorials printed by other sheets which played down the pits.

At World Wireless, we sent out a memo to all stringers: "File no more enterpriser dispatches on black pit story. Mail queries should be sent to regional desk if a new angle breaks in your territory." We got about ten mail queries, mostly from journalism students acting as string men, and we turned them all down. All the older hands got the pitch, and didn't bother to file it to us when the town drunk or the village old maid loudly reported that she saw a pit open up on High Street across from the drugstore. They knew it was probably untrue, and that furthermore nobody cared.

I wrote Benson about all this, and humbly asked him what his prediction for next summer was. He replied, obviously having the time of his life, that there would be at least one more summer phenomenon like the last three, and possibly two more—but none after that.

It's so easy now to reconstruct, with our bitterly earned knowledge!

Any youngster could whisper now of Benson: "Why, the damned fool! Couldn't anybody with the brains of a louse see that they wouldn't keep it up for two years?" One did whisper that to me the other day, when I told this story to him. And I whispered back that, far from being a damned fool, Benson was the one person on the face of the earth, as far as I know, who had bridged with logic the widely separated phenomena with which this reminiscence deals.

Another year passed. I gained three pounds, drank too much, rowed incessantly with my staff, and got a tidy raise. A telegrapher took a swing at me midway through the office Christmas party, and I fired him. My wife and kids didn't arrive in April when I expected them. I phoned Florida, and she gave me some excuse or other about missing the plane. After a few more missed planes and a few more phone calls, she got around to telling me that she didn't *want* to come back. That was okay with me. In my own intuitive way, I knew that the upcoming silly season was more important than who stayed married to whom.

In July, a dispatch arrived by wire while a new man was working the night desk. It was from Hood River, Oregon. Our stringer there reported that more than one hundred "green capsules" about fifty yards long had appeared in and around an apple orchard. The new desk man was not so new that he did not recall the downhold policy on silly-season items. He killed it, but left it on the spike for my amused inspection in the morning. I suppose exactly the same thing happened in every wire service newsroom in the region. I rolled in at 10:30 and riffled through the stuff on the spike. When I saw the "green capsules" dispatch I tried to phone Portland, but couldn't get a connection. Then the phone buzzed and a correspondent of ours in Seattle began to yell at me, but the line went dead.

I shrugged and phoned Benson, in Fort Hicks. He was at the police station, and asked me: "Is this it?"

"It is," I told him. I read him the telegram from Hood River and told him about the line trouble to Seattle.

"So," he said wonderingly, "I called the turn, didn't I?"

"Called what turn?"

"On the invaders. I don't know who they are—but it's the story of the boy who cried wolf. Only this time, the wolves realized—" Then the phone went dead.

But he was right.

The people of the world were the sheep.

We newsmen—radio, TV, press, and wire services—were the boy, who should have been ready to sound the alarm.

But the cunning wolves had tricked us into sounding the alarm so many times that the villagers were weary, and would not come when there was real peril.

The wolves who then were burning their way through the Ozarks, utterly without opposition, the wolves were the Martians under whose yoke and lash we now endure our miserable existences.

Or Else

by Henry Kuttner

Miguel and Fernandez were shooting inaccurately at each other across the valley when the flying saucer landed. They wasted a few bullets on the strange airship. The pilot appeared and began to walk across the valley and up the slope toward Miguel, who lay in the uncertain shade of a cholla, swearing and working the bolt of his rifle as rapidly as he could. His aim, never good, grew worse as the stranger approached. Finally, at the last minute, Miguel dropped his rifle, seized the machete beside him, and sprang to his feet.

"Die then," he said, and swung the blade. The steel blazed in the hot Mexican sun. The machete rebounded elastically from the stranger's neck and flew high in the air, while Miguel's arm tingled as though from an electric shock. A bullet came from across the valley, making the kind of sound a wasp's sting might make if you heard it instead of feeling it. Miguel dropped and rolled into the shelter of a large rock. Another bullet shrieked thinly, and a brief blue flash sparkled on the stranger's left shoulder.

"Estoy perdido," Miguel said, giving himself up for lost. Flat on his stomach, he lifted his head and snarled at his enemy.

The stranger, however, made no inimical moves. Moreover, he seemed to be unarmed. Miguel's sharp eyes searched him. The man was unusually dressed. He wore a cap made of short, shiny blue feathers. Under it his face was hard, ascetic and intolerant. He was very thin, and nearly seven feet tall. But he did seem to be unarmed. That gave Miguel courage. He wondered where his machete had fallen. He did not see it, but his rifle was only a few feet away.

The stranger came and stood above Miguel.

"Stand up," he said. "Let us talk."

He spoke excellent Spanish, except that his voice seemed to be coming from inside Miguel's head.

"I will not stand up," Miguel said. "If I stand up, Fernandez will shoot me. He is a very bad shot, but I would be a fool to take such a chance. Besides, this is very unfair. How much is Fernandez paying you?"

The stranger looked austerely at Miguel.

"Do you know where I came from?" he asked.

"I don't care a centavo where you came from," Miguel said, wiping sweat from his forehead. He glanced toward a nearby rock where he had cached a goatskin of wine. "From *los estados unidos,* no doubt, you and your machine of flight. The Mexican government will hear of this."

"Does the Mexican government approve of murder?"

"This is a private matter," Miguel said. "A matter of water rights, which are

53

very important. Besides, it is self-defense. That *cabrón* across the valley is trying to kill me. And you are his hired assassin. God will punish you both." A new thought came to him. "How much will you take to kill Fernandez?" he inquired. "I will give you three pesos and a fine kid."

"There will be no more fighting at all," the stranger said. "Do you hear that?"

"Then go and tell Fernandez," Miguel said. "Inform him that the water rights are mine. I will gladly allow him to go in peace." His neck ached from staring up at the tall man. He moved a little, and a bullet shrieked through the still, hot air and dug with a vicious splash into a nearby cactus.

The stranger smoothed the blue feathers on his head.

"First I will finish talking with you. Listen to me, Miguel."

"How do you know my name?" Miguel demanded, rolling over and sitting up cautiously behind the rock. "It is as I thought. Fernandez has hired you to assassinate me."

"I know your name because I can read your mind a little. Not much, because it is so cloudy."

"Your mother was a dog," Miguel said.

The stranger's nostrils pinched together slightly, but he ignored the remark. "I come from another world," he said. "My name is—" In Miguel's mind it sounded like Quetzalcoatl.

"Quetzalcoatl?" Miguel repeated, with fine irony. "Oh, I have no doubt of that. And mine is Saint Peter, who has the keys to heaven."

Quetzalcoatl's thin, pale face flushed slightly, but his voice was determinedly calm. "Listen, Miguel. Look at my lips. They are not moving. I am speaking inside your head, by telepathy, and you translate my thoughts into words that have meaning to you. Evidently my name is too difficult for you. Your own mind has translated it as Quetzalcoatl. That is not my real name at all."

"De veras," Miguel said. "It is not your name at all, and you do not come from another world. I would not believe a *norteamericano* if he swore on the bones of ten thousand highly placed saints."

Quetzalcoatl's long, austere face flushed again.

"I am here to give orders," he said. "Not to bandy words with—Look here, Miguel. Why do you suppose you couldn't kill me with your machete? Why can't bullets touch me?"

"Why does your machine of flight fly?" Miguel riposted. He took out a sack of tobacco and began to roll a cigarette. He squinted around the rock. "Fernandez is probably trying to creep up on me. I had better get my rifle."

"Leave it alone," Quetzalcoatl said. "Fernandez will not harm you."

Miguel laughed harshly.

"And you must not harm him," Quetzalcoatl added firmly.

"I will, then, turn the other cheek," Miguel said, "so that he can shoot me through the side of my head. I will believe Fernandez wishes peace, *Señor* Quetzalcoatl, when I see him walking across the valley with his hands over his head.

Even then I will not let him come close, because of the knife he wears down his back."

Quetzalcoatl smoothed his blue steel feathers again. His bony face was frowning.

"You must stop fighting forever, both of you," he said. "My race polices the universe and our responsibility is to bring peace to every planet we visit."

"It is as I thought," Miguel said with satisfaction. "You come from *los estados unidos.* Why do you not bring peace to your own country? I have seen *los señores* Humphrey Bogart and Edward Robinson in *las películas.* Why, all over Nueva York gangsters shoot at each other from one skyscraper to another. And what do you do about it? You dance all over the place with *la señora* Betty Grable. Ah yes, I understand very well. First you will bring peace, and then you will take our oil and our precious minerals."

Quetzalcoatl kicked angrily at a pebble beside his shiny steel toe.

"I must make you understand," he said. He looked at the unlighted cigarette dangling from Miguel's lips. Suddenly he raised his hand, and a white-hot ray shot from a ring on his finger and kindled the end of the cigarette. Miguel jerked away, startled. Then he inhaled the smoke and nodded. The white-hot ray disappeared.

"Muchas gracias, señor," Miguel said.

Quetzalcoatl's colorless lips pressed together thinly. "Miguel," he said, "could a *norteamericano* do that?"

"Quién sabe?"

"No one living on your planet could do that, and you know it."

Miguel shrugged.

"Do you see that cactus over there?" Quetzalcoatl demanded. "I could destroy it in two seconds."

"I have no doubt of it, *señor.*"

"I could, for that matter, destroy this whole planet."

"Yes, I have heard of the atomic bombs," Miguel said politely. "Why, then, do you trouble to interfere with a quiet private little argument between Fernandez and me, over a small water hole of no importance to anybody but—"

A bullet sang past.

Quetzalcoatl rubbed the ring on his finger with an angry gesture.

"Because the world is going to stop fighting," he said ominously. "If it doesn't we will destroy it. There is no reason at all why men should not live together in peace and brotherhood."

"There is one reason, *señor.*"

"What is that?"

"Fernandez," Miguel said.

"I will destroy you both if you do not stop fighting."

"El señor is a great peacemaker," Miguel said courteously. "I will gladly stop fighting if you will tell me how to avoid being killed when I do."

"Fernandez will stop fighting too."

Miguel removed his somewhat battered sombrero, reached for a stick, and carefully raised the hat above the rock. There was a nasty crack. The hat jumped away, and Miguel caught it as it fell.

"Very well," he said. "Since you insist, *señor,* I will stop fighting. But I will not come out from behind this rock. I am perfectly willing to stop fighting. But it seems to me that you demand I do something which you do not tell me how to do. You could as well require that I fly through the air like your machine of flight."

Quetzalcoatl frowned more deeply. Finally he said, "Miguel, tell me how this fight started."

"Fernandez wishes to kill me and enslave my family."

"Why should he want to do that?"

"Because he is evil," Miguel said.

"How do you know he is evil?"

"Because," Miguel pointed out logically, "he wishes to kill me and enslave my family."

There was a pause. A road runner darted past and paused to peck at the gleaming barrel of Miguel's rifle. Miguel sighed.

"There is a skin of good wine not twenty feet away—" he began, but Quetzalcoatl interrupted him.

"What was it you said about the water rights?"

"Oh, that," Miguel said. "This is a poor country, *señor.* Water is precious here. We have had a dry year and there is no longer water enough for two families. The water hole is mine. Fernandez wishes to kill me and enslave—"

"Are there no courts of law in your country?"

"For such as us?" Miguel demanded, and smiled politely.

"Has Fernandez a family too?" Quetzalcoatl asked.

"Yes, the poors," Miguel said. "He beats them when they do not work until they drop."

"Do you beat your family?"

"Only when they need it," Miguel said, surprised. "My wife is very fat and lazy. And my oldest, Chico, talks back. It is my duty to beat them when they need it, for their own good. It is also my duty to protect our water rights, since the evil Fernandez is determined to kill me and—"

Quetzalcoatl said impatiently, "This is a waste of time. Let me consider." He rubbed the ring on his finger again. He looked around. The road runner had found a more appetizing morsel than the rifle. He was now to be seen trotting away with the writhing tail of a lizard dangling from his beak.

Overhead the sun was hot in a clear blue sky. The dry air smelled of mesquite. Below, in the valley, the flying saucer's perfection of shape and texture looked incongruous and unreal.

"Wait here," Quetzalcoatl said at last. "I will talk to Fernandez. When I call, come to my machine of flight. Fernandez and I will meet you there presently."

"As you say, *señor,*" Miguel agreed. His eyes strayed.

"And do not touch your rifle," Quetzalcoatl added with great firmness.

"Why, no *señor,*" Miguel said. He waited until the tall man had gone. Then he crawled cautiously across the dry ground until he had recaptured his rifle. After that, with a little searching, he found his machete. Only then did he turn to the skin of wine. He was very thirsty indeed. But he did not drink heavily. He put a full clip in the rifle, leaned against a rock, and sipped a little from time to time from the wineskin as he waited.

In the meantime the stranger, ignoring fresh bullets that occasionally splashed blue from his steely person, approached Fernandez' hiding place. The sound of shots stopped. A long time passed, and finally the tall form reappeared and waved to Miguel.

"Yo voy, señor," Miguel shouted agreeably. He put his rifle conveniently on the rock and rose very cautiously, ready to duck at the first hostile move. There was no such move.

Fernandez appeared beside the stranger. Immediately Miguel bent down, seized his rifle and lifted it for a snap shot.

Something thin and hissing burned across the valley. The rifle turned red-hot in Miguel's grasp. He squealed and dropped it, and the next moment his mind went perfectly blank.

"I die with honor," he thought, and then thought no more.

. . . When he woke, he was standing under the shadow of the great flying saucer. Quetzalcoatl was lowering his hand from before Miguel's face. Sunlight sparkled on the tall man's ring. Miguel shook his head dizzily.

"I live?" he inquired.

But Quetzalcoatl paid no attention. He had turned to Fernandez, who was standing beside him, and was making gestures before Fernandez' masklike face. A light flashed from Quetzalcoatl's ring into Fernandez' glassy eyes. Fernandez shook his head and muttered thickly. Miguel looked for his rifle or machete, but they were gone He slipped his hand into his shirt, but his good little knife had vanished too.

He met Fernandez' eyes.

"We are both doomed, Don Fernandez," he said. "This *señor* Quetzalcoatl will kill us both. In a way I am sorry that you will go to hell and I to heaven, for we shall not meet again."

"You are mistaken," Fernandez replied, vainly searching for his own knife. "You will never see heaven. Nor is this tall *norteamericano* named Quetzalcoatl. For his own lying purposes he has assumed the name of Cortés."

"You will tell lies to the devil himself," Miguel said.

"Be quiet, both of you," Quetzalcoatl (or Cortés) said sharply. "You have seen a little of my power. Now listen to me. My race has assumed the high duty of seeing that the entire solar system lives in peace. We are a very advanced race, with power such as you do not yet dream of. We have solved problems which your people have no answer for, and it is now our duty to apply our power for the good of all. If you wish to keep on living, you will stop fighting immediately and forever, and from now on live in peace and brotherhood. Do you understand me?"

"That is all I have ever wished," Fernandez said, shocked. "But this off-spring of a goat wishes to kill me."

"There will be no more killing," Quetzalcoatl said. "You will live in brotherhood, or you will die."

Miguel and Fernandez looked at each other and then at Quetzalcoatl.

"The *señor* is a great peacemaker," Miguel murmured. "I have said it before. The way you mention is surely the best way of all to insure peace. But to us it is not so simple. To live in peace is good. Very well, *señor.* Tell us how."

"Simply stop fighting," Quetzalcoatl said impatiently.

"Now that is easy to say," Fernandez pointed out. "But life here in Sonora is not a simple business. Perhaps it is where you come from—"

"Naturally," Miguel put in. "In *los estados unidos* everyone is rich."

"—but it is not simple with us. Perhaps in your country, *señor,* the snake does not eat the rat, and the bird eat the snake. Perhaps in your country there is food and water for all, and a man need not fight to keep his family alive. Here is is not so simple."

Miguel nodded. "We shall certainly all be brothers some day," he agreed. "We try to do as the good God commands us. It is not easy, but little by little we learn to be better. It would be very fine if we could all become brothers at a word of magic, such as you command us. Unfortunately—" he shrugged.

"You must not use force to solve your problems," Quetzalcoatl said with great firmness. "Force is evil. *You will make peace now.*"

"Or else you will destroy us," Miguel said. He shrugged again and met Fernandez' eyes. "Very well, *señor.* You have an argument I do not care to resist. *Al fin,* I agree. What must we do?"

Quetzalcoatl turned to Fernandez.

"I too, *señor,*" the latter said, with a sigh. "You are, no doubt, right. Let us have peace."

"You will take hands," Quetzalcoatl said, his eyes gleaming. "You will swear brotherhood."

Miguel held out his hand. Fernandez took it firmly and the two men grinned at each other.

"You see?" Quetzalcoatl said, giving them his austere smile. "It is not hard at all. Now you are friends. Stay friends."

He turned away and walked toward the flying saucer. A door opened smoothly in the sleek hull. On the threshold Quetzalcoatl turned.

"Remember," he said. "I shall be watching."

"Without a doubt," Fernandez said. *"Adiós, señor."*

"Vaya con Dios," Miguel added.

The smooth surface of the hull closed after Quetzalcoatl. A moment later the flying saucer lifted smoothly and rose until it was a hundred feet above the ground. Then it shot off to the north like a sudden flash of lightning and was gone.

"As I thought," Miguel said. "He was from *los estados unidos.*"

Fernandez shrugged.

"There was a moment when I thought he might tell us something sensible," he said. "No doubt he had great wisdom. Truly, life is not easy."

"Oh, it is easy enough for him," Miguel said. "But he does not live in

Sonora. We, however, do. Fortunately, I and my family have a good water hole to rely on. For those without one, life in indeed hard."

"It is a very poor water hole," Fernandez said. "Such as it is, however, it is mine." He was rolling a cigarette as he spoke. He handed it to Miguel and rolled another for himself. The two men smoked for a while in silence. Then, still silent, they parted.

Miguel went back to the wineskin on the hill. He took a long drink, grunted with pleasure, and looked around him. His knife, machete and rifle were carelessly flung down not far away. He recovered them and made sure he had a full clip.

Then he peered cautiously around the rock barricade. A bullet splashed on the stone near his face. He returned the shot.

After that, there was silence for a while. Miguel sat back and took another drink. His eye was caught by a road runner scuttling past, with the tail of a lizard dangling from his beak. It was probably the same road runner as before, and perhaps the same lizard, slowly progressing toward digestion.

Miguel called softly, *"Señor* Bird! It is wrong to eat lizards. It is very wrong."

The road runner cocked a beady eye at him and ran on.

Miguel raised and aimed his rifle.

"Stop eating lizards, *Señor* Bird. Stop, or I must kill you."

The road runner ran on across the rifle sights.

"Don't you understand how to stop?" Miguel called gently. "Must I explain how?"

The road runner paused. The tail of the lizard disappeared completely.

"Oh, very well," Miguel said. "When I find out how a road runner can stop eating lizards and still live, then I will tell you, *amigo*. But until then, go with God."

He turned and aimed the rifle across the valley again.

The Venus Hunters

by J.G. Ballard

When Dr. Andrew Ward joined the Hubble Memorial Institute at Mount Vernon Observatory he never imagined that the closest of his new acquaintances would be an amateur stargazer and spare-time prophet called Charles Kandinski, tolerantly regarded by the Observatory professionals as a madman. In fact, had either he or Professor Cameron, the Institute's Deputy Director, known just how far he was to be prepared to carry this friendship before his two-year tour at the Institute was over, Ward would certainly have left Mount Vernon the day he arrived and would never have become involved in the bizarre and curiously ironic tragedy which was to leave an ineradicable stigma upon his career.

Professor Cameron first introduced him to Kandinski. About a week after Ward came to the Hubble he and Cameron were lunching together in the Institute cafeteria.

"We'll go down to Vernon Gardens for coffee," Cameron said when they finished dessert. "I want to get a shampoo for Edna's roses and then we'll sit in the sun for an hour and watch the girls go by." They strolled out through the terrace tables towards the parking lot. A mile away, beyond the conifers thinning out on the slopes above them, the three great Vernon domes gleamed like white marble against the sky. "Incidentally, you can meet the opposition."

"Is there another observatory at Vernon?" Ward asked as they set off along the drive in Cameron's Buick. "What is it—an Air Force weather station?"

"Have you ever heard of Charles Kandinski?" Cameron said. "He wrote a book called 'The Landings from Outer Space.' It was published about three years ago."

Ward shook his head doubtfully. They slowed down past the check-point at the gates and Cameron waved to the guard. "Is that the man who claims to have seen extra-terrestrial beings? Martians or—"

"Venusians. That's Kandinski. Not only seen them," Professor Cameron added. "He's talked to them. Charles works at a cafe in Vernon Gardens. We know him fairly well."

"He runs the other observatory?"

"Well, an old 4-inch MacDonald Refractor mounted in a bucket of cement. You probably wouldn't think much of it, but I wish we could see with our two-fifty just a tenth of what he sees."

Ward nodded vaguely. The two observatories at which he had worked previously, Cape Town and the Milan Astrographic, had both attracted any number of cranks and charlatans eager to reveal their own final truths about the cosmos, and the prospect of meeting Kandinski interested him only slightly. "What is he?" he asked. "A practical joker, or just a lunatic?"

Professor Cameron propped his glasses onto his forehead and negotiated a tight hairpin. "Neither," he said.

Ward smiled at Cameron, idly studying his plump cherubic face with its puckish mouth and keen eyes. He knew that Cameron enjoyed a modest reputation as a wit. "Has he ever claimed in front of you that he's seen a . . . Venusian?"

"Often," Professor Cameron said. "Charles lectures two or three times a week about the landings to the women's societies around here, and put himself completely at our disposal. I'm afraid we had to tell him he was a little too advanced for us. But wait until you meet him."

Ward shrugged and looked out at the long curving peach terraces lying below them, gold and heavy in the August heat. They dropped a thousand feet and the road widened and joined the highway which ran from Vernon Gardens across the desert to Santa Vera and the coast.

Vernon Gardens was the nearest town to the Observatory and most of it had been built within the last few years, evidently with an eye on the tourist trade. They passed a string of blue and pink-washed houses, a school constructed of glass bricks and an abstract Baptist chapel. Along the main thoroughfare the shops and stores were painted in bright jazzy colors, the vivid awnings and neon signs like street scenery in an experimental musical.

Professor Cameron turned off into a wide tree-lined square and parked by a cluster of fountains in the center. He and Ward walked toward the cafes—Al's Fresco Diner, Ylla's, the Dome—which stretched down to the sidewalk. Around the square were a dozen gift-shops filled with cheap souvenirs: silverplate telescopes and models of the great Vernon dome masquerading as ink-stands and cigar-boxes, plus a juvenile omnium gatherum of miniature planetaria, space helmets and plastic 3-D star atlases.

The cafe to which they went was decorated in the same futuristic motifs. The chairs and tables were painted a drab aluminum grey, their limbs and panels cut in random geometric shapes. A silver rocket ship, ten feet long, its paint peeling off in rusty strips, reared up from a pedestal among the tables. Across it was painted the cafe's name.

'The Site Tycho.'

A large mobile had been planted in the ground by the side-walk and dangled down over them, its vanes and struts flashing in the sun. Gingerly Professor Cameron pushed it away. "I'll swear that damn thing is growing," he confided to Ward. "I must tell Charles to prune it." He lowered himself into a chair by one of the open-air tables, put on a fresh pair of sunglasses and focused them at the long brown legs of a girl sauntering past.

Left alone for the moment, Ward looked around him and picked at a cellophane transfer of a ringed planet glued to the table-top. The Site Tycho was also used as a small science fiction exchange library. A couple of metal bookstands stood outside the cafe door, where a soberly dressed middle-aged man, obviously hiding behind his upturned collar, worked his way quickly through the rows of paperbacks. At another table a young man with an intent, serious face was reading a magazine. His high cerebrotonic forehead was marked across the temple by a ridge of pink tissue, which Ward wryly decided was a lobotomy scar.

"Perhaps we ought to show our landing permits," he said to Cameron when after three or four minutes no one had appeared to serve them. "Or at least get our pH's checked."

Professor Cameron grinned. "Don't worry, no customs, no surgery." He took his eyes off the side-walk for a moment. "This looks like him now."

A tall, bearded man in a short-sleeved tartan shirt and pale green slacks came out of the cafe towards them with two cups of coffee on a tray.

"Hello, Charles," Cameron greeted him. "There you are. We were beginning to think we'd lost ourselves in a time-trap."

The tall man grunted something and put the cups down. Ward guessed that he was about 55 years old. He was well over six feet tall, with a massive sunburnt head and lean but powerfully muscled arms.

"Andrew, this is Charles Kandinski." Cameron introduced the two men. "Andrew's come to work for me, Charles. He photographed all those Cepheids for the Milan Conference last year."

Kandinski nodded. His eyes examined Ward critically but showed no signs of interest.

"I've been telling him all about you, Charles," Cameron went on, "and how we all follow your work. No further news yet, I trust?"

Kandinski's lips parted in a slight smile. He listened politely to Cameron's banter and looked out over the square, his great seamed head raised to the sky.

"Andrew's read your book, Charles," Cameron was saying. "Very interested. He'd like to see the originals of those photographs. Wouldn't you, Andrew?"

"Yes, I certainly would," Ward said.

Kandinski gazed down at him again. His expression was not so much penetrating as detached and impersonal, as if he were assessing Ward with an utter lack of bias, so complete, in fact, that it left no room for even the smallest illusion. Previously Ward had only seen this expression in the eyes of the very old. "Good," Kandinski said. "At present they are in a safe-deposit box at my bank, but if you are serious I will get them out."

Just then two young women wearing wide-brimmed Rapallo hats made their way through the tables. They sat down and smiled at Kandinski. He nodded to Ward and Cameron and went over to the young women, who began to chatter to him animatedly.

"Well, he seems popular with them," Ward commented. "He's certainly not what I anticipated. I hope I didn't offend him over the plates. He was taking you seriously."

"He's a little sensitive about them," Cameron explained. "The famous dustbin-lid flying saucers. You mustn't think I bait him, though. To tell the truth I hold Charles in great respect. When all's said and done, we're in the same racket."

"Are we?" Ward said doubtfully. "I haven't read his book. Does he say in so many words that he saw and spoke to a visitor from Venus?"

"Precisely. Don't you believe him?"

Ward laughed and looked through the coins in his pocket, leaving one on the table. "I haven't tried to yet. You say the whole thing isn't a hoax?"

"Of course not."

"How do you explain it then? Compensation-fantasy or—"

Professor Cameron smiled. "Wait until you know Charles a little better."

"I already know the man's messianic," Ward said dryly. "Let me guess the rest. He lives on yogurt, weaves his own clothes, and stands on his head all night, reciting the Bhagavadgita backwards."

"He doesn't," Cameron said, still smiling at Ward. "He happens to be a big man who suffers from barber's rash. I thought he'd have you puzzled."

Ward pulled the transfer off the table. Some science fantast had skilfully pencilled in an imaginary topography on the planet's surface. There were canals, craters and lake systems named Verne, Wells and Bradbury. "Where did he see this Venusian?" Ward asked, trying to keep the curiosity out of his voice.

"About twenty miles from here, out in the desert off the Santa Vera highway. He was picnicking with some friends, went off for a stroll in the sandhills and ran straight into the spaceship. His friends swear he was perfectly normal both immediately before and after the landing, and all of them saw the inscribed metallic tablet which the Venusian pilot left behind. Some sort of ultimatum, if I remember, warning mankind to abandon all its space programs. Apparently someone up there does not like us."

"Has he still got the tablet?" Ward asked.

"No. Unluckily it combusted spontaneously in the heat. But Charles managed to take a photograph of it."

Ward laughed. "I bet he did. It sounds like a beautifully organized hoax. I supposed he made a fortune out of his book?"

"About 150 dollars. He had to pay for the printing himself. Why do you think he works here? The reviews were too unfavorable. People who read science fiction apparently dislike flying saucers, and everyone else dismissed him as a lunatic." He stood up. "We might as well get back."

As they left the cafe Cameron waved to Kandinski, who was still talking to the young women. They were leaning forward and listening with rapt attention to whatever he was saying.

"What do the people in Vernon Gardens think of him?" Ward asked as they moved away under the trees.

"Well, it's a curious thing, almost without exception those who actually know Kandinski are convinced he's sincere and that he saw an alien spacecraft, while at the same time realizing the absolute impossibility of the whole story."

" 'I know God exists, but I cannot *believe* in him'?"

"Exactly. Naturally, most people in Vernon think he's crazy. About three months after he met the Venusian, Charles saw another UFO chasing its tail over the town. He got the Fire Police out, alerted the Radar Command chain and even had the National Guard driving around town ringing a bell. Sure enough, there were two white blobs diving about in the clouds. Unfortunately for Charles, they were caused by the headlights of one of the asparagus farmers in the valley doing some night spraying. Charles was the first to admit it, but at 3 o'clock in the morning no one was very pleased."

"Who is Kandinski, anyway?" Ward asked. "Where does he come from?"

"He doesn't make a profession of seeing Venusians, if that's what you mean. He was born in Alaska, for some years taught psychology at Mexico City Univeristy. He's been just about everywhere, had a thousand different jobs. A veteran of the private evacuations. Get his book."

Ward murmured non-committally. They entered a small arcade and stood for a moment by the first shop, an aquarium called 'The Nouvelle Vague,' watching the Angel fish and Royal Brahmins swim dreamily up and down their tanks.

"It's worth reading," Professor Cameron went on. "Without exaggerating, it's really one of the most interesting documents I've ever come across."

"I'm afraid I have a closed mind when it comes to interplanetary bogeymen," Ward said.

"A pity," Cameron rejoined. "I find them fascinating. Straight out of the unconscious. The fish too," he added, pointing at the tanks. He grinned whimsically at Ward and ducked away into a horticulture store halfway down the arcade.

While Professor Cameron was looking through the sprays on the hormone counter, Ward went over to a newsstand and glanced at the magazines. The proximity of the observatory had prompted a large selection of popular astronomical guides and digests, most of them with illustrations of the Mount Vernon domes on their wrappers. Among them Ward noticed a dusty, dog-eared paperback, 'The Landings from Outer Space,' by Charles Kandinski. On the front cover a gigantic space vehicle, at least the size of New York, tens of thousands of portholes ablaze with light, was soraing majestically across a brilliant backdrop of stars and spiral nebulae.

Ward picked up the book and turned to the end cover. Here there was a photograph of Kandinski, dressed in a dark lounge suit several sizes too small, peering stiffly into the eye-piece of his MacDonald.

Ward hesitated before finally taking out his wallet. He bought the book and slipped it into his pocket as Professor Cameron emerged from the horticulture store.

"Get your shampoo?" Ward asked.

Cameron brandished a brass insecticide gun, then slung it, buccaneer-like, under his belt. "My disintegrator," he said, patting the butt of the gun. "There's a positive plague of white ants in the garden, like something out of a science fiction nightmare. I've tried to convince Edna that their real source is psychological. Remember the story 'Leningen vs the Ants'? A classic example of the forces of the Id rebelling against the Super Ego." He watched a girl in a black bikini and lemon-colored sunglasses move gracefully through the arcade and added meditatively: "You know, Andrew, like everyone else my real vocation was to be a psychiatrist. I spend so long analyzing my motives I've no time left to act."

"Kandinski's Super-Ego must be in difficulties," Ward remarked. "You haven't told me your explanation yet."

"What explanation?"

"Well, what's really at the bottom of this Venusian he claims to have seen?"

"Nothing is at the bottom of it. Why?"

Ward smiled helplessly. "You will tell me next that you really believe him."

Professor Cameron chuckled. They reached his car and climbed in. "Of course I do," he said.

When, three days later, Ward borrowed Professor Cameron's car and drove down to the rail depot in Vernon Gardens to collect a case of slides which had followed him across the Atlantic, he had no intention of seeing Charles Kandinski again. He had read one or two chapters of Kandinski's book before going to sleep the previous night and dropped it in boredom. Kandinski's description of his encounter with the Venusian was not only puerile and crudely written but, most disappointing of all, completely devoid of imagination. Ward's work at the Institute was now taking up most of his time. The Annual Congress of the International Geophysical Association was being held at Mount Vernon in little under a month, and most of the burden or organizing the three-week program of lectures, semesters and dinners had fallen on Professor Cameron and himself.

But as he drove away from the depot past the cafes in the square he caught sight of Kandinski on the terrace of the Site Tycho. It was 3 o'clock, a time when most people in Vernon Gardens were lying alseep indoors, and Kandinski seemed to be the only person out in the sun. He was scrubbing away energetically at the abstract tables with his long hairy arms, head down so that his beard was almost touching the metal tops, like an aboriginal half-man prowling in dim bewilderment over the ruins of a futuristic city lost in an inversion of time.

On an impulse, Ward parked the car in the square and walked across to the Site Tycho, but as soon as Kandinski came over to his table he wished he had gone to another of the cafes. Kandinski had been reticent enough the previous day, but now that Cameron was absent he might well turn out to be a garrulous bore.

After serving him Kandinski sat down on a bench by the bookshelves and stared moodily at his feet. Ward watched him quietly for five minutes, as the mobiles revolved delicately in the warm air, deciding whether to approach Kandinski. Then he stood up and went over to the rows of magazines. He picked in a desultory way through half a dozen and turned to Kandinski. "Can you recommend any of these?"

Kandinski looked up. "Do you read science fiction?" he asked matter-of-factly.

"Not as a rule," Ward admitted. When Kandinski said nothing he went on: "Perhaps I'm too skeptical, but I can't take it too seriously."

Kandinski pulled at a blister on his palm. "No one suggests you should. What you mean is that you take it too seriously."

Accepting the rebuke with a smile at himself, Ward pulled out one of the magazines and sat down at a table next to Kandinski. On the cover was a placid suburban setting of snugly eaved houses, yew trees, and children's bicycles. Spreading slowly across the roof-tops was an enormous pulpy nightmare, blocking out the sun behind it and throwing a weird phosphorescent glow over the roofs and lawns. "You're probably right," Ward said, showing the cover to Kandinski. "I'd hate to want to take that seriously."

Kandinski waved it aside. "I have seen 11th century illuminations of the pentateuch more sensational than any of these covers." He pointed to the cinema theater on the far side of the square, where the four-hour Biblical epic 'Cain and Abel' was showing. Above the trees an elaborate technicolored hoarding showed Cain, wearing what appeared to be a suit of Roman armor, wrestling with an immense hydraheaded boa constrictor.

Kandinski shrugged tolerantly. "If Michelangelo were working for MGM today would he produce anything better?"

Ward laughed. "You may well be right. Perhaps the House of the Medicis should be re-christened '16th Century-Fox.' "

Kandinski stood up and straightened the shelves. "I saw you here with Godfrey Cameron," he said over his shoulder. "You're working at the Observatory?"

"At the Hubble."

Kandinski came and sat down beside Ward. "Cameron is a good man. A very pleasant fellow."

"He thinks a great deal of you," Ward volunteered, realizing that Kandinski was probably short of friends.

"You mustn't believe everything that Cameron says about me," Kandinski said suddenly. He hesitated, apparently uncertain whether to confide further in Ward, and then took the magazine from him. "There are better ones here. You have to exercise some discrimination."

"It's not so much the sensationalism that puts me off," Ward explained, "as the psychological implications. Most of the themes in these stories come straight out of the more unpleasant reaches of the unconscious."

Kandinski glanced sharply at Ward, a trace of amusement in his eyes. "That sounds rather dubious and, if I may say so, second-hand. Take the best of these stories for what they are: imaginative exercises on the theme of tomorrow."

"You read a good deal of science fiction?" Ward asked.

Kandinski shook his head. "Never. Not since I was a child."

"I'm surprised," Ward said. "Professor Cameron told me you had written a science fiction novel."

"Not a novel," Kandinski corrected.

"I'd like to read it," Ward went on. "From what Cameron said it sounded fascinating, almost Swiftian in concept. This spacecraft which arrives from Venus and the strange conversations the pilot holds with a philosopher he meets. A modern morality. Is that the subject?"

Kandinski watched Ward thoughtfully before replying. "Loosely, yes. But, as I said, the book is not a novel. It is a factual and literal report of a Venus landing which actually took place, a diary of the most significant encounter in history since Paul saw his vision of Christ on the road to Damascus." He lifted his huge bearded head and gazed at Ward without embarrassment. "As a matter of interest, as Professor Cameron probably explained to you, I was the man who witnessed the landing."

Still maintaining his pose, Ward frowned intently. "Well, in fact Cameron did say something of the sort, but I . . ."

"But you found it difficult to believe?" Kandinski suggested ironically.

"Just a little," Ward admitted. "Are you seriously claiming that you did see a Venusian spacecraft?"

Kandinski nodded. "Exactly." Then, as if aware that their conversation had reached a familiar turning, he suddenly seemed to lose interest in Ward. "Excuse me." He nodded politely to Ward, picked up a length of hose-pipe connected to a faucet and began to spray one of the big mobiles.

Puzzled but still skeptical, Ward sat back and watched him critically, then fished in his pockets for some change. "I must say I admire you for taking it all so calmly," he told Kandinski as he paid him.

"What makes you think I do?"

"Well, if I'd seen, let alone spoken to a visitor from Venus I think I'd be running around in a flat spin, notifying every government and observatory in the world."

"I did," Kandinski said. "As far as I could. No one was very interested."

Ward shook his head and laughed. "It is incredible, to put it mildly."

"I agree with you."

"What I mean," Ward said, "is that it's straight out of one of these science fiction stories of yours."

Kandinski rubbed his lips with a scarred knuckle, obviously searching for some means of ending the conversation. "The resemblance is misleading. They are not my stories," he added parenthetically. "This cafe is the only one which would give me work, for a perhaps obvious reason. As for the incredibility, let me say that I was and still am completely amazed. You may think I take it all calmly, but ever since the landing I have lived in a state of acute anxiety and foreboding. But short of committing some spectacular crime to draw attention to myself I don't see now how I can convince anyone."

Ward gestured with his glasses. "Perhaps. But I'm surprised you don't realize the very simple reasons why people refuse to take you seriously. For example, why should you be the only person to witness an event of such staggering implications? Why have *you* alone seen a Venusian?"

"A sheer accident."

"But why should a spacecraft from Venus land here?"

"What better place than near Mount Vernon Observatory?"

"I can think of any number. The UN Assembly, for one."

Kandinski smiled lightly. "Columbus didn't make his first contacts with the North American Indians at the Iroquois-Sioux Tribal Conference."

"That may be," Ward admitted, beginning to feel impatient. "What did this Venusian look like?"

Kandinski smiled wearily at the empty tables and picked up his hose again. "I don't know whether you've read my book," he said, "but if you haven't you'll find it all there."

"Professor Cameron mentioned that you took some photographs of the Venusian spacecraft. Could I examine them?"

"Certainly," Kandinski replied promptly. "I'll bring them here tomorrow. You're welcome to test them in any way you wish."

That evening Ward had dinner with the Camerons. Professor Renthall, Director of the Hubble, and his wife completed the party. The table-talk consisted almost entirely of good-humored gossip about their colleagues retailed by Cameron and Renthall, and Ward was able to mention his conversation with Kandinski.

"At first I thought he was mad, but now I'm not so certain. There's something rather too subtle about him. The way he creates an impression of absolute integrity, but at the same time never gives you a chance to tackle him directly on any point of detail. And when you do manage to ask him outright about this Venusian his answers are far too pat. I'm convinced the whole thing is an elaborate hoax."

Professor Renthall shook his head. "No, it's no hoax. Don't you agree, Godfrey?"

Cameron nodded. "Not in Andrew's sense, anyway."

"But what other explanation is there?" Ward asked. "We know he hasn't seen a Venusian, so he must be a fraud. Unless you think he's a lunatic. And he certainly doesn't behave like one."

"What is a lunatic?" Professor Renthall asked rhetorically, peering into the facetted stem of his raised hock glass. "Merely a man with more understanding than he can contain. I think Charles belongs in that category."

"The definition doesn't explain him, sir," Ward insisted. "He's going to lend me his photographs and when I prove those are fakes I think I'll be able to get under his guard."

"Poor Charles," Edna Cameron said. "Why shouldn't he have seen a spaceship? I think I see them every day."

"That's just what I feel, dear," Cameron said, patting his wife's matronly, brocaded shoulder. "Let Charles have his Venusian if he wants to. Damn it, all it's trying to do is ban Project Apollo. An excellent idea, I have always maintained; only the professional astronomer has any business in space. After the Rainbow tests there isn't an astronomer anywhere in the world who wouldn't follow Charles Kandinski to the stake." He turned to Renthall. "By the way, I wonder what Charles is planning for the Congress? A Neptunian? Or perhaps a whole delegation from Proxima Centauri. We ought to fit him out with a space suit and a pavilion—'Charles Kandinski—New Worlds for Old'."

"Santa Claus in a space suit," Professor Renthall mused. "That's a new one. Send him a ticket."

The next weekend Ward returned the twelve plates to the Site Tycho.

"Well?" Kandinski asked.

"It's difficult to say," Ward answered. "They're all too heavily absorbed. They could be clever montages of light brackets and turbine blades. One of them looks like a close-up of a clutch plate. There's a significant lack of any really corroborative details, which you'd expect somewhere in so wide a selection." He paused. "On the other hand, they could be genuine."

Kandinski said nothing, took the paper package, and went off into the cafe.

The interior of the Site Tycho had been designed to represent the control room of a spaceship on the surface of the Moon. Hidden fluorescent lighting glimmered through plastic wall fascia and filled the room with an eerie blue glow. Behind the bar a large mural threw the curving outline of the Moon onto an illuminated starscape. The doors leading to the rest rooms were circular and bulged outwards like air locks, distinguished from each other by the symbols ♂ and ♀. The total effect was ingenious but somehow reminiscent to Ward of a twenty-fifth century cave.

He sat down at the bar and waited while Kandinski packed the plates away carefully in an old leather briefcase.

"I've read your book," Ward said. "I had looked at it the last time I saw you, but I read it again thoroughly." He waited for some comment upon this admission, but Kandinski went over to an old portable typewriter standing at the far end of the bar and began to type laboriously with one finger. "Have you seen any more Venusians since the book was published?" Ward asked.

"None," Kandinski said.

"Do you think you will?"

"Perhaps." Kandinski shrugged and went on with his typing.

"What are you working on now?" Ward asked.

"A lecture I am giving on Friday evening," Kandinski said. Two keys locked together and he flicked them back. "Would you care to come? Eight-thirty, at the high school near the Baptist chapel."

"If I can," Ward said. He saw that Kandinski wanted to get rid of him. "Thanks for letting me see the plates." He made his way out into the sun. People were walking about through the fresh morning air, and he caught the clean scent of peach blossom carried down the slopes into the town.

Suddenly Ward felt how enclosed and insane it had been inside the Tycho, and how apposite had been his description of it as a cave, with its residential magician incanting over his photographs like a down-at-heel Merlin manipulating his set of runes. He felt annoyed with himself for becoming involved with Kandinski and allowing the potent charisma of his personality to confuse him. Obviously Kandinski played upon the instinctive sympathy for the outcast, his whole pose of integrity and conviction a device for drawing the gullible towards him.

Letting the light spray from the fountains fall across his face, Ward crossed the square towards his car.

Away in the distance 2,000 feet above, rising beyond a screen of fir trees, the three Mount Vernon domes shone together in the sun like a futuristic Taj Mahal.

Fifteen miles from Vernon Gardens the Santa Vera highway circled down from the foot of Mount Vernon into the first low scrub-covered hills which marked the southern edge of the desert. Ward looked out at the long banks of coarse sand stretching away through the haze, their outlines blurring in the afternoon heat. He glanced at the book lying on the seat beside him, open at the map printed between its end covers, and carefully checked his position, involuntarily slowing the speed of the Chevrolet as he moved nearer to the site of the Venus landings.

In the fortnight since he had returned the photographs to the Site Tycho, he had seen Kandinski only once, at the lecture delivered the previous night. Ward had deliberately stayed away from the Site Tycho, but he had seen a poster advertising the lecture and driven down to the school despite himself.

The lecture was delivered in the gymnasium before an audience of forty or fifty people, most of them women, who formed one of the innumerable local astronomical societies. Listening to the talk around him, Ward gathered that their activities principally consisted of trying to identify more than half a dozen of the constellations. Kandinski had lectured to them on several occasions and the subject of this latest installment was his researches into the significance of the Venusian tablet he had been analyzing for the last three years.

When Kandinski stepped onto the dais there was a brief round of applause. He was wearing a lounge suit of a curiously archaic cut and had washed his beard, which bushed out above his string tie so that he resembled a Mormon patriarch or the homespun saint of some fervent evangelical community.

For the benefit of any new members, he prefaced his lecture with a brief account of his meeting with the Venusian, and then turned to his analysis of the tablet. This was the familiar ultimatum warning mankind to abandon its preparations for the exploration of space, for the ostensible reason that, just as the sea was a universal image of the unconscious, so space was nothing less than an image of psychosis and death, and that if he tried to penetrate the interplanetary voids man would only plunge to earth like a demented Icarus, unable to scale the vastness of the cosmic zero. Kandinski's real motives for introducing this were all too apparent—the expected success of Project Apollo and subsequent landings on Mars and Venus would, if nothing else, conclusively expose his fantasies.

However, by the end of the lecture Ward found that his opinion of Kandinski had experienced a complete about face.

As a lecturer Kandinski was poor, losing words, speaking in a slow ponderous style and trapping himself in long subordinate clauses, but his quiet, matter-of-fact tone and absolute conviction in the importance of what he was saying, coupled with the nature of his material, held the talk together. His analysis of the Venusian cryptograms, a succession of intricate philological theorems, was well above the heads of his audience, but what began to impress Ward, as much as the painstaking preparation which must have preceded the lecture, was Kandinski's acute nervousness in delivering it. Ward noticed that he suffered from an irritating speech impediment that made it difficult for him to pronounce 'Venusian,' and he saw that Kandinski, far from basking in the limelight, was delivering the lecture only out of a deep sense of obligation to his audience and was greatly relieved when the ordeal was over.

At the end Kandinski had invited questions. These, with the exception of the chairman's, all concerned the landing of the alien space vehicle and ignored the real subject of the lecture. Kandinski answered them all carefully, taking in good part the inevitable facetious questions. Ward noted with interest the audience's curious ambivalence, simultaneously fascinated by and resentful of Kandinski's exposure of their own private fantasies, an expression of the same ambivalence which had propelled so many of the mana-personalities of history towards their inevitable Calvarys.

Just as the chairman was about to close the meeting, Ward stood up.

"Mr. Kandinski. You say that this Venusian indicated that there was also life on one of the moons of Uranus. Can you tell us how he did this, if there was no verbal communication between you?"

Kandinski showed no surprise at seeing Ward. "Certainly; as I told you, he drew eight concentric circles in the sand, one for each of the planets. Around Uranus he drew five lesser orbits and marked one of these. Then he pointed to himself and to me and to a patch of lichen. From this I deduced, reasonably I maintain, that—"

"Excuse me, Mr. Kandinski," Ward interrupted. "You say he drew five orbits around Uranus? One for each of the moons?"

Kandinski nodded. "Yes. Five."

"That was in 1960," Ward went on. "Three weeks ago Professor Pineau at Brussels discovered a sixth moon of Uranus."

The audience looked around at Ward and began to murmur.

"Why should this Venusian have omitted one of the moons?" Ward asked, his voice ringing across the gymnasium.

Kandinski frowned and peered at Ward suspiciously. "I didn't know there was a sixth moon . . ." he began.

"Exactly!" someone called out. The audience began to titter.

"I can understand the Venusian not wishing to introduce any difficulties," Ward said, "but this seems a curious way of doing it."

Kandinski appeared at a loss. Then he introduced Ward to the audience. "Dr. Ward is a professional while I am only an amateur," he admitted. "I am afraid I cannot explain the anomaly. Perhaps my memory is at fault. But I am sure the Venusian drew only five orbits." He stepped down from the dais and strode out hurriedly, scowling into his beard, pursued by a few derisory hoots from the audience.

It took Ward fifteen minutes to free himself from the knot of admiring, white-gloved spinsters who cornered him between two vaulting horses. When he broke away he ran out to his car and drove into Vernon Gardens, hoping to see Kandinski and apologize to him.

Five miles into the desert Ward approached a nexus of rock cuttings and causeways which were part of an abandoned irrigation scheme. The colors of the hills were more vivid now, bright siliconic reds and yellows, crossed with sharp stabs of light from the exposed quartz veins. Following the map on the seat, he turned off the highway onto a rough track which ran along the bank of a dried-up canal. He passed a few rusting sections of picket fencing, a derelict grader half-submerged under the sand, and a collection of dilapidated metal shacks. The car bumped over the potholes at little more than ten miles an hour, throwing up clouds of hot ashy dust that swirled high into the air behind him.

Two miles along the canal the track came to an end. Ward stopped the car and waited for the dust to subside. Carrying Kandinski's book in front of him like a divining instrument, he set off on foot across the remaining three hundred yards. The contours around him were marked on the map, but the hills had shifted several hundred yards westward since the book's publication and he found himself wandering about from one crest to another, peering into shallow depressions only as old as the last sandstorm. The entire landscape seemed haunted by strange currents and moods; the sand-swirls surging down the aisles of dunes and the proximity of the horizon enclosed the whole place of stones with invisible walls.

Finally he found the ring of hills indicated and climbed a narrow saddle leading to its center. When he scaled the thirty-foot slope he stopped abruptly.

Down on his knees in the middle of the basin with his back to Ward, the studs of his boots flashing in the sunlight, was Kandinski. There was a clutter of tiny objects on the sand around him, and at first Ward thought he was at prayer, making his oblations to the tutelary deities of Venus. Then he saw that Kandinski was slowly scraping the surface of the ground with a small trowel. A circle about 20 yards in diameter had been marked off with pegs and string into a series of wedge-shaped allotments. Every few seconds Kandinski carefully decanted a small heap of grit into one of the test tubes mounted in a wooden rack in front of him.

Ward put away the book and walked down the slope. Kandinski looked around and then climbed to his feet. The coating of red ash on his beard gave him a fiery, prophetic look. He recognized Ward and raised the trowel in greeting.

Ward stopped at the edge of the string perimeter. "What on earth are you doing?"

"I am collecting specimens." Kandinski bent down and corked one of the tubes. He looked tired but worked away steadily.

Ward watched him finish a row. "It's going to take you a long time to cover the whole area. I thought there weren't any gaps left in the Periodic Table."

"The spacecraft rotated at speed before it rose into the air. This surface is abrasive enough to have scratched off a few minute filings. With luck I may find one of them." Kandinski smiled thinly. "262. Venusiam, I hope."

Ward started to say: "But the transuranic elements decay spontaneously . . ." and then walked over to the center of the circle, where there was a round indentation, three feet deep and five across. The inner surface was glazed and smooth.

It was shaped like an inverted cone and looked as if it had been caused by the boss of an enormous spinning top. "This is where the spacecraft landed?"

Kandinski nodded. He filled the last tube and then stowed the rack away in a canvas satchel. He came over to Ward and stared down at the hole. "What does it look like to you? A meteor impact? Or an oil drill, perhaps?" A smile showed behind his dusty beard. "The F-109's at the Air Force Weapons School begin their target runs across here. It might have been caused by a rogue cannon shell."

Ward stooped down and felt the surface of the pit, running his fingers thoughtfully over the warm fused silica. "More like a 500-pound bomb. But the cone is geometrically perfect. It's certainly unusual."

"Unusual?" Kandinski chuckled to himself and picked up the satchel.

"Has anyone else been out here?" Ward asked as they trudged up the slope?

"Two so-called experts." Kandinski slapped the sand off his knees. "A geologist from Gulf-Vacuum and an Air Force ballistics officer. You'll be glad to hear that they both thought I had dug the pit myself and then fused the surface with an acetylene torch." He peered critically at Ward. "Why did you come out here today?"

"Idle curiosity," Ward said. "I had an afternoon off and I felt like a drive."

They reached the crest of the hill and he stopped and looked down into the basin. The lines of string split the circle into a strange horological device, a huge zodiacal mandala, the dark patches in the arcs Kandinski had been working telling its stations.

"You were going to tell me why you came out here," Kandinski said as they walked back to the car.

Ward shrugged. "I suppose I wanted to prove something to myself. There's a problem of reconciliation." He hesitated, and then began: "You see, there are some things which are self-evidently false. The laws of common sense and every day experience refute them. I know a lot of the evidence for many things we believe is pretty thin, but I don't have to embark on a theory of knowledge to decide that the Moon isn't made of green cheese."

"Well?" Kandinski shifted the satchel to his other shoulder.

"This Venusian you've seen," Ward said. "The landing, the runic tablet. I can't believe them. Every piece of evidence I've seen, all the circumstantial details, the facts given in this book . . . they're all patently false." He turned to one of the middle chapters. "Take this at random—'A phosphorescent green fluid pulsed through the dorsal lung-chamber of the Prime's helmet, inflating two opaque fan-like gills . . . '" Ward closed the book and shrugged helplessly. Kandinski stood a few feet away from him, the sunlight breaking across the deep lines of his face.

"Now I know what you say to my objections," Ward went on. "If you told a 19th century chemist that lead could be transmuted into gold he would have dismissed you as a medievalist. But the point is that he'd have been right to do so—."

"I understand," Kandinski interrupted. "But you still haven't explained why you came out here today."

Ward stared out over the desert. High above, a stratojet was doing cuban eights into the sun, the spiral vapor trails drifting across the sky like gigantic fragments of an apocalyptic message. Looking around, he realized that Kandinski must have walked from the bus-stop on the highway. "I'll give you a lift back," he said.

As they drove along the canal he turned to Kandinski. "I enjoyed your lecture last night. I apologize for trying to make you look a fool."

Kandinski was loosening his bootstraps. He laughed unreproachfully. "You put me in an awkward position. I could hardly have challenged you. I can't afford to subscribe to every astronomical journal. Though a sixth moon would have been big news." As they neared Vernon Gardens he asked: "Would you like to come in and look at the tablet analysis?"

Ward made no reply to the invitation. He drove around the square and parked under the trees, then looked up at the fountains, tapping his fingers on the windshield. Kandinski sat beside him, cogitating into his beard.

Ward watched him carefully. "Do you think this Venusian will return?"

Kandinski nodded. "Yes. I am sure he will."

Later they sat together at a broad rolltop desk in the room above the Tycho. Around the wall hung white cardboard screens packed with lines of cuneiform glyphics and Kandinski's progressive breakdown of their meaning.

Ward held an enlargement of the original photograph of the Venusian tablet and listened to Kandinski's explanation.

"As you see from this," Kandinski explained, "in all probability there are not millions of Venusians, as everyone would expect, but only three or four of them altogether. Two are circling Venus, a third Uranus and possibly a fourth is in orbit around Neptune. This solves the difficulty that puzzled you and antagonizes everyone else. Why should the Prime have approached only one person out of several hundred million and selected him on a completely random basis? Now obviously he had seen the Russian and American satellite capsules and assumed that our race, like his own, numbered no more than three or four, then concluded from the atmospheric H-bomb tests that we were in conflict and would soon destroy ourselves. This is one of the reasons why I think he will return shortly and why it is important to organize a worldwide reception for him on a governmental level."

"Wait a minute," Ward said. "He must have known that the population of this planet numbered more than three or four. Even the weakest telescope would demonstrate that."

"Of course, but he would naturally assume that the millions of inhabitants of the Earth belonged to an aboriginal subspecies, perhaps employed as work animals. After all, if he observed that despite this planet's immense resources the bulk of its population lived like animals, an alien visitor could only decide that they were considered as such."

"But space vehicles are supposed to have been observing us since the Babylonian era, long before the development of satellite rockets. There have been thousands of recorded sightings."

Kandinski shook his head. "None of them has been authenticated."

"What about the other landings that have been reported recently?" Ward asked. "Any number of people have seen Venusians and Martians."

"Have they?" Kandinski asked skeptically. "I wish I could believe that. Some of the encounters reveal marvelous powers of invention, but no one can accept them as anything but fantasy."

"The same criticism has been leveled at your spacecraft," Ward reminded him.

Kandinski seemed to lose patience. "I *saw* it," he exclaimed, impotently tossing his notebook onto the desk. "I *spoke* to the Prime!"

Ward nodded non-committally and picked up the photograph again. Kandinski stepped over to him and took it out of his hands. "Ward," he said carefully. "Believe me. You must. You know I am too big a man to waste myself on a senseless charade." His massive hands squeezed Ward's shoulders and almost lifted him off the seat. *"Believe* me. Together we can be ready for the next landings and alert the world. I am only Charles Kandinski, a waiter at a third-rate cafe, but you are Dr. Andrew Ward of Mount Vernon Observatory. They will listen to you. Try to realize what this may mean for mankind."

Ward pulled himself away from Kandinski and rubbed his shoulders.

"Ward, do you believe me? Ask yourself."

Ward looked up pensively at Kandinski towering over him, his red beard like the burning, unconsumed bush.

"I think so," he said quietly. "Yes, I do."

A week later the 23rd Congress of the International Geophysical Association opened at Mount Vernon Observatory. At 3:30 p.m., in the Hoyle Library amphitheater, Professor Renthall was to deliver the inaugural address welcoming the 92 delegates and 25 newspaper and agency reporters to the fortnight's program of lectures and discussions.

Shortly after 11 o'clock that morning Ward and Professor Cameron completed their final arrangements and escaped down to Vernon Gardens for an hour's relaxation.

"Well," Cameron said as they walked over to the Site Tycho, "I've got a pretty good idea of what it must be like to run the Waldorf Astoria." They picked one of the sidewalk tables and sat down. "I haven't been here for weeks," Cameron said. "How are you getting on with the Man in the Moon?"

"Kandinski? I hardly ever see him," Ward said.

"I was talking to the Time Magazine stringer about Charles," Cameron said, cleaning his sunglasses. "He thought he might do a piece about him."

"Hasn't Kandinski suffered enough of that sort of thing?" Ward asked moodily.

"Perhaps he has," Cameron agreed. "Is he still working on his crossword puzzle? The tablet thing, whatever he calls it."

Casually, Ward said: "He has a theory that it should be possible to see the lunar bases. Refueling points established there by the Venusians over the centuries."

"Interesting," Cameron commented.

"They're sited near Copernicus," Ward went on. "I know Vandone at Milan is mapping Archimedes and the Imbrium. I thought I might mention it to him at his semester tomorrow."

Professor Cameron took off his glasses and gazed quizzically at Ward. "My dear Andrew, what has been going on? Don't tell me you've become one of Charles' converts?"

Ward laughed and shook his head. "Of course not. Obviously there are no lunar bases or alien spacecraft. I don't for a moment believe a word Kandinski says." He gestured helplessly. "At the same time I admit I have become involved with him. There's something about Kandinski's personality. On the one hand I can't take him seriously—"

"Oh, I take him seriously," Cameron cut in smoothly. "Very seriously indeed, if not quite in the sense you mean." Cameron turned his back on the sidewalk crowds. "Jung's views on flying saucers are very illuminating, Andrew; they'd help you to understand Kandinski. Jung believes that civilization now stands at the conclusion of a Platonic Great Year, at the eclipse of the sign of Pisces which has dominated the Christian epoch, and that we are entering the sign of Aquarius, a period of confusion and psychic chaos. He remarks that throughout history, at all times of uncertainty and discord, cosmic space vehicles have been seen approaching Earth, and that in a few extreme cases actual meetings with their occupants are supposed to have taken place."

As Cameron paused, Ward glanced across the tables for Kandinski, but a relief waiter served them and he assumed it was Kandinski's day off.

Cameron continued: "Most people regard Charles Kandinski as a lunatic, but as a matter of fact he is performing one of the most important roles in the world today, the role of a prophet alerting people to this coming crisis. The real significance of his fantasies, like that of the ban-the-bomb movements, is to be found elsewhere than on the conscious plane, as an expression of the immense psychic forces stirring below the surface of rational life, like the isotactic movements of the continental tables which heralded the major geological transformations."

Ward shook his head dubiously. "I can accept that a man such as Freud was a prophet, but Charles Kandinski—?"

"Certainly. Far more than Freud. It's unfortunate for Kandinski, and for the writers of science fiction for that matter, that they have to perform their task of describing the symbols of transformation in a so-called rationalist society, where a scientific, or at least a pseudo-scientific explanation is required *a priori*. And because the true prophet never deals in what may be rationally deduced, people such as Charles are ignored or derided today."

"It's interesting that Kandinski compared his meeting with the Venusian with Paul's conversion on the road to Damascus," Ward said.

"He was quite right. In both encounters you see the same mechanism of blinding unconscious revelation. And you can see too that Charles feels the same overwhelming need to spread the Pauline revelation to the world. The Anti-Apollo movement is only now getting underway, but within the next decade it will recruit millions, and men such as Charles Kandinski will be the fathers of its apocalypse."

"You make him sound like a titanic figure," Ward remarked quietly. "I think he's just a lonely, tired man obsessed by something he can't understand. Perhaps he simply needs a few friends to confide in."

Slowly shaking his head, Cameron tapped the table with his glasses. "Be warned, Andrew, you'll burn your fingers if you play with Charles' brand of fire. The mana-personalities of history have no time for personal loyalties—the founder of the Christian church made that pretty plain."

Shortly after seven o'clock that evening Charles Kandinski mounted his bicycle and set off out of Vernon Gardens. The small room in the seedy area where he lived always depressed him on his free days from the Tycho, and as he pedaled along he ignored the shouts from his neighbors sitting out on their balconies with their crates of beer. He knew that his beard and the high, ancient bicycle with its capacious wicker basket made him a grotesque, Quixotic figure, but he felt too preoccupied to care. That morning he had heard that the French translation of 'The Landings from Outer Space', printed at his own cost, had been completely ignored by the Paris press. In addition a jobbing printer in Santa Vera was pressing him for payment for 5,000 anti-Apollo leaflets that had been distributed the previous year.

Above all had come the news on the radio that the target date of the first manned Moonflight had been advanced to 1965, and on the following day would take place the latest and most ambitious of the instrumented lunar flights. The anticipated budget for the Apollo program (in a moment of grim humor he had calculated that it would pay for the printing of some 1000 billion leaflets) seemed to double each year, but so far he had found little success in his attempt to alert people to the folly of venturing into space. All that day he had felt sick with frustration and anger.

At the end of the avenue he turned onto the highway which served the asparagus farms lying in the 20-mile strip between Vernon Gardens and the desert. It was a hot empty evening and few cars or trucks passed him. On either side of the road the great lemon-green terraces of asparagus lay seeping in their moist paddy beds, and occasionally a marsh-hen clacked overhead and dived out of sight.

Five miles along the road he reached the last farmhouse above the edge of the desert. He cycled on to where the road ended 200 yards ahead, dismounted and left the bicycle in a culvert. Slinging his camera over one shoulder, he walked off across the hard ground into the mouth of a small valley.

The boundary between the desert and the farm-strip was irregular. On his left, beyond the rocky slopes, he could hear a motor-reaper purring down one of the mile-long spits of fertile land running into the desert, but the barren terrain and the sense of isolation began to relax him and he forgot the irritations that had plagued him all day.

A keen naturalist, he saw a long-necked sand-crane perched on a spur of shale fifty feet from him and stopped and raised his camera. Peering through the finder he noticed that the light had faded too deeply for a photograph. Curiously, the sand-crane was clearly silhouetted against a circular glow of light which emanated from beyond a low ridge at the end of the valley. This apparently sourceless corona fitfully illuminated the darkening air, as if coming from a lighted mineshaft.

Putting away his camera, Kandinski walked forward, within a few minutes reached the ridge, and began to climb it. The face sloped steeply, and he pulled himself up by the hefts of brush and scrub, kicking away footholds in the rocky surface.

Just before he reached the crest he felt his heart surge painfully with the exertion, and he lay still for a moment, a sudden feeling of dizziness spinning in his head. He waited until the spasm subsided, shivering faintly in the cool air, an unfamiliar undertone of uneasiness in his mind. The air seemed to vibrate strangely with an intense inaudible music that pressed upon his temples. Rubbing his forehead, he lifted himself over the crest.

The ridge he had climbed was U-shaped and about 200 feet across, its open end away from him. Resting on the sandy floor in its center was an enormous metal disc, over 100 feet in diameter and 30 feet high. It seemed to be balanced on a huge conical boss, half of which had already sunk into the sand. A fluted rim ran around the edge of the disc and separated the upper and lower curvatures, which were revolving rapidly in opposite directions, throwing off magnificent flashes of silver light.

Kandinski lay still, as his first feelings of fear retreated and his courage and presence of mind returned. The inaudible piercing music had faded, and his mind felt brilliantly clear. His eyes ran rapidly over the spaceship, and he estimated that it was over twice the size of the craft he had seen three years earlier. There were no markings or ports on the carapace, but he was certain it had not come from Venus.

Kandinski lay watching the spacecraft for ten minutes, trying to decide upon his best course of action. Unfortunately he had smashed the lens of his camera. Finally, pushing himself backwards, he slid slowly down the slope. When he reached the floor he could still hear the whine of the rotors. Hiding in the pools of shadow, he made his way up the valley, and two hundred yards from the ridge he broke into a run.

He returned the way he had come, his great legs carrying him across the ruts and boulders, seized his bicycle from the culvert and pedaled rapidly towards the farmhouse.

A single light shone in an upstairs room and he pressed one hand to the bell and pounded on the screen door with the other, nearly tearing it from its hinges. Eventually a young woman appeared. She came down the stairs reluctantly, uncertain what to make of Kandinski's beard and ragged, dusty clothes.

"Telephone!" Kandinski bellowed at her, gasping wildly as he caught back his breath.

The girl at last unlatched the door and backed away from him nervously.

Kandinski lurched past her and staggered blindly around the darkened hall. "Where is it?" he roared.

The girl switched on the lights and pointed into the sitting room. Kandinski pushed past her and rushed over to it.

Ward played with his brandy glass and discreetly loosened the collar of his dress shirt, listening to Dr. MacIntyre of Greenwich Observatory, four seats away on his right, make the third of the after-dinner speeches. Ward was to speak next, and he ran through the opening phrases of his speech, glancing down occasionally to con his notes. At 34 he was the youngest member to address the Congress banquet, and by no means unimpressed by the honor. He looked at the venerable figures to his left and right at the top table, their black jackets and white shirt fronts reflected in the table silver, and saw Professor Cameron wink at him reassuringly.

He was going through his notes for the last time when a steward bent over his shoulder. "Telephone for you, Dr. Ward."

"I can't take it now," Ward whispered. "Tell them to call later."

"The caller said it was extremely urgent, Doctor. Something about some people from the Neptune arriving."

"The Neptune?"

"I think that's a hotel in Santa Vera. Maybe the Russian delegates have turned up after all."

Ward pushed his chair back, made his apologies and slipped away.

Professor Cameron was waiting in the alcove outside the banquetting hall when Ward stepped out of the booth. "Anything the trouble, Andrew? It's not your father, I hope—"

"It's Kandinski," Ward said hurriedly. "He's out in the desert, near the farm-strip. He says he's seen another space vehicle."

"Oh, is that all." Cameron shook his head. "Come on, we'd better get back. The poor fool!"

"Hold on," Ward said. "He's got it under observation now. It's on the ground. He told me to call General Wayne at the air base and alert the Strategic Air Command." Ward chewed his lip. "I don't know what to do."

Cameron took him by the arm. "Andrew, come on. MacIntyre's winding up."

"What can we do, though?" Ward asked. "He seemed all right, but then he said that he thought they were hostile. That sounds a little sinister."

"Andrew!" Cameron snapped. "What's the matter with you? Leave Kandinski to himself. You can't go now. It would be unpardonable rudeness."

"I've got to help Kandinski," Ward insisted. "I'm sure he needs it this time." He wrenched himself away from Cameron.

"Ward!" Professor Cameron called. "For God's sake, come back!" He followed Ward out onto the balcony and watched him run down the steps and disappear across the lawn into the darkness.

As the wheels of the car thudded over the deep ruts, Ward cut the headlights and searched the dark hills which marked the desert's edge. The warm glitter of Vernon Gardens lay behind him and only a few isolated lights shone in the darkness on either side of the road. He passed the farmhouse from which he assumed Kandinski had telephoned, then drove on slowly until he saw the bicycle Kandinski had left for him.

It took him several minutes to mount the huge machine, his feet well clear of the pedals for most of their stroke. Laboriously he covered a hundred yards, and after careening helplessly into a clump of scrub was forced to dismount and continue on foot.

Kandinski had told him that the ridge was about a mile up the valley. It was almost night and the starlight reflected off the hills lit the valley with fleeting, vivid colors. He ran on heavily, the only sounds he could hear those of a thresher rattling like a giant metal insect half a mile behind him. Filling his lungs, he pushed on across the last hundred yards.

Kandinski was still lying on the edge of the ridge, watching the spaceship and waiting impatiently for Ward. Below him in the hollow the upper and lower rotor sections swung around more slowly, at about one revolution per second. The spaceship had sunk a further ten feet into the desert floor and he was now on the same level as the observation dome. A single finger of light poked out into the darkness, circling the ridge walls in jerky sweeps.

Then out of the valley behind him he saw someone stumbling along towards the ridge at a broken run. Suddenly a feeling of triumph and exhilaration came over him, and he knew that at last he had his witness.

Ward climbed up the slope to where he could see Kandinski. Twice he lost his grip and slithered downwards helplessly, tearing his hands on the gritty surface. Kandinski was lying flat on his chest, his head just above the ridge. Covered by dust, he was barely distinguishable from the slope itself.

"Are you all right?" Ward whispered. He pulled off his bow tie and ripped open his collar. When he had controlled his breathing he crawled up besides Kandinski.

"Where?" he asked.

Kandinski pointed down into the hollow.

Ward raised his head, levering himself up on his elbows. For a few seconds he peered out into the darkness, and then drew his head back.

"You see it?" Kandinski whispered. His voice was short and labored. When Ward hesitated before replying he suddenly seized Ward's wrist in a vice-like grip. In the faint light reflected by the white dust on the ridge Ward could see plainly his bright inflamed eyes.

"Ward! Can you see it?"

Ward nodded. "Yes," he said. "Yes, I see it."

The powerful fingers remained clamped to his wrist as he lay beside Kandinski and gazed down into the darkness.

Below the compartment window one of Ward's fellow passengers was being seen off by a group of friends, and the young women in bright hats and bandanas and the men in slacks and beach sandals made him feel that he was leaving a seaside resort at the end of a holiday. From the window he could see the observatory domes of Mount Vernon rising out of the trees, and he identified the white brickwork of the Hoyle Library a thousand feet below the summit. Edna Cameron had brought him to the station, but he had asked her not to come onto the platform, and she had said goodbye and driven off. Cameron himself he had seen only once, when he had collected his books from the Institute.

Trying to forget it all, Ward noted thankfully that the train would leave within five minutes. He took his bankbook out of his wallet and counted the last week's withdrawals. He winced at the largest item, 600 dollars which he had transferred to Kandinski's account to pay for the cablegrams.

Deciding to buy something to read, he left the car and walked back to the newsstand. Several of the magazines contained what could only be described as discouraging articles about himself, and he chose two or three newspapers.

Just then someone put a hand on his shoulder. He turned and saw Kandinski.

"Are you leaving?" Kandinski asked quietly. He had trimmed his beard so that only a pale vestige of the original bloom remained, revealing his high bony cheekbones. His face seemed almost fifteen years younger, thinner and more drawn, but at the same time composed, like that of a man recovering slowly from the attack of some intermittent fever.

"I'm sorry, Charles," Ward said as they walked back to the car. "I should have said goodbye to you but I thought I'd better not."

Kandinski's expression was subdued but puzzled. "Why?" he asked. "I don't understand."

Ward shrugged. "I'm afraid everything here has more or less come to an end for me, Charles. I'm going back to Princeton until the spring. Freshman physics." He smiled ruefully at himself. "Boyle's Law, Young's Modulus, getting right back to fundamentals. Not a bad idea, perhaps."

"But why are you leaving?" Kandinski pressed.

"Well, Cameron thought it might be tactful of me to leave. After our statement to the Secretary-General was published in *The New York Times* I became very much *persona non grata* at the Hubble. The trustees were on Professor Renthall again this morning."

Kandinski smiled and seemed relieved. "What does the Hubble matter?" he scoffed. "We have more important work to do. You know, Ward, when Mrs. Cameron told me just now that you were leaving I couldn't believe it."

"I'm sorry, Charles, but it's true."

"Ward," Kandinski insisted. "You can't leave. The Primes will be returning soon. We must prepare for them."

"I know, Charles, and I wish I could stay." They reached the car and Ward put his hand out. "Thanks for coming to see me off."

Kandinski held his hand tightly. "Andrew, tell me the truth. Are you afraid of what people will think of you? Is that why you want to leave? Haven't you enough courage and faith in yourself?"

"Perhaps that's it," Ward conceded, wishing the train would start. He reached for the rail and began to climb into the car but Kandinski held him.

"Ward, you can't drop your responsibilities like this!"

"Please, Charles," Ward said, feeling his temper rising. He pulled his hand away but Kandinski seized him by the shoulder and almost dragged him off the car.

Ward wrenched himself away. "Leave me alone!" he snapped fiercely. "I saw your spaceship, didn't I?"

Kandinski watched him go, a hand picking at his vanished beard, completely perplexed.

Whistles sounded, and the train began to edge forward.

"Goodbye, Charles," Ward called down. "Let me know if you see anything else."

He went into the car and took his seat. Only when the train was twenty miles from Mount Vernon did he look out of the window.

Exposure

by Eric Frank Russell

The Rigelian ship came surreptitiously, in the deep of the night. Choosing a heavily forested area, it burned down a ring of trees, settled in the ash, sent out a powerful spray of liquid to kill the fires still creeping outward through the undergrowth.

Thin coils of smoke ascended from dying flames. Now adequately concealed from all directions but immediately above, the ship squatted amid towering conifers while its tubes cooled and contracted with metallic squeaks. There were strong smells of wood smoke, pine resin, acrid flamekiller and superheated metal.

Within the vessel there was a conference of aliens. They had two eyes apiece. That was their only positive feature: two eyes. Otherwise they had the formlessness, the almost liquid sloppiness of the completely malleable. When the three in the chart room consulted a planetary photograph they gestured with anything movable, a tentacle, pseudopod, a long, stump-ended arm, a mere digit, anything that struck their fancy at any given moment.

Just now all three were globular, shuffled around on wide, flat feet and were coated with fine, smooth fur resembling green velvet. This similarity was due to politeness rather than desire. During conversation it is conventional to assume the shape of one's superior and, if he changes, to change with him.

So two were spherical and furry solely because Captain Id-Wan saw fit to be spherical and furry. Sometimes Id-Wan was awkward. He'd give himself time to do a difficult shape such as that of reticulated molobater then watch them straining their innards in an effort to catch up.

Id-Wan said: "We've recorded this world from far out on its light side and not a spaceship came near to challenge our presence. They have no spaceships." He sniffed expressively and went on, "The blown-up pictures are plenty good enough for our purpose. We've got the lay of the land and that's as much as we need."

"There appears to be a lot of sea," remarked Chief Navigator Bi-Nak, peering at a picture. "Too much sea. More than half of it is sea."

"Are you again belittling my conquests?" demanded Id-Wan, producing a striped tail.

"Not at all, captain," asured Bi-Nak, dutifully imitating the tail. "I was simply pointing out—"

"You point too much," snapped Id-Wan. He turned to the third Rigelian. "Doesn't he, Po-Duk?"

Pilot Po-Duk played safe by remarking, "There are times and there are times."

"That is truly profound," commented Id-Wan, who had a robust contempt for neutrals. "One points while the other functions as a fount of wisdom. It would be a pleasant change if for once you did the pointing and let Bi-Nak be the oracle. I could stand that. It would make for variety."

"Yes, captain," agreed Po-Duk.

"Certainly, captain," endorsed Bi-Nak.

"All right." Id-Wan, turning irritably to the photographs, said: "There are many cities. That means intelligent life. But we have seen no spaceships and we know they've not yet reached even their own satellite. Hence, their intelligence is not of high order." He forced out a pair of mock hands so that he could rub them together. "In other words, just the sort of creatures we want—ripe for the plucking."

"You said that on the last planet," informed Bi-Nak, whose strong point was not tact.

Id-Wan pulled in his tail and bawled, "That was relative to worlds previously visited. Up to that point they were the best. These are better."

"We haven't seen them yet."

"We shall. They will give us no trouble." Id-Wan cooled down, mused aloud, "Nothing gives us trouble and I doubt whether anything is capable of it. We have fooled half a hundred successive life forms, all utterly different from any known in our home system. I anticipate no difficulties with another. Sometimes I think we must be unique in creation. On every world we've explored the creatures were fixed in form, unchangeable. It would appear that we alone are not the slaves of rigidity."

"Fixedness of form has its advantages," denied Bi-Nak, a glutton for punishment. "When my mother first met my father in the mating-field she thought he was a long-horned nodus, and—"

"There you go again," shouted Id-Wan, "criticizing the self-evident." Sourly, Id-Wan turned back to the photographs, indicated an area toward the north of a great landmass. "We are located there, well off the beaten tracks, yet within individual flying distance of four medium-sized centers. The big cities which hold potential dangers—though I doubt any real dangers—are a good way off. Nearer villages are too small to be worth investigating. The medium-sized places are best for our purpose and, as I've said, there are four within easy reach."

"Which we'll proceed to inspect?" suggested Po-Duk, mostly to show that he was paying attention.

"Of course. The usual tactics—two scouts in each. One day's mixing among the natives and they'll get us all we need to know, while the natives themselves learn nothing. After that—"

"A demonstration of power?" asked Po-Duk.

"Most certainly." Id-Wan extended something like a hair-thin tentacle, used it to mark one of the four near towns. "That place is as good as any other. We'll scrape it clean off Earth's surface, then sit in space and see what they do about it.

A major blow is the most effective way of persuading a world to reveal how highly it is organized."

"If the last six planets are anything to go by," ventured Po-Duk, "we won't see much organization here. They'll panic or pray or both."

"Much as we did when the Great Spot flared in the year of—" began Bi-Nak. His voice trailed off as he noted the gleam in Id-Wan's eyes.

Id-Wan turned to Po-Duk: "Summon the chief of the scouts and tell him to hurry. I want action." Staring hard at Bi-Nak, he added, "Action—not talk!"

The fat man whose name was Ollie Kampenfeldt waddled slowly through the dark toward the log hut whence came the thrum of a guitar and the sound of many voices. He was frowning as he progressed, and mopping his forehead at regular intervals.

There were other log huts scattered around in the vicinity, a few showing lights, but most in darkness. A yellow moon hung only a little above the big stockade of logs which ran right around the encampment; it stretched the shadows of the huts across neatly trimmed lawns and grassy borders.

Kampenfeldt lumbered into the noisy hut and yelped in shrill tones. The guitar ceased its twanging. The talking stopped. Presently the lights went out. He emerged accompanied by a small group of men, most of whom dispersed.

Two stayed with him as he made toward the building nearest the only gate in the heavy stockade. One of them was expostulating mildly.

"All right. So guys need sleep. How were we to know it was that late? Why don'tcha put a clock in the place?"

"The last one got snitched. It cost me fifty."

"Hah!" said the grumbler. "So time doesn't matter. What do I care about it? There's plenty of it and I'm going no place. Make less noise and get to bed. We've got no clock because the place is full of thieves. You'd think I was back in the jug."

His companion on the other side of Kampenfeldt perked up with sudden interest. "Hey, I didn't know you'd been in clink."

"After ten years on the night beat for a big sheet you've been everywhere," said the first. "Even in a crackpotorium—even in a cemetery, for that matter." Then he stopped his forward pacing, raised himself on his toes, stared northward. "What was *that?*"

"What was what?" inquired Kampenfeldt, mopping his brow and breathing heavily.

"Sort of ring of brilliant red light. It floated down into the forest."

"Meteor," suggested Kampenfeldt, not interested.

"Imagination," said the third, having seen nothing.

"Too slow for a meteor," denied the observer, still peering on tiptoe at the distant darkness. "It floated down, like I said. Besides, I've never heard of one that shape or color. More like a plane in flames. Maybe it was a plane in flames."

"We'll know in an hour," promised Kampenfeldt, a little disgruntled at the thought of further night-time disturbances.

"How?"

"The forest will be ablaze on a ten-mile front. It's drier than I've ever known it, and ripe for the kindling." He made a clumsy gesture with a fat hand. "No fire, no plane."

"Well, what else might it be?"

Kampenfeldt said wearily: "I neither know nor care. I have to get up in the morning."

He waddled into his hut, yawning widely. The others stood outside a short time and stared northward. Nothing extraordinary was visible.

"Imagination," repeated one.

"I saw something queer. Dunno what could be out there in all that timber, but I saw something—and I've got good eyes." He removed his gaze, shrugged. "Anyway, the heck with it."

They went to bed.

Captain Id-Wan gave his orders to the chief of the scout. "Bring in some local life forms. The nearest and handiest will do providing they're assorted, small and large. We want to test them."

"Yes, captain."

"Collect them only from the immediate neighborhood. There is a camp to the south which undoubtedly holds superior forms. Keep away from it. Orders concerning that camp will be given you after the more primitive forms have been tested."

"I see, captain."

"You do not see," reproved Id-Wan. "Otherwise you would have noted that I have created flexible digits upon my feet."

"I beg your pardon, captain," said the chief, hastening to create similar extensions.

"The discourtesy is overlooked, but do not repeat it. Send in the head radio technician, then get on with your task."

To the radio officer, who made toes promptly, he said: "What have you to report?"

"The same as we noted upon our approach—they fill the air."

"What?" Id-Wan pulled surprisedly at an ear which he had not possessed a moment before. The ear stretched like soft rubber. "I was not informed of that during the approach."

"I regret, I forgot to—" commenced Bi-Nak, then ceased and strained himself before Id-Wan's eyes could catch him without a rubber ear.

"They fill the air," repeated the radio technician, also dutifully eared. "We've picked up their noises from one extreme to the other. There seem to be at least ten different speech patterns."

"No common language," Bi-Nak mourned. "That complicates matters."

"That simplifies matters," Id-Wan flatly contradicted. "The scouts can masquerade as foreigners and thus avoid speech troubles. The Great Green God could hardly have arranged it better."

"There are also other impulse streams," added the technician. "We suspect them of being pictorial transmissions."

"Suspect? Don't you *know?*"

"Our receivers cannot handle them, captain."

"Why not?"

The radio officer said patiently: "Their methods do not accord with ours. The differences are technical. To explain them would take me a week. In brief, our receivers are not suitable for their transmitted pictures. Eventually, by trial-and-error methods, we could make them suitable, but it would take a long time."

"But you do receive their speech?"

"Yes—that is relatively easy."

"Well, it tells us something. They've got as far as radio. Also, they're vocal and therefore unlikely to be telepathic. I would cross the cosmos for such bait." Dismissing the radio officer, he went to the lock, looked into the night-wrapped forest to see how his scouts were doing.

His strange Rigelian life-sense enabled him to detect their quarry almost at a glance, for life burned in the dark like a tiny flame. There was just such a flame up a nearby tree. He saw it come tumbling down when the paralyzing dart from a scout's gun struck home. The flame flickered on landing but did not die out. The hunter picked it up, brought it into the light. It was a tiny animal with prick ears, coarse, reddish fur and a long, bushy tail.

Soon eight scouts struggled in bearing a huge, thickly furred form of ferocious aspect. It was big-pawed, clawed, and had no tail. It stank like molobater blood mixed with aged cheese. Half a dozen other forms were brought in, two of them winged. All were stiffened by darts, had their eyes closed, were incapable of movement. All were taken to the examiners.

One of the experts came to Id-Wan in due course. He was red-smeared and had an acrid smell.

"Nonmalleable. Every one of them."

"Bhingho!" exclaimed Id-Wan. "As are the lower forms, so will be the higher."

"Not necessarily, but very probably," said the expert, dodging the appearance of contradiction.

"We will see. Had any of these creatures possessed the power of imitative and ultra-rapid reshaping, I should have had to modify my plans. As it is, I can go right ahead."

The other responded, "So far as can be judged from these simple types you should have little trouble with their betters."

"That's what I think," agreed Id-Wan. "We'll get ourselves a sample."

"We need more than one. Two at least. A pair of them would enable us to determine the extent to which individuals differ. If the scouts are left to draw upon their own imaginations in creating differences, they may exaggerate sufficiently to betray themselves."

"All right, we'll get two," said Id-Wan. "Call in the chief of the scouts."

* * *

To the chief of the scouts, Id-Wan said: "All your captures were of unalterable form."

"Excellent!" The chief was pleased.

"Pfah!" murmured Bi-Nak.

Id-Wan jerked around. "What was that remark?"

"Pfah, captain," admitted Bi-Nak, mentally cursing the efficiency of the rubber ear. As mildly as possible, he added, "I was considering the paradox of rigid superiority, and the pfah popped out."

"If I were telepathic," answered Id-Wan, very deliberately, "I would know you for the liar you are."

"Now there's something," offered Bi-Nak, sidetracking the insult. "So far we've encountered not one telepathic species. On this planet there are superior forms believed to be rigid—so whence comes their superiority? Perhaps they are telepathic."

Id-Wan complained to the chief scout, "Do you hear him? He points and pops out and invents obstacles. Of all the navigators available I had to be burdened with this one."

"What could be better could also be worse," put in Po-Duk, for no reason whatsoever.

Id-Wan yelled, "And this other one hangs around mouthing evasions." His fur switched from green to blue.

They all went blue, Po-Duk being the slowest. He was almost a color-cripple, as everyone knew. Id-Wan glared at him, swiftly changed to a reticulated molobator. That caught all three flat out. Id-Wan excelled at molobators and gained much satirical satisfaction from their mutual writhings as each strove to be first. "See," he snapped, when finally they had assumed the new shape. "You are not so good, any of you."

"No, captain, we are very bad," endorsed Bi-Nak, oozing the characteristic molobator stench.

Id-Wan eyed him as if about to challenge the self-evident, decided to let the matter drop, returned his attention to the chief of the scouts. He pointed to the photographs. "There is that encampment a little to our south. As you can see, it is connected by a long, winding path to a narrow road which ambles far over the horizon before it joins a bigger road. The place is pretty well isolated; that is why we picked it."

"Picked it?" echoed the chief.

"We chose it and purposefully landed near it," Id-Wan explained. "The lonelier the source of samples, the less likelihood of discovery at the start, and the longer before an alarm can be broadcast."

"Ah," said the chief, recovering the wits strained by sudden molobating. "It is the usual technique. We are to raid the camp for specimens?"

"Two of them," confirmed Id-Wan. "Any two you can grab without rousing premature opposition."

"That will be easy."

"It cannot be otherwise. Would we be here, doing what we are doing, if all things did not come easy to our kind?"

"No, captain."

"Very well. Go get them. Take one of the radio technicians with you. He will first examine the place for signs of a transmitter or any other mode of ultra-rapid communication which cannot be detected on this photograph. If there proves to be a message-channel, of any sort at all, it must be put out of action, preferably in a manner which would appear accidental."

"Do we go right now?" asked the chief. "Or later?"

"At once, while it remains dark. We have observed how their cities dim by night, watched their lights go out, the traffic thin down. Obviously they are not nocturnal. They are most active in the daytime. Obtain those samples now and be back here before dawn."

"Very well, captain." The chief went out, still a molobator, but not for long.

Bi-Nak yawned and remarked, "I'm not nocturnal either."

"You are on duty," Id-Wan reminded him severely, "until I see fit to say that you are not on duty. And furthermore, I am disinclined to declare you off duty so long as I remain at my post."

"Example is better than precept," approved Po-Duk, currying favor.

Id-Wan promptly turned on him and bawled, "Shut up!"

"He was only pointing out," observed Bi-Nak, picking his not-teeth with fingers that weren't.

Kampenfeldt lumbered with elephantine tread to where three men were lounging full length on the grass. He wiped his forehead as he came, but it was from sheer habit. The sun was partway up and beginning to warm. The cool of the morning was still around. Kampenfeldt wasn't sweating, nevertheless he mopped.

One of the men rolled lackadaisically onto one side, welcomed him with, "Always on the run, Ollie. Why don'tcha flop down on your fat and absorb some sun once in a while?"

"Never get the chance." Kampenfeldt mopped, looked defeated. "I'm searching for Johnson and Greer. Every morning it's the same—somebody's late for breakfast."

"Aren't they in their hut?" inquired a second man, sitting up with an effort and plucking idly at blades of grass.

"Nope. First place I looked. Must've got up mighty early because nobody saw them go. Why won't guys tell me they're going out and might be late? Am I supposed to save something for them or not?"

"Let 'em do without," suggested the second man, lying down again and shading his eyes.

"Serves them right," added the first.

"They're not anywhere around," complained Kampenfeldt, "and they didn't go out the gate."

"Probably climbed the logs," offered one. "They're both batty. Most times they climb the logs when they go moonlight fishing. Anyone who wanders around like that in the middle of the night has got a hole in his head." He glanced at the other. "Were their rods in the hut?"

"Didn't think to look," admitted Kampenfeldt.

"Don't bother to look. They like to show they're tough. Let 'em be tough. It's a free country."

"Yeah," admitted Kampenfeldt reluctantly, "but they ought to have told me about their breakfasts. Now they'll be wasted unless I eat them myself."

They watched him waddle away, still worried, and mopping himself at regular intervals.

One said: "That silhouette shows there isn't much wasted."

Another said: "Hah!" and shaded his eyes with one hand and tried to look at the sun.

An examiner appeared, red-smeared and acrid-smelling as before. "They're like all the others—fixed."

"Unalterable?" insisted Id-Wan.

"Yes, captain." Distastefully he gazed down at the lurid stains upon himself, added, "Eventually we separated them, putting them in different rooms, and revived them. We killed one, then the other. The first fought with his limbs and made noises, but displayed no exceptional powers. The other one, in the other room, was already agitated but did not become more so during this time. It was obvious that he had no notion of what was happening to his companion. We then killed him after he had resisted in the same manner. The conclusion is that they are neither hypnotic nor telepathic. They are remarkably ineffectual even at the point of death."

"Good!" exclaimed Id-Wan, with great satisfaction. "You have done well."

"That is not all, captain. We have since subjected the bodies to a thorough search and can find no organs of life-sense. Evidently they have no way of perceiving life."

"Better still," enthused Id-Wan, "no life-sense means no dynamic receivers—no way of tuning an individual life and tracing its whereabouts. So those in the camp cannot tell where these two have gone."

"They couldn't in any case, by this time," the other pointed out, "since both are dead." He tossed a couple of objects onto a table. "They had those things with them. You may wish to look at them."

Id-Wan picked up the articles as the examiner went away. They were a pair of small bags or satchels made of treated animal hide, well finished, highly polished, and attached to adjustable belts.

He tipped out their contents upon the table, pawed them over: A couple of long, flat metal cases containing white tubes stuffed with herbs. Two metal gadgets, similar but not the same, which could be made to spark and produce a light. A thin card with queer, wriggly writing on one side and a colored picture of a tall-towered city on the other. One small magnifying glass. Two writing instruments, one black, the other silvery. A crude time meter with three indicators and a loud tick. Several insectlike objects with small, sharp hooks attached. Four carefully folded squares of cloth of unknown purpose.

"Humph!" He scooped the lot back, tossed the satchels to Po-Duk. "Take them to the workshop, tell them to make six reasonably good copies complete with contents. They must be ready by next nightfall."

"Six?" queried Po-Duk. "There will be eight scouts."

"Imbecile! You are holding the other two."

"So I am," said Po-Duk, gaping fascinatedly at the objects as if they had just materialized from thin air.

"There are times and there are times," remarked Bi-Nak as Po-Duk departed.

Id-Wan let it pass. "I must have a look at these bodies. I am curious about them." He moved off to the operating room, Bi-Nak following.

The kidnapped and slaughtered creatures proved to be not as repulsive as some they'd found on other worlds. They lay side by side, long, lean, brown-skinned, with two arms, two legs, and with dark, coarse hair upon their heads. Their dead eyes were very much like Rigelian eyes. Their flesh was horribly firm despite the fact that it was full of red juice.

"Primitive types," pronounced Id-Wan, poking at one of them. "It's a marvel they've climbed as high as they have."

"Their digits are surprisingly dexterous," explained the head examiner. "And they have well-developed brains, more so than I had expected."

"They will need all their brains," promised Id-Wan. "We are too advanced to be served by idiots."

"That is true," endorsed Bi-Nak, gaining fresh heart.

"Although sometimes I wonder," added Id-Wan, staring hard at him. He shifted his attention back to the examiner: "Give these cadavers to the scouts and tell them to get in some practice. I'll pick out the eight best imitators tonight. They had better be good!"

"Yes, captain."

The sinking sun showed no more than a sliver of glowing rim on a distant hill when the chief of the scouts reported to Id-Wan. There was a coolness creeping over the land, but it was not coldness. Here, at this time, the nights were merely less warm than the days.

Id-Wan inquired: "Did you have any difficulty in obtaining those two specimens this morning?"

"No, captain. Our biggest worry was that of getting there before broad daylight. It took longer than we'd anticipated to reach the place. In fact dawn was already showing when we arrived. However, we were lucky."

"In what way?"

"Those two were already outside the camp, just as if the Great Green God had provided them for us. They bore simple apparatus for trapping water game and evidently intended an early-morning expedition. All we had to do was plant darts in them and take them away. They had no chance to utter a sound. The camp slumbered undisturbed."

"And what about the message channels?"

"The technician could find none," said the chief. "No overhead wires, no underground cables, no antenna, nothing."

"That is peculiar," remarked Bi-Nak. "Why should creatures so forward be so backward? They *are* superior types, aren't they?"

"They are relatively unimportant in this world's scheme of things," declared Id-Wan. "Doubtless they serve these trees in some way, or watch for fires. It is of little consequence."

"Sitting down on their dirt is not of little consequence," grumbled Bi-Nak to himself. "I'll be happier after we've blasted one of their towns, or ten of them, or fifty. We can then get their reaction and beat it home with the news. I am more than ready to go home even if I am chosen to return with the main fleet sometime later."

"Are the scouts ready for my inspection?" Id-Wan asked the chief.

"Waiting now, captain."

"All right, I'll look them over." Going to the rear quarters, he studied the twenty Rigelians lined up against a wall. The two corpses reposed nearby for purposes of comparison. Subjecting each scout to long and careful scrutiny, he chose eight, whereupon the remaining twelve promptly switched to his own shape. The eight were good. Four Johnsons and four Greers.

"It is a simple form to duplicate," commented the chief. "I could hold it myself for days on end."

"Me, too," agreed Id-Wan. He addressed the row of two-armed, brown-skinned bipeds who could be whatever he wanted them to be. "Remember the most stringent rule: In no circumstances will you change shape before your task is done. Until then, you will retain that precise form and appearance, even under threat of destruction."

They nodded silently.

He continued, "All your obejctives have large parks into which you will be dropped shortly before dawn. You will then merge as unobtrusively as possible with the creatures appearing in each awakening town. After that, do as you've done many a time before—dig up all the useful data you can get without arousing suspicion. Details of weapons and power sources are especially needed. Enter no building until you are sure that your entry will not be challenged. Do not speak or be spoken to if it is avoidable. In the last resort, respond with imitations of a different speech pattern."

"Fanziki moula? Sfinadacta bu!" said Bi-Nak, concocting an example.

Id-Wan paused to scowl at him before he went on, "Above all, there are eight of you, and one may find what another has missed."

They nodded again, bipeds all of them, but with the Rigelian life-flame burning up within them.

He finished, "If absolutely imperative, give up the quest and hide yourselves until the time for return. Be at your respective dropping-points in the parks at the mid-hour of the following night. You will then be picked up." He raised his voice in emphasis. "And do not change shape before then!"

They didn't. They had not altered by as much as one hair when they filed impassively into the ship's lifeboat between the mid-hour and dawn. Id-Wan was there to give them a final lookover. Each walked precisely as the now-dead samples had walked, swinging his arms in the same manner, using the same bearing, wearing the same facial expression. Each had a satchel complete with alien contents, plus a midget dart gun.

The lifeboat rose among the trees into the dark, bore them away. A few creatures in the trees resented the brief disturbance, made squawking sounds.

"Not one other ship in the night," remarked Id-Wan, looking upward. "Not one rocket trail across the stars. They've got nothing but those big, clumsy air machines which we saw toiling through the clouds." He gave a sigh. "In due time we'll take over this planet like taking a karda-fruit from a nodus. It is all too easy, too elementary. Sometimes I feel that a little more opposition might be interesting."

Bi-Nak decided to let that point go for what it was worth, which wasn't much. Two days and nights on continual duty with the indefatigable Id-Wan had tired him beyond argument. So he yawned, gave the stars a sleepless, disinterested eye, and followed Id-Wan into the ship.

Making for the dynamic receivers, Id-Wan had a look at their recording globes, each of which had been tuned to a departing scout. Each globe held a bright spot derived from a distant life-glow. He watched the spots shrink with distance until eventually they remained still. A bit later the lifeboat came back, reported all landed. The spots continued to shine without shifting. None moved until the sun stabbed a red ray in the east.

Planting another filled glass on the tray, Ollie Kampenfeldt gloomed at a night-shrouded window and said: "It's been dark two hours. They've been gone all day. No breakfast, no dinner, no supper, nothing. A feller can't live on nothing. I don't like it."

"Me neither," approved somebody. "Maybe something's happened."

"If one had broken his leg or his neck, the other would be here to tell us," another pointed out. "Besides, if it were anyone else, I'd suggest a search for them. But you know those two coots. Isn't the first time Johnson and Greer have taken to the jungle. Reckon they've seen too many Tarzan pictures. Just a pair of overgrown, muscle-bound kids."

"Johnson's no kid," denied the first. "He's an ex-navy heavyweight who still likes to jump around."

"Aw, probably they've got lost. It's the easiest thing in the world to get lost if you wander a bit. Four times I've had to camp out all night, and—"

"I don't like it," interjected Kampenfeldt, firmly.

"O.K., you don't like it. What are you going to do about it? Phone the cops?"

"There's no phone, as you know," said Kampenfeldt. "Who'd drag a line right up here?" He thought it over, frowning fatly, and wiped his forehead. "I'll give 'em to morning. If they're not back by then, I'll send Sid on his motorcycle to tell the forest rangers. Nobody's going to say I did nothing about it."

"That's the spirit, Ollie," one of them approved. "You look after nature's children and they'll look after you."

Several laughed at that, heartily. Within half an hour Johnson and Greer were forgotten.

It was early in the afternoon when the tracer operators rushed into the main cabin and so far forgot themselves as not to match Id-Wan's shape. Remaining rotund, tentacular and pale purple, the leading one of the three gestured excitedly as he spoke.

"Two have gone, captain."

"Two what have gone where?" demanded Id-Wan, glowering at him.

"Two dynamic sparks."

"Are you certain?" Without waiting for a reply, Id-Wan ran to the receivers.

It was true enough. Six globes still held their tiny lights. Two were dull, devoid of any gleam. Even as he watched, another became extinguished. Then, in rapid succession, three more.

The chief of the scouts came in saying: "What's the matter? Is there something wrong?"

Slowly, almost ponderously, Id-Wan said, "Six scouts have surrendered life in the last few moments." He breathed heavily, seemed to have trouble in accepting the evidence of the globes. "These instruments say they are dead, and if indeed they are dead they cannot retain shape. Their bodies automatically will revert to the form of their fathers. And you know that means—"

"A complete giveaway," said the chief of the scouts, staring grimly at the globes.

Both remaining lights went out.

"Action stations!" yelled Id-Wan, electrified by the sight. "Close all ports! Trim the tubes! Prepare for takeoff!" He turned savagely upon Po-Duk. "You're the pilot. Don't squat there gaping like an ebelmint halfway out of its egg! Get into the control seat, idiot—we've no time to lose!"

Something whisked overhead. He caught a fleeting glimpse of it through the nearest observation port. Something long, shapely and glistening, but much too fast to examine. It had gone almost before it registered. Seconds later its noise followed a terrible howl.

The radio technician said: "Powerful signals nearby. Their sources seem to be—"

The ship's tubes coughed, spluttered, shot fire, coughed again. A tree began to burn. Id-Wan danced with impatience. He dashed to the control room.

"Blast, Po-Duk, blast!"

"There is not yet enough lift, captain, and until the meters show that—"

"Look!" screamed Bi-Nak, pointing for the last time.

They could see what was coming through the facing port; seven ultra-rapid dots in V-formation. The dots lengthened, sprouted wings, swept immediately overhead without a sound. Black lumps fell from their bellies, came down, struck the ship and all around the ship.

The badly lagging noise of the planes never got that far. Their leading waves were repulsed by the awful blast of the bombs.

For the final change, the Rigelians became a cloud of scattered molecules.

Settling himself more comfortably in the chair, the roving video reporter griped, "I'd no sooner shown my face in the office than the area supervisor grabbed me, told me to chase up here and give the breathless world a candid close-up of mad Martians on the rampage. I'm partway here when the Air Force chips in, holds me back a couple of hours. When I do get here what do I find?" He sniffed sourly, "Some timber smoking around a whacking big crater. Nothing else. Not a pretzel."

Dragging an almost endless handkerchief from his pocket, Kampenfeldt smeared it across his brow. "We keep civilization at arm's length here. We've no radio, no video. So I don't know what you're talking about."

"It's like this," explained the reporter. "They dumped their spies in the parks during the night. They weren't around long because they got picked up with the milk. Twenty steps and Clancy had 'em."

"Eh?"

"The cops," elucidated the other. "We put the faces of the first pair on the breakfast-time videocast. Ten people phoned through in a hurry and identified them as Johnson and Greer. So we assumed that said Johnson and Greer were nuts." He gave a lugubrious laugh.

"Sometimes I've thought so myself," Kampenfeldt offered.

"Then, half an hour later, the next station on the chain infriged our copyright by also showing Johnson and Greer. Another followed suit ten minutes later still. By ten o'clock there were four pairs of them, as alike as two of you, and all grabbed in similar circumstances. It looked like the whole cockeyed world wanted to be Johnson or, alternatively, Greer."

"Not me," denied Kampenfeldt. "Neither of them."

"The news value of that was, of course, way up. We planted the entire eight of them on the midmorning boost, which is nationwide, our only thought being that we'd got something mighty queer. Military intelligence boys in Washington saw the videocast, pestered local cops for details, put two and two together and made it four, if not eight."

"And then?"

"They clamped heavy pressure on all these Johnsons and Greers. They talked all right, but nothing they said made sense. Eventually one of them tried a fast out, got killed on the run. He was still Johnson when he flopped, but a couple of minutes later his body turned to something else, something right out of this world. Boy, it would have turned your stomach!"

"In that case, I want no description," said Kampenfeldt, defensively nursing his outsize paunch.

"That was an eye-opener. Anything not of this world obviously must be of some other. The authorities bore down on the remaining seven, who acted as before until they realized that we knew what we knew. Forthwith they put death before dishonor, leaving us with eight dollops of goo and no details."

"Ugh!" said Kampenfeldt, hitching his paunch.

"Our only clue lay in Johnson and Greer. Since these creatures had copied real people, the thing to do was find the last known whereabouts of said people. Chances were good that alien invaders would be found in that vicinity. A shout went up for Johnson and Greer. Fifty friends of theirs put them here, right here. The forest rangers chipped in saying you'd just reported them missing."

"I did," admitted Kampenfeldt. "And if I'd known where they'd gone, I'd be missing myself—and still running."

"Well, the Air Force took over. They were told to look-see. If an alien ship was down, it was to stay down. You know those boys. They swoop around yipping. They overdid the job, left not a sliver of metal as big as my finger. So what do I put on the videocast? Just a crater and some smoking tree stumps."

"Which is no great pity," opined Kampenfeldt. "Who wants to see things that could climb into your bed as Uncle Willie? You wouldn't know who was who with creatures like that around."

"You would not." The reporter pondered awhile, added, "Their simulation was perfect. They had the power to lead us right up the garden path if only they'd known how to use it. Power is never much good unless you know how to use it. They made a first-class blunder when they grabbed their models." He scratched his head, eyed the other speculatively. "It sure beats me that of all the places in this wide world they had to pick on a nudist camp."

"Solar health center," corrected Kampenfeldt, primly.

What Is This Thing Called Love?

by Isaac Asimov

But these are two species," said Captain Garm, peering closely at the creatures that had been brought up from the planet below. His optic organs adjusted focus to maximum sharpness, bulging outwards as they did so. The color patch above them gleamed in quick flashes.

Botax felt warmly comfortable to be following color-changes once again, after months in a spy cell on the planet, trying to make sense out of the modulated sound waves emitted by the natives. Communication by flash was almost like being home in the far-off Perseus arm of the Galaxy. "Not two species," he said, "but two forms of one species."

"Nonsense, they look quite different. Vaguely Perse-like, thank the Entity, and not as disgusting in appearance as so many outforms are. Reasonable shape, recognizable limbs. But no color-patch. Can they speak?"

"Yes, Captain Garm," Botax indulged in a discreetly disapproving prismatic interlude. "The details are in my report. These creatures form sound waves by way of throat and mouth, something like complicated coughing. I have learned to do it myself." He was quietly proud. "It is very difficult."

"It must be stomach-turning. Well, that accounts for their flat, unextensible eyes. Not to speak by color makes eyes largely useless. Meanwhile, how can you insist these are a single species? The one on the left is smaller and has longer tendrils, or whatever it is, and seems differently proportioned. It bulges where this other does not. —Are they alive?"

"Alive but not at the moment conscious, Captain. They have been psycho-treated to repress fright in order that they might be studied easily."

"But are they worth study? We are behind our schedule and have at least five worlds of greater moment than this one to check and explore. Maintaining a time-stasis unit is expensive and I would like to return them and go on—"

But Botax's moist spindly body was fairly vibrating with anxiety. His tubular tongue flicked out and curved up and over his flat nose, while his eyes sucked inward. His splayed three-fingered hand made a gesture of negation as his speech went almost entirely into the deep red.

"Entity save us, Captain, for no world is of greater moment to us than this one. We may be facing a supreme crisis. These creatures could be the most dangerous life-forms in the Galaxy, Captain, just *because* there are two forms."

"I don't follow you."

"Captain, it has been my job to study this planet, and it has been most difficult, for it is unique. It is so unique that I can scarcely comprehend its facets. For instance, almost all life on the planet consists of species in two forms. There are no words to describe it, no concepts even. I can only speak of them as first form and second form. If I may use their sounds, the little one is called 'female,' and the big one, here, 'male,' so the creatures themselves are aware of the difference."

Garm winced, "What a disgusting means of communication."

"And, Captain, in order to bring forth young, the two forms must cooperate."

The Captain, who had bent forward to examine the specimens closely with an expression compounded of interest and revulsion, straightened at once. "Cooperate? What nonsense is this? There is no more fundamental attribute of life than that each living creature bring forth its young in innermost communication with itself. What else makes life worth living?"

"The one form does bring forth life but the other form must cooperate."

"How?"

"That has been difficult to determine. It is something very private and in my search through the available forms of literature I could find no exact and explicit description. But I have been able to make reasonable deductions."

Garm shook his head. "Ridiculous. Budding is the holiest, most private function in the world. On tens of thousands of worlds it is the same. As the great photobard, Levuline, said, 'In budding-time, in budding time, in sweet, delightful budding time; when . . .' "

"Captain, you don't understand. This cooperation between forms brings about somehow (and I am not certain exactly how) a mixture and recombination of genes. It is a device by which in every generation, new combinations of characteristics are brought into existence. Variations are multiplied; mutated genes hastened into expression almost at once where under the usual budding system, millennia might pass first."

"Are you trying to tell me that the genes from one individual can be combined with those of another? Do you know how completely ridiculous that is in the light of all the principles of cellular physiology?"

"It must be so," said Botax nervously under the others pop-eyed glare. "Evolution is hastened. This planet is a riot of species. There are supposed to be a million and a quarter different species of creatures."

"A dozen and a quarter more likely. Don't accept too completely what you read in the native literature."

"I've seen dozens of radically different species myself in just a small area. I tell you, Captain, give these creatures a short space of time and they will mutate into intellects powerful enough to overtake us and rule the Galaxy."

"Prove that this cooperation you speak of exists, Investigator, and I shall consider your contentions. If you cannot, I shall dismiss all your fancies as ridiculous and we will move on."

"I can prove it." Botax's color-flashes turned intensely yellow-green. "The creatures of this world are unique in another way. They foresee advances they have not yet made, probably as a consequence of their belief in rapid change which, after all, they constantly witness. They therefore indulge in a type of literature involving the space-travel they have never developed. I have translated their term for the literature as 'science-fiction.' Now I have dealt in my readings almost exclusively with science-fiction, for there I thought, in their dreams and fancies, they would expose themselves and their danger to us. And it was from that sience-fiction that I deduced the method of their inter-form cooperation."

"How did you do that?"

"There is a periodical on this world which sometimes publishes science-fiction which is, however, devoted almost entirely to the various aspects of the cooperation. It does not speak entirely freely, which is annoying, but persists in merely hinting. Its name as nearly as I can put it into flashes is 'Recreationland.' The creature in charge, I deduce, is interested in nothing but inter-form cooperation and searches for it everywhere with a systematic and scientific intensity that has roused my awe. He has found instances of cooperation described in science-fiction and I let material in his periodical guide me. From the stories he instanced I have learned how to bring it about.

"And Captain, I beg of you, when the cooperation is accomplished and the young are brought forth before your eyes, give orders not to leave an atom of this world in existence."

"Well," said Captain Garm, wearily, "bring them into full consciousness and do what you must do quickly."

Marge Skidmore was suddenly completely aware of her surroundings. She remembered very clearly the elevated station at the beginning of twilight. It had been almost empty, one man standing near her, another at the other end of the platform. The approaching train had just made itself known as a faint rumble in the distance.

There had then come the flash, a sense of turning inside out, the half-seen vision of a spindly creature, dripping mucus, a rushing upward, and now—

"Oh, God," she said, shuddering. "It's still here. And there's another one, too."

She felt a sick revulsion, but no fear. She was almost proud of herself for feeling no fear. The man next to her, standing quietly, but still wearing a battered fedora, was the one who had been near her on the platform.

"They got you, too?" she asked. "Who else?"

Charlie Grimwold, feeling flabby and paunchy, tried to lift his hand to remove his hat and smooth the thin hair that broke up but did not entirely cover the skin of his scalp and found that it moved only with difficulty against a rubbery but hardening resistance. He let his hand drop and looked morosely at the thin-faced woman facing him. She was in her middle thirties, he decided, and her hair was nice and her dress fit well, but at the moment, he just wanted to be somewhere else and it did him no good at all that he had company; even female company.

He said, "I don't know, lady. I was just standing on the station platform."

"Me, too." Marge said quickly.

"And then I see a flash. Didn't hear nothing. Now here I am. Must be little men from Mars or Venus or one of them places."

Marge nodded vigorously, "That's what I figure. A flying saucer? You scared?"

"No. That's funny, you know. I think maybe I'm going nuts or I *would* be scared."

"Funny thing. I ain't scared, either. Oh, God, here comes one of them now. If he touches me, I'm going to scream. Look at those wiggly hands. And that wrinkled skin, all slimy; makes me nauseous."

Botax approached gingerly and said, in a voice at once rasping and screechy, this being the closest he could come to imitating the native timbre, "Creatures! We will not hurt you. But we must ask you if you would do us the favor of cooperating."

"Hey, it talks!" said Charlie. "What do you mean, cooperate."

"Both of you. With each other," said Botax.

"Oh?" He looked at Marge. "You know what he means, lady?"

"Ain't got no idea whatsoever," she answered loftily.

Botax said, "What I mean—" and he used the short term he had once heard employed as a synonym for the process.

Marge turned red and said, "What!" in the loudest scream she could manage. Both Botax and Captain Garm put their hands over their mid-regions to cover the auditory patches that trembled painfully with the decibels.

Marge went on rapidly, and nearly incoherently. "Of all things. I'm a married woman, you. If my Ed was here, you'd hear from *him*. And you, wise guy," she twisted toward Charlie against rubbery resistance, "Whoever you are, if you think—"

"Lady, lady," said Charlie in uncomfortable desperation. "It ain't my idea. I mean, far be it from me, you know, to turn down some lady, you know; but me, I'm married, too. I got three kids. Listen—"

Captain Garm said, "What's happening, Investigator Botax? These cacophonous sounds are awful."

"Well," Botax flashed a short purple patch of embarrassment. "This forms a complicated ritual. They are supposed to be reluctant at first. It heightens the subsequent result. After that initial stage, the skins must be removed."

"They have to be *skinned?*"

"Not really skinned. Those are artificial skins that can be removed painlessly, and must be. Particularly in the smaller form."

"All right, then. Tell it to remove the skins. Really, Botax, I don't find this pleasant."

"I don't think I had better tell the smaller form to remove the skins. I think we had better follow the ritual closely. I have here sections of those space-travel tales which the man from the 'Recreationland' periodical spoke highly of. In those tales the skins are removed forcibly. Here is a description of an accident, for instance 'which played havoc with the girl's dress, ripping it nearly off her slim body. For a second, he felt the warm firmness of her half-bared bosom against his cheek—' It goes on that way. You see, the ripping, the forcible removal, acts as a stimulus."

"Bosom?" said the Captain. "I don't recognize the flash."

"I invented that to cover the meaning. It refers to the bulges on the upper dorsal region of the smaller form."

"I see. Well, tell the larger one to rip the skins off the smaller one. —What a dismal thing this is."

Botax turned to Charlie. "Sir," he said, "rip the girl's dress nearly off her slim body, will you? I will release you for the purpose."

Marge's eyes widened and she twisted toward Charlie in instant outrage. "Don't you dare do that, you. Don't you *dast* touch me, you sex maniac."

"Me?" said Charlie plaintively, "It ain't my idea. You think I go around ripping dresses? Listen," he turned to Botax, "I got a wife and three kids. She finds out I go around ripping dresses, I get clobbered. You know what my wife does when I just look at some dame. *Listen—*"

"Is he still reluctant?" said the Captain, impatiently.

"Apparently," said Botax. "The strange surroundings, you know, may be extending that stage of the cooperation. Since I know this is unpleasant for you, I will perform this stage of the ritual myself. It is frequently written in the space-travel tales that an outer-world species performs the task. For instance, here," and he riffled through his notes finding the one he wanted, "they describe a very awful such species. The creatures on the planet have foolish notions, you understand. It never occurs to them to imagine handsome individuals such as ourselves, with a fine mucous cover."

"Go on! Go on! Don't take all day," said the Captain.

"Yes, Captain. It says here that the extraterrestrial 'came forward to where the girl stood. Shrieking hysterically, she was cradled in the monster's embrace. Talons ripped blindly at her body, tearing the kirtle away in rags.' You see, the native creature is shrieking with stimulation as her skins are removed."

"Then go ahead, Botax, remove it. But please, allow no shrieking. I'm trembling all over with the sound waves."

Botax said politely to Marge, "If you don't mind—"

One spatulate finger made as though to hook onto the neck of the dress.

Marge wiggled desperately. "Don't touch. Don't touch! You'll get slime on it. Listen, this dress cost $24.95 at Ohrbach's. Stay away, you monster. Look at those eyes on him." She was panting in her desperate efforts to dodge the groping, extraterrestrial hand. "A slimy, bug-eyed monster, that's what he is. Listen, I'll take it off myself. Just don't touch it with slime, for God's sake."

She fumbled at the zipper, and said in a hot aside to Charlie, "Don't you dast look."

Charlie closed his eyes and shrugged in resignation.

She stepped out of the dress. "All right? You satisfied?"

Captain Garm's fingers twitched with unhappiness. "Is that the bosom? Why does the other creature keep its head turned away?"

"Reluctance. Reluctance," said Botax. "Besides, the bosom is still covered.

Other skins must be removed. When bared, the bosom is a very strong stimulus. It is constantly described as ivory globes, or white spheres, or otherwise after that fashion. I have here drawings, visual picturizations, that come from the outer covers of the space-travel magazines. If you will inspect them, you will see that upon every one of them, a creature is present with a bosom more or less exposed."

The Captain looked thoughtfully from the illustrations to Marge and back. "What is ivory?"

"That is another made-up flash of my own. It represents the tusky material of one of the large sub-intelligent creatures on the planet."

"Ah," and Captain Garm went into a pastel green of satisfaction. "That explains it. This small creature is one of a warrior sect and those are tusks with which to smash the enemy."

"No, no. They are quite soft, I understand." Botax's small brown hand flicked outward in the general direction of the objects under discussion and Marge screamed and shrank away.

"Then what other purpose do they have?"

"I think," said Botax with considerable hesitation, "that they are used to feed the young."

"The young eat them?" asked the Captain with every evidence of deep distress.

"Not exactly. The objects produce a fluid which the young consume."

"Consume a fluid from a living body? Yech-h-h." The Captain covered his head with all three of his arms, calling the central supernumerary into use for the purpose, slipping it out of its sheath so rapidly as almost to knock Botax over.

"A three-armed, slimy, bug-eyed monster," said Marge.

"Yeah," said Charlie.

"All right you, just watch those eyes. Keep them to yourself."

"Listen, lady. I'm trying not to look."

Botax approached again. "Madam, would you remove the rest?"

Marge drew herself up as well as she could against the pinioning field. "Never!"

"I'll remove it, if you wish."

"Don't touch! For God's sake, don't touch. Look at the slime on him, will you? All right, I'll take it off." She was muttering under her breath and looking hotly in Charlie's direction as she did so.

"Nothing is happening," said the Captain, in deep dissatisfaction, "and this seems an imperfect specimen."

Botax felt the slur on his own efficiency. "I brought you two perfect specimens. What's wrong with the creature?"

"The bosom does not consist of globes or spheres. I know what globes or spheres are and in these pictures you have shown me, they are so depicted. Those are large globes. On this creature, though, what we have are nothing but small flaps of dry tissue. And they're discolored, too, partly."

"Nonsense," said Botax. "You must allow room for natural variation. I will put it to the creature herself."

He turned to Marge, "Madam, is your bosom imperfect?"

Marge's eyes opened wide and she struggled vainly for moments without doing anything more than gasp loudly. *"Really!"* she finally managed. "Maybe I'm no Gina Lollobrigida or Anita Ekberg, but I'm perfectly all right, thank you. Oh, boy, if my Ed were only here." She turned to Charlie. "Listen, you, you tell this bug-eyed slimy thing here, there ain't nothing wrong with my development."

"Lady," said Charlie, softly. "I ain't looking, remember?"

"Oh, sure, you ain't looking. You been peeking enough, so you might as well just open your crummy eyes and stick up for a lady, if you're the least bit of a gentleman, which you probably ain't."

"Well," said Charlie, looking sideways at Marge, who seized the opportunity to inhale and throw her shoulders back, "I don't like to get mixed up in a kind of delicate matter like this, but you're all right—I guess."

"You *guess?* You blind or something? I was once runner-up for Miss Brooklyn, in case you don't happen to know and where I missed out was on waist-line, *not* on—"

Charlie said, "All right, all right. They're fine. Honest." He nodded vigorously in Botax's direction. "They're okay. I ain't that much of an expert, you understand, but they're okay by me."

Marge relaxed.

Botax felt relieved. He turned to Garm. "The bigger form expresses interest, Captain. The stimulus is working. Now for the final step."

"And what is that?"

"There is no flash for it, Captain. Essentially, it consists of placing the speaking-and-eating apparatus of one against the equivalent apparatus of the other. I have made up a flash for the process, thus: kiss."

"Will nausea never cease?" groaned the Captain.

"It is the climax. In all the tales, after the skins are removed by force, they clasp each other with limbs and indulge madly in burning kisses, to translate as nearly as possible the phrase most frequently used. Here is one example, just one, taken at random: 'He held the girl, his mouth avid on her lips.' "

"Maybe one creature was devouring the other," said the Captain.

"Not at all," said Botax impatiently. "Those were burning kisses."

"How do you mean, burning? Combustion takes place?"

"I don't think literally so. I imagine it is a way of expressing the fact that the temperature goes up. The higher the temperature, I suppose, the more successful the production of young. Now that the big form is properly stimulated, he need only place his mouth against hers to produce young. The young will not be produced without that step. It is the cooperation I have been speaking of."

"That's all? Just this—" The Captain's hands made motions of coming together, but he could not bear to put the thought into flash form.

"That's all," said Botax. "In none of the tales; not even in 'Recreationland,' have I found a description of any further physical activity in connection with young-bearing. Sometimes after the kissing, they write a line of symbols like little stars, but I suppose that merely means more kissing; one kiss for each star, when they wish to produce a multitude of young."

"Just one, please, right now."

"Certainly, Captain."

Botax said with grave distinctness, "Sir, would you kiss the lady?"

Charlie said, "Listen, I can't move."

"I will free you, of course."

"The lady might not like it."

Marge glowered. "You bet your damn boots, I won't like it. You just stay away."

"I would like to, lady, but what do they do if I don't? Look, I don't want to get them mad. We can just—you know—make like a little peck."

She hesitated, seeing the justice of the caution. "All right. No funny stuff, though. I ain't in the habit of standing around like this in front of every Tom, Dick and Harry, you know."

"I know that, lady. It was none of my doing. You got to admit that."

Marge muttered angrily, "Regular slimy monsters. Must think they're some kind of gods or something, the way they order people around. Slime gods is what they are!"

Charlie approached her. "If it's okay now, lady." He made a vague motion as though to tip his hat. Then he put his hands awkwardly on her bare shoulders and leaned over in a gingerly pucker.

Marge's head stiffened so that lines appeared in her neck. Their lips met.

Captain Garm flashed fretfully. "I sense no rise in temperature." His heat-detecting tendril had risen to full extension at the top of his head and remained quivering there.

"I don't either," said Botax, rather at a loss, "but we're doing it just as the space travel stories tell us to. I think his limbs should be more extended— Ah, like that. See, it's working."

Almost absently, Charlie's arm had slid around Marge's soft, nude torso. For a moment, Marge seemed to yield against him and then she suddenly writhed hard against the pinioning field that still held her with fair firmness.

"Let go." The words were muffled against the pressure of Charlie's lips. She bit suddenly, and Charlie leaped away with a wild cry, holding his lower lip, then looking at his fingers for blood.

"What's the idea, lady?" he demanded plaintively.

She said, "We agreed just a peck, is all. What were you starting there? What's going on around here? First these slimy creatures make like they're gods and now this. You some kind of playboy or something?"

Captain Garm flashed rapid alternations of blue and yellow. "Is it done? How long do we wait now?"

"It seems to me it must happen at once. Throughout all the universe, when you have to bud, you bud, you know. There's no waiting."

"Yes? After thinking of the foul habits you have been describing, I don't think I'll ever bud again. —Please get this over with."

"Just a moment, Captain."

But the moments passed and the Captain's flashes turned slowly to a brooding orange, while Botax's nearly dimmed out altogether.

Botax finally asked hesitantly, "Pardon me, madam, but when will you bud?"

"When will I *what?*"

"Bear young?"

"I've got a kid."

"I mean bear young now."

"I should say not. I ain't ready for another kid yet."

"What? What?" demanded the Captain. "What's she saying?"

"It seems," said Botax, weakly, "she does not intend to have young at the moment."

The Captain's color patch blazed brightly. "Do you know what I think, Investigator? I think you have a sick, perverted mind. Nothing's happening to these creatures. There is no cooperation between them, and no young to be borne. I think they're two different species and that you're playing some kind of foolish game with me."

"But Captain—" said Botax.

"Don't 'but Captain' me," said Garm. "I've had enough. You've upset me, turned my stomach, nauseated me, disgusted me with the whole notion of budding and wasted my time. You're just looking for headlines and personal glory and I'll see to it that you don't get them. Get rid of these creatures now. Give that one its skins back and put them back where you found them. I ought to take the expense of maintaining Time-stasis all this time out of your salary."

"But, Captain—"

"Back, I say. Put them back in the same place and at the same instant of time. I want this planet untouched, and I'll see to it that it stays untouched." He cast one more furious glance at Botax. "One species, two forms, bosoms, kisses, cooperation, BAH— You are a fool, Investigator, a dolt as well and, most of all, a sick, sick, sick creature."

There was no arguing. Botax, limbs trembling, set about returning the creatures.

They stood there at the elevated station, looking around wildly. It was twilight over them, and the approaching train was just making itself known as a faint rumble in the distance.

Marge said, hesitantly, "Mister, did it really happen?"

Charlie nodded. "I remember it. Listen, I'm sorry you was embarrassed. It was none of my doing. I mean, you know, lady, you wasn't really bad. In fact, you looked good, but I was kind of embarrassed to say that."

She smiled. "It's all right."

"You want maybe to have a cup of coffee with me just to relax you. My wife, she's not really expecting me for a while."

"Oh? Well, Ed's out of town and my little boy is visiting at my mother's. I don't have to rush home."

"Come on, then. We been kind of introduced."

"I'll say." She laughed.

They had a couple of cocktails and then Charlie couldn't let her go home in the dark alone, so he saw her to her door. Marge was bound to invite him in for a few moments.

Meanwhile, back in the spaceship, the crushed Botax was making a final effort to prove his case. While Garm prepared the ship for departure Botax hastily set up the tight-beam visiscreen for a last look at his specimens. He focused in on Charlie and Marge in her apartment. His tendril stiffened and he began flashing in a coruscating rainbow of colors.

"Captain Garm! Captain! Look what they're doing now!"

But at that very instant the ship winked out of Time-stasis.

Shadows In the Sun
by Chad Oliver

1

At first it had been plain stubbornness, disguised as scientific curiosity, that had kept Paul Ellery going. It was different now.

He *had* to know.

He sat at the corner table of the Jefferson Springs Cafe, alone as he had always been alone in Jefferson Springs. There wasn't much to look at in the small dining room—a grimy electric clock that had been exactly six minutes slow for the past two months, a somewhat battered jukebox, with tired technicolored bubbles, dying on its feet, the inevitable painting of Judge Roy Bean's *Law West of the Pecos,* a greenish-glass case filled with warm candy bars. Paul Ellery looked anyway, with restrained desperation. Then he pushed back his plate with its remnants of chicken-fried steak and French fries, and began to draw wet circles on the varnished table with the bottom of his beer bottle.

There was a boxlike air-conditioner stuck in one window, consisting of a fan that blew wet air into the room. Ellery could hear the water from the fan hose dripping down to the ground on the other side of the wall; and inside the cafe it was so humid that even the wood was sweating.

Except for the hum and drip of the air-conditioner, there wasn't a sound. It was like sitting in a cave, miles beneath the earth.

Waiting for an earthquake.

Ellery tried to ignore the unwanted little animal that kept shivering up and down his spine on multiple ice-sheathed feet. He tried to remind himself that the animal was imaginary. He tried to tell himself that he had nothing to fear. He tried to look calmer than he felt.

It was incredible.

The month was August, the day was Thursday. He was in Jefferson Springs, a town of six thousand inhabitants, in the state of Texas, a part, usually, of the United States of America. It was eight o'clock in the evening and it was hot. Some one hundred and twenty miles to the north was the city of San Antonio, where the Alamo had given way to the Air Force. Sixty miles to the south was Eagle Pass, and on across the river was Piedras Negras, in Mexico. Everything seemed perfectly ordinary. Indeed, Jefferson Springs could hardly have been a more average town if it had tried.

On the surface, there was no cause for alarm.

He finished his beer, and it was as hot and sticky as the rest of the cafe. He briefly considered ordering another one, but abandoned the idea. Instead, with great deliberation, he dug his pipe out of his back pocket, where he carried it like a .45, and filled it with tobacco from a cloudy plastic pouch. He lit it with a wood stick match, broke the match, and dropped it artistically into the beer bottle. Then he aimed a wobbly smoke ring in the general direction of Judge Roy Bean and watched it battle the current from the air-conditioner.

"The hell with all of you," he said, silently but inclusively.

He was the only customer in the Jefferson Springs Cafe. He had been the only customer, so far as he could tell, for the past sixty-one days. Cozy.

The first week he had been in Jefferson Springs he had played the jukebox religiously. It had seemed like sound field technique, and it had helped to fill up the emptiness with a semblance of life. As he was somewhat selective in his choice of popular music, however, this hadn't proved precisely a sedative to his nerves. The jukebox in the cafe was typical of those in small Texas towns. There were a number of nasal cowboy standards, including *When My Blue Moon Turns to Gold Again* and *San Antonio Rose*. There were several old Bing Crosby records: *White Christmas* and *Don't Fence Me In*. There were a number of year-old blues sides, featuring honking one-note saxes and leering pseudo-sexual lyrics leading up to inevitable anticlimaxes. There was a haphazard collection of middle-aged hit-parade agonies, notably *Doggie in the Window* and *Till I Waltz Again with You*. And finally, slipped in by mistake, there was an old Benny Goodman sextet number, *Rose Room*. He played that ten times during the first week, and then gave up.

In a way he could not quite understand, the record had violated an unseen pattern. It was not a simple and obvious case of the record's being out of place in Jefferson Springs; rather, it was the fact that music was being played at all, *any* music. The pattern was a subtle one, but he had been trained to be sensitive to just such cultural harmonies and configurations.

Paul Ellery had often remarked elsewhere that he would just as soon eat his food without the collective sobbings of the music industry in the background, to say nothing of an endless babble of human voices earnestly reciting the current cliches. Now that he found himself faced with total silence, however, he found the experience unexpectedly unpleasant. The silence cut him off, isolated him. It put him in the middle of a bright stage, without a script or an orchestra, alone, with the curtain going up.

He sat for what seemed to him to be a long time, smoking his pipe. Somehow, only fifteen slow minutes crawled by on the greasy electric clock above the doorway. The doorway led to a small alcove, which faced both the kitchen and the dark, deserted beer bar. He listened closely, but could hear nothing. The other door led outside, into the town.

He was afraid to go out.

He shoved back his chair and got to his feet, annoyed with himself. He told himself that there was nothing to fear. He remembered a time many years before, when he was just a kid. He had gone to a midnight show with another boy to see *Son of Frankenstein*. Then he had had to walk home, through the city of Austin. He and the other boy had walked all the way back to back, one walking frontward and the other backward, in order to keep an eye peeled in both directions at once. It wasn't that they *believed* in such things, of course, it wasn't that they were afraid—

You know.

It was that way now. What was he afraid of? No one had tried to harm him in Jefferson Springs. After all, it was just a little Texas town, just like a thousand others drowsing on the highway or tucked away on a back road, wasn't it? *Wasn't it?*

He left a dollar bill and two quarters on the damp table and walked out of the cafe. After the gloomy humidity of the dining room, the dry heat outside was a tonic. It wasn't cool yet by a long shot, and the sidewalk was still warm under his feet, but the burning sun had gone down. There was even the ghost of a breeze rustling in from the desert and trying to work its way down the street.

He stood in front of the whitewashed cafe and considered. He was a big man, standing a shade under six feet and pushing two hundred pounds. His brown eyes were shrewd and steady. He was dressed in the local uniform—khaki shirt and trousers, capped with a warped, wide-brimmed felt hat at one end and cowboy boots at the other. His Ph.D. didn't show, and he didn't look like the kind of a man who had often been frightened.

Jefferson Springs waited for him quietly. The cafe was at the northern end of the town, on Main Street. Main Street was split down the middle by the railroad, with its little station and loading platforms. Orange trees were planted on both sides of the tracks. To his right, two blocks away, he could see the lights of the Rialto, where a Mitzi Gaynor movie was now in progress. There were a few street lights, a few passing cars moving very slowly, but Jefferson Springs was dark and shadow-crossed.

Jefferson Springs. To the casual onlooker, it was nothing. A place to drive through on your way to the city. A place to get gas, if you were lucky enough to find a station open after dark.

Paul Ellery knocked the ashes out of his pipe against the curb. He had read many books written by men in search of the unknown, the mysterious. They had looked in the Arctic. They had looked in the jungles of South America. They had looked in Africa, in Egypt, in Polynesia. They had taken telescopes and spectroscopes and looked out into space, at the moon, at Mars, at Jupiter, at the stars beyond. They had invented the electroencephalograph and had looked in the human brain.

No one had ever looked in Jefferson Springs. Jefferson Springs was no place to look for the unknown. How known could you get?

Paul Ellery had spent the summer in Jefferson Springs. He hadn't merely lived there—he had studied the town. He had made schedules and charts and investigations, because that was his job. He had asked questions and checked up on the answers. He had read the paper, examined the records, interviewed the people. He had looked at Jefferson Springs the way he would at an Eskimo settlement or an African village.

And Jefferson Springs didn't add up. Jefferson Springs wasn't what it seemed to be. Jefferson Springs was—different. Unknown? You could call it that, all right, and more.

He looked up and down the street. There was not a single human in sight. He walked around the corner slowly, and got into his car, a Ford. He stuck the key in the ignition and just sat there, not knowing where to go. He was beaten, and had he been anyone else he would have admitted the fact and gone his way. Paul Ellery, however, was a stubborn man.

"The joint is jumping," he said aloud, staring at the empty town. "I wonder what's doing down at the morgue."

The stars were coming out above him now. He could smell the fragrance of the orange trees along the railroad tracks. It was a lonely smell, and a nostalgic one. It made him think of Anne, less than two hundred miles away in Austin. Two hundred miles—that was four hours' driving time. If he left now, he could be there a little after midnight. And why not? What was he accomplishing here?

But he knew he wouldn't go. He couldn't go, not yet. Not until he knew.

He had read a few lines, years ago, that had intrigued him enough to start him out on a career. He thought of them now, as he had thought of them many times the past two months in Jefferson Springs.

The fact is, like it or not, that we know more about the Crow Indians than we do about the average citizen of the United States. We know more about Samoan villages than we do about American cities. We know a thousand times as much about the Eskimos as we do about the people who live in the small towns of the so-called civilized world. Who lives there, in those unexplored communities we drive through on our way to and from the great cities? What do they do, what do they think, where do they come from, where are they going?

A shocking handful of small American villages have been scientifically studied by cultural anthropologists and rural sociologists. The sample is so small as to be meaningless. The data are hopelessly inadequate. We know as much about the planet Mars as we do about ninety-nine percent of our own country.

Look at the towns and villages and whistle-stops of America. Go into them with your eyes open, take nothing for granted, and study them as objectively as you would a primitive tribe. There is no man on this planet who can predict what you may find.

Well, he had found plenty, if he could only put it all together and make some kind of sense out of it. He had found more than the author of those lines had ever dreamed of.

He started the motor, cut in the lights, and began to drive aimlessly through the dark streets. He made the long square of Main Street first, not sure what he was looking for, not even sure he wanted to find it.

He drove down past the drugstore, which was open but deserted, past the bank and the dry-goods store and the jewelry shop and the Rialto. The Rialto was bright with lights, and he caught a fragment of tinny music and deep, mechanical voices as he drove by. There was a girl sitting in the glass ticket booth, doing her nails.

He turned left, bouncing across the railroad tracks, and then left again down the other side of Main Street. It was much the same, with minor variations: another drug store, this one closed, a Humble gas station, an "American Club" that was actually a combination pool hall and domino parlor, the Hot Chili Cafe, a grocery store, a few houses, and the Catholic Church. He turned left again at the big, square icehouse, jounced across the tracks, and looked over into the Mexican section of town. There was a little more life there—a few scattered lights, a woman laughing somewhere, the faint strumming of a guitar.

Paul Ellery pulled up along the curb, put the Ford in neutral, and left the motor running. He refilled his pipe and lit it. He didn't want to go back to his hotel room at the Rocking-T. He just couldn't face another long night of sitting alone and wrestling with the senseless data he had got in Jefferson Springs.

He constructed a newspaper headline for his own amusement: YOUNG SCIENTIST BAFFLES LEARNED SOCIETIES; MIXES FACTS IN LABO-RATORY AND GETS NOTHING.

He noticed that his hands were sweating, and it wasn't that hot now. He tried to analyze his fear. Partly, it was the result of two months of overt and covert hostility from Jefferson Springs. Partly, it was the result of working on a research grant and not coming up with the right dope. Partly, it was the pattern that always just eluded him—the pattern that would make sense of his charts and files and statistics.

Mostly, it was a feeling. He had lived in Texas all his life, except for a stretch in the army and two years at the University of Chicago. He knew his state pretty well. It was a diverse state, despite all the stereotypes. The coastal city of Galveston was utterly unlike the capital city of Austin, just as booming Houston was quite different from Abilene or Amarillo or Fort Worth or Laredo. Nevertheless, happily or otherwise, a man knew when he was in Texas.

Jefferson Springs didn't belong. It wasn't quite Texas. It wasn't even quite America. In fact, it wasn't quite—

What was he thinking of?

"Cut that out, boy," he said to himself. "You're headed for the funny factory."

He made up his mind. He wasn't going back to the hotel, not yet. Somewhere, there had to be the clue he needed. Somewhere, there had to be an answer. Somewhere—but where?

There was one possibility.

He cut the car into gear and drove back along Main Street, and on out of town. He drove south, along the highway that led eventually to Eagle Pass and Mexico, toward the Nueces River. The land was flat but rolling, and his headlights picked out the dark twistings of mesquite trees and brush. The night was almost cool now, and the breeze slanting in from the window vents was fresh and crisp. The Ford hummed along the empty highway. Ahead of him, the lights stabbed a path through the early darkness. Behind him, the night shadows flowed in again and filled up the hole.

Paul Ellery knew, with complete certainty, that there was something terribly wrong with the town of Jefferson Springs. He meant to find out what it was.

2

Five miles outside of town, he turned off the highway to the left. The car purred along, still on a paved road, with plowed fields on either side. The stars were coming out above him.

Trying to calm himself, he switched on the car radio. The faded yellow light on the dial clicked on, together with a vast humming. Ellery hadn't been able to afford the standard radio when he had bought the car, so he had installed a special model he had found on sale. It had its drawbacks, but it worked. It warmed up and the first thing he got, naturally, was one of the huckster stations with mailing addresses in Texas and transmitters in Mexico, where they could pour on the power:

Yes sir, friends, I want to remind you again tonight of our big special offer. My daughter and I are offering you absolutely the biggest hymn book you've ever seen. This beautiful book, which will give you hours and days of pleasure and consolation, is two feet high and one foot wide. Yes sir, that's feet we're talking about—and remember that there are twelve inches in every single foot. And now, before my daughter sings one of these grand old hymns for you, just let me mention the price of this huge hymn book. The price is the best part of all, my friends, and remember that it's your contributions that keep this faith broadcast on the air—

Ellery tried again, and picked up a network show out of a San Antonio station:

(Burst of crashing music.) *Oh ho! And our next contestant, whose name is Ambrose Earnest, is from none other than Sulfur Creek, Colorado!* (Wild applause.) *Well now, Mr. Earnest, you're not nervous are you?* (Laughter) *Oh ho! Now then, Mr. Earnest, for two hundred and sixty-eight dollars in new quarters, can you tell me under what name William Frederick Cody became famous in the West?* (Long pause) *What's that? Speak right up, please. Oh ho, I'm sorry—Billy the Kid is not the correct answer.* (Moan) *But we don't want you to go away yet—*

Ellery turned the radio off. Nevertheless, his mood had brightened considerably. It was all so utterly prosaic—the peaceful country road, the night, the radio. How could there be subtle terror in a world of two-foot-high hymn books? How could there be horror in the land of Ambrose Earnest from Sulfur Creek, Colorado?

He rumbled across the old bridge that spanned the Nueces, and turned sharply to the right along the river. The road was gravel now, and his tires crunched through the ruts, although there was no need to slow down. A screen of trees blocked his view of the Nueces on his right, and a fenced pasture stretched away into the darkness on his left. He was getting close to the ranch road.

What was there, really, that alarmed him in Jefferson Springs? Paul Ellery told himself that he was neither wildly imaginative nor given to flights of occult speculation. He was an anthropologist working on a community study, and he had experience both as a teacher and as a research scientist.

Apart from his profession, he was skeptical by temperament. He liked facts and was apt to ask embarrassing questions to get them. He had a habit of being right, and a rather poor memory for the few times he had been wrong. This led him to a certain cynical bullheadedness, which wasn't as objectionable as it might

have been, because he was saved by a lively sense of humor and a pleasant un-
pretentious personality.

In any event, he wasn't given to seeing ghosts.

Okay. Rule out the supernatural. Chins up, and all that rot. How could be explain the facts?

ITEM: When he had first chosen Jefferson Springs as the subject for a community study, and had got a grant from the Norse Fund in New York to carry it
out, he had met with nothing but hostility from the inhabitants of the town. When
that happened, in ordinary circumstances, an anthropologist with only a few
months for research usually picked out another town where he could get quicker
returns for the time invested. Ellery, however, had been stubborn. He wasn't to be
licked by Jefferson Springs.

ITEM: After a few weeks, the people had changed their tactics. Instead of
clamming up, they had talked willingly and volubly. They had told him everything. Unfortunately, hardly a word of what they said rang true.

ITEM: There was not one single person in the town of Jefferson Springs who
had lived there longer than fifteen years. The town had a population of six thousand. Now, Jefferson Springs, for all its woebegone appearance to a stranger, was
no ghost town. It had been continuously occupied for one hundred and thirty-two
years. There had been no disasters, no social upheavals, no plagues, no crop failure, no nothing.

ITEM: That meant, in a nutshell, that the entire population—six thousand
men, women, and children—had been *replaced*. What other word was there to
use? The original citizens, one by one, had moved out. The last had left only a few
years ago. At the same time, different people had moved in. None of them had
been there longer than fifteen years, and most of them had lived in Jefferson
Springs a much shorter time than that. It was a totally new population.

ITEM: In view of the average Texan's devotion to his land and his town; in
view of the old families who lived in all such small towns, resolutely facing the
past; in view of a million things this unexplained shift in population was impossible.

ITEM: But there it was. What do your learned books have to say on the subject? Nothing? How sad.

ITEM: The culture of Jefferson Springs, as described to him by informants
after everyone had decided to talk, was a lovely textbook example of a typical
Texas small town. Everything was in precisely the right place and in the right
amounts. It was exactly as though you had read that three out of four men wore
chlorophyll bags in their ears, and then you went out into a busy street and there
they were. One, two, three men with chlorophyll bags; one without, doubtless
self-conscious. One, two, three men with chlorophyll bags; one without. As regular as clockwork. And as phony as hell.

ITEM: The people of Jefferson Springs just didn't *feel* right. Paul Ellery was
ready to swear that they were not the genuine article. They said the right things
at the right times, and more or less did the right things at the right times. But it
wasn't spontaneous. They were play-acting. The stage setting was absolutely

authentic, and they had all memorized their lines. But the play was a fraud. It was a soap opera with no soap.

ITEM: *Why?*

He came to the Thorne Ranch gate and stopped the car. He left his headlights on, got out, and slid the wooden bar back to release the gate. He pushed it back and drove the car through, then rode the gate back shut and fastened it again. The night was very still. Except for the frogs down along the Nueces, croaking their ancient song, and the gentle breeze sighing across the fields, there wasn't a sound. The stars were bright now, and diamond-hard. There was no moon.

He eased the Ford along the dirt ranch road, taking it slow. When he had gone almost a mile, he topped a small rise and looked down on the buildings of the Thorne Ranch ahead of him. They were completely dark, without a light on anywhere. Either everyone was asleep or away, or else they could see in the dark. It was an indication of Ellery's frame of mind that he rather favored the latter view. As a matter of fact, he had noticed that there were far too few lights burning in Jefferson Springs at night. The town was kept dark, and once you got off the main highway it was exceptional to see a lighted window after eight or nine o'clock. What did that mean, if anything? Was it significant?

He stopped the car, pulling into the rut by the side of the road. Trying to organize his thoughts, he cut the motor and turned off his lights. Whatever was going on at the Thorne Ranch, he had neither excuse nor authority for prowling around the grounds in the dark. His mission was hardly urgent enough to rout Thorne out of bed—or was it? How could he tell? He would have lied to examine the grounds further, just on the off-chance of picking up something useful, but that was a good way to stop a bullet on any ranch, mysterious or not.

He was reluctant to turn back. There was no place to go. He sat and listened to the frogs, welcoming their familiar music. He watched the stars, clean in the smoke-free air.

Melvin Thorne was a big, gruff, soft-spoken Texan. Correction: *appeared* to be. Ellery wasn't taking anything on faith anymore. Nobody, he decided, ever questioned the obvious. Therefore, if you were trying to put a fast one over, the obvious was a good place to start.

Thorne was something of a leader in Jefferson Springs—neither rich nor poor, but a man who commanded respect. He had been cordial enough to Ellery when Ellery had interviewed him, and had urged him to drop in again. He had even made the more or less inevitable suggestion that when Ellery got tired of fooling around with all them books he could always get an honest job on the Thorne Ranch.

The stuff that Thorne had told him abut the ranch was average information, and absolutely identical with the information given him by Jim Walls, who had the place out near Comanche Lake. As usual, it was *too* identical. It was a carbon copy.

Ellery had decided to try an experiment. He would fake all the data given him by Walls, making it flatly contradict what Thorne had told him of ranching conditions, and then ask Thorne to explain the discrepancies. It wasn't much, but it might be a lead.

He sat in the darkness, feeling a little foolish. It was all so incongruous, really. That was one thing that made the whole problem so tough: it didn't *look* like a problem. You had to go back constantly to your notes to make certain it was really there, and not just a figment of imagination, or a rationalization for sloppy work. The setting was all wrong for a mystery—no dark castles, no murders, no thunder and lightning, no mad scientist, no beautiful girl.

Just a soft summer night on a country road. Just a sleepy ranch and frogs by the river. Just earth and air and stars.

It was then that he got the feeling.

He couldn't place it at first. He sat up straight, suddenly tense. He held the steering wheel tightly in his hands, ready to move. What was wrong?

He listened. There was only the breeze, and the frogs in the distance.

He looked. There was the ranch, dark and deserted. There was the land around him. There was the night, frosted with stars.

And something else.

He held his breath. His heart thudded in his throat. He looked up, above the outbuildings of the Thorne Ranch, into the night sky.

There was something there—something enormous.

Paul Ellery released his breath in a hissing whisper. He felt the cold sweat pop out on his forehead and his hands felt sticky on the plastic of the steering wheel. Very quietly, he opened the door of his Ford and stepped out on the dirt road. Free from the distortion effect of the windshield, he looked up again.

The thing was still there.

Actually, it wasn't what he *saw* that frightened him. It was what he *didn't* see. He couldn't really see the thing at all, but he could feel its presence in the skies.

His neck ached but he kept his head back, staring. It was a perfectly clear night—he must remember that. There wasn't a cloud in the sky. The moon was just rising, but it was still swelling on the horizon and did not interfere with his line of sight. There were millions of stars burning in the darkness.

Except, of course, where they were blotted out.

That was what he saw. There was a dark mass in the sky over his head that covered up the stars. He could trace its outlines without difficulty, but he could not actually *see* it, apart from an occasional dull glint of reflected light. Its outlines were long and slender, rather pointed at one end, rounded off at the other. It was difficult to judge, because he could not tell for certain what its altitude was, but he roughly estimated its length as at least five hundred yards. It hung in the sky, completely motionless. It neither threatened nor promised. It was just there.

Paul Ellery did not know how long he stood in the dirt road, but it was a long time. Finally, he was rewarded by a flash of muted flame under the cylindrical shadow. A small shadow detached itself from the larger one, and started to float down. Unmistakably, it was headed for the Thorne Ranch.

Ellery's first impulse was to run. He felt utterly helpless, utterly alone.

Worst of all, he felt insignificant. But he stood his ground. This was his chance. If he let it go by, he would never sleep soundly again. If he took advantage of it—

He stood very still, watching.

He could see the descending shape fairly clearly now. It was spherical, featureless, about ten feet in diameter. It looked like nothing so much as a huge metal beach ball.

It landed without a sound in the yard of the ranch house, not a quarter of a mile from Ellery's Ford. Five figures got out of it. They didn't speak. In the light of the rising moon, he saw that one of them, unmistakably, was the rancher, Melvin Thorne. The other four, at least at that distance, were strangers to Ellery—a man and a woman and two children. They went into the ranch house and closed the door behind them. Surprisingly, they turned a light on.

The metal globe hummed very slightly and floated back into the air, where it rejoined the massive shadow above. There was a flicker of light, so brief that Ellery could hardly be sure that he had seen it, and that was all.

The shadow in the sky was gone. The stars looked down on him, twinkling.

Paul Ellery got back into his car and carefully closed the door. He was completely stunned, and it took a real effort to keep his hands from trembling. He looked at his watch. It was half-past ten.

He couldn't think. Nothing made sense to him, not now. The most important thing in the world to him at that moment was to get his mind back on the tracks. He had to make some sanity out of the world in which he found himself—a different world, surely, than the one he had thought he knew. Otherwise, he was just an animal—a rat in a maze.

It might be that he was not entirely rational that night. He had been through a lot, and subtle pressures can sometimes build up and explode with frightening violence. He had always thought of himself as an essentially practical man. Certainly he was not the hero type. And yet—

He had been treated like a fool. He didn't like it.

He clamped an iron grip on his mind, refusing to panic. He started the engine. He turned his headlights on bright. Making plenty of noise, he drove straight down the dirt road toward the ranch house. He would have to do it some time, or go crazy.

He had driven out here tonight to ask Melvin Thorne some questions, and that was what he was going to do.

3

Ellery knocked on the door. There was a long heartbeat while the world held its breath. Then heavy footsteps thudded along from inside the house, coming toward the door.

The door opened.

Melvin Thorne stood there in the yellow frame of light. He could not have looked less mysterious. He was a big man, bigger than Ellery. He stood a good six-feet-three, and he was solid. He might have weighed two hundred and twenty pounds, and it was all rock-hard. His hair was brown and thinned down against his skull as a result of years of wearing a hat to shade his pale eyes from the sun. He was dressed in style—khaki trousers, light shirt with the throat open, boots. He needed a shave.

A *perfect imitation,* thought Ellery.

"Howdy, Paul," said Melvin Thorne. His voice was slow and friendly, and the drawl was unmistakable. "What can I do for you this time of night?"

Easy now. Take it slow.

"I'd like to ask you a few more questions, Mr. Thorne, if you could spare me a few minutes."

"My name is Mel," said Melvin Thorne. He paused. "Kinda late," he suggested.

"I know this is a poor time to come calling, Mel, but I surely would appreciate your help. I'm running into some things that are like to tying me in knots."

"Well, now, Paul, that would be a shame."

Ellery said nothing. His hands were wet with sweat.

"Well, come along in, son," Thorne said, smiling. "Reckon a few minutes won't hurt none."

Ellery followed Thorne inside the house, and Thorne locked the door behind him. Ellery pretended not to notice—why shouldn't a man lock the door in his own house? Why shouldn't a *man*—

The house seemed deserted; Ellery couldn't see a sign of the four people who had come in with Thorne from the sphere. He listened, but all he heard was the sound of his own footsteps and a big, noisy clock ticking in the living room. The house was typical of small Texas ranch houses, which meant that it resembled a standard frame farmhouse. There were no wagon wheels, buffalo rugs, or brands on the furniture. The rooms were comfortable, but hardly flamboyant. It was a clean, middle-class, town-on-Saturday, church-on-Sunday house. It had a no-nonsense air about it.

Thorne led him into the kitchen, of course. There was the big farm icebox in the corner, the big iron stove against the wall, the shelves of mugs and plain dishes, the battered wood table with a fresh red-and-white checked table cloth. They sat down at the table. There were salt and pepper shakers on the table, each of which was inscribed with a deathless bit of verse. The salt shaker said: "I'm full of SALT, all nice and white; some use me heavy, some use me light." The pepper shaker said: "I'm full of PEPPER, don't shake me a lot; use me sparingly, I'm pretty hot."

Mystery?

"Coffee?" asked Melvin Thorne.

Ellery nodded. "Please," he said.

Thorne poured from the big black pot on the stove. *Where did the coffee come from?* Paul Ellery wondered. *There hadn't been time to make any fresh.*

Ellery drank it black. It was warm, but not really hot. He decided that Thorne must have just turned the fire on under the old coffee when he had heard the knock on the door.

Thorne made a face. "Coffee's right poor," he said. "The missus hasn't been feeling none too well lately. Anyhow, you know how women are—they all like weak coffee. Now *I* always say the more coffee the better. You're not drinkin' the stuff to taste the *water.*"

"That's sure right," Ellery agreed, searching for an opening. What could he say to this man? *By the way, Mel, I've just been wondering—are you a Martian?*

That would hardly do.

"Well, son," Thorne said, "start firin' in those questions of yours. I can't read your mind, you know."

Paul Ellery looked at him sharply, but the other's face was smiling and unsuggestive.

It was very quiet in the house. The big clock ticked in the living room, and that was all. Four people had come inside with Thorne, had come down out of the sky. Where were they? Hiding behind the door? Under the bed? In a secret passage?

Absurd. It was all absurd. And the ship—

Ellery licked his lips slowly. He was good and tired of beating around the bush. He was afraid and uncertain and confused, for the first time in his life, but he knew he had two choices in Jefferson Springs: he could go on with the farce, write up the data he knew to be false, and go on his way; or, if he dared, he could go after the truth, no matter where it led him.

He smiled. He knew that he had no choice at all. "Mel," he said, "I need your help."

Thorne poured more coffee for himself and refilled Ellery's cup. This time, it was steaming hot, and a big improvement over the first batch.

"Happy to help out, son," Thorne said. "'Course, I don't claim to know nothing about all this stuff of yours, but I know Jefferson Springs as well as the next man and better than some."

Ellery nodded, feeling his way. "Look here, Mel, did you ever notice anything—well, strange—peculiar, about Jefferson Springs?"

"I'm not real sure I follow you there."

"Don't you?"

"Well now, you take that Pebbles woman, lives over there by the high school. I'd be the last man in the world to say that woman was *crazy,* but it's a fact that she's plumb peculiar. Now, I recollect one time, I was driving along in my pick-up, and I looked over thataway, and there she is, in broad daylight, pushing that old lawnmower of hers, and she was plain naked, naked as the day she was born—"

"I don't mean that kind of peculiar, Mel."

"Well, you're dealing this hand. What kind of peculiar *do* you mean?"

Ellery retreated to his favorite defense mechanism—his pipe. He was smoking too much these days, but it gave him a chance to collect his thoughts and look occupied when he wasn't really doing anything. Anyhow, the most mundane statement took on a certain profundity when it was pushed around the stem of a briar. He lit it, broke the match, and dropped it into his wet saucer.

"Here's the kind of peculiar I mean, Mel," he said slowly.

"You ever been anywhere where things just didn't feel right, even when you couldn't quite put your finger on what was wrong? I remember one time—wasn't far from here, either, up around Sabinal—I was riding a one-eyed white mare down the road one afternoon, just as calm and peaceful as you please. Well, all of a sudden that mare shied away from her blind side so quick she almost jerked me out of the saddle, and the next thing I knew she took off like a bat out of hell. Took me a good ten minutes to stop that mare."

Thorne laughed. "Nothin' to it," he said. "She seen a snake or something on her blind side and it scared her. Happens all the time."

"Suppose," suggested Paul Ellery, "that there was no snake there? Suppose there was nothing there?"

Thorne shrugged. "So she was jumpy, son. What's peculiar about that? Don't *you* never get jumpy?"

"Sometimes," Ellery admitted. He looked evenly at the man who sat across the table from him. "I've had a funny feeling about Jefferson Springs almost ever since I got here," he said. "In fact, it's more than a feeling. I'm absolutely positive there's something wrong with this town."

"Wrong?" There was a long silence. "With Jefferson Springs?"

"You've never noticed it, I suppose."

"Can't say as I have. Course, there's Mayor Cartwright. I've heard tell the man's a little slippery, but he's a politician, after all. You take that mess in Washington now—I'm not too surprised at anything I might see here at home."

Ellery blew an uncertain smoke ring at the salt shaker. Clearly, he wasn't going to trick Thorne into saying anything revealing. The man was refusing to talk about anything important. And he was a good actor, no doubt about that. Already, despite what he had seen, Ellery began to feel unsure of himself.

Well, he'd just have to get blunter—hit him over the head with it and see what happened. No one had tried to harm him yet in Jefferson Springs, and until they did he meant to keep digging.

He leaned forward. "Cards on the table now, Mel," he said evenly. "I was parked down the road in my Ford when you came home tonight."

The silence deepened. Outside, the summer wind whispered across the land.

Melvin Thorne didn't bat an eye. "What's that got to do with it?"

Ellery took a deep breath. "You came down out of the sky," he said. The words bounced around the prosaic ranch kitchen, trying to find a place to fit.

"I don't follow you, son, not at all. What might you be trying to say?"

"Four other people were with you," Ellery went on doggedly, "a man, a woman, and two children. They came into this house."

Melvin Thorne grinned, big and confident and completely at his ease. "Is this a game, Paul, or have you been hitting the old bottle? Come down out of the *sky!*"

Ellery kept talking. He felt as though he were on a treadmill and couldn't get off. "You came down in a metal sphere. I saw you. What's it all about?"

Ellery felt like a fool, like a complete sap. *Yes, that's the way you're supposed to feel. That's the best defense in the world—the fear of ridicule.*

"You can't be serious. More coffee?"

"Thanks. I'm serious. Damn it, you *know* I'm serious!"

Thorne laughed. "Sphere? Ain't no sphere in *my* yard. Got a old oil drum out in the shed yonder, if that'll help any."

Laugh it up, buddy, Ellery thought, getting mad. *Make with the truisms and the phony accent.* "Stuff a cold and starve a fever," he said. "Still water runs deep. All that glitters is not gold."

Thorne looked at him with concern in his pale eyes. "You're not making very good sense, Paul."

"Neither are you."

"No call to get riled up. I tell you what—if you think there's one of these spheres in my yard, why don't we just go outside and have a look? If you find one, you can keep it and take it home with you."

"I didn't *say* it was in your yard now. I said you came down here in it. I said you came down with four other people out of the sky. Don't humor me, Mel. I know what I saw."

Thorne shrugged. "Anything you say, son. I might as well tell you the truth, since you already know part of it." He smiled. "Fact is, I been herdin' my cattle from a flying saucer. Traded in my jeep and my ridin' stock and bought one out of a mail-order catalogue. They're right nice, too, exceptin' that I always fall off when I try to do any ropin'."

"Cut it out, Mel," Ellery said.

"It was your idea, son. I was just trying to give you some more good ideas."

"I'm mighty grateful." Paul Ellery got to his feet, his fists clenched. He looked the big man in the eye. "I want you to know something, though."

Melvin Thorne got to his feet also. "Yes?"

"I want you to know that I don't believe one damned thing I've heard since I walked into this house. I don't believe one damned thing I've heard since I got to Jefferson Springs. I don't *believe* in Jefferson Springs. I saw you get out of some kind of metal sphere tonight, right out there in your yard, and I saw the ship up above it too. I don't know what the hell is going on around here, but I mean to find out. I don't take kindly to being treated like a two-year-old. I want you to know I'm not leaving this town until I know the score, if it takes me the rest of my life. And spare me the Texas drawl, what say? It stinks."

The big man looked at him. "I'd say you got powerful bad manners, son. I don't know what they're teachin' in the schools these days, but it sure ain't neighborliness."

"Can it," Ellery said. "You're not fooling anybody."

The two men stared at each other across the kitchen table.

Somewhere, far out on the range, a coyote cried.

Melvin Thorne laughed, abruptly. It was a big laugh, a loud laugh. It rebounded around the room, sure and confident and unconcerned.

"I like you, Paul," Mel Thorne said. "You oughta give up them books before you go completely loco, and come and work for me."

Paul Ellery felt tears of helpless rage well up in his eyes. How could you fight an enemy who refused to act like an enemy? How could you deal with a man who refused to meet you on any terms except his own? He measured the man before him carefully.

"Steady," said Melvin Thorne calmly. "You better run along home before you do something foolish. You'll feel better in the morning."

Paul Ellery was not inexperienced, and had been a competent-enough athlete in his time. He wasn't in really poor condition, but Mel Thorne could probably tear him apart if he felt so inclined. He knew the type. Socking him on the jaw would be like kicking a tank in a moment of irritation.

"Okay, Mel," he said. "Thanks for the coffee."

"You're surely welcome," said Melvin Thorne. "Come back any old time."

He led him back through the living room to the front door, unlocked it, and saw him out. The door closed behind him and the lock clicked.

Paul Ellery looked at his watch. A quarter to twelve. Less than four hours ago, he had been finishing up his meal in the Jefferson Springs Cafe.

He walked over to his Ford and got in. He started up the motor and turned around in the dirt drive. His brain spinning, he started back toward town.

It was still a beautiful night, soft and clear and sprinkled with stars. The moon had climbed high above him now, like a great pale eye in the darkness. Everything was so normal, it hurt. The frogs were still croaking down along the Nueces, in splendid unconcern. Maybe that was the answer: be a frog.

It was, Paul Ellery thought, like a movie in a nightmare. The people didn't go with the scenery, and the dialogue didn't go with the plot.

What *was* the plot?

He drove fast, and he did not look back.

4

The next day was exactly like the previous sixty-two: hot.

The blazing white sun hung in the sky, almost motionless, as though it too were too hot to move. No cloud braved that furnace, and the heat beat down like boiled, invisible rain. Heat waves shimmered like glass in the still air and the parched earth took on the consistency of forgotten pottery.

Jefferson Springs, from the coolest corner in the thick, square icehouse to the baked metal of the top of the water tower, held its breath and waited for evening.

In his room at the Rocking-T, Paul Ellery sweated. His room was an uninspired boxlike affair, and the resemblance to an oven was more than fleeting. He sat on the thin, plain bed and nursed a pitcher of ice water from the drug store three doors down. His notebooks were scattered over the floor in unscholarly confusion, liberally sprinkled with spilled tobacco. The morning paper, from San Antonio, was stuffed in the wastebasket, and the symbolism was intentional.

He was trying to think. The heat didn't help, and neither did the events of the preceding night. But he knew the trouble now, knew it clearly: the whole situation was completely outside human experience. The human mind is so constructed that it works on past experiences; these are the data which it tries to utilize. Human beings store up past experiences, both those of the individual and those of the group, and carry them as integral parts of cultures. When a man runs up against a situation, even a novel one for him, he doesn't really have to deal with it alone. He has at least *heard* of such situations, he at least has *some* facts he can bring to bear, he at least has *some* notion of how to proceed.

Most situations, that is.

Not this one.

This one was unique. In a nutshell, that meant he had to figure it out for himself. That sounds easy enough, being one of the familiar figures of speech of the English language, but Paul Ellery knew that it was not so simple. Most people live and die without ever having to solve a totally new problem. Do you wonder how to make the bicycle stay up? Daddy will show you. Do you wonder how to put the plumbing in your new house? The plumber will show you. Would it be all right to pay a call on Mrs. Layne, after all that scandal about the visiting football player? Well, call up the girls and talk it over. Should you serve grasshoppers at your next barbecue? Why, nobody does that. Shall you come home from the office, change to a light toga, and make a small sacrifice in the back yard? What would the neighbors think!

But—how do you deal with a Whumpf in the butter?

What do you do about Grlzeads on the stairs?

How much should you pay for a new Lttangnuffel?

Is it okay to abnakave with a prwaatz?

Why, how silly! I never heard of such things. I have enough problems of my own without bothering my head about such goings on. A Whumph in the butter! I declare.

A situation completely outside human experience.

Paul Ellery could see just how lovely the situation would appear from the other side of the fence. If you wish to devise a problem that cannot be solved, the simplest way is to make it appear that there *is* no problem. So long as everyone is convinced that all the answers are on file, nobody bothers to devise new answers. And if the problem is so constructed that you cannot even accept it as real without doubting your own sanity—?

How *could* the Earth go around the Sun? Any fool could see that it was the other way around, just by watching. How *could* there be anything alien and inexplicable in a little Texas town right on the San Antonio highway? Any fool could drive through it and see that it was just like any other town.

But when you introduced astronomy and mathematics—

Or anthropology and community-study techniques—

Paul Ellery frowned at his scattered notebooks. It was all there, the whole pat, unbelievable story.

There was the expected class structure, ranging from "that no-good trash" through the various ethnic groups to "those big shots who think they're better than anyone else." The pattern was closer to what West reported from Plainville than to Warner's elaborate class divisions from Yankee City, but that was in line with the size of the communities involved.

There was the expected emphasis on the high school as an upward-mobility mechanism. Clyde Kluckhohn and others had long ago pointed out that education had tended to supplant the frontier as a pet way to get along in the world, and this seemed to be as true in Jefferson Springs as elsewhere. Americans expected their children to get a better deal than they had, and the high school was usually the ladder that led upstairs.

There were the expected racial stereotypes about Negroes and Mexicans, and it was depressing to see that so little had changed since Powdermaker had written her *After Freedom* in 1939. There was the expected rural-urban ecology, the expected small-town kin ties, the expected suspicion of "those crooks in Washington."

But, somehow, it didn't fit together into a coherent whole—or more precisely, it fitted together *too* well. The neighborhood maps, the statistics, the symbol systems, the values—they added up to a perfect, ideal "type" that simply could not exist in reality. Social science was one devil of a long way from being that precise in its predictions. No one had ever found an ideal "folk" society as conceptualized by Redfield, and no one could expect to find a community as typical in every way as Jefferson Springs.

Still, he had found one. There were no ragged edges, no individual peculiarities, no human unpredictability.

It was, in a word, faked data.

It was a false face.

The entire population of Jefferson Springs had been replaced within the last fifteen years. Even a superficial look at courthouse records, supplemented with names and dates from Austin, had told him that much. The town had been taken over. The old residents had moved out—under what kind of pressure?

Okay.

Say it. Are you afraid of the words? This little town is in contact with—something—out in space. Thorne knows. They all know.

The cowboy hats and the boots and the Texas drawls and the inane weekly paper meant nothing. They were clothes worn to a costume party. Whose party?

Toward evening, when the intolerable heat eased off to become merely acutely uncomfortable, he left the hotel and endured another meal at the Jefferson Springs Cafe. Whatever the things were he was up against, he reflected, they had certainly learned the secret of Texas cooking: fry it in too much grease, add day-old French-fries, allow to cool, serve on soiled plate. When he had finished, he went back to his hotel.

There were two men in his room.

They were pleasant enough in appearance, quite unsinister, young, and casually dressed in sport clothes. They might have wandered in from a yacht club. One of them smoked a pipe. Ellery had never seen either one of them before.

"Hello, Ellery," said the man with the pipe, as though Ellery had just dropped in for a visit. "I hope we haven't alarmed you by waiting for you here."

"You've scared me to death. So what?"

"The fact is, Ellery, that we'd like to talk to you, if you're not too busy investigating us." He gestured at the notebooks with his pipe. "Interesting reading."

"Thanks," said Ellery. He stuck his hands in his pockets. "Make yourselves at home, gentlemen. My time is your time."

The men hesitated. "We'd rather hoped you'd come with us," offered the one without the pipe finally. "We think we can save you some time, if you're interested."

"I'm interested," Ellery looked them over carefully. "Where are we going?"

The pipe-smoker smiled. "To the ship," he said. "I believe you caught a glimpse of it last night, isn't that correct? I'm sure you'll find it interesting."

Paul Ellery lit a cigarette; he smoked them whenever his pipe got too foul even for him. He felt as though he were caught up on a treadmill, pushed and pulled by forces over which he had no control. And yet, the choice was his. The two men had asked him if he wanted to come along, and seemingly that was what they meant. They had not told him that he *must* go with them.

Strangely, much of his fear had left him. He didn't know whether it was because he was getting used to the situation or because the situation was too implausible to be feared. You can't fear the totally unknown—what you fear is something within your experience that you cannot fully understand but have reason to believe is dangerous.

These people were X factors—unknowns.

Obviously, they were not melodrama villains, twisting their black mustaches while they fed the babies to the meat grinders. They seemed reasonable enough. If Jefferson Springs had wished to harm him, there had been many chances. And if these people had really come from a ship in space, they were probably more intelligent than he was, or at least had far superior knowledge. If they were out to get him, they could deliver the goods at their own convenience. If not—

The ship, up there under the stars.

"Would you object if I carried a gun?" asked Ellery. "You gentlemen are strangers to me, you know."

The man with the pipe shrugged cheerfully. "You'll be perfectly safe with us," he assured him, "but by all means take a gun along if it makes you feel better."

Humor the native, Paul Ellery thought wryly. *If he wants to take his spear, let him take it.*

Well, it would make him feel better. He walked over to the dresser and took his .38 from the middle drawer, where he kept it hidden under his shirts. As a man who had to do a lot of moving around, Ellery kept the revolver with him as a precaution. He checked the cartridges, smiled at the two men who were watching him, and dropped a spare box of ammunition in his pocket. Then he stuck the gun in his belt and changed his shirt to a short-sleeved seersucker, replete with designs of palm trees and improbable dancing girls. He left the shirt-tail out, which at least served to make the .38 a little less conspicuous.

"Lead on, MacDuff," said Paul Ellery.

The man with the pipe nudged his companion. "That's him," he said, in perfect seriousness. "That's Shakespeare, remember? Misquoted, I believe, from *Macbeth*."

Ellery stared at the man, but said nothing. He switched out the light and followed the two men out of the hotel. The air was pleasant now, dry and warm but invigorating after the blistering sunlight.

They got into a perfectly ordinary black Buick and drove out of town. The two strangers sat in the front seat, leaving Ellery alone in the back. He could have shot them both without any difficulty, but of course he had no reason to—yet. The Buick went the other way from Thorne Ranch, out the San Antonio highway for seven or eight miles, and then veered off to the right along a dirt road. They went two miles on that—Ellery checked the speedometer over the driver's shoulder—and then purred to a stop.

Ellery spotted it instantly.

The big ten-foot globe, looking like a giant metal beach ball, swayed lightly in the middle of a plowed field.

They left the Buick by the side of the road, wriggled under a barbed-wire fence, and walked across the field to the gray sphere. A sliding panel lifted at their approach, and white light spilled out. They stepped inside and the panel closed. There was a sensation of lifting, very much the same as riding in a smooth elevator.

The interior of the globe was unremarkable. It was simply a hollow sphere, with a flat floor section built in, furnished with a soft gray wall-to-wall carpet, and two comfortable green couches. There was a very faint smell of electricity—or something like electricity—in the air. The globe hummed slightly, and there was a barely discernible vibration.

The two men sat on one couch, clearly not thinking about the ride at all. Paul Ellery sat on the other one and tried not to look like a country boy on his first trip to the big city.

His heart was thumping much too fast for his peace of mind, and his blood sang in his ears. What he felt was not fear, nor even wonder. He accepted it, all of it, because there was nothing else he could do. Here he was, and that was that. It was quite beyond his comprehension, and he knew it.

There was no name for what he felt, floating through the night sky with two men who were not of Earth.

The sphere stopped, very gently. There was a muffled thump as something locked into place. The two men stood up, and Ellery followed their example. The sliding panel opened. Outside, there was a glow of subdued yellowish light.

"After you," said the man with the pipe, smiling.

Somehow, Paul Ellery walked through the door. He passed through a short corridor—out of the garage, he thought rather wildly—and then he was inside of it. Inside the great shadow that had blotted out the stars.

Say it. A spaceship.

A long hallway stretched before him, with soothing indirect lighting in the walls. The floor was spotlessly clean and polished. There were panels along the sides, evidently leading to rooms of some sort. What could be in those rooms?

How many secrets did this ship hold, secrets as yet unguessed by the men of Earth? Where had this ship been built, and when, and what ports had it seen as it cruised the greatest sea of all?

The hallway ahead was deserted and silent.

They don't want to scare me, he thought. *Caution! Do not frighten the aborigine!*

"Just walk straight ahead," said one of the men behind him. "You have nothing to fear, I assure you."

Paul Ellery walked straight ahead. Superficially, it was not unlike walking along an air-conditioned corridor in some modern skyscraper. Almost, you could imagine that you could stroll over to a window and look out, and there would be the familiar towers and gray, honking streets of a large city.

Except that there weren't any windows.

Except that you were hanging in the air, far above the cities of Earth.

Except that the .38 in your belt suddenly seemed an amusing toy, nothing more.

He walked for what seemed to be a long time, with the footsteps of the two men clicking behind him in the hallway. Actually, by his watch, it took him a little over one minute.

But it was a long minute.

At the end of the corridor, there was a heavy door, set flush with the wall. There was no knob on it.

"Just go right on in," said the man with the pipe. "The door will open and let you through. We'll be back for you a little later."

The two men turned and walked down the corridor, and disappeared into a branching passage. Paul Ellery was alone.

"Here goes nothing," he said, not giving himself time to hesitate.

He stepped forward and the big door swung open without a sound.

He walked inside.

5

A little red-faced fat man was waiting for him.

"Ellery!" he exclaimed, extending a stubby hand and getting up from behind a large and untidy desk. "Damn glad to see you—been really looking forward to making your acquaintance. Say, haven't you been the stubborn devil though! I like that, I admire that. Have a drink?"

Paul Ellery got his own hand out in time to have it pumped up and down with enough enthusiasm to make him worry about his shoulder socket. He could not have been more surprised if he had encountered an alligator in a spacesuit. This jovial little fat man simply didn't fit the bill as a mysterious alien. He was about as mysterious as Lassie.

"What the hell," said the fat man, hands on his hips. "Don't stare at me like that, Ellery. This isn't a zoo, old man, and I have always flattered myself on a roughly humanoid appearance."

"Sorry," Paul Ellery managed to say. "I didn't mean to stare. It's just—well, you sort of caught me off base, that's all."

The fat man frowned with what seemed to be genuine petulance. "What do you want me to do, confound it—act inscrutable or something?"

"Or something," Ellery admitted.

The fat man laughed. "Well, anyhow," he said, "my name here is John. Frightfully original, hey? And now that we've been formally introduced, how about that drink? Permit me to assure you that it is not mere hospitality that speaks—I, the amazing monster from beyond the stars, am thirsty."

Paul Ellery hesitated. This was all coming at him so fast that he hardly knew how to react to it. The behavior pattern just didn't exist. It was just last night that he had stood on the dirt road on the Thorne Ranch, looking up—

But he felt himself relaxing. John seemed an amiable enough old buzzard. At least he wasn't a second-hand Texan, and that was a relief.

Careful. He may be a trick.

"What kind of a drink?" he asked cautiously.

The man called John laughed again. "What kind of a drink? Why, there's only one possibility, of course! I'll let you in on it, because I'm really not John at all—my name is Buster, and I'm an undercover man from the F.B.I.!"

Incredibly, the little fat man began to pace the floor, making wild theatrical passes at the air and frowning hideously. "The drink—ah, yes, the drink. You want to know about the drink?"

Ellery caught himself gaping again. Was the man a lunatic? A—what was the phrase—a mad scientist? Oh no, that would be the last straw! *Call the attendant, Doctor. I'm ready.*

"The drink," announced John, rubbing his small hands together with great relish, "is none other than a magic potion which will make you our willing slave in our diabolical scheme to turn the Earth into roast beef!"

Ellery laughed out loud, unable to control himself. It sounded a little hysterical.

John abandoned his pose and pretended disgust, but it was evident that he had enjoyed playing his brief role. "Damn it all, Paul," he said, "you're a rational man. You've got to get hold of yourself and calm down. We're banking on your intelligence, old man. Pray don't disappoint us. There's nothing up my sleeve, and I'm not going to turn into a spider and feed you to my young. You chaps, if you don't mind my saying so, have the most monstrous stories about us. There's a whole literature down here that's positively stuffed with invading monsters, ghouls, and a frightfully dull army of dim-witted supermen who dash about through the air thinking at each other and throwing things about with mental force, whatever that is—you read science fiction, of course?"

"Well, no," Ellery admitted. "I haven't had much time for that sort of thing."

John clucked sadly. "Deplorable. The worser sort, that is. Well, no matter. When I say a drink, I mean a *drink*—in your terms, of course. I rather like your Scotch—do you?"

"Yes," said Ellery. "Yes I do, and I could use some." He sat down in a chair in front of the large messy desk. He couldn't pretend to himself that he knew what the score was, but at least he could try not to make a fool of himself.

The little fat man sat down in a plush, padded chair on the other side of the desk and produced a bottle and two glasses from a drawer. The bottle was a familiar one—White Horse. John filled two glasses and handed one to Ellery.

"To sin," he said, and swallowed a good two jiggers in one gulp.

Ellery matched John's drink with one of his own, and the Scotch felt good. He needed it. He looked around the room, trying to get a line on the man who occupied it. The place was jammed with books—all kinds of books. Many of them were totally unfamiliar to him, alien in language and design, but there were others that he had seen before: Thomas Wolfe's *Of Time and the River,* Mark Twain's *Huckleberry Finn,* Ernest Hemingway's *The Sun Also Rises,* A. E. Housman's *A Shropshire Lad,* Thomas Mann's *The Magic Mountain,* Books by Chekhov and Dostoevski, de Maupassant and Sartre, Eliot and Shakespeare. Detective stories by Conan Doyle, Chesterton, Cornell Woolrich. Science fiction by Arthur Clarke, Ray Bradbury, Edgar Pangborn, Clifford Simak. And magazines and newspapers and tapes and cans of film. Ellery even spotted Kroeber's *Anthropology* and Howell's *Mankind So Far*—two books by anthropologists who knew how to write.

"You read a lot," he commented without brilliance.

John grinned and refilled both glasses. "I know you're wondering about many things, Paul."

"Wouldn't you be?"

"Of course." The little man produced a cigarette which glowed into a light when he puffed on it. He frowned. "I'm not playing with you, Paul. I hope you'll excuse my ham acting when you came in—you have no idea how it feels to shake hands with someone and all the time have him look at you as if you were about to sprout wings and squirt fire in his eyes." He drummed his fingers on the untidy desk. Almost, he looked nervous and ill at ease. "You see, Paul, this is rather a ticklish situation. Hard to explain, hard to get across. This isn't easy for me, either. Doing the best I can, do you see?"

Paul Ellery thought he saw. *No use kidding myself. He's the anthropologist and I'm the aborigine.*

"Maybe I can help," he said.

"Maybe you can," John agreed. "I hope you'll try."

"Question one," Ellery said, "what am I doing here?"

John frowned again and puffed on his cigarette. "Look at it this way—and please understand that there is nothing personal in what I say. The fact is that we regard you as an intelligent man. Further, you are a patient man, a persistent man. You even have a basic grounding in the scientific approach to phenomena. All right. You have blundered into a situation, quite by accident, and you've been smart enough to see through the window dressing and formulate a problem. That in itself is remarkable, and we are properly impressed. You are not, frankly, dangerous to us. You *are* a nuisance, if you will excuse my bluntness. Therefore, we have decided to do the only logical thing from our point of view."

"Which is?"

"Remove the nuisance, of course."

Paul Ellery raised his eyebrows. "What do I do—walk the plank?"

John frowned, changed his mind, and laughed. He laughed rather too much for comfort, Ellery thought. But then, he seemed concerned about Ellery's feelings, not his own. Sincerity, or part of the job? Or both?

"Nonsense," the little fat man said. He tossed his cigarette into a small depression in his desk and the cigarette disappeared. "Utter rot. Our methods are hardly so crude as all that. As a matter of fact, Paul, I can set your mind at ease a bit by telling you one simple fact. It is this: we are forbidden by the laws under which we live to harm physically any native of your planet. Ah, I see this surprises you! You find it hard to imagine that the monsters from space live under laws of their own?"

"To tell you the truth," said Ellery, "I never thought about it."

"Ummm. Well, be that as it may, the fact is that you probably have less to fear from us than from your own people. So do try to relax. You're making *me* nervous."

Paul Ellery savored the Scotch in his mouth. He tried to picture the scene he was enacting: a young man sitting across the table from some sort of an alien, an alien with what almost amounted to an inferiority complex about being an alien, in a spaceship hanging over the Earth, discussing the nuisance value of the aborigines. It wasn't easy to visualize. It was still less easy to accept as reality—it had all happened too fast. But only an idiot could bury his head in the sand and convince himself that what was happening *couldn't* happen.

"Question two," said Paul Ellery. "Are the people in Jefferson Springs—well, human?"

John poured more Scotch. He must, Ellery thought, have a capacity like a storage tank. What did they drink where *he* came from?

"You'll have to define 'human,' I'm afraid, before your question will make much sense," John said, inserting another cigarette in his mouth. "Do you mean, to employ your own terminology, a creature that may be classified as kingdom Animal, phylum Chordata, class Mammal, subclass Eutheria, order Primate, sub-order Anthropoidea, family Hominidae, genus Homo, species sapiens? Do you mean a divine creature with a soul, and do you care to specify any particular religious faith? Do you mean the highest product of evolution? Do you mean people born on Earth, or in America, or perchance in Texas? Do you mean a highly complex animal which, by means of glandular interaction, possesses rare spiritual qualities? Do you mean an essence, a vapor, an ultimate this-or-that? Do you mean something, say, with a cranial capacity of over a thousand cubic centimeters? Do you mean someone with whom you are not at war at the present time?"

Paul Ellery digested that slowly. To cover his own confusion, he resorted again to his pipe, filling it and lighting it with slow deliberation. Whatever else he might be, the little fat man was no fool. All right, then—what did *he* mean by "human?"

"Suppose we rephrase my somewhat childish question," he said. "First of all, as to your physical type, if I can use the term, I should judge that these people are indeed Homo sapiens, at least externally. Right?"

"You have answered your own question," John said. "Isn't it surprising how much you know if you will just stop half a second and think?"

"Okay," Ellery went on. "Next, were you born on Earth? I presume not. Next, if you weren't born on Earth, where *were* you born? More important, are you the product of a completely different evolutionary chain, unconnected in any way with Earth? As an anthropologist, I find it hard to understand how man could be repeated so precisely somewhere else in the universe. The line of development that produced man is so improbable and twisted—"

"If I may say so," John interrupted him, "there are a good many things anthropologists do not understand."

"I would be the last to deny that," Ellery admitted. He felt relaxed now, almost at his ease. It was like a bull session in college—except that college was a spaceship, high above the sleeping Earth.

"No offense, Paul," the fat man assured him. "Anthropologists are no worse than other natives of your planet. In fact, they are less certain than others, which means they are almost on the road to average intelligence. But we digress, my friend. The Scotch has loosened your tongue, and it has made me arrogant."

"It hasn't made you answer my question, however."

"Ummm. Well, it's no secret. The galaxy has spawned man many times, although its motive for doing so, if I may anthropomorphize a bit, seems obscure. In fact, man is a rather common animal. All it seems to require is a planet that closely resembles your own—and planets are a dime a dozen, you know—and a sun of the proper type; and man, by one road or another, becomes disgustingly inevitable. One of man's attributes, by the way, is that until a certain rather low level of development, he always is quite certain that his own planet is the only fortunate one in the universe, being blessed with his presence."

Ellery downed his Scotch and puffed on his pipe. "Let's try another question, then," he said. "The gentlemen you sent for me mentioned saving me some time. I was given to understand you had some concrete proposal you were going to make to me. What were they talking about?"

John refilled both glasses and then got to his feet. He began pacing up and down behind his desk. Ellery got the distinct impression that the little fat man really had been enjoying their talk, just as he had enjoyed acting out the role of one of Frankenstein's afterthoughts when Ellery had first come in. Now, he was working again, and none too happy about it. Why?

"It's quite simple, Paul," he said, jamming his hands into the pockets of his loose-fitting gray tunic. "You are, to put it candidly, an investigator who has been annoying our people. Now, suppose our positions were reversed. Suppose that you found an investigator who went around bothering *your* people—one without official immunity, let us say. What would you do with him?"

"Try to get rid of him, I suppose," Ellery said.

"Precisely. And how would you get rid of the investigator?"

"Well, you could lock him up if he had performed any criminal act. Or you could make things so hot for him he would have to go away and leave you alone. Or, failing all else, you might try to buy him off."

"Logical enough," John admitted, still pacing up and down. "Logical, but rather crude. I might almost say primitive—nothing personal, you understand."

"Naturally," said Ellery.

"Yes," said John. "We think we have a much more efficient method for getting unwanted investigators out of our hair."

"Which is?"

"Simplicity itself, old man. We simply take the problem that the investigator is trying to solve, and solve it for him! After that, we present him with the solution, with our compliments. Then, you see, the investigator finds himself in the untenable position of having nothing left to investigate. He has got the answers he was looking for and—presuming that he is an honest investigator—he can leave us in peace."

Ellery stared at the little man. "You mean you brought me up here to tell me what I've been trying to find out?"

"That's the general idea." John walked back to his desk and sat down. "There are things in the town of Jefferson Springs which you do not understand and which bother you. You've seen ranchers come down out of the sky in a metal sphere, and you have seen this ship. You might think, incidentally, that Thorne was a bit careless in letting himself be spotted that way, but sometimes it *is* necessary to transport people back and forth. After all, it was done at night on Thorne's own ranch, and Thorne's land does not lie along a main road, you know. Even if it did, most people wouldn't spot that shadow in the sky. The few that might would be dismissed as flying-saucer addicts, and in any event we'd be gone before any lasting harm was done. Well! I'm going to tell you the works, Paul, the true story. After that, I'm going to make you an offer. Clear enough?"

"Clear so far."

"Okay," said John. "Here we go."

6

The story the fat man told was a strange mixture of the familiar and the unique. It was man—another race of man, perhaps, but man for all of that—writing the old, old stories on new paper with new machines.

There were many earthlike planets in the galaxy—rather small, unspectacular planets, orbited about quite ordinary suns. On every one, the alchemy of life had produced miracles in the seas, and the chain had begun. From the sea to the land, from reptile to amphibian to mammal; from simple to complex; from tiny, scuttling animal, sneaking a living from the domain of monsters, to man, proud and powerful and almost intelligent enough to be a long-term success instead of a flash in the pan.

The details were often different, but the generalized outline was the same. If you started with an Earthlike planet, you got an Earthlike man. Man was not quite an accident, and neither was he planned. He was the result of a set of conditions.

Each group of men, when they arrived at a stage when they began to wonder about such things, naturally assumed that they were altogether too remarkable ever to be duplicated elsewhere in the known universe. Therefore, man's first inevitable contact with other men—for all men looked out at the stars, and all men wondered—always came as something of a shock.

People who had been living in villages found themselves also in a universe.

People who worried about nations discovered galaxies.

People who had learned to live in one world were dismayed to learn of a hundred thousand more.

Eventually, of course, great organizations and federations developed—man was an organizing animal. Planets which had reached a relatively high level of culture joined forces with other advanced planets. This was not easy, and took many centuries, for of course each planet felt that it had unique qualities; and it was difficult to trust foreigners. Each planet knew that it was superior and, what was more, each could prove it to its own satisfaction.

But civilization, which was another name for complexity and larger social aggregates, spread. At first, it was a few planets that had banded together, each for selfish purposes and each speaking loudly of brotherhood. Then it was many planets—for how could one lone planet survive against the power of many?

Man was an animal with big ideas.

The federation, loose and suspicious at first, thrived. Ideas were exchanged, and fresh viewpoints. Cultures flowered. A vast galactic government evolved, weak in the beginning, and then strong. Man could not live without organization.

When man on Earth was a clumsy thing climbing down from the trees, the first civilized planets were making overtures to each other.

When man on Earth found himself with a brain of sorts, and learned to make fire and pick up rocks with which to bash in other brains, a tenuous galactic federation was struggling to be born.

When man on Earth was yet a Neanderthal, slowly evolving the ideas of religion and an afterlife, other men he could not see had a civilization that spanned the known universe.

When man on Earth was a Cro-Magnon painting the walls of caves, he might look up at night, perhaps walking homeward from a mammoth hunt, and see the stars. Out there, a hundred thousand planets were jockeying for position on a galactic scale.

When man on Earth was an Indian, coming into an empty America across the Bering Strait from Asia, the star-civilization was running into difficulties.

When man on Earth was developing agriculture and cities and mushrooming technologies, the galactic troubles grew.

They had to be solved.

The interstellar civilization had thrived. When man thrives, he multiplies. The birth rate had gone up with the cultural vitality. Man filled up his planets, and the civilized planets of the galaxy became overcrowded.

The expanding population had to find some place to go. At first, non-human planets had been tried. Unfortunately, this had not worked out. The existing lifeforms which occupied these other planets had been part of the trouble, but only a small part. For the most part, they were so utterly different that they had no interest in human beings one way or the other, and competition with them was out of the question—different life-forms lived different lives, and required different things.

The basic problem, however, was the planets themselves. If a planet was naturally suitable for human life, human life evolved there. If it wasn't naturally suitable, the mere question of survival for men posed tremendously difficult problems. It had been said many times that man was an extremely adaptable animal, and so he was—on his own planet, or on one closely resembling it. He didn't adapt very well to a planet with twenty gravities; he didn't exactly thrive on a methane atmosphere; he didn't find temperatures that melted rock very pleasant.

To be sure, there were some relatively unoccupied planets that man could exist on. He could build atmosphere domes and enclosed villages; he could substitute his technologies for nature. But only up to a point. Human populations didn't do well in plastic bowls. In some cases, they managed to stay alive, but they—changed.

Obviously, the "different" planets were no solution. Man needed Earthlike planets for his homes, because it had been Earthlike planets that had spawned him. On the right kind of a planet, on *his* kind of a planet, man worked. On other kinds, he didn't work, because he was a man. It was that simple.

The population continued to expand. The galactic civilization had to have Earthlike planets, had to have colonies that could drain off the overflow of men. Where could it find them?

There was only one place. If you want an Earthlike planet, a Marslike planet won't do. You can irrigate a desert and make it green, but you can't turn Jupiter into England with a slide rule. If you want an Earthlike planet, you must pick an Earthlike planet in the first place and go there.

It was unfortunate that *all* of the Earthlike planets were occupied.

It was more fortunate that all the Earthlike planets were not at the same level of cultural advancement. Many of them were quite primitive, others were just experiencing the growth pangs of civilizations.

Now, cultural simplicity has consequences over and beyond any moral condemnation or exaltation of the noble savage. It has consequences in terms of populations. A culture that exists by hunting and gathering, on the average, must be a small one. If the population of New York City alone had to live in New York State by hunting wild animals, it is a safe bet that the population would be drastically reduced. A culture that has farming can support more people on the available land surface. With the beginnings of machine technology, still more people can live on the same amount of land.

But it takes a galactic civilization *really* to fill up a planet. As a result, most of the Earthlike planets which had not yet become a part of the larger civilization still had some room left for expansion.

Earth was one of those planets.

The galactic civilization found itself in an odd position. On the one hand, it had developed to a point which made the ruthless conquering and exploiting of other worlds unthinkable. Its own citizens would never stand for such an action. On the other hand, it had to drain off population, and there were only the occupied Earthlike planets which offered any possibilities in that direction.

They did the best they could. Man, when forced into it, is a compromising animal. They decided to colonize the undeveloped Earthlike planets left in the galaxy, but their colonization was no crude and slapdash affair. In order to appease public opinion within the federation, they had to work within a framework of principles, restrictions, and laws.

First of all, the primitive planet must not be aware that it had been colonized, for that would destroy initiative and rob whole worlds of their futures. Secondly, the natives could not be harmed in any way, and could not be interfered with except in the initial setting up of the colony, when various psychological techniques were permitted. Finally, there was a limit to the percentage of a planet that could be colonized. This percentage varied with the planet, but in no case could it exceed fifteen percent.

Earth was one of the primitive planets selected.

There was nothing intentionally cruel about this idea, although it had its imperfections and unforeseen consequences. It was just an emergency solution to a pressing problem, and it postponed, at least, the necessity for long-term, sweeping reorganization and restriction. It was a practical program for thousands of years, in most cases, and as for the future—well, perhaps they would have other solutions then.

They were not *proud* of their solution, but they were stuck with it.

Ironically enough, there was a precise parallel on Earth itself, if on a more limited scale. On many parts of the planet, expanding Western civilization had reached out and enfolded more primitive cultures. In some cases, it had simply exterminated the natives, in others, it had just taken away their land and deposited the aborigines on reservations. It had happened quite strikingly in North America, among other places. The Europeans came in, and the Indians were presented with the short end of the stick.

We weren't a vicious people, the Europeans said afterward. *We weren't bloodthirsty fiends. But it was inevitable—all that land, supporting only a fraction of the people it could support. And we needed land, needed it badly. Perhaps we were wrong, in an abstract sense, but what happened couldn't be helped. No practical man could imagine leaving a whole continent to the Indians. We didn't always like it, but what else could we do?*

What, indeed?

And, argued the civilized peoples of the galaxy a few hundred years later, *what else could we do?*

When civilization came furtively to Earth, sneaking in by the back door as it were, it was all done with great finesse and subtlety. Advanced peoples employ advanced methods. There was no drum-thumping invasion, no excitement, no death rays, no battling space fleets. No one got hurt. The Earth never even knew it had company.

Planets had been colonized before. Methods were smooth and routine. No fuss, no muss, no bother.

Defense? How could there be a defense? Defense against what? Where was the offense?

Naturally, the colonists confined themselves to the small towns and villages. They had other uses for the cities.

Picture a small town, any small town. A Main Street and a drugstore and a movie. Houses with unpainted, honest fronts and hamburgers cooking in the kitchen. Snow in the winter, sun in the summer. Rain on the night of the big dance. Rotary Clubs and gas stations. Gray ladies worried about the new preacher—he smokes, you know. A boy and a girl on a night in spring, the family car kissed by magic, a soft moon forgotten among the stars.

The town, though caught in the web of nation and state, is isolated. The people there see the same people every day. The next town is twenty miles away, and of course the people in the next town are hardly the *proper* sort. Strangers aren't wanted, because strangers always want to change things. We like our town the way it is.

The small town has a reputation in the city. The people who live and die there are ignorant, so the legend goes. They are fifty years behind the times. You can't ever tell about small towns—they're funny. They're full of local color and strange rural customs and the damnedest characters you ever saw.

An isolated society, then. A clannish society that doesn't want strangers poking around. A backward society where odd things and unusual-looking people are a part of life. Building all up, crops all planted, stores all stocked. A rustic colony. Ideal conditions. Ready for immediate occupancy.

The scientific experts from an unsuspected civilization go to work. Buy here, sell there. Tamper with a crop here, dust a few cattle there. Alter the rainfall, just a little. Spread a few pointed stories around—why, they're cleaning up down the road in Oakville, or out in Indiana, or right over there in the city. Opportunity!

And new people move into your little town. Funny people. They don't mix. Why, they're taking over the town, I declare! It's all poor Mrs. Smith can do to keep body and soul together. And so many of your friends moving on, after all these years, selling out, going to the city.

It's just not the same in your town any more. And you've heard of such wonderful chances somewhere else—the Wilsons went there, remember, and the Wades and the Flahertys—

Will, I've been wondering—

It was a snap. Duck soup for the experts from the stars. One population moved out, another population moved in.

A colony.

Of course, it was unfortunately true that if you moved the natives off their land you had to be sure they had somewhere to go. Fifteen percent of a planet was a lot of real estate. There had to be, in a sense, reservations for the natives.

Earth was ideal. Earth already had its reservations, ready and waiting. They were called cities.

Where did the unabsorbed small-town people go when they left home? Where had they always gone? Into the cities, of course.

The cities of Earth became preserves for the aborigines.

It was beautiful, really. What sane man would prefer to live in the shrieking chaos of a city, stacked in like sardines with his neighbors in the smoke and the dirt and the sweat? What sane man would voluntarily leave the sunshine and the green fields and the quiet companionship of home for a factory and a tenement and the grinding of machinery?

Answer: almost all of them. Wasn't it the thing to do? Wasn't the city the place to go to get ahead? Wasn't the city where all the smart people were? Weren't you an ignorant hick if you stayed at home?

There was nothing new in this. Man had always gone to the city. But he could be helped along if necessary, and he was. Psychological conditioning techniques, when administered by a really advanced culture, were remarkable things.

If you want to build an escape-proof prison, there is a way. Just don't tell the prisoners that they're in jail. Make them compete with each other for life-sentences.

Call it home.

There was one colossal irony in what was happening on the Earth, and it afforded the colonists with no end of amusement. The technicians of Earth were busily engaged in trying to build a spaceship of their own—one of the first primitive types, of course, with chemical fuels. With this spaceship of theirs, if it ever got off the drawing boards, they hoped to transport colonies of *natives* to other planets! They were bravely hoping one day to go out and "conquer" and populate the galaxy—a galaxy that was already so overcrowded that it had overflowed to Earth!

Naturally, they would find that the other planets of their solar system were quite unsuited for colonies of any sort, and they were still many centuries away from a workable interstellar drive. Still, it was amusing.

Since Earth was now entering a primitive phase of what might be termed pre-civilization, with savage war patterns coupled with semi-advanced destructive techniques, it might well be that an atomic war could occur. Earth was at a crisis period in her history, and could easily go either forward or backward. Many of the Earthlike planets had reached this stage many times, only to be blown back to the beginning for another start. Some planets never did get any further.

Now, an atomic war, under present conditions, would primarily affect only the large cities. This was not a pleasant prospect, of course, but for the colonists it was far from being a tragedy. The longer it took Earth to evolve a true civilization, the more time the colonies had to live their lives undisturbed.

Mind you, they would not start the war. They were not immoral beasts. Starting a war would be very unethical. On the other hand, they were forbidden to interfere. They just wouldn't *prevent* the war. Savages were so warlike.

The town of Jefferson Springs, obviously, was one of the alien colonies. It went through the typical well-trained motions of an American village, but this was no village of Earth.

This was different.

And that was the story the fat man told.

7

There was a brief silence while John paused for breath. He occupied himself by refilling the neglected glasses with Scotch and indulging in another cigarette. He looked just faintly bored—the look of a college professor explaining evolution to a freshman.

"Well, that's that," he said. "I hope I haven't bored you?"

"Not at all," said Paul Ellery. *When all else is gone,* he told himself, *put up a good front.*

"No monsters, no fiends, no wicked prime ministers," the fat little man observed, rather sadly. "Not even much drama, I'm afraid, to say nothing of melodrama. Just expediency. Just politics. Just human littleness in the face of something big." He sipped his drink. "I sometimes think that men are too small for their universe, Paul. We have such a magnificent backdrop, and our plays are so confoundedly uninspired and monotonous."

"Yeah," said Paul Ellery. "Monotonous."

"I'm quite serious," John said. "You will find that life on a galactic scale can be every bit as humdrum as life confined to a planetary anthill. Sam still loves Mary, and Mary still wants Sam to be a bigger wheel than Philip. It's all damnably dull if you ask me, which you didn't."

Paul Ellery, Ph.D., born in Austin, Texas, and raised on the planet Earth, puffed on his pipe in a spaceship room, hanging in the night. It was his fourth pipe, and his mouth felt like sandpaper. The rest of him felt worse.

He felt numb with what he had heard. It was not so much that it had come as a complete surprise, for much of his information had pointed the same way. Rather, it was the fact that his wildest conjectures, his most fantastic guesses, had been reduced to the level of a commonplace, everyday existence.

Little green men living in your furnace? Why, of course! Didn't you know?

John's matter-of-fact attitude toward the whole thing had made him feel oddly distant from the whole problem. It was like an intellectual exercise, a bedtime story in bedlam, a motion picture about another world.

It wasn't easy to remember that *he* was an aborigine. Ph.D.? He had never been unduly proud of it, but it *was* disconcerting to have it calmly reduced to the level of Witch Doctor, Third Class. *Some of his herbs really work, you know, but all that mumbo-jumbo is just too much for me.*

He couldn't doubt the story he had heard. It fitted the evidence too well, and the quiet ship that surrounded him squelched any qualms he might have had with complete authority. There was no reason for John to lie to him. He had heard the truth and he knew it.

He had one question, however.

"Look, John," he said slowly. "You kept talking about the inevitability of these colonies. You kept speaking of the necessity for what you did, and you used some examples from our own history to justify your viewpoint. But isn't there a basic difference? After all, this outfit of yours is a galactic civilization. It's big business. Wouldn't birth control have solved your whole population problem very neatly?"

John smiled. "No, it wouldn't," he said.

"Why? Surely your people are sophisticated enough—"

"That's not the point, Paul. Look here—you have birth control available and widely practiced right in the United States, isn't that right? And has the population gone up or down since the introduction of birth control techniques?"

"Up," Ellery had to admit. "But I still think—"

"No, my friend. It isn't that simple. Many other factors are involved. For one thing, the galactic federation is not a dictatorial set-up—and it takes a dictatorship to impose that sort of a rigid restriction on people. You will find that as people advance they insist on a certain amount of individual freedom; they will submit voluntarily to some things, but not to others. Birth control is practiced to some extent, just as it is in the United States, and you will observe that the birth rate in Jefferson Springs is actually lower than in most American towns. That isn't enough, however—it's a phony solution."

"Why?"

"You know the answer to that one, Paul. Permit me to refer you to one of your own scientists, V. Gordon Childe. What has *always* happened when there is a technological advance? What happened in the Neolithic? What happened during the Industrial Revolution?"

Ellery saw the point. "The population expands," he admitted.

"Check. And you are *sitting* right smack in the middle of a technological advance—a spaceship. Spaceflight *always* means more population, not less. That's just the way it is. If there's a method of cutting down population without killing the culture, we haven't found it yet. It's a problem for the future. We don't know all the answers, Paul, and we never will."

Ellery let that sink in a minute. There was just one thing he could say. He said it. "You spoke of an offer, John."

John put the tips of his fingers together and twiddled his thumbs. "Paul, you're an intelligent man. The fact that I am from what we have modestly described as a high civilization and you are a citizen of, shall we say, a less developed culture, has no bearing on your *intelligence*. We respect your brains. We know our own self-interest when we see it, and we think we could find a place for you in Jefferson Springs. Not much of a place at first, to be candid, but with hope for the future. We want you to work for us. That way, we gain and you gain. The other way, nobody gains. You have a saying on your planet, I believe, one of the few that makes a modicum of sense: If you can't beat 'em, join 'em. Crude, but I'm sure you see the point."

Ellery looked at the fat little man—the friendly blue eyes, the lines in the pink forehead, the earnestness that filtered through the easy mannerisms. Whatever else he was, John was an intelligent man. More to the point, he seemed to be an honest man. "Suppose I don't accept your offer?"

"You are indeed a suspicious man," John sighed. "I'm afraid you still think of me as a monster of some sort."

"Not a monster, John," Ellery said truthfully. "I'm trying to deal with you as a human being."

"What is there to say, my friend? If you don't accept our offer, you don't accept our offer. That's all. Nothing will happen to you—although the psychological effects are apt to be rather overpowering. You are free to leave here, go anywhere you want to go, say anything you want to say. We think you have a brain, and we hope you use it. It's up to you."

Ellery hesitated. "You mean I am actually free to leave, after what you've told me?"

John nodded at the door. "There's the exit. You will be escorted back to your room, unconditioned and uninfluenced. You're a free agent—or as much of one as a human being ever is. You know Mel Thorne. If you want to take us up on our offer, go out and see him. If not, I wish you well."

Paul Ellery got to his feet, slowly.

"So long, Paul," John said, shaking his hand firmly.

"So long—and thanks. I appreciate—well, everything."

"It was a pleasure, my friend." John looked as though he meant it.

The big door opened silently for him. He left the fat man alone at his desk. He seemed a little lonely, a little sad. The two escorts were waiting in the long, cool corridor.

Ellery followed them down the timeless, deserted tunnel, past the side panels that lined the walls. There was the door, the short passage, another door—and he was back in the sphere. He sat down on the green couch on the gray carpet, and the humming vibration came again.

When the sliding panel opened again, he emerged into the moist coolness of false dawn. He heard crickets chirping in the damp grass. He looked at his watch. It was five o'clock in the morning. There was the ride in the Buick, hardly remembered, and then he was back in his hotel room. His two guides left, and he was alone.

He sat down on the edge of the bed, in the darkness. He felt terrible. Too much Scotch, too much tobacco, too much everything. At long last, a hollow reaction caught up with him. He had left one world a short two months ago, his life secure and his future comfortable. He had come back to a new world this morning. His future might be—anything.

He got up, pulled the .38 from his belt, and stuck it back in the dresser drawer. Then he fell down on the bed, clothes and all, and stared at the gray light of morning until he fell into a light and fitful sleep.

He twisted and turned as the hours passed and the blistering heat came again. Twice, he cried out.

He woke up shortly after noon; it was too hot to sleep any more, and his pillow was wet with sweat. He managed to shave and take a cold shower in the bathroom at the end of the hall, and when he had put on fresh clothes he felt a little better.

He didn't even try to think until after he had downed four cups of black coffee at the cafe, and managed to choke down two overdone eggs and some passable sausage. Then he got into his car, opened all the windows, and just drove. He wasn't going anywhere, he just wanted the air to circulate a little. The sun was like a big brass shield in an absolutely empty sky.

He thought, briefly, of going to Austin, but he couldn't quite face it.

He had dimly hoped that when he woke up, despite John's assurances, he wouldn't remember a thing that had happened the night before. But he remembered it.

All of it.

He simply couldn't go into the city yet.

He recognized, with painful clarity, the utter hopelessness of his position. Things weren't the same any more, and they would never be the same again, not for him.

Sure, he had the whole story now—or most of it. There was no more problem. He had the answer he had sought.

Great.

Fabulous.

What could he do with it? *Nothing.* Absolutely nothing. He thought of every conceivable angle. He analyzed every possible course of action. He planned at least fifty different moves, and promptly discarded every one of them.

It was impossible for him, being what he was, just to put Jefferson Springs and all that it meant out of his mind, leave the place for good, and try to find any meaning in the life he would have to lead. It was a shock, to put it mildly, to find out that he was a primitive, a savage, sitting in his little village and calmly assuming that he was king of all he surveyed. A man—or at least Ellery's kind of man—couldn't go on with his work, knowing that all he was working for was thousands of years old-hat to a civilization of which he could never be a part. He couldn't face his friends every day, working, laughing, dreaming their dreams—when all the time he knew.

He would look up at the stars at night, and one night he would pull the trigger.

He could not write up what he had discovered in a technical paper. The idea was laughable. *Some Evidence Pertaining to an Alien Colony in Texas, with Suggestions about a Galactic Civilization.* No reputable journal would touch such an article for a million dollars. And if it were published, what difference would it make? Who would believe it? Even if the world's most famous scientist seriously advanced such a theory, he would be quietly carted off to an insane asylum.

And Paul Ellery was not the world's most famous scientist. There were several hundred thousand or so ahead of him.

He could not go to the newspapers or to the police. What could he say? He could hear himself: "Look, do you know the town of Jefferson Springs? It's been taken over by aliens, people from out of space. That's right, *space.* You know. You see, they took me into their spaceship one night and told me the whole story. It's like this . . ."

He couldn't even tell his best friend. "Look, Joe, a funny thing happened to me while I was working in Jefferson Springs. I know this sounds nuts, but . . ."

It was hopeless.

It was hopeless precisely because the colonists really *were* far more advanced than the cultures of Earth. The whole problem that the colony posed, a problem in philosophy and psychology and ethics as well as in survival, was virtually inconceivable as a serious situation to a planet at Earth's development stage. It was precisely analogous to a Neanderthal shouting into his cave that he had just split the atom.

Hopeless, too, because there *was* no Earth. There were only the hostile nations, glaring at each other in armed truce. There was only the U.N., fighting to be born in a world that needed it desperately but wasn't ready for it yet.

Could you address the United States Senate and suggest that aliens from outer space made up many of the senators' constituents? Ellery didn't even want to think about that possibility.

A revolution as an answer was sophomoric. Who would revolt? Against what? The plain fact was that Earth had evolved no technique even faintly suitable to handling the situation. It was outside Earth's experience, outside her expectations. It was even worse than trying to stop a tank with a bow and arrow. Earth could not even recognize that the tank *existed*.

There was only one thing he could do, obviously. There was no answer to the new problem that had been created by the solution to the old problem. All right, accept that. Therefore, his job was easily stated: *find one.*

He actually knew little or nothing about what really went on in the town of Jefferson Springs. He knew the familiar patterns designed for public consumption, and he knew at least something of the true story behind the colony. Beyond that, he was ignorant. The inner life of the colony, the genuine, functioning community culture—all that was unknown.

What was the actual relationship of the colony to Earth? Was it at worst a harmless parasite, as John had suggested? Or were these people human enough to want their colony to continue for always? Would the colonists *really* leave Earth alone to work out its own affairs? How could they be controlled that closely?

And how did the damned thing *work*? How could people, real people, live out their lives in a masquerade, pretending to be virtual savages from their point of view? Roughing it was fine for a vacation, even for a year or two. But for a lifetime?

Paul Ellery thought about Jefferson Springs—the real Jefferson Springs that he had never penetrated. Possibly—just possibly—there was a clue there. If he could find it.

He didn't really think he could. It was a needle in a haystack, at best. He wasn't even sure what it was he would have to look for. It was a million-to-one shot. But Paul Ellery was a stubborn man. He was also a practical man. He repeated the words to himself: *If you can't beat 'em, join 'em.*

He told himself that he was motivated by pure self-interest. He told himself that he was too sensible to try to save the world. Saving the world was a large order, with or without colonists from the stars. The hydrogen bomb was a tough opponent in a debate.

If he could come up with no solution, he would just have to make the best of things. He would have to adjust. He had been given a chance. Many a native before him had had to leave his tribe and try to learn the strange ways of civilization. He remembered his friend Two Bears, his interpreter among the Hawks. Two Bears was one of many Indians he had known, caught between two opposing lifeways. What were they called in the literature?

Marginal men.

He would try to find a flaw in the colony's armor. He would do the best he could. That was all he could do.

It was evening when he turned his Ford around and drove back to Jefferson Springs. The long shadows lay like soft fingers across the fields and the brush and the cactus. The faint breeze was only another shadow, whispering over the clean, sweet land. Jefferson Springs baked in the late sun, one hundred and twenty miles from San Antonio, sixty miles from the Rio Grande and Mexico.

Paul Ellery had made up his mind.

He had become a hired man. Not a *hired* man, he reminded himself, but a hired *man*. There was a difference.

Tomorrow, he would drive out again to see Melvin Thorne.

8

The next day was like all the rest. The burning sun was up early, sucking the night moisture out of the air, and again turning Paul Ellery's hotel room in the Rocking-T into a boxlike oven. It was wrong, somehow, that the day should still be the same. So much had happened, so much had changed, that the most incredible thing of all, the most difficult fact to accept, was that the world went on, inevitable and unimpressed.

Ellery ate a perfectly ordinary breakfast—no worse than usual—and was faintly surprised to find that he had a good appetite. In fact, he felt fine. The pressure was off, and if what was left was mainly resignation—well, that was still an improvement.

He went back to his hotel room, took off his shirt, and propped himself up on the bed, using a bulky copy of *Anthropology Today* as a writing desk. His handwriting was none too beautiful, but his typing was worse.

He had three letters to write.

The first was to Winans University. Winans was a small, privately endowed school, a few miles north of Austin, near Round Rock. It had been established thirty years ago by old Edgar V. Winans, an eccentric Texas millionaire who had, surprisingly, graduated from Harvard. Winans had failed to see why his native state could not support a really *good* small college, and to prove his point he had built Winans University. Winans was a man who knew what he was doing, and when he was through he had a first-class school on his hands, and one that attracted high-caliber students. Ellery, who had been teaching at the University of Texas, had resigned before coming to Jefferson Springs on the Norse grant. He had an offer from Winans University, which he had tentatively accepted because he liked small schools and the pay was good.

That, of course, had been in the other world.

Now, he dropped a note to Bud Winans, the old gentleman's capable son, and told him that he couldn't make it by September. He said that his plans were indefinite for a while, but that he would give him a definite answer as soon as he could. Hardly standard operating procedure, but Bud was a good guy, and would pull the necessary strings.

The second letter was to his parents. This was a more conventional item, hinting broadly at hard work and unexpected complications, and said in effect that he would be very busy for a while, but would try to see them soon.

The third letter was to Anne. This one required more skill. He had to prevent her from getting lonesome and coming to see him; and on the other hand he had to keep in her good graces in case he should decide to see *her*. This wasn't too difficult, being a type of letter that all young men learn to write to their girls, although Ellery had a sneaking suspicion that Anne was never fooled a bit.

He thought of Anne, only a short distance away in Austin, and felt a strong desire to go to her, be with her. But he rejected the idea almost before it was born. Nice, yes—but the answer to *his* problem wasn't in Austin.

He took his camera off the dresser and loaded it. It was a most unspectacular box Brownie. Ellery wasn't certain what he intended to do with it, but he figured that a few pictures here and there wouldn't hurt anything.

He dropped the letters in the slot at the ramshackle post office, across the street near the Rialto. Now showing at the Rialto: *Rocketship X-M.* Ellery guessed that *that* one would be well attended. Coincidence—or did all the colonists have an odd sense of humor?

He got into his Ford, stopped and bought gas at the Humble station, and tried to tell himself that the station attendant was an alien colonist. It didn't work. The overalls, the clumsy shoes, the red bandanna hanging out of a back pocket—the man was just too damned *ordinary*.

He had to keep telling himself: *This is not real, this is an alien colony, this is not real—*

The words were not real, either.

He drove off, back out of town and out across the Nueces bridge to the Thorne Ranch. He did his best to choke off both his mood and his train of thought. The treadmill thinking that kept rolling off *this-can't-be-real-but-it-is-real-but-it-doesn't-LOOK-real* wasn't helping a bit. He had to keep his mind clear.

For himself, of course. He came first.

He drove along through the familiar country, along the familiar gravel road, and turned off at the dirt road that led to the ranch house. He looked up, half expecting to see a great ship swimming in the air, but the pale blue sky was empty. There was only the sun, relentlessly pressing the attack.

He pulled into the ranch driveway and parked. No pictures yet, he decided. He got out and knocked on the door. He heard footsteps, but they were not those of Thorne's clumping boots. His wife, maybe?

The door opened. It wasn't his wife.

"Hello," said the girl, smiling. "Are you Paul Ellery?"

"I used to be," Paul said.

"Please come in, Paul. I'm Cynthia. I'll call Mel."

Ellery followed her into the house, caught off base again. The girl was a surprise. She was a blonde, with her hair piled up on top of her head, careless of her looks because she had them to spare. She wore a man's white shirt with the sleeves rolled up, and gray shorts. Her feet were bare.

"Sit down, Paul," she said.

Ellery sat down. He was in the living room this time, on a brown couch. The big clock ticked monotonously in the heat.

"Mel's out in the barn," Cynthia said. Her voice was soft, but it had a definite Texas slur in it. "Don't go 'way."

She left, and Ellery heard her call. She had a good pair of lungs, among other things. Ellery tried to add her into the equation. Mistress? New colonist from the ship? Bait? Friend of the family? Vampire?

Cynthia came back. "My God, it's hot here," she said.

That, Ellery reflected, was a statement with at least two hidden jokes in it. Who or what her God might be, he had not the foggiest notion. And the way she said "here" suggested strongly that she had just arrived from elsewhere. However, if nothing else, the sentence neatly destroyed the picture of her as a *femme fatale* he had been building up in his mind.

"It is hot," he said wittily. Then, ashamed of himself, he tried to do better. "Do you live here?" Not much of an improvement.

"Yes," she said, sitting down next to him on the couch. "In town," she added. "I teach home economics in the high school."

Ellery let that digest a minute, and discovered that her eyes were the standard blue. Age? Early twenties, probably.

"That's nice," he said. "For the students, I mean."

She smiled. "Thank you, Paul," she said demurely.

The back door slammed and there were more footsteps. Clumping ones, this time. Melvin Thorne walked into the room, big and solid and sweating. He held his hat in his hand, and he was wearing tight, faded blue jeans and a dirty khaki shirt. The cowboy boots were scuffed.

"Howdy, Paul," he drawled. "Mighty glad to see you again."

Oh no, thought Ellery a little wildly. *Not the dialect again.*

"Hello, Mel. How are you?"

"Fine, mighty fine." The big man paused. "Cynthia, you get the hell out of here." He said it in exactly the tone of voice he would have used to say, "Cynthia, please pour me another cup of coffee."

Cynthia raised her neat eyebrows but made no objection. She stood up, looking very cool and slim next to Thorne. "See you later, Paul," she said, and left the room.

"You want to watch out for that one, son," Melvin Thorne said. "She's trouble. Come on into the kitchen where we can talk."

They went back into the kitchen and sat down at the battered wood table with the red-and-white checked tablecloth. The salt and pepper shakers still carried their inane legends, unashamed. Before Thorne had a chance to say anything, his wife padded into the kitchen. She was dumpy, white-haired, scrubbed. She had nice brown eyes.

"Pour us some coffee, Martha," Melvin Thorne said.

Martha obliged, pouring from the big black pot on the stove into two mugs that had seen better days. She didn't bother about sugar or cream. She eyed Ellery for a moment, and then put a strong hand on his shoulder.

"You'll be Mr. Ellery," she said. "You look like a nice young man, and I hope you like it here with us."

"Thank you, Mrs. Thorne," Ellery said. "Thanks a lot."

Again, he looked at Mr. and Mrs. Melvin Thorne. Could these people really be "alien," and what did that mean? If they had evolved on a planet that circled another sun, was that so horrible? What was the difference?

Why is there a threat to Earth at all? A threat to me? Why shouldn't they live here, the same as anybody else?

But he remembered, even there in that cozy kitchen. He remembered all those primitive peoples who had come face to face with the white man. The white man had evolved on the same planet they had, and was indistinguishable from them except for a few minor traits. Where were those primitive peoples now? These aliens, or whatever they were, said that they had no desire to "conquer" the Earth. As far as Ellery could tell, that was true. But more of them were coming all the time, looking for living space. They were not machines. They had their weaknesses the same as other people.

Some day, that meant trouble.

Paul Ellery wondered: *Had any colonized planet ever climbed out of savagery? Or were they—helped—to stay where they were?*

He thought, too, of the hydrogen bombs and all that they represented. The civilized aliens could prevent those bombs from ever going off, could wipe war from the Earth forever. But they wouldn't. Here, if anywhere, they would not interfere. What chance did Earth have, on its own?

Paul Ellery clenched his fists. Well, here was one way out—for him.

"I guess John told you the story," he said.

"I heard from old John, that's right," Melvin Thorne said, drinking his coffee. "Reckon you've decided to tie up with us, that right?"

"That's right," Ellery said. He swallowed his coffee more out of politeness than desire. Gulping hot coffee in the middle of the day in summer was one Texas custom he had never made his own. "He told me you'd tell me what I needed to know."

"Mighty glad to help, Paul," Thorne said slowly. "Though there ain't an all-fired lot to tell."

Melvin Thorne was still employing his Texas drawl, and Ellery suddenly realized that it wasn't faked at all. *This was the only English the man knew.* He had been trained for this particular culture—for how long? Ellery began to appreciate something of the stake that Thorne and the rest had in staying in Jefferson Springs. Where else could they go?

"It will have to be sort of odd jobs at first, Paul, until we're sure and you're sure that you want to stay on with us," Mel said, pouring more coffee. "You understand, I reckon, that it will take you a spell to fit into the *real* life of our town. You've got a lot to learn, just like I had a lot to learn before I came down here and set me up a ranch. I think the paper would be a good place for you to start, since you like readin' and all that stuff anyhow. We'll keep you at that a spell, and then

give you a shot at something else. It won't be very exciting at first, Paul, but we
think we've got a nice little town here and we're proud of it."

Ellery listened in growing wonderment. Thorne was just the same as he had
been before—evidently he really *was* more or less what he appeared to be on the
surface. Personality type screening? Right man for the right job? Somehow, he
hadn't expected an alien from an advanced civilization to be of no better than average intelligence. But why not? It was the civilization that was advanced, not the
citizen. The fact that Joe Blow lives in the same culture as Albert Einstein does
not mean that Joe Blow can't be a Grade-Q moron. And Mel Thorne seemed to
be—what? A Texas Babbitt from another planet? It was a vaguely frightening
thought.

"I'll do my best, Mel," he said.

"I'm sure you will, son. And later on, if you get along okay, they may send
you—back—for the full treatment."

"Back?"

"That's right—back. You know. But for right now it'll have to be the newspaper."

"Well," Ellery said, "it could be worse. They used to have a standard joke in
college that all the guys with a Ph.D. wound up digging ditches."

Melvin Thorne laughed—a big, booming, noisy laugh. "That's a good one,
son," he said. "I always said that there book learnin' was a waste of time."

Ellery sighed. The man *meant* it. It was no act. "Well, I'll try to rise above
it," he said.

Mrs. Thorne came back into the kitchen, smiled vacantly, and padded out
again.

"One thing we *can* do for you right at the start," Mel told him, "and that's
get you out of that Rocking-T hotel. That place is just to scare the tourists off."

He laughed. Ellery laughed with him, unamused.

"You just go on into that little white house across from the high school,"
Thorne said. "Ain't nobody living there, so that's your house now. You'll find the
key in the mailbox."

"Thanks again," Ellery said. His mind set up a pleasant equation: house plus
high school equals Cynthia.

"And keep an eye out for Cynthia, son," Thorne said. "She's trouble, like I
said. She teaches high school, you know."

"I know," Ellery said. "I'll wear my armor."

"Uh huh," Thorne said doubtfully. "Well, that's about it, Paul. I want you
to feel free to come out here and see me any old time. And remember this, son:
you're not a prisoner here. This is your *home*, if you want it. You're free to leave
whenever you want to. We're right proud of what we've done in Jefferson
Springs; we've worked hard for what we've got. Just remember, it ain't half as
funny to you as it was to us when we first came here."

Ellery caught just a glimpse then of Jefferson Springs the way the colonists
saw it. An alien town on a strange and distant world, a tiny spot torn out of a hostile wilderness, a fragile container into which they poured their lives and their

loves and their hopes. An adventure on another world, as surely as though it had been men from Earth journeying to the stars. . . .

"Thanks, Mel," he said.

"Don't mention it, son."

Paul Ellery went back through the living room and out the door. He didn't see Cynthia. He gunned his Ford down the dirt road. The brilliant sunshine touched the blue sky with gold, and the heat was heavy with the rich smell of the river and the cypress trees.

He breathed deeply of summer and tried not to think.

9

His first day on the weekly newspaper was singular enough for any man.

The *Watchguard* office, located across from the Community Hall, was a long, narrow, and magnificently drab shed. It was so palpably ancient that Ellery half expected to find that all the writing was done by hooded scribes with goose-quill pens.

Instead, it was done by Abner Jeremiah Stubbs.

Mr. Stubbs was tall, stooped, and thin. He was pleasantly grotesque. His hair was a precise nothing-color, and it was kept out of his eyes by a faded green eye shade. He dressed in a black suit. His shapeless coat was hung on a hook on the door, and he worked in a shiny vest. He had a big gold watch, and Ellery knew without checking that it was scrupulously accurate.

Abner spoke in funereal tones, when he spoke at all. Everything he said came out sounding like, "Ah, the pity of it all, the *vast* pity of it all."

To Ellery, he said: "Typewriter's in the next room. Telephone's there too. List of stories on the pad. You know makeup?"

"Only the kind that goes on girls' faces," Ellery confided.

Mr. Stubbs nodded wearily. Another day, another burden. "You'll learn. Get ink in your blood."

Ellery nodded. Mr. Stubbs leaned back in his swivel chair and gazed blankly at the wall, so Ellery decided that the interview was over. He went into his office, if it could be dignified by that name, and risked the wrath of ageless gods by wrestling up a window that acted as if it had been shut since the Flood. The Flood hadn't washed it any too clean, either.

The heat was stifling. Outside the window, a single forlorn oak tree drooped in the sun and tried to remember what rain looked like. Ellery sat at a small, un-painted table and contemplated a typewriter that must have been older than he was.

He had, of course, studied the paper intensively in his work in Jefferson Springs. Every item in it for months before he had arrived in the town had been classified and filed. The news items had given him information on kinship con-nections, meetings, parties. They had furnished valuable interview leads. The ed-itorials of Mr. Stubbs had yielded insights into the value system of Jefferson Springs.

Ellery knew the paper. He had never been much of a writer, but he felt supremely confident that he could attain the required stylistic excellence. The paper was called *The Jefferson Springs Watchguard*. Its slogan: OUR FIGHT FOR THE RIGHT IS ETERNAL AS THE PLAINS.

Not much of a slogan, he reflected, but better than some he had seen. There was one town in East Texas with a paper called the *Jimplecute: Join Industry, Manufacturing, Planting, Labor, Energy, Capital (in) Unity Together Everlasting.*

He studied the scrawled pad for thirty minutes and then stuck a yellow sheet in the typewriter. In three hours he wrote four stories, and between the battered typewriter and his own unskilled fingers he managed to produce a mess worthy of any seasoned reporter. Casting inexperience to the winds, he composed four headlines to go with the stories. He was happily ignorant of word-counts and allied trivia, but he caught the tone of the *Watchguard* to perfection:

MILDEW IS COMMON PROBLEM OF SUMMER.
LITTLE JODY DAVIS IMPROVED AFTER BEING KICKED IN FACE BY HORSE.
A 4-H CAMPER WRITES HOME TO MOM.
LIONS CLUB BANQUET IS VERY ENJOYABLE EVENT.

His day's work done, Ellery examined the last issue of the paper, trying to find something in it that would prove useful to him. Here again was the basic anomaly of Jefferson Springs. The town was an alien colony but there was nothing advanced about it that he could see. It was as average as dirt. Now, acting or no acting, false-face or not, the colonists actually *were* living in Jefferson Springs. No matter how insincere—and it did not strike Ellery that they were insincere at all in the lives they led—the mere business of going through the motions of life in Jefferson Springs took time, a lot of time. These people spent, without any doubt, the majority of their lives acting out the parts of small-town Texas citizens.

And that didn't make sense.

These colonists were human enough, as far as Ellery could tell. No group of people would willingly spend at least seventy percent of every single day pretending to live in a culture without meaning for them.

Ellery reversed a few positions in order to see the problem more clearly. Suppose that the cultures concerned were those of the present-day United States and a Southeastern Indian group, say the Natchez who had once lived on the lower Mississippi. The gulf between the two cultures was roughly comparable to the gulf between a galactic civilization and the United States, though possibly not as profound. Okay, that was the setup. On one hand, modern industrialized America. On the other, seven villages of thatched huts, agricultural, with temple mounds and undying-fire ceremonies, together with a well-defined class system ranging from a supreme Sun down through Nobles, Honored Men, and commoners, the last known as Stinkards. Now, suppose that for some reason the present-day Americans wish to set up a colony among the Natchez, and do it in such a way that the Natchez are unaware of the colony's presence. First, of course, there would have to be an intensive period of detailed training, to say nothing of time travel. But, assuming that the United States citizens could turn themselves into a reasonable facsimile of Natchez Indians, how long would they be willing to *live* like the Indians, cut off from all the comforts and conveniences and values of the life they had known? Not for a week or so, not for a summer's outing, but for *keeps?*

Ellery could see only one possibility there: if the United States citizens were taken as children and brought up as Indians, then they would, of course, be perfectly content with the Indian culture, since they would, in effect, *be* Indians. They would not, however, be typical United States citizens any longer.

That was the possibility. It was unfortunate that the aliens weren't working it that way.

Quite clearly, it wouldn't work in their case. Their problem was considerably more complex. They must both fit their citizens for life in a primitive colony and at the same time retain them as participants in a galactic civilization. Simply dumping them down in Jefferson Springs as children wouldn't do the trick, and in any event he had already seen enough to indicate that the procedure was quite different. Some of the colonists came to Jefferson Springs as young adults; that called for one technique. Some of them came as children; that meant another technique. And some, apparently, were born in Jefferson Springs and then trained as full galactic citizens elsewhere.

Sent "back for the full treatment," as Thorne had intimated that Ellery would be eventually?

The question remained: how could they be both? How could they live in and *enjoy*—for they must enjoy it—Jefferson Springs, and at the same time maintain their unity with a vast and complex interstellar civilization?

Ellery had no answer for that one.

He read the paper carefully, digesting every last "personal" ("Mr. and Mrs. Joe Walker spent too happy days last week visiting in Garner State Park") and advertisement ("Mr. Merchant: Don't Preach Home Patronage then Send Your Printing Elsewhere"). In the entire paper, he found only one small item that was at all suggestive. It was suggestive only because it was cryptic; there was nothing blatantly mysterious about it. It was a small square on the back page:

THORNE RANCH
COMPULSORY
AUGUST 25   9 P.M.

That was all. And the date was the day after tomorrow. Paul Ellery didn't know what it was, or even what it might be.

He did know that he was going to be there.

He walked out of his office and handed his completed stories to Mr. Stubbs, who was still seated in his swivel chair gazing with complete absorption at the wall. Stubbs fished out his gold watch, shook his head sadly, and said nothing.

Ellery chose to interpret this as both approval and dismissal, and left for the day. He drove home to his new white house across from the high school, which was deserted for the summer. The house was just beginning to cool off from the afternoon roasting, but it was still plenty warm. There was a slight breeze out of the north, but Ellery had no instruments delicate enough to detect it.

The house was plain but comfortable: living room, bathroom, bedroom, kitchen, a few closets, all put together without a single trace of either ingenuity or imagination. There was one painting in the place, a waxen floral study, and when it had been carefully turned to face the wall it was passable.

Ellery fried himself a hamburger, preferring even his own cooking to that of the Jefferson Springs Cafe, and opened a bottle of beer. He armed himself with a notebook and a pencil and sat down at the kitchen table.

He asked himself what he, as an anthropologist, knew about the problems of culture contact that would be useful to him. He was not given to getting in over his head and asking questions afterward; he had found that it was to his advantage to figure things out ahead of time. If he could.

When the knock on the door came, he was halfway through the hamburger. On the problems of culture contact, his progress was less remarkable. He stuck the notebook in a drawer in the kitchen table and opened the front door.

It was Cynthia. The equation ran through his mind again: house plus high school equals Cynthia. Well, better late than never. And better early than late.

"Are you busy?" asked Cynthia, smiling.

"Not that busy," Ellery assured her. "Won't you come in? I'm just finishing up my caviar."

She came in, and Ellery closed the door. She was wearing a dark green skirt and a white silk blouse, and her blond hair was down. She was slim and tanned and she looked good.

Very good.

"Now that you're a reporter," she said, "I thought I'd bring you a story."

"Fine," said Ellery. "Bring it on into the kitchen and I'll give you a beer for a reward."

She followed him into the kitchen and sat down at the table, wrinkling her nose slightly at the hamburger. She accepted the beer without complaint, but she didn't look like the beer-drinking type.

"Sorry I don't have anything better," Ellery said. "I just moved in here, and I haven't stocked the cellar yet. In fact, I haven't got a cellar."

She laughed gently. It was a pleasant laugh. It said: "That wasn't a bit funny, but it was a reasonable try."

"Do you eat hamburgers every night?" Cynthia asked.

"Not at all," Ellery assured her. "I fry a mean egg too, so there's no monotony in my diet."

"Poor man," Cynthia said. "You need a cook. Will I do?"

There it was. No stalling, no fumbling for invitations, no beating around the bush. Cynthia wasn't being coy, and she wasn't kidding. Ellery decided that he and Cynthia were going to get along fine.

"Lady," he said, "you will do splendidly. I won't even ask for references."

"That's good," she said, "because I haven't got any."

Ellery finished his beer and opened another. "When do we start this charming arrangement?" he asked.

Cynthia smiled her man-killer smile. "Let's make it tomorrow night," she suggested. "I'll bring the groceries and see if I can impress you."

"With or without groceries," Ellery assured her, "you will impress me."

"Good," said Cynthia. She crossed her legs pleasantly. "Let's not forget about the story, Paul."

Ellery, who had done just that, nodded. He went into the living room and got an empty notebook. "Let's have it," he said, sitting down again. "I'll phone Stubbs and have him stop the presses."

"No hurry," Cynthia said. "It's about the high school. It opens on the third of September, and all new students will have to have a birth certificate, small-pox vaccination, and diphtheria immunization."

Ellery stared at her. She wasn't fooling, so he wrote it down. He remembered that Cynthia taught home economics in the high school. My God, maybe she *was* going to cook him a dinner!

Period.

"That all?" he asked.

"That's all." She smiled. "I just thought I'd save you a little work."

"Well, thanks. Thanks a lot."

Ellery took a long pull on his beer. Just when you thought you had these people all figured out they always pulled another rabbit out of the hat.

No matter. Cynthia could be useful. Anyway, he liked rabbits.

"Cynthia," he said, "I wonder if you'd tell me something."

"I'm sure you do," Cynthia said.

Ellery ignored that one. "Look," he said earnestly, "I'm in a tough spot here—you know that. You're about the only person I've met who's acted—well, who's acted—"

"Human?" Cynthia suggested.

"Friendly," Ellery corrected. "I don't feel so much like a freak when you're around."

Cynthia laughed. "What do you want to know, Paul?"

Ellery put it on the line; he had a nagging suspicion that it would be a stupid man indeed who thought he could put over a fast one on Cynthia. "I saw a notice in the paper, last week's paper," he said, "about a compulsory something at the Thorne Ranch the day after tomorrow. I saw you out there, and I wonder—"

"What it's all about," finished Cynthia. She patted her hair.

"Check," said Ellery. "If I'm going to play on your team, I've got to know the signals."

Cynthia pursed her lips. "I don't know, Paul," she said. "I'd like to tell you, but I'm not sure that it's permitted. Tell you what I'll do, though—I'll find out just where you stand on this, and if I can get an okay I'll do better than explain it. I'll take you out there with me, and you can watch."

"Fair enough," Cynthia. "Thanks."

She finished her beer and stood up. "We'll see what we see," she said. "Thanks for the beer. Have to run now."

"So soon?"

"So soon." She walked toward the door, the green skirt rustling around her legs.

Ellery caught her at the door, touched her cool arm with his hand. He could smell the perfume in her hair.

"Cynthia—"

"Good night, Paul," she said, softly but firmly. "See you tomorrow."

And she was gone, into the gathering shadows of night.

10

Next morning, Paul Ellery was up early. It was still cool from the night before, but the sun was already climbing into the sky for the day's bombardment.

However, he did notice, on his way to the newspaper office, that there were just the bare suggestions of gray clouds hanging on the horizon. They might mean nothing, but there was a chance they spelled a break in the heat. August was a hot month in Texas, but usually the rains came in by September. They were long overdue.

The cadaverous Mr. Stubbs had not yet arrived, so Ellery went into his office and hacked out a story on the high school's opening. He finished just as Stubbs came in, and he took it in and placed it on his desk.

A. Jeremiah Stubbs looked at him as he might have looked at a stray goldfish in his drinking water and said nothing. Very carefully, he took off his shapeless black coat and hung it on the hook on his door. He then rolled up his sleeves, freeing his white, skinny arms for action, and donned his green eye shade. His work for the day presumably finished, he lowered himself wearily into his swivel chair behind the editor's desk and resumed his fascinated contemplation of the empty wall.

"If you don't have anything urgent that needs doing," Ellery said, "I'm going out to look for some news."

Mr. Stubbs gazed at him in mild astonishment. He blinked his eyes as though he had difficulty keeping him in focus. "Look for news?" he repeated.

Ellery nodded.

Mr. Stubbs concentrated mightily and one corner of his upper lip twitched. The unaccustomed smile almost fractured his jaw. "Only one real story in this town, sonny," he said, "and that's the one we can't print."

Ellery waited respectfully, but that was all there was. Mr. Stubbs spoke mainly in silences, and it was up to his listener to figure out the drift of his inaudible conversations. Having no real evidence either way, Ellery again chose to interpret the silence as approval, and so he left. In truth, there was very little that needed to be done on *The Jefferson Springs Watchguard,* and Paul Ellery found it hard to take the job too seriously.

There must be something more than this.

And yet, weren't there still the tiresome little jobs filled by colorless people, even in interstellar civilizations? Surely not *everybody* spent his time cruising around in spaceships. If Earth joined the galactic league, wouldn't someone still have to work in the gas station, clerk in the grocery store, take tickets at the movie?

Ellery drove home, without the vaguest intention of looking for any news. He had his own work to do. He noticed hopefully that the gray clouds were massed more thickly on the horizon. It might—just *might*—rain.

At home, he sat down at the kitchen table and sipped his coffee. Everything was happening so fast that it was getting away from him. He didn't like the prospect of getting swept along by the current. He wanted to steer a little.

What did he, as an anthropologist, know that might help him in the life he found himself living?

The cards were all stacked against him in Jefferson Springs, no matter how much the dealer smiled. If he wanted a wild card in his hand, he would have to pull it out of his own sleeve. If he wanted to win, or only to break even—

The first step was finding the right question to ask. After that, he had to be able to recognize the answer when he saw it.

Well, this was clearly a problem in culture contact, and that had a name: acculturation. Unhappily, however, the problem wasn't really an acculturation problem. Of the two cultures—correction, more than two; this thing wasn't limited to the United States—one was unaware of the contact!

And, in a very real sense, they weren't in contact.

Still, *he* was in an acculturation situation. He was a savage, rubbing his nose in civilization. The principles of acculturation must apply to him as well as to all the other primitive peoples who had found themselves in the same boat. Could he make the jump, blowgun to atom bomb? Cave to skyscraper?

What were the choices open to him?

He sweated it out. There had been a great deal of work done on problems of acculturation, but very little of it seemed applicable to the fix he was in. Facts were more insistent than theories: his thoughts constantly returned to Two Bears, his old interpreter. He had done his first field work among the Hawk Indians of Montana, and he had made many friends there. The Hawks were a former Plains tribe, with the customary bison-hunting economy, and they had never taken too kindly to agriculture. The old people still had a security of a sort, living in the past. But the younger men and women were trapped between the old and the new. Two Bears was inclined to be a little contemptuous of the ways of his ancestors, and in any event their culture was practically extinct. At the same time, he was enough of an Indian, culturally speaking, so that he didn't fit into the pattern of American life around him.

Two Bears was a very mixed-up man, trying to fit fragments of opposing lifeways together into a meaningful whole.

He spent a lot of time getting drunk. He spent a lot of time, too, off in the hills by himself—alone with the gods that he could not quite accept.

Paul Ellery understood him a little better now.

He took a fast, cold shower, and shaved too quickly, nicking himself twice. He got dressed, abandoning his work clothes for a pair of brown slacks, white shirt, and tie, and loafers with noisy yellow argyle socks.

At a quarter after six, Cynthia drove up outside.

He lifted two large sacks out of the front seat and carried them into the house, setting them down on the kitchen table. One clinked and one didn't.

"I didn't expect you to have an apron," Cynthia said, "so I brought one of my own." She took a plastic apron out of her purse and tied it around her hips. "Now you get out of here, and I'll start supper."

"Yes, master?" Paul Ellery said. He walked into the living room and sat down, reflecting that of all the mysteries in Jefferson Springs Cynthia certainly wasn't the least. He fired up his pipe and listened to Cynthia's heels clicking around in the kitchen. He timed her. In fifteen minutes flat she was out, a glass in each hand.

"I hope you like Martinis," she said, handing him one.

"I'm enchanted," Ellery said. He examined his glass. "And two olives! You've read my mind."

"No," Cynthia said seriously. "Just guessed."

She sat down next to him on the couch. Ellery could feel his pulse thudding like a schoolboy's, but he let it thud. He couldn't figure Cynthia out, and for now he was content to let it go at that. Of course, it was flattering to think that he was just plain irresistible, but if that were the case then he could think of a large number of females in the past who much have been blind.

Cynthia had on a smooth but simple black dress, nothing fancy, and she had a green ribbon in her soft blond hair. Her dress caught the light and rustled when she moved, and she seemed quite conscious of the effect.

Ellery sipped his Martini, which was extremely dry and extremely potent. "What did you find out about tomorrow night?" he asked. "Am I included out?"

Cynthia patted his knee. "Not at all, Paul," she said. "I talked to John and he fixed it up. You can come."

"You know John?"

"Of course. Have another?"

"Sold."

She went back into the kitchen, bustled around a bit, and came back with two fresh Martinis. This time, his had three olives in it.

"This," Paul Ellery said sincerely, "is the life. I'm converted. Where do I go to enlist?"

"I'm not trying to sell you anything, Paul," Cynthia said, with a directness he found disconcerting. "I'm here on my own. Wait until tomorrow night, then see what you think of us."

"What *happens* out there tomorrow? Black Mass?"

She laughed, the Martini putting a flush in her cheeks. "Not exactly," she said. She had nice white teeth. "It's sort of a—well, sort of a ceremony. Only not exactly that. Not a ritual either, really. And not quite a political meeting. It—draws us together, all of us, on all the worlds. Do you understand that, Paul?"

"Not exactly," Ellery admitted. "But I'll say Rite of Intensification; that sounds good."

"To tell the truth," Cynthia said, downing her Martini, "I think the whole thing is kind of corny."

There it was again. The offbeat note. The wrong chord. If these people would just be human or alien, one or the other, it wouldn't be so bad. But when they were both—

"You won't find it corny, though," Cynthia added. "I promise you that. The first time is apt to be—uncomfortable."

"You hold my hand," Ellery suggested. "I won't be scared."

"We'll see," Cynthia said. "And now we'll eat."

She vanished into the kitchen again. Five minutes later she called him, and there it was. Thick steaks covered with mushrooms. Mashed potatoes with natural gravy. A crisp green salad. A glass of cold water and another Martini.

Ellery pitched in. "By God," he said, "you *can* cook."

"I have my talents," Cynthia said, and met his eyes without wavering.

After supper, with the dishes stacked in the sink and another Martini under his belt, Ellery was feeling amorous.

"And now," Cynthia said, "we cool off a little. Let's take a walk."

"Walk?"

"Walk."

They walked.

They walked under a darkening sky, through a hushed and breathless night. They walked along the street toward town, arm in arm, like any two lovers since time began.

He thought: *just like two average people in an average sort of town. How could you doubt it?*

Cynthia was warm and soft in his arm. They walked down past the icehouse and across the tracks. Ellery could smell the orange trees, their fragrance suspended in the electric air. They turned to the right and walked on into Mexican Town. The pavement ended, and they walked on a dirt road, like a path, but there were more lights now, and laughter floated out of the night.

Someone, somewhere, was strumming a guitar. The sound was happy, and a little lonely too.

They passed several Mexican couples, strolling along, talking in Spanish. The Mexicans nodded, friendly but reserved. They were better dressed than the native Texans of the town; the men with ties and sport clothes, the women with bright, flowing dresses that were designed to please. Ellery liked them, as he had always liked Mexico.

A distant rumble ruffled the still air. The night tensed itself, waiting.

"These people," Ellery said quietly, "Are they—part of it?"

Cynthia laughed, her voice faintly husky. "Yes, Paul. They're part of it too, all of them."

"But—well, are they happy here? I mean, the lot of most Mexicans in Texas leaves something to be desired. I'd think that people of your civilization—"

She squeezed his arm. "You can't understand us yet, can you? Paul, there are all sorts of physical types in the universe. On one planet, one type is running the show, and somewhere else it's a different group. It's purely a matter of historical accident, and if you *know* that, it doesn't matter. These people know that they're just as good as we are, and we know it too, so the tension isn't there. It isn't where you live that counts, it's how other people think of you. We go where we can, and live as we must."

"Thanks for the anthropology lesson."

"You're welcome, love."

There was a deeper lush, sudden and complete. Then the thunder crashed, and there was no doubt about it this time. A small, cool breeze began to whimper along the street.

"We'd better get back," Ellery said.

"Yes. Come on."

They walked back down the dirt road, and back to the paved highway again. They crossed the tracks and hurried past the big square icehouse, squatting like a cement monster in the darkness. They could see the lightning now, flashing down in livid forks out of the massed black clouds that blotted out the stars. The thunder was a continuous rumble in the north.

They walked faster, and the wet breeze became a wind, sighing down the street. The smell of rain clogged the air, rich and sweet and heavy.

Ellery rolled up the windows in Cynthia's Nash, and they half ran up to the little porch of his house.

They just made it.

There was a flash of lightning that charged the air, quick and close and turning the night into pale silver. Then the thunder that crashed down, splitting the skies. A gathering, a hush, a pause—

And then the rain.

Sheets of it, smashing down in big fat drops. Buckets and tubs and rivers of it, gushing into the dry gray street. The street glistened and little brooks gurgled down the gutters.

Ellery caught his breath, his arm holding Cynthia close. The lightning flashed and flickered and the thunder rolled. The storm roared in from the desert wastes, and the wind and the rain washed through the streets of Jefferson Springs.

They went inside and closed the door behind them. The storm pattered and surged on the roof, and the air was released and fresh. Ellery flicked on the light.

Cynthia smiled at him and Ellery could feel the tightness in his stomach, the blood in his veins.

She reached up, slowly, and untied the green ribbon in her hair. She shook her hair gently and it caressed her shoulders. He could smell its subtle perfume.

She came to him and loosened his necktie, her hands cool and sure.

"Well," she whispered softly, "what are you waiting for, Paul?"

11

Next morning, it was still raining—a gentle rain now, that pattered against the window panes and splashed into little puddles off the roof. Thunder muttered furtively, far away and lonely, rumbling around on the horizon, looking for a way back to town.

Cynthia was already up and dressed when Ellery opened his eyes, and he could smell breakfast cooking in the kitchen. He lay quietly for a long minute, sniffing the rich aroma of percolating coffee and the fresh tang of frying bacon, and then he eased himself out of bed and into his bathrobe.

He felt good. He felt better than he had felt in a long time. He told himself that he was certainly satisfied, and probably happy.

Still, he wasn't positive he liked everything he remembered about the night just past.

What do you want, boy, he thought, *egg in your beer?*

When he walked into the kitchen, after more or less combing his hair, Cynthia had her back to him, frying eggs. Her blond hair was tied back again with the green ribbon and she looked cool, beautiful, and collected. He kissed her on the ear and she smiled.

"I think I'll call you Cyn for short," Ellery said. "Spelled with an 's' and an 'i' and an 'n'."

"I'm flattered, Paul. Two eggs or three?"

"Make it three," Ellery said. He found himself feeling playful, but he sensed that Cynthia wasn't having any.

Breakfast it was, then.

"Will the rain hurt things tonight?" he asked, working on his second cup of coffee.

"Not too much, Paul, unless it rains harder than it's raining this morning. It's too important to call off, you know. They'll be electing delegates."

"Delegates?"

"You'll see. You mustn't be impatient, love."

"Okay. All things come to him who waits, so I'm told."

"Well," said Cynthia, "you wait for me this evening and we'll test your proverb."

"You can't stay?"

"Sorry. You know I'd like to. But I've got—things—to do before tonight. Can you wash the dishes and make the bed? I'll be back for you about eight."

"Fair enough," said Ellery.

Cynthia got to her feet and smoothed her dress down over her hips. She picked up her purse and glanced at her watch.

"Cyn?"

"Yes?"

"Is anything wrong? You seem so—well, different."

Cynthia put her purse down. She came to him and put her arms around his neck. She kissed him, hard and expertly. Her body was cool as silk, and Ellery began to tremble. She let him go and smiled, her white teeth very sharp.

"See you at eight, love. Don't forget about me."

Ellery laughed, a little hoarsely, and she was gone. Ellery stood at the door and watched her drive away. The blue Nash turned left at the high school and vanished into the gray mist.

The gray day darkened and became night, and still the drizzle came. There was more rain in the sky, more real rain, but it was holding off.

Waiting.

Ellery found himself afraid again, and stuck the .38 in his pants pocket. He hoped it wouldn't show under the raincoat.

Exactly at eight o'clock, Cynthia came back. He had hoped that she would come in, but she honked the horn for him and he went out. The street was glistening under the car's headlights.

"All set?" she asked.

"All set," he said. He wished that it were true.

The Nash purred off through the drizzle, its windshield wipers ticking and shushing against the tiny, hesitant rain-spray. Cynthia looked inviting as ever, in brown slacks and a gray sweater, with a raincoat tossed over her shoulders; but she seemed distant and preoccupied, so Ellery didn't try to talk.

It was hard to believe that just sixteen hours ago—

Well, the hell with it. Ellery watched the yellow headlights cut wetly through the town, licking at the empty glass windows and the pale gasoline pumps, and then they were on the highway, the tires hissing through the dampness.

Before he was really ready, they were at the Thorne Ranch.

They got out. There were already at least one hundred cars parked around the ranch yard, glistening dully in the drizzle, but otherwise the ranch looked normal enough. There weren't even any lights on inside. The cars in the yard might have been sitting in a parking lot outside a fair or a stock show or a football game.

Cynthia set off with a quick, determined stride, out across a wet field, away from the ranch buildings. Ellery, feeling rather like a faithful dog curious about a missing bone, turned up his coat collar and followed her dark shadow. The soaking rain of the previous night hadn't been a drop in the bucket to the thirsty fields, and the ground was not muddy, although it was a trifle slick.

The thunder rumbled distantly, promising to do better.

They worked their way along toward a bend in the river, and Ellery could sense other figures moving along with them through the night. They topped a slight rise, too small to qualify as a hill, and at first there was nothing.

And then there it was.

It was a large square of pale blue lights, invisible until you were almost on top of them. Pale blue lights, like glowing, bloated bugs hanging in the mist. Beyond them, the poplars and cypress that fringed the river made a black wall. Inside them was the population of Jefferson Springs, Texas.

They were all there, or soon would be. All six thousand of them. Ellery's first reaction was one of surprise—surprise that a whole town could fit in that pale blue square. But then he recalled that it was nothing for fifty or sixty thousand to watch a football game.

There seemed to be a screen of some sort around the square, a wall of invisible force. Cynthia had to take his hand and lead him through. The citizens of Jefferson Springs stood quietly, waiting. A few had brought along canvas chairs. The people were all different in their attitudes. Ellery saw old women, dressed in black funeral dresses, who were rapt and consecrated. He saw wide-eyed children, and children who clearly had their minds on other things. He saw thoughtful men, impatient men, bored men. One portly gentleman with a cigar was loudly issuing orders that nobody listened to.

And there was Mr. Stubbs, looking gloomy. Clearly, Stubbs expected a hurricane at any moment. He was prepared to be blown away.

Ellery started to relax a little. Nothing alarming here. Just like a big meeting, or even a picnic.

The music started.

It was soft, subtle, insidious. Ellery couldn't see where it was coming from. It throbbed and beat softly, almost inaudibly. You had to strain to hear it, and yet you couldn't get away from it. It was inside your head—searching.

Ellery thought of stars.

He heard the voices now. People were talking. They weren't talking English; they were speaking their own language. It had tones and buzzes and clicks.

Ellery shivered. He wished that it hadn't been quite so dark. The pale blue lights tricked the eyes. He wished that it would start to rain. Really rain. He would like to hear rain now.

"I'll have to leave you," Cynthia's voice said. Hers was the only voice speaking in English. "Enjoy yourself, love."

She was gone. He was alone. He had never been so alone. The music began to beat at him. The pale blue lights began to blur. Sweat trickled down under his arms, icily. He was afraid to move.

A hand touched him on the elbow.

Ellery crouched without thinking, his hand clutching for the butt of his .38. He almost drew it out, and then he saw who it was.

A jovial little fat man with shrewd, laughing eyes.

John.

"Still hunting monsters, Paul?" he whispered.

"No. Sorry! Yes. Dammit, am I glad to see *you*!"

"Not so loud, old man. You just try to keep your eyes open, and I'll cue you in when I can on what is going on. Deal?"

"Deal," agreed Ellery gratefully.

A pickup truck came jouncing across the field toward the square of blue lights, feeling its way with only its parking lights on. It came inside and two men unloaded a large metallic box. They placed it carefully on the ground in the middle of the square. It had no connections, dials, knobs, or levers of any kind, as far as Ellery could make out. It was just a box.

All the lights winked out but one blue eye, staring at him. The beat of the music throbbed through his veins.

"News report," John whispered.

The box talked.

It talked for perhaps fifteen minutes. The voice was not unduly loud, but it had a compelling quality to it. Ellery could not understand a word of it, but it did not *sound* terribly different from an ordinary news summary coming over an ordinary radio.

John whispered: "More attention promised for colonials . . . that old bunk . . . some economic difficulties in Capella Sector . . . a scrunch play won the

Sequences; you wouldn't get that . . . a new treaty with the Transformists . . . a suspected sighting of the Others . . . a Two Representative says there is corruption in Arcturus Sector . . . some guff about the traditional planetwide conference coming up in Sol Sector; that's a special tossed on the line to inflate our egos— they'll never hear it outside the system . . . the Evolutionaries agree to a compromise on Spicus Six, just opened up . . . the usual stuff."

Oh sure. The usual stuff.

The box stopped.

A smooth-shaven, portly man moved to the center of the square. Ellery recognized him as Samuel Cartwright, mayor of Jefferson Springs. He began to talk persuasively in the alien tongue—persuasively, but with just a hint of a lisp that Ellery had noticed before, as though Cartwright were having trouble with his false teeth. He talked for ten minutes, pausing now and then to wipe the mist from his face.

When he stopped, there was scattered finger-snapping, which Ellery took to be applause, and several quite Earthly catcalls. A lively wrangle ensued, and some of the citizens appeared to be getting hot under the collar.

Clearly, they were electing some representatives.

"Delegates to the big conference," John whispered, confirming Ellery's guess. "They're going to discuss our colonial policy toward Earth. Want to come?"

"You're kidding," Ellery said.

"Not at all, Paul. I can fix it up. I carry some weight around here, you know. Anyway, it's high time you got an education. I'll notify you."

The election was over, with two men and a woman picked to represent Jefferson Springs. Ellery waited, wondering what was coming next. For a long minute, there was nothing.

The people, however, were very quiet. Ellery could hear the tiny ticks of the rain on his coat. Suddenly, the one blue light winked out. There was total darkness. The beat of the music, almost forgotten, picked up. It grew stronger, much stronger.

And stronger still.

Ellery felt himself swaying on his feet and tried to steady himself.

"Don't fight it, Paul," came John's voice from far away.

He was floating on a gray cloud, a warm gray cloud. He could feel the cloud in his hands. He could pick it up and shred it like cotton.

He drifted, lost and entranced.

He saw colors, smelled smells, tasted tastes. He spun lazily, a moth in the summer night, swallowed in euphoria.

He saw his home with a strange, distorted clarity. He smelled fried chicken in the kitchen. He saw his old books on the shelf in the room he had grown up in: *The Wind in the Willows, Just-So Stories, The Wizard of Oz*. He saw his old model airplanes suspended from the ceiling, their tissuepaper wings shredding where the glue was wearing off. He saw his mother, young again, and his father, snorting at the evening paper.

The scene shifted, noiselessly and completely. He was playing football for the Austin Maroons, racing down the green field under the lights. He heard the crowd, on its feet and yelling. He shook off one tackler, throwing a hip into him, and angled off to his right. The broken strap on his rib pads twisted sweatily. He saw that he wasn't going to make it past the safety man, who wasn't going to be faked out of the way. He set himself to run over him, fighting for the extra yard, and then there was a *smack* as the safety man went down in a heap, blocked out by his end. He cut for the goal stripe. He was going all the way—

Again the scene shifted. He caught his breath. There was a planet, a blue and green and brown planet, hanging like a jewel in black velvet. It was his planet. His vision flickered, and the scene expanded fantastically. His field of sight was enormous, vast beyond imagination, and yet the whole thing was crystal-clear. There were many suns, and many planets. Together, they formed a Titanic design that he could barely grasp. Between the worlds, almost invisible, were spun gossamer silver threads, tying them together. Atoms, atoms of worlds—

Something else. Something down in the corner, down dark in the corner. Something vague, amorphous—

He wanted to scream. Perhaps he did. He whirled, twisted, spun. Dizziness and mist. . . .

It was over. He blinked his eyes and saw that John was holding him up. The blue light snapped back on. The spray of rain cooled his forehead.

"All right?"

"I—think so."

"It's a little strange at first. You didn't get it all, old man. Designed to reinforce, do you see, rather than to dramatize. You've got to supply most of the images, and you won't see what the others see until you go to a Center and get the full treatment. You should have picked up the drift, though: nostalgia for home, the relation of the one to the many, the unity of civilized life—that sort of thing. Quite unimaginative, really."

Ellery listened to John's clipped, matter-of-fact voice and was more than ever grateful to him for being on hand. The rotund little man with the fringe of hair around his pink skull looked like a worldly friar out of Chaucer. He was something solid and real to hang onto. He was a man you could deal with as a man, without worrying about culture or status or formalities. In a word, Ellery thought, John was one hell of a good guy.

An old woman, gray-haired and earnest, stood up in the glow of the blue lights and intoned some syllables, letting them collapse from her thin lips in monotonous cadences. There was considerable shuffling of feet among the audience.

"Poem," said John. "Very bad."

The old woman sat down. The blue lights brightened, almost imperceptibly. The music switched its key. It sounded proud, and a little sad. It swelled up in stirring sweeps, suggesting ancient kings and magnificent temples and acts of bravery long forgotten.

"You'll get more of this," John whispered. "It's the first landing here, the first colonists."

The music pounded, then faded to a low murmur.

The blue lights dimmed, and then began to brighten again, very slowly and steadily.

The people chanted, their voices filling the great night silences.

Ellery saw Earth through alien eyes—wonderful, mysterious, frightening, compelling.

He saw a hidden ship in the night, a globe that floated down in a deserted field, a handful of colonists turned loose near a waiting car. The men and women alone in a strange world, ready to carve a life for themselves out of a primitive planet.

The colonists walked to the car, got inside. They were well trained and they knew what to do, how to move in. They were part of a superlatively well-organized immigration. They knew every step they had to make.

Still, they were afraid.

This was a new world for them, a new home, a chance for their children. They were pioneers in an occupied land.

The car started. They drove toward town, a square of lights far away but clear in the clean, cool air. They were dressed like the natives, they looked like the natives, they talked like the natives. They were ready, and their eyes shone with a hard determination.

They must not fail.

They *would* not fail.

The car purred on down the highway, through a strange and marvelous land. . . .

The music stopped. The chant died. Ellery opened his eyes.

He saw them all around him, the people of Jefferson Springs, ghostly in the pale blue light and the drizzle of the rain. The people of Jefferson Springs, the colonists—proud, confident, superior.

And, somehow, a million million miles away.

Ellery felt sick and tired. He was not a part of them. He was not *one* of them. He was just—

Nothing.

Nobody.

He looked at Cynthia, on the other side of the square. Blond hair, blue eyes, brown slacks, gray sweater, a raincoat tossed over her shoulders. She was lost in pride. She was smiling, as a queen might smile. She was *somebody*. She didn't even look at him. She wouldn't have seen him if she had.

He felt John's firm hand on his arm. There were words. He felt the field, moist and earthy under his feet. A car, and the highway again. His house, dark and empty and alone.

"You'll be all right, Paul."

"I know."

"It takes a little time."

"Sure."

"I'll be back in a few days."

"Thanks, John."

John was gone. He went inside and turned on the lights. He threw himself down on the couch in the living room. He lay very still and listened to the cold sound of thunder rumbling in from the other side of the world.

12

Sleep did not come.

At three in the morning he got up, changed his clothes, packed a bag and left. It was cool in the morning mist, and very dark. He started his car and drove out of Jefferson Springs. By five, he was through San Antonio, circling by way of Loop 13. He stopped to get gas, drank a coke, and drove on down the Austin highway.

He was not quitting. He knew he would go back. But right now he needed a break.

He needed Anne.

He smiled a little. He always ran to Anne when he was in trouble, and Anne was always there. Someday, she wouldn't be. He knew that. No girl would wait forever.

But that was in the other world.

By half-past six, he was in Austin. It was sultry already, and he opened all the windows. He drove past Hill's—how many steaks had he eaten at Hill's?—and past Irving's, and crossed the bridge over the Colorado River. He drove down the broad sweep of Congress Avenue, almost deserted in the early-morning gloom. He stopped at the P-K Grill, which was open all night, and drank three cups of coffee. Then he drove down and parked on the corner, across from the Capitol Dome, and just sat. Anne wouldn't be up yet, and he didn't want to go home.

He watched the city wake up. Austin was his city. He tried to remember that. It wasn't easy.

The sky lightened to a gray glare. He looked back down Congress. Humphrey Bogart at the State, James Stewart at the Paramount, Roy Rogers at the Queen. The bulk of the Austin Hotel dominating the street. Shoe stores, department stores, ten-cent stores, banks, cafes, offices. The Capitol Building, with its big Lone Star Flag. Newspapers stacked on the corners. And—yes, there was Norman, the thinnest and most energetic newspaper seller in the United States, already hawking the morning headlines. How many papers had he bought from Norman, over on the Drag in front of the University?

The cars came first, and then the people. The cars dribbled down the street in the beginning, fed into Congress Avenue by a network of side streets. As the sun climbed higher into the leaden sky, the cars came faster. They squirted into the street, and then flowed like rivers, compressed and controlled by the dams of traffic lights. The horns honked, the brakes screeched, the gears ground. Hot-rods and motorcycles charged up and down the street with a clatter and a bang, and vacant-eyed female drivers consistently managed to turn right from the left lanes. By eight o'clock, the first ambulance had moaned through the street, scattering the cars like toys. Somewhere, energetically, a cop blew a whistle.

The people seeped out of the walls. At first, there had been only a scattered few: a neatly dressed man with a cane, who was undoubtedly never late to his office; a pale woman gazing into store windows; a tired young man in need of a shave who had come hurriedly out of a hotel via the side entrance. Then, as though the few had divided like cells to become many, the sidewalks were jammed. Big ones, little ones, fat ones, thin ones. A blind man sitting hopefully with his box of pencils. A girl and her mother getting new clothes for school. The lights clicked through their memorized routine, and human beings and cars took turns testing the pavement.

The heat hit like a bombardment. It was an unseasonal, humid heat. The hot air was caught between the cement and the gray clouds. Whatever god was responsible for such matters fumbled around for the rain trigger and couldn't find it.

Ellery felt choked, and his hands were shaking. His hair felt sticky. His eyes burned. He felt like hell.

It wasn't all the heat.

He looked at his city and didn't recognize it. The city had changed. It had been comfortable and soft and familiar. It was now distressing, hard, and alien.

It was a reservation for savages.

It *had* changed—if only in his mind. And he had changed, too. He wasn't the same Paul Ellery who had left Austin to spend the summer justifying a research grant. He didn't quite know what to make of Paul Ellery Number Two. He did know one thing: he wasn't very comfortable to live with.

He started the car and drove slowly out past the University of Texas, a collection of vaguely Spanish structures dominated and presided over by a white skyscraper with a Greek temple perched in perpetual surprise on top of it, and on to the greenish apartment house on King Street where Anne lived.

He went up the outside stairs and rang the bell. There was a short pause and the door opened. It wasn't Anne.

"Paulsy!" exclaimed Peg, Anne's eternal roommate. "My dear, you look like the *wrahth of Gawd,* I mean you *really* do."

"Thank you, Dale Carnegie," Ellery said. "Is Anne around?"

"But of *coawse!* Come in for heaven's sakes, I'll *call* her."

"Fine," said Ellery. He walked inside and slumped in the chair by the phonograph.

"Now you be careful of my etchings," Peg said. "They smear *dreadfully.*"

"No more rug-weaving?"

"Oh, heavens no! I gave that up months ago. Paulsy, it's so good to see you."

"It's good to see you, Peg," Ellery said, and he meant it.

Peg disappeared to attempt the Herculean feat of waking Anne up, and Ellery reflected that he had always liked Peg, and didn't quite know why. She was a dizzy blonde, not devastating but well informed, and she had an arty personality that in anyone else he would have detested cordially. But Peg never took herself any more seriously than she deserved, and she was one of those curious and wonderful people who were always just "around" when you particularly needed a friend. You had to take Peg on her own terms, but she wore well.

Ellery took in the well-remembered apartment with real affection, and felt himself beginning to relax a little. There were books all over the place, and they were stacked in untidy piles that indicated they were being read instead of exhibited.

But the place was clean, comfortable, and quiet. It was subtly feminine, with unexpected frills and flowers popping out here and there, but its sex wasn't flaunted. It was an apartment resigned to being a girl, and enjoying it, but still given to playing tomboy now and then.

There was a swish and Anne was in his arms.

"Ell," she whispered. "I've been so lonesome."

"Me too," said Ellery.

He looked at her, holding her at arm's length. Her dark hair was mussed and she didn't have any make-up on. Only her clear gray-green eyes hinted that she could be beautiful when she wanted to. She had on a shapeless blue bathrobe, and from underneath it peeked a sleazy pink silk nightgown. Anne's pet vice was an addiction to secret-agent nightgowns and harem pajamas, and Ellery had never objected yet.

"You look good," he said. "You look wonderful."

"You don't, Ell. I love you, but you look shot. Want some breakfast?"

"I could use some."

Anne went into the kitchen, taking Ellery with her. She brewed up sausages and poached eggs and toast and coffee. Suspecting a hangover, she made a quart of orange juice and made him drink most of it. He did feel better when he finished, and his nervousness turned into weariness.

"Now, you lazy man," she said, kissing him lightly, "You're going to bed. I've got to work this afternoon, and tonight we're going out. I refuse to go out with somnambulists. I'll wake you up when I get home."

She put him to bed, firmly. She kissed him again, picked up clothes from various places, and disappeared into the bathroom to get dressed. Ellery stretched, feeling tired and delighted.

He heard Anne come out of the bathroom after a while, and he heard her phone somebody named Ralph and break her date for that night. He heard the door open and she sneaked in and kissed his nose.

"Good night, or good day or something," she whispered. "Nice to have you back in the house of ill-repute."

"Night, hon," he said. "I think I love you."

"What, again? It must have been something you ate."

And she was gone. Peg had kept discreetly out of the way, and he didn't know whether or not she was still in the apartment. He yawned, hugely.

Jefferson Springs seemed far, far away.

He slept.

Hours later, he awoke when Anne shook his shoulder. "Rise and shine, handsome," she said. "You're taking me out to supper tonight, or didn't you know?"

"I didn't know," Ellery mumbled. "I thought perhaps your magic touch in the kitchen—"

"No thanks, pal. I get tired, you know—it's one of my little idiosyncracies.

If I'm supposed to be charming, gay, and lovable tonight, then you're supposed to dig down in the vault and buy me some eats."

"I'll pay," Ellery said. "Don't beat me any more."

They changed clothes and went out to Irving's, where they disposed of two charcoal-broiled filets. Then they drove out to Lake Austin and stopped at the Flamingo. It was still hot and overcast, with no stars in sight. They bought a fifth of Scotch from the adjoining liquor store before going inside—the quaint Texas liquor laws ruling mixed drinks evil and corrupting unless you bring your own fifth and pour it in yourself.

They got a quiet booth at the Flamingo, held hands, and Ellery settled down to some serious drinking. The Flamingo was pleasant and modern, and its most distinctive attribute was a painting of a sensational nude, which hung over the piano. Confirmed barflies had a legend that after twenty-five beers, no more and no less, you could watch closely and see the nude roll over. Ellery had tried it one time, in his younger days, but had been rewarded with only a slight twitch of the right shoulder.

It seemed that everyone in the Flamingo knew Anne, and stopped to say hello. Anne was a girl with a lovely split personality. About half the time she was the gayest of the party-party crowd, and the other half she holed up in her apartment and read. Ellery was about the only man who had seen both sides of her character, which gave him a certain distinction.

"Anything wrong, Ell?"

"Wrong? Of course not."

"You're the worst liar I know. I must remember that. What is it—work going badly, bored with me again, just ornery?"

"Ornery, I guess. Let's pretend it isn't there, okay?"

"Okay. Laugh and be merry, for tomorrow we will have hangovers."

She was merry, too, at least on the outside. She took Ellery in hand, made him dance, and poured Scotch into him. It was a therapy that had worked before, and tonight it was *almost* successful. Except that Ellery got too high.

He took to monopolizing the jukebox, feeding it with handfuls of quarters. He started out with good swing, showing marked favoritism to records cut prior to the bop mania, and then, with more Scotch, proceeded to sloppy ballads that would have sickened him if he had been sober.

"I love you, Annie," he said along about midnight. "I really love you. You're the finest, sweetest—"

"There, there," Anne said, patting his hand. "You always love me when you're drunk. You love everybody when you're drunk."

Ellery downed another drink, hurrying to get it in before the midnight curfew. "I don't know about that," he said slowly. "I just don't *know* about that." He was feeling very wise and lucid. "It's my theory that drink reveals a man's character. You see, Annie, when I get drunk I *do* love everybody. I love *everybody.* You see?"

"That's wonderful," Anne said.

"You *do* see. You see, if *everybody* loved everybody when everybody was drunk, you see, why then, everybody . . . everybody . . ."

"I see," Anne said, as Ellery trailed off into uncharted vistas of the mind.

Finally, Ellery surged to his feet. "We go!" he announced.

"Goody," said Anne. She carefully picked up her purse and tipped the waitress.

Ellery set himself in motion toward the door. He was confident that he had never walked with more dignity. Anne artfully removed a forgotten paper napkin from his belt to add to the illusion. He paused once before the jukebox and listened with great concentration.

"Terrific," he announced, after due deliberation. And then, at the top of his lungs, he added: "Oh, play that THING!"

Anne steered him to the car and shortly they were home.

Ellery mounted the stairs, singing lustily, and carried Anne over the threshold into her own apartment. He dropped her on the floor, missing the chair with great precision, and then carefully dived at the couch, and made it.

He didn't move. His eyes were open, but decidedly glassy.

Peg came out of the bedroom, rubbing her eyes. "Oh, bro-*ther!* Do I have to put *both* of you to bed?"

Anne picked herself up off the floor, laughing. "Nope. Just lend a hand with Junior here."

"Well," said Peg, "at least I don't get tossed out of my bed tonight."

"Hush," said Anne.

They went to work, trying to arrange two hundred pounds of inert mass. The inert two hundred pounds said, quite distinctly: "I am thoroughly capable of putting my own self in the sack." It said it twelve more times before they got him arranged on the couch and tossed a sheet over him.

"Night, baby," Anne said, and kissed him.

She undressed and went to sleep in the other room. She slept soundly as always. Once, very early in the morning, she thought she woke up and heard someone crying in the living room.

13

The next morning was on the miserable side, and by the time Ellery really began to sit up and take an interest in things, the girls had to go to work.

Ellery sat in the apartment and wondered what to do.

Jefferson Springs sat there with him, smiling.

Last night, he had managed to shut out Jefferson Springs. He had stuffed it down into a back corner in his mind and poured alcohol on top of it. It had worked, too—

Except for the dreams.

"Damn it," he said. "Damn *me*."

He wished, fervently, that he could forget all about Jefferson Springs, and forget everything that had happened there. He wished that he could simply unpack his bag where he was and never go back. He could go on and live a life, some kind of a life, and tell himself that it was none of his business. He didn't have to go on being a scientist; science was not a religion to him. He could just relax and persuade himself that a few facts didn't really matter. He would just say to himself, "I once knew a town less than two hundred miles from my home, a town where people lived who thought of me as a savage. I once knew such a town, but the hell with it."

He liked the idea.

Too bad that it was impossible.

Impossible for *him*. Paul Ellery had been cursed with a mind that asked questions, looked for answers. His mind worked whether he wanted it to or not, and he had never been able to find the button that would turn it off. He had been cursed with a stubborn streak a yard wide, and he had never been broken. He had been cursed with a cynical soul that he wasn't proud of; he had always thought that he should have been better than he was, or at least dumber.

He could no more walk out of Jefferson Springs, licked, than Cortez could have walked out of Mexico, or Columbus could have quit before sighting land. It wasn't heroism, and it wasn't noble. It was selfish pride, and he knew it.

Either he was going to beat Jefferson Springs or Jefferson Springs was going to beat him. If he won, which he knew was impossible, then he had done something for his people and for himself. If *they* won, which was certain, then he would be one of them, and he would have done something for himself.

Neat.

He wished he believed it in his guts instead of in his head.

Okay, bright boy, he told himself. *You came up here to think things out. Start thinking.*

The flash of illumination, the insight that would have made the impossible easy, didn't come. Ellery paced the floor, swearing diligently under his breath. He looked out the window at the hot gray sky and cursed that explicitly. Why didn't it rain?

He picked up the morning paper and stared at it glumly. The same old crud. He read the story over, and a thought waded around below the surface and tried to be born.

He sat down, his head in his hands. He had three hours left before Anne came home. Three hours. Had he made any more progress, really, toward understanding what went on in Jefferson Springs? He told himself that he had not, and then he wasn't so sure.

For one thing, now that he thought about it, that ritual in the blue lights at the Thorne Ranch had told him plenty. It had given him a needed clue into the workings of the colony culture. If that was a prime source after the "full treatment," and if the citizens of the colony spent all or most of the rest of their time in living the lives of small-town Texans, then there was only one possible technique they could be following.

If all human beings in all their variety had to start with an almost identical skeleton—

Well, leave that for the moment.

Take that story in the paper about China. That was interesting, definitely. What *was* the attitude of the United States toward China? That depended. Which

China did he mean—the one on the island or the one in China? Did he mean the official policy of the United States Government? Which administration—past, present, or future? Did he mean the individual states? Which ones? Did he mean the "man in the street?" Which man? What street?

That was interesting. That was another clue.

So—how about the alien culture? What was he up against there, and how could he come to terms with it? What was the attitude of the whole alien civilization toward its colonial policy? John had hinted of friction there, hadn't he? Wasn't that what the big conference was going to be about?

What did they think of savages who climbed up the ladder?

Had John told him the *whole* truth about Jefferson Springs?

Questions. Always questions. Find the right question and you get the right answer. Questions—

How about the aliens, the people? Were *they* all identical robots, thinking alike, speaking alike, looking alike? The little fat man, high above the Earth, reading bad science fiction with a persecution complex? Mel Thorne, running his ranch in the sun? A. Jeremiah Stubbs, sitting on the one story he could never send out to the A. P. wire?

Cynthia?

And how about the *billions* of others, out there beyond his imagination? No conflicts, no disagreements, no factions? Nothing that he could use, nothing that he could turn to his own advantage?

Well, leave *that* for the moment. But don't forget it.

Of course, the whole problem posed by Jefferson Springs was a problem in acculturation, a problem created by the contact of cultures. One culture was extremely advanced, so advanced that he could hardly do better than to catch tantalizing, unsatisfying hints as to its true nature. The other culture was his own.

Or had been.

There was the catch he had thought of before: there was no acculturation problem for the two *cultures* involved, since one of them wasn't even aware that the other existed. But there was acculturation for *him*. He knew.

He thought, again, of Two Bears.

What happened to men caught between two cultures? What happened to a savage when civilization reared its metallic head? Well, he could be killed, of course, either literally or spiritually. He might try his luck with a spear against a tank, or he might watch his people die and smile. He might make himself useful to the civilized men, might even go to school and become one of them. He might run away, if there was any place to go. What else might he do? Was there *anything?*

Maybe. Just maybe.

In spite of himself, Paul Ellery felt a growing excitement. He was a man again. He would go back. This time, he knew what he was looking for.

By the time Anne and Peg came home, Ellery had shaved and taken a shower and put on clean clothes. He even managed to stick a smile on his face that was almost as good as the genuine article.

"Whee!" said Peg, kicking off her shoes and rubbing her ankles. "He's *alive* again! I like you so much better that way, Paulsy. I mean I really do."

Ellery kissed each girl impartially. "I'll make some coffee," he said. "You all sit down and radiate."

"My," said Anne, obeying orders. "What are we supposed to radiate— gamma rays?"

She looked trim and provocative in a white blouse and dark skirt with a red silk handkerchief around her throat. Ellery kissed her again for good measure. "You radiate beauty, of course," he told her. "Maybe a bath would help, but right now you do the best you can."

"Wait until you see that different, mysterious me," she said. "I come on after five, or at least that's what it said in the glamour magazine. Right now I *do* stink a little. You feeling better, hon?"

"Wait and see," he said cryptically and went out to make the coffee.

He proved it to her, taking the rest of the night for a demonstration. They didn't do anything spectacular, but when they were right they didn't have to do anything at all. They had something to eat at Dirty Bill's Drive-In, and then they just drove, outside of Austin, out in the hills.

There was beauty around Austin, an unsuspected beauty that waited patiently for someone to come out and look at it. It was not a sensational, color-postcard kind of beauty. It was a beauty that asked for a pair of seeing eyes.

There was a long, comfortable lake, made by a dam across the Colorado. There were low hills, blanketed in sweet-smelling cedar. There was empty farmland, rolling away into the shadows. They drank it in, and neither talked of it. Then he drove Anne home.

"Paul," said Anne, "will you ever come back for me?"

"I don't know," Ellery said, hating himself. "I hope so. I want to, Anne. Remember that."

"I wish I knew what had happened to you down there. You're different, Ell. It's not just another woman this time."

"No. Maybe I'm growing up."

"Don't grow away from me, Paul. We're not so young any more, and it's lonely sometimes. You need me, too."

"Yes. No one else would put up with me."

"Could I come and see you?"

"No, baby. I don't want you down there. Don't make me explain."

"I'm only human, Paul."

"That's enough. Don't say any more. Don't talk."

It was three o'clock when he took her home.

"Come back to me, Ell. I can help, whatever it is. I've always helped you, haven't I, Paul?"

"Always," he said. "You're my girl."

"You'll come back, Paul? Please say you'll come back."

"I'll try, Annie. That's all I can say."

"Okay, hon. Sorry I love you so much. 'Night."

"Good night, Annie."

He drove away, trying to ignore the knot in his stomach.

He stopped at the University and walked across the gray campus, deserted in the early morning hours. He walked to steady himself, to clear his head.

And he walked to remember.

The cold gray buildings that he knew so well were like a living past. He knew them all, from Waggoner Hall, where he had taken his first course in anthropology, to the Tower that housed the library. He even knew buildings that were no longer there, like old B Hall, now just a plot of grass.

And the old faces came back, laughing and crying and unconcerned.

An icy melancholy crept over him as he walked and his blood was cold in his veins. With an almost numbing shock, Paul Ellery began to understand that his problem was far more than it had appeared to be. All his life he had rejected, questioned, rebelled. Not altogether, of course, and perhaps mainly in his mind. Maybe, even, it went with his kind of mind. Maybe it was necessary, if he was ever to understand. But the fact remained that even this was not wholly his.

He was an outsider not to one culture, but to two.

He shook the feeling off and went back to his car. He got in and drove through the sleeping city, back out the San Antonio highway and on toward Jefferson Springs.

And all through the night he thought. He thought of the Osage, who had discovered oil on their reservation. . . .

14

September hurried by, trailing rain and a crispness in the morning air. The land turned green, hurriedly, and the cactus flowers bloomed. The hot afternoon sun blazed down recklessly, not knowing what month it was, and tried to suck the moisture from the ground. But the rains had come and the rivers flowed, and then, quite suddenly, it was October.

John sent the same two men to escort Ellery to the ship. One of them was still smoking a pipe, and Ellery got the distinct impression that it had not gone out since he had last seen him. They came for him while he was at work.

"We must be quick," the man with the pipe said. "The delegates are already aboard, and we have a lot of territory to cover before the conference."

"On my way," Ellery said, yanking a sheet from his typewriter and handing it to Mr. Stubbs. "Here's the story on the garden club."

A. Jeremiah Stubbs did not look up. He slowly extracted his big gold watch from its nest and examined it with marked distaste. He adjusted his green eye shade and hooked his fingers in his black vest. "Young cub," he said gloomily. "When I was your age—"

Ellery slapped him on the back, startling him to such an extent that he actually tilted his swivel chair a full inch from its usual position. "I'll bet you were a demon!" Ellery assured him. And then to the two men: "Let's go."

Time twisted back on itself and played a remembered scene again. There was the black Buick and the country road, and then there was the ten-foot globe.

He sat on the same green couch on the same gray carpet, and there was the same faint smell of electricity in the air. The globe lifted through the golden sunlight, carrying him very high this time, and then the panel slid open and there was a glare of gentle yellow light.

He was back in the giant spaceship, floating over the Earth.

Back down the long polished corridor, and even as he walked he felt a new vibration in the ship. It was subdued, but it carried a hint of power that was beyond his comprehension. For the first time, he was on the ship while it was in flight. He knew a fleeting moment of terror. He pictured the massive silver tube of the ship standing on her tail and pointing her nose up and out, flashing into the abyss of space, leaving the Earth far behind her, a dot in the infinite, and then nothing, nothing at all—

He pulled himself together. The ship would only be circling the Earth, picking up representatives from the star colonies.

He laughed shortly. That was all. Just alien delegates. How strange it was, he thought, this endless adaptability of the human mind . . .

Back to the heavy door set flush in the end of the corridor, the door that swung open without a sound as he approached it. Back to the familiar room, the padded chairs, the cluttered desk.

And John.

The fat little man beamed. He chuckled, hugely, like Santa Claus. He got out his bottle of Scotch and poured out two glassfuls. *He's glad to see me,* Ellery thought, and he was grateful. *He's really glad to see ME.*

"Ellery, old man!" John exclaimed. "Welcome back to the den of the fat monsters!"

"Howdy, John," Paul Ellery said, taking his drink and sitting down. "Thanks for not forgetting me."

"Nothing, nothing at all," John said, tossing down half a glass of straight Scotch at a swallow. "Ah! The delicate glow of hot machine oil. I've missed you, Paul. You have no idea how deadly dull it is to have to sneak around and be mysterious all the time. Damn it, I hate mysteries! I'm a straightforward man. How do you like being an alien, son?"

Ellery hesitated. "I don't know," he said finally.

"Fine!" said John. "How was Austin?"

"Strange," Ellery said truthfully. "Strange, and rather wonderful. How the devil did you know I was in Austin?"

John shrugged, his bald dome gleaming above its fringe of hair. "Elementary, my dear Paul. Nothing omniscient about it at all. I left you in a state of shock, and the next day it was noticed that your car was missing. I know you pretty well, old man; and it wasn't hard to guess that you'd go home. As a matter of fact, it's easier to keep track of you out of the colony than in it."

"Meaning?"

John pulled out a big black cigar and stuck it in his mouth. "Follow your instincts, Paul. At its somewhat primitive level, your science doesn't much believe in instincts any more, but you follow 'em anyhow."

"You're hinting at something, John-boy. What?"

John ignored the question. "I want you to see the ship before the yak-yak starts. And I want you to meet Withrow. He's been in the same situation you're in, and you two should have a lot in common."

They started to walk, with John leading the way. Ellery could feel the ship sliding to stops and then easing into motion again.

Picking up passengers, around the Earth.

They walked until Ellery's legs ached. John plunged on like a plump, eager puppy, and he never seemed to tire. Ellery once had estimated the length of the ship at five hundred yards, but he decided now that he would have to revise his estimate upward.

Way upward.

What he saw was astonishing enough—astonishing in its vastness and in its cool, comfortable efficiency. But what he could only sense was more astonishing still: a million engineering problems solved and hidden under his feet, problems as yet unformulated in the world he had known. A million answers to questions that might never be asked . . .

There were computers and planetwide survey graphs. There were acres of files on unbelievable subjects. There were libraries and compact weapons that could wipe out a world at a touch of a button. There were hospitals and galactic communications equipment, bewildering in its complexity.

But he saw only the simple stuff, the toys.

And there were men and women, more alert and intense than those he had known in Jefferson Springs, technicians and engineers, and men who had long ago made a science out of anthropology and psychology and sociology, and then had gone on to something else.

When he saw the navigation room, he caught his breath. Three-dimensional mock-ups of galactic sectors, with stars and planets and moons and asteroids moving frigidly in magnetic fields, a universe stuck in a glass cage. And when two of the technicians computed a drive line, a triangular segment of star systems blurred eerily, so that the eye could not follow it, and the three dimensions that Paul Ellery had lived with turned into—something else.

He not only knew, now, that this ship could go a long, long way, he *felt* it.

"Don't forget, Paul," John said, watching his eyes when they were alone together for a brief moment "they're just people. Take a jackass and give him an automobile, and he's still a jackass."

Just people. What was he trying to say? "This conference," Ellery said. "It's about colonial policy, right?"

"Check. Maybe that's too much of an inflated term, though. This is just one planet, son. Peanuts. Strictly peanuts."

"I've been wondering," Ellery said slowly. "I'm not sure I understand your part in all this. What are *your* views about Earth?"

John looked him right in the eye and didn't smile. "Me? Why, I'm absolutely non-political. I have no views. I leave thinking to the smart men."

"Oh," said Paul Ellery. *Damn liar*, he thought.

"And now," John said, "you get to meet Withrow. Come along."

Ellery moved his legs again and wondered when the numbness would go away. "Who's Withrow?"

"Well, he used to be a writer—quite a popular one, as a matter of fact. He got to poking around in a little town in Maine about six years ago, and we made him the same offer that was made to you. He took us up on it, and he's been to the Center, so now he's one of us. You can probably learn a lot from Withrow."

Ellery was intrigued. Maybe here at last was someone who could be closer to him than either of the two cultures, a man who had been in the same boat that he was in. Maybe—

I need a friend, he thought. *I need one in the worst way.*

They found Withrow in a scanning cube, studying. Ellery sized him up. He was a thin, confident man with iron-gray hair, perhaps forty years old. He had cold, flinty eyes. He nodded at John and introduced himself to Ellery.

"Paul," he said, extending a businesslike hand, "I've heard a lot about you. I'm Hamilton Withrow. I hope very much that I can be of some help to you; I know how confusing things can seem at first." He smiled.

"I'm sure we'll get along," Paul Ellery said.

"Mr. Withrow has consented to do us a favor," John said. "Since you can't understand our language as yet, Hamilton has kindly offered to stay with you during the conference and let you know what is going on. I'll be busy elsewhere, being a non-political person."

"That's mighty nice of you," Ellery said.

"Not at all," said Hamilton Withrow.

John left them, presumably to go back to his office.

"Strange man," observed Withrow.

"John? He seems like a pretty good guy."

Withrow shrugged and didn't pursue the subject. "You know, Paul," he said, "I was in exactly your position once. I know the difficulties you're going through. If I may say so, all your doubts will vanish utterly after a short time at the Center. Your old life—and I mean no offense by this—will seem an amusing childhood, and your old friends just fondly remembered children. We must learn to take the long view, Paul, the *long* view."

"I appreciate your advice, Mr. Withrow."

"Please! My name is Hamilton—or even Ham, if you prefer." He laughed.

Ellery laughed, dutifully.

The hours passed, and the great ship swam around the Earth, scooping up her passengers like fish from a shallow sea. In what was really a remarkably short time, Hamilton Withrow led Ellery to the conference room, where things were starting.

It was a long, low room, staggering in its immensity. It was filled to overflowing with the strangest people Ellery had ever seen.

There were Chinese, English, American, French. There were Africans, Danes, Brazilians, Poles, Swedes, Japanese. There were Filipinos, Swiss, Australians, Russians. There were Negroids, Whites, Mongoloids. There were rich men, poor men. Men in business suits and men who were half naked. Women with rings through their noses, women with rings in their lips, women with rings on their fingers.

But the strangeness was more than their diversity. The strangeness was in their *similarity*. They were all self-assured, sophisticated, well-behaved. Even a bit smug, perhaps. They had a tangible sense of belonging, an unconscious air of superiority, an aura of power.

The people were human, all right. If a man could apply strictly objective criteria, they were undoubtedly the most human people on Earth. But they were not human beings as Paul Ellery had known them. They were somehow different, somehow alien. Almost, they were the Cro-Magnons as seen by the Neanderthals.

"Look at them!" Withrow exclaimed, his cold eyes shining. "Aren't they splendid?"

Ellery hesitated. "Splendid" wasn't quite the word that he would have used, but he decided against saying so. "Remarkable, no doubt of that," he said.

There was a great deal of soft conversation, filled with buzzes and clicks, and Ellery couldn't understand a word of it.

"We can't speak to each other in our adopted Earth tongues, you know," Withrow told him. "Each group knows only its own local language. So, when we get together, we have to use the mother tongue."

"Oh," said Ellery, glancing at Withrow. "The mother tongue."

Hamilton Withrow, however, failed to notice the speculative look. He was thoroughly wrapped up in the conference, his thin body proud and alert. Occasionally, he exchanged words with someone he knew, speaking quite fluently in the clicks and buzzes of the alien language. Ellery began to feel uncomfortable.

The conference started.

Ellery was unable to fathom the rules of procedure. Small groups appeared to work together, examining documents and talking softly, and then the various different groups would compare notes. Periodically, and seemingly apart from the group arrangements, someone would address the convention. While he spoke, perhaps five or six of the delegates would pause and listen to him. This, too, seemed to be somehow prearranged.

On one wall, there was a large white square, bordered in some black metallic substance. As the conference wore on, colored lights flickered into life on the square. They arranged themselves into flowing patterns, and altered after each speech. From time to time, a small group would send someone over to check the pattern against a small black gadget that fitted into the hand, and when the checker went back to his group there would be a renewed flurry of activity.

To Ellery, the whole thing took on a hypnotic, lulling quality. Very important and all that, but a little removed. Withrow could not translate a fiftieth of what was said, and Ellery could not understand a fourth of what was translated.

He listened and did his best.

"All automatic, you know," Withrow said. "All the variables are integrated, and then the free-choice element is factored out and manipulated."

"Ummmm," said Ellery. *And don't put the bananas in the refrigerator!*

"He's saying, essentially, that we must be practical about this thing. He says that our colonial policy was not a choice, but a necessity. He says we should give the colonials a greater voice in galactic administration. He suggests that Earth will soon blow itself back a thousand years, and then we can safely bring in more colonists. He says we must think of our children, and of our children's children."

"I see," said Ellery.

"This one's a bit wild. He says that our whole solution to the problem of overpopulation is nothing more than sticking our head in the sand. He says he isn't any aborigine-lover, but just the same he thinks we're headed for trouble. He says we should resurvey the whole galactic colonial system. I wonder where he thinks *he* would go if we left all the planets for the savages! You can see how muddy his thinking is, Paul."

"Sure," said Ellery.

"The next speaker—see him, the one with the abominable haircut—is saying—well, he is saying—you see, it's about the relation of the Prime Force to the Quadrant—I mean—well, I'm afraid it's a bit over your head."

"Don't worry about it," Ellery said.

He listened, and the meeting seemed to go on endlessly. There was a great deal of bickering about local problems: the position of the colony in the galactic economy, the possible importation of luxury items into backward areas, the problem of fraternization with the local savages. Ellery just couldn't take it all in. He had to keep telling himself, over and over: *This is Earth they are talking about, this is—was—my home they are discussing, my people—*

The voice droned on in his ear: "This one is advocating more interference to maintain the status quo . . . this one wishes to send missionaries among the savages; that's a good one . . . this one thinks we should send all colony-born children back to the Center *before* the high-school ages . . . this one . . . this one . . . this one . . . "

After an eternity, it was over.

The pattern of lights on the board flowed, steadied, and stopped. The result was announced.

"Same old thing." Withrow yawned. "The galactic colonial policy is approved, and more attention is requested for local problems. Doesn't mean a thing, but it keeps the colonists happy."

Ellery looked at Withrow. Unbidden, an image came into his mind. An image from many years ago, from high school. A boy who had come out for football during the last month of the season, when it was too late for him even to get in shape, and had thenceforth referred to himself as "one of the team."

"You can probably learn a lot from Withrow," John had said.

John was subtler than he looked.

"I appreciate your help, Hamilton," Ellery said.

He was exhausted, mentally and physically. He let Withrow lead him out of the conference room, and back to John's office. He was glad when Withrow left him alone; he simply didn't feel up to talking to the man.

John wasn't in. Ellery thought dimly that this might be a good time to pick up some secret information from John's desk, but he rejected the idea. He already had more information than he could possibly handle; he was flooded with a deluge of information. His problem, he knew, was never going to be solved by any remarkable item filched from a desk.

There were no magic formulae.

Ellery compromised by walking over to a wall couch, stretching out, and going to sleep in seconds. It was the only retreat he had left, and it was good to get away for a while.

John woke him up, hours later, and brought him a cup of hot coffee, which he drank thankfully. He was stiff and sore, and he felt thoroughly insignificant.

"Jefferson Springs," John said quietly. "Time to go home."

"Thanks, John. What do I owe you for the room?"

"Not much, my boy. Shall we settle for your grandmother's arm and the mortgage on the family homestead?"

"It's a deal."

John himself escorted him down the long corridor, walking with deceptive speed. "You know, Paul," the little fat man said, "you're just beginning to get an insight into the size of this mess. That whole conference you witnessed was classed as a strictly rural affair. Maybe it'll get one line in the Galactic Administration Report, and nobody'll even read it. It's a bit shocking at times—did you know that more than ninety-nine percent of the civilized people of this galaxy do not know that the planet Earth exists? It's strictly specialized information."

Ellery started. *Ninety-nine percent did not know—*

Well, how could they?

"Quite stupid," John said, shaking his head. "The conference didn't even have the guts to *mention* the real problem."

Ellery raised his eyebrows.

"There are the Others, you know. I believe you caught a glimpse of them at the little gathering on the Thorne Ranch?"

Ellery remembered. *The galaxy, with gossamer silver threads. Atoms of worlds. And something else. Something down in the corner, down dark in the corner.*

Had he screamed?

They came to the panel that led to the metallic sphere which Ellery was beginning to think of as an elevator.

"You'll be sent to a Center soon, Paul," John said. "Don't sleep too long."

Ellery stared at the fat man, waiting, but John said nothing more. The panel slid open and Ellery walked into the globe. He sat down on the same green couch, but this time it was more crowded. The two ship escorts were there, one of them still with his pipe in his mouth, and in addition there were the three conference delegates from Jefferson Springs, two men and a woman. The men wore boots and big hats, and the woman wore a black dress and a shawl. They sat next to him and made small talk, but the atmosphere was strained.

The great floating globe touched down, and they stepped out into a plowed field. It was night, and the blackness was frosted with stars. There was a cold moon, coating the Earth with silver. Ellery wasn't sure what night it was.

They got into the black Buick, and the car jolted over the dirt road, and then purred down the highway toward Jefferson Springs. Ellery sat in the back seat, crowded in with the three colonists. He didn't look at them and he avoided their eyes.

Too big, too big, he thought. *Too big to fight.*

He felt himself growing tense as the little town came closer. He sensed the vast bulk of the spaceship, lost in the stars over his head. He felt very small.

He couldn't beat them. Being what he was, he couldn't ignore them. After seeing Withrow, he wasn't even sure he could join them, and stay sane.

He thought about Anne, and wondered what she was doing.

He tried to think about Indians who had found oil on reservations.

He was very tired, and the big black Buick rushed on, into the shadows and the night and the pale splashes from an empty moon.

15

Autumn flowed softly by, easing its way toward winter. The land lost its brief flush of green and stood nakedly before the wind, but there would be no real freeze until January.

Paul Ellery kept digging, looking for the chink in the armor of Jefferson Springs. He knew that he was not learning fast enough, and he knew that it would not be long until they shipped him off to the Center for the "full treatment."

After that, he wouldn't care.

He saw Cynthia, occasionally, using her to fight the empty loneliness he felt in the town that was not his own.

Once, out walking on a country road, he spotted a piece of worked flint half buried in the dry, hard-packed earth. He picked it up and looked at it. It was a crudely made, pointed artifact about five inches long, bearing the characteristic flake scars of human workmanship. It was too long for an arrow point; it might have been a spear point, a dart point, or a stone knife. Probably not Comanche or Apache. Ellery wasn't certain, not being an archaeologist, but the flint had probably been used by one of the nameless hunting-and-gathering Indian groups that had been common throughout Texas before the beginnings of the written historical records.

Another way of life—vanished in the dust.

He stood in the chill wind and shivered.

The humble, long-overlooked bit of flint called forth a host of memories. He remembered the kick he had got out of his first anthropology courses. He remembered the long, all-night discussions, and the books that had seemed to open up wonderful, uncharted vistas of the mind—the excitement of Malinowski, the sweep and daring of White, the vision of Linton dedicating a work of social science to the next generation. He remembered his young confidence, his certainty that he had a key that would unlock doors that others could not see. And he remembered the subsequent plodding of graduate school, the hot digs, the quizzes on bone fragments, the wrestling with German. Fun, all of it; but what had happened to the excitement and the hope and the promise for the future?

When had it turned into uncertainty and caution and even fear? When had the kick in his work gone out the window?

Was it the apathy of his students? Was it the preoccupation with trivia of many of the scientists? Was it the discovery that social science had many questions but few answers?

Was it the flowering hell of the hydrogen bomb that reduced what he was trying to do to hopeless insignificance?

Was it a climate of cultural hysteria in which a scientist could not work?

Or had he failed himself, somewhere along the line?

He stood for a long time, the old artifact in his hand, and then walked back to town under the thin, pale sun.

He kept trying. And one day he found something.

It was late in the afternoon of a warm day. He stepped into the American Club for a beer. There was a little bell on the screen door, and it jingled as he walked through. The front room was furnished with four faded green pool tables and a few crooked wire stools. There were calendars on the walls, showing bathing beauties in love with Coca-Cola, cowboys in love with horses, and business executives in love with trout. There was a stained bar along one wall, made of plywood. There was no one in the room.

There were voices coming from the back room, behind a thin wood partition. Voices, and the click of dominoes.

He moved quietly over to the wall and stood with his ear pressed against it. He kept his eyes open. He could hear the voices clearly:

"I don't care what you say, dammit, the Administration is gonna throw us to the wolves."

Administration? That would be the galactic government.

"What're we supposed to do—just sit on our tails and let 'em take our homes away from us? You listen here to what I'm tellin' you boys—"

"Me, I say we oughta do more—a hell of a lot more! So maybe the Preventers are illegal—so what? They're workin' for *us,* and they're the only ones who give a good goddam about us."

Preventers? He had come across references to them before—an organization that believed in preventing a colonized planet from ever reaching civilized status, as opposed to the Evolutionaries who felt that colonized planets must be left alone to progress as best they could, without interference.

"Ahh, you take yourself too blamed serious. They'll blow their ratholes sky high without any help from us. Let the Preventers stick their necks out if they're a mind to. Me, I ain't forgettin' that ship up yonder, and don't *you* forget it neither. You remember what happened to that colony down south, don't yuh? Polio, they said—"

"They're a pack of damn Evolutionists in One Sector, if you want *my* opinion. I ask you, what do them jokers know about *practical* problems?"

"Take it easy, there, you're not yellin' into a tornado."

"Ahh, what're yuh scared of—the F.B.I.?"

Laughter.

"Yeah, the hell with it. Bill, what say to a couple more beers?"

The sound of a chair scraping the floor. Footsteps.

Ellery hurried across the room and out through the screen door. He had forgotten the little bell, and it tinkled as the door swung. He walked down the sidewalk, then crossed the street and entered a narrow alley. He stopped by a garbage can and listened.

Nothing.

He kept moving, back on Main Street, down the block to his car. He got in, backed into the street, and drove past the club. There was no excitement there. No one was in the front room. Either he hadn't been seen or else they didn't care.

He went home to get dressed for a date with Cynthia. While he dressed, he thought over what he had heard.

The pieces were beginning to fall into place a little.

If only he had more time . . .

Evidently, the aliens had not been able to eliminate an old, old problem in the field of government. There was a marked conflict between basic administrative policy, set by the Galactic Administration, and the colonies actually living in the field. The basic policy was fair and even altruistic. The great spaceship was there to see that the hands-off policy was followed to the letter. Unfortunately, the ship couldn't be everywhere at once, and some colonists didn't think too highly of basic policy. They were human enough to think of themselves first and ethical questions later, if at all. If the Preventers could only prod the native planets into atomic wars that would blast the city reservations, then the colonies were safe from eventual interference.

Probably, the Administration could handle the Preventers. Ellery was sure that John and the rest knew all about them, and were quite competent to deal with the problem. For Ellery, the important fact was simply that the colonists were divided in their sentiments.

That could be helpful.

Cynthia picked him up at eight. He climbed into her blue Nash and gave her a kiss.

"Hi love," she said. "In a dancing mood?"

"More or less. But I'm getting old for that sort of thing."

"You're not old, Paul."

"I feel old," he said, and meant it.

"We'll see if we can't rejuvenate you."

"You're the doctor."

They pulled up in front of the Community Hall, which was a drab, barnlike structure rearing up out of a lot of bare ground and a few earnestly struggling blades of grass. Her arm in Ellery's, Cynthia swished up the cement walk, cool and aloof in an off-the-shoulder dress of green taffeta. Ellery didn't mind dancing, and the Community Hall struck him as genuinely quaint, but walking into a building full of colonists still made him nervous. It was not fear so much as it was awkwardness and a sense of uncertainty, much as he had felt as a child when he had been cajoled into performing in a grammar-school play before an audience of adults. He had, he recalled all too vividly, dropped his spear and tripped on his toga.

He hoped that the inevitable punch was spiked, but he knew that it wouldn't be.

They made their entrance. Cynthia took the frankly admiring glances of the men in stride, accepting them as her due, and she returned the critical looks from the older females with icy disdain. She held Ellery's arm tightly, possessively.

It seemed to take forever, but eventually the buzz of conversation picked up again and filled up the sudden hush.

The inside of the Community Hall easily fulfilled the promise of its unglittering exterior. Primarily, it was empty space. Along the sides were folding chairs, and upon the chairs were seated the old women of Jefferson Springs. There were two doors at the back of the Community Hall which led to a kitchen. Music was provided by a portable phonograph plugged into a light socket. The phonograph was manned mainly by the high-school crowd, who watched Cynthia with frank speculation. Ellery wondered what she taught the kiddies in home economics.

The records in the Community Hall were somewhat dated, which suited Ellery fine. There was a lot of Glenn Miller, a sprinkling of Harry James, and a minimum of trick novelty records produced for the moron market.

The music played: *On a Little Street in Singapore. At Last. Serenade in Blue.*

Ellery danced, or at least shuffled his feet around. Cynthia politely turned down men who tried to cut in on them, and she felt light and pleasant in his arms. Ellery tried to forget where he was and just enjoy himself. All things considered, he did rather well.

The Community Hall simply wasn't very alien. And the girl in his arms was a beautiful young woman.

Along about eleven o'clock, after too much sweet and fruity punch, one of the boys decided to liven things up a bit. He seemed to be a standard Jefferson Springs product, with huge, rawboned hands dangling out of a too-tight and unfamiliar blue suit, but he had a taste for an upbeat tempo in his music. He diligently plowed through the Community Hall record stacks and turned up a dozen instrumentals. He risked the wrath of the football coach—who wasn't visible at the moment—by lighting a cigarette with airy unconcern. Then he proceeded to play the records, one by one.

He started off with *In the Mood,* and the dance floor cleared as if by magic, Paul started to join the exodus, but Cynthia pulled him back.

"Come on, love," she urged, her face flushed. "Show your stuff."

Ellery did his best, reluctantly at first, but warming to his task as he danced. He had never been the best fast dancer in the world, jitterbugging being an art that he had mastered solely to save himself embarrassment, and it had been a long time since he had really had to work up a sweat on the dance floor.

Watching the few remaining dancers out of the corner of his eye, however, he began to feel better about the whole thing. Unsensational though he was, he was better than *they* were. They were going through the motions easily enough, but they weren't letting themselves go. They seemed slightly uneasy, like a group of wrestlers dancing the minuet.

So, he thought, *there's one thing I know more about than they do!*

The music went from *No-Name Jive,* with its hackneyed but effective tenor sax solo, to Harry James's old *Two O'Clock Jump.*

Paul Ellery and Cynthia were alone on the dance floor.

Ellery began to show off. He twirled Cynthia around like a top, and she loved the chance to show off her legs. Ellery really got with it, closing his eyes in pseudo-ecstasy, and contorting himself. Cynthia kept up with him, but by God he was the star of *this* show!

He strutted half the length of the floor, and then the record stopped.

He laughed, his heart thumping merrily.

Then he heard the applause. It came at him from all sides, waves of it. Jefferson Springs was impressed.

Even Cynthia was clapping.

Paul Ellery stopped laughing.

The applause ended, and there was a sudden silence. Conversations started up, a little too quickly, and someone went over to the phonograph and put on a slow record.

Ellery stood very still.

"Oh, Paul!" exclaimed Cynthia, breathing hard. "You were positively *unique!*"

"Shut up," said Ellery.

"Why what's wrong, Paul?" She was smiling.

"*Shut up.*" His voice was louder than he had intended.

Some of the old ladies were looking at him.

He heard a whisper: "Savage!"

Blindly, Paul Ellery pushed his way outside, out of the building, into the cool night air. He stood alone, leaning against the wall. His sweat chilled and he clenched his fists.

Fool! I did it, right there in the middle of them. I did it, and I was proud of myself!

An exhibition. An exhibition of primitive dancing.

She made me do it. Damn her soul, she knew what she was doing. She tricked me, showed me off like a smart animal.

Paul Ellery saw red.

He looked around him in the starlight and found two rocks, one for each hand. He gripped them tightly.

He started for the door, where Cynthia stood framed in the yellow light.

He moved through a red haze, step by step.

And then he stopped. The whisper stuck, stinging his ears: *"Savage!"*

He dropped the rocks, listening to them thud when they hit the ground. He stood still, trying to control himself. He stood there for a long time, until he was sure that he was calm.

He was going to show them something about savages.

He didn't have his pipe, so he settled for a cigarette. He lit it with a steady hand, and blew a smoke ring up into the still air. He breathed deeply.

Then, quite casually, he strolled back into the Community Hall. There were three men watching him closely, but he didn't even look at them. He went straight to Cynthia and took her hand. She tensed, first in fear and then in surprise.

Paul Ellery smiled pleasantly. "Come on, dear," he said softly. "Let's go home."

Her blue eyes widened. "So—soon?"

His smile widened. "Not afraid of *me,* are you, Cyn?"

She hesitated. "Of course not."

"Then let's go."

"All right," she said. "All right, Paul."

They went home, to the little house across from the high school. It was a long night, and Ellery never touched her.

By morning, there was a certain respect in Cynthia's eyes.

16

Paul Ellery kept digging.

His job on *The Jefferson Springs Watchguard* didn't take up much of his time. He checked in almost every morning, typed up a story or two, and left. Mr. Stubbs handled the advertising, which was the biggest job on the paper, and how he did it was a mystery to Ellery. He never saw Stubbs move from his precisely tilted chair, and the old gentleman's eyes remained fixed on the blank wall, as though searching for impudent termites.

As a matter of fact, he supposed that Stubbs had his paper down to such a routine that it was virtually automatic. All of the accounts were handled by mail, and whenever anyone had a bit of news he always brought it in to Stubbs, like a faithful dog with a dead duck.

For a long time, Ellery had been puzzled by the absence of lights at night in Jefferson Springs. The town was never completely dark, except after midnight when everyone was asleep, but on the other hand it was never illuminated properly, either. The houses, particularly, were darker than they should have been. By eight or nine o'clock, there were seldom more than a dozen lights to be seen away from Main Street, and frequently there were none at all. In a town of six thousand, that didn't make sense.

The problem did not turn out to be unduly difficult to solve, once Ellery decided to investigate it. It was surprising, really, he thought, how many questions could be answered if only someone would go out and look. His method was simple, if unheroic. He became a Peeping Tom. He felt like an idiot, but he got his answer.

He spent two nights prowling through the dark streets of Jefferson Springs. He walked by houses first, to find out whether or not there was a dog around, and if he didn't draw any canine howls of fury he went back. The streets were poorly lighted, and except for passing cars, there wasn't enough light to pick him out. He just walked through the yard to the side of the house and looked through the windows. Or tried to.

All the windows had blinds over them, covering what was inside. The blinds were old-fashioned roller types, however, and he could usually find enough of a gap at the sides to look through. He saw very little at first, because the houses were dark, but he stuck with it, and eventually began to spot things.

A glimpse here, a hurried look there. The back of a head, a table, a shadowy figure.

And the blue lights.

Many of the houses were empty, but whenever he found one with people in it he found the blue lights with them. They were simple blue bulbs, as far as he could see, which were screwed into ordinary sockets. They gave off a pale blue light, identical with the blue light he had seen before, that night at the Thorne Ranch.

Around the blue lights were seated the people of Jefferson Springs, ten or more to each occupied house. They sat very still, in chairs or on the floor, and they never spoke. Their eyes were open—he could see them glinting dully in the eerie light—but they were fixed and unseeing.

Ellery listened closely, but he could not hear a sound. If there were any transmitters in operation, they were very quiet.

He never saw one of the meetings start, because they began early and he was afraid to risk sneaking around while it was still light. He did see two of them break up. At an invisible signal—evidently a time lapse of some sort, since it hit them all at the same moment—the people came out of their trances. The host turned off the blue lights and replaced them with plain white light bulbs. There was coffee and casual talk, and then the visitors went back to their own homes.

Ellery stayed hidden. As long as he was careful (and didn't leave town) no one would spot him. The colonists were not omnipotent.

He had enough data now to make some sense out of what he saw. Clearly, the colonists took turns acting as hosts for small groups of people; one night at one house, the next night at another. The blue lights had been used at the community ritual at the Thorne Ranch, and evidently these smaller gatherings served much the same purpose. They were ceremonies, ceremonies with a distinct religious flavor.

How did they work? There was no talk, and no apparatus that Ellery could see. The people just sat down, the blue lights went on, and the people entered into a state of trance. What happened then? Well, the colonists must have been conditioned in such a manner that they could go into a kind of direct voluntary hypnosis by looking into the pale blue lights. Something more than hypnosis, probably, but certainly related to it. What did it accomplish? Ellery was certain that it served to open their minds to some form of suggestion that had been previously implanted in them. Sitting there in the blue lights, they looked at nothing. And they saw—

Who could say? Scenes and events and commands that tied them to the larger whole of which they were a part, experiences that Paul Ellery could only guess at. Experiences he could never know, until he went to the Center.

That was what Centers were for.

The citizens of Jefferson Springs. Watching scenes undreamed of on Earth.

Back in *his* house. Ellery sat alone at the kitchen table and wondered about Cynthia. She, for one, passed up a lot of rituals. Perhaps she wasn't a good citizen. But she had gone to one ceremony, and she had done her bit.

Ellery was making progress. He knew that, and felt a certain satisfaction in it. But he knew, too, that he wasn't making progress fast enough. Still—

He had the key to the alien culture now. His notebook was paying off. His notebook and the long, lonely hours. He had the key.

What made it possible for members of a galactic civilization to live in a primitive culture? How could they possibly spend their lives going through the motions of what was, to them, an alien life? How did the galactic colonial system *work*?

It wasn't a masquerade. That was the first thing to remember. These people, up to a certain point, believed in the lives they were living. These were their lives, and this was their culture. It had to be.

But it wasn't their *only* culture. That was the catch.

What the galactic administration had done was to indoctrinate its colonists with a hard core of civilized premises and beliefs. That was the skeleton, the same for every citizen, no matter where he might live. On top of that core of culture, the administration had grafted the customs and habits of the area to which the colonist was to be sent. That was the face and flesh and fingerprints, different for every citizen as it was for every human being.

It took some doing, of course. There was plenty of opposition. The whole scheme would have been utterly impossible in an uncivilized society. That, however, was just the point: these people were civilized.

They had learned, long ago, that it was the cultural core that counted—the deep and underlying spirit and belief and knowledge, the tone and essence of living. Once you had that, the rest was window dressing. Not only that, but the rest, the cultural superstructure, *was relatively equal in all societies.*

Human beings, by virtue of being human beings, had certain structural "musts" that had to find outlets. They had to eat and sleep and mate. All societies provided for such needs. And if you were conditioned to live in one specific society, you did it in the way the society specified, and you liked it—because that was your way, too. Beyond those basic needs, all cultures provided systems of handling the products of group living. Families? They could be monogamous or polygamous, matrilineal or patrilineal. You liked the one you were brought up in. Economy? It might be hunting or fishing or raising crops or buying food in a can. You liked what you were used to. The arts? They might include beating on a log drum, dancing in masks, or reading books. You were pleased by what you had been trained to like.

The colonists had the core. Beyond that, they could be taught to live with any cultural trapping—*and they could be happy in any society in which human beings could be happy.*

The core of civilized culture was reinforced and kept alive by community rituals that maintained contact with the mother culture. The techniques varied from society to society, but the purpose was always the same, and it worked, within human limits. It worked because the galactic administration knew what it was doing. It worked because the civilization involved had learned enough to pull it off.

It worked, too, because the really intelligent and successful citizens attained responsible positions in their native cultures. In a word, they stayed home, or worked in the Galactic Fleet. The ones who were farmed out to the colonies as population overflow were the weak and the dull and the uncaring—and the misfits. That wasn't the way it was planned, but that was the way it worked.

Adults were conditioned in the Centers before they were permitted to move into colonies. Children who were born in the colonies were indoctrinated by the colonies at the same time that they received instruction in the culture in which they found themselves and then before maturity they were sent "home" for intensive training and conditioning for a period of three Earth-years.

Paul Ellery had the key to the alien culture. He understood it as well as any outsider could ever hope to understand it.

But what could he do with his key?

How could he *use* it?

He didn't know.

And so he went on, doing the best he could, while time ran out on him. He was convinced now that he wasn't going to *find* any secret weapon that would turn defeat into victory. He didn't give up, but he did reaffirm his earlier decision.

He did it, oddly enough, at a football game. It was the last one of the season, and it was played on Thanksgiving. Jefferson Springs was playing Eagle Pass. The game was played at night, as always, under the lights. This was because the merchants were all busy on Saturday or holiday afternoons, when the ranchers came to town; and the games drew bigger crowds at night.

Ellery went with Cynthia, who looked fresh and young and almost innocent in skirt and sweater and loafers. He had a good seat and he enjoyed the game. Texas high-school football was rough, tough, and fast. It was played for blood. The fields were apt to be pitted and rock-strewn, the bands were customarily out of tune, and the pep squads were more strident than effective. But the games were good and hard and well played.

Cynthia watched with complete detachment, although she uttered the correct noises at the proper times. Ellery, who had been under the lights himself a long time ago, was quieter than he should have been, because he was rooting for the wrong team. He was pulling, desperately, for Eagle Pass.

They had two brothers, Dave and Tom Toney, at quarterback and halfback. They were good, giving all they had and then some, and Ellery cheered them silently.

Come on, Dave, he thought, *come on Tom. Sock it to 'em!*

Dave and Tom socked it.

Ellery felt a thrill of pride. The Jefferson Springs boys played earnestly, but they lacked the sparkle. They felt a bit superior, and that was deadly. Eagle Pass surprised them, with a bruising line and a tricky backfield.

Come on Dave, come on Tom!

The lights on the towers soaked the field and hid the stars. The creaky wooden grandstands swayed whenever the fans stood up and hollered. The referee blew his whistle, and the yardage chain moved up and down the sidelines, following the ball.

Ellery kept his fingers crossed. He was still an outsider. He didn't belong to Jefferson Springs. He didn't even belong to Eagle Pass, but he felt closer to them. They, at least, had been his kind.

Ellery watched the field and wrestled with his thoughts. He decided, again, what he had to do.

Sock it to 'em!

He could not go on living a life without meaning. He could not go back to Anne and live a life in a zoo. He could not bring children into a world in which they would live on a reservation, devoting their lives to finding out things already a million years forgotten by others, facing a frightful future in which cities disappeared in a searing flash.

There was no secret weapon that he could find. The galactic set-up was simply too prodigious to be overthrown by one man, and particularly not by an ignorant savage.

He would keep trying, yes, because he had to. But if he could not come up with a real solution to his problem by the time the aliens decided to send him to the Center, there was just one thing to do. He would go to the Center and make no fuss about it.

After that, he wouldn't be Paul Ellery any more.

Come on Dave, come on Tom!

Now that it was lost to him, his world looked pretty good. He thought of it, with all its laughter and sadness and beauty and squalor, and he wanted it. He wanted it very much.

But not a world without purpose or meaning. Life was too tough if it was all for nothing.

Maybe he wouldn't have to be another Hamilton Withrow—Withrow, probably, hadn't been any prize specimen even before the "full treatment." Maybe he could even be another John. He liked John. It would be better than the life he was living now—tolerated, but not a part of things. Any culture was better than none, if you believed in it. And he *would* believe in it, after the Center. No doubt about that.

Attaboy, Dave! Attaway, Tom!

Eagle Pass won, and whooped jubilantly off the field. It was Thanksgiving, and in his own way Ellery gave thanks. He was proud of his boys.

Dammit, there must be *some* way! If only he had more time . . .

Someone tapped him on the shoulder as he stood up. He turned around. It was Samuel Cartwright, portly and with his pink face gleaming with shaving lotion. The mayor of Jefferson Springs.

" 'Lo, Cynthia," he said, with just the trace of a lisp in his speech. "Good to see you, Paul. How are you getting along?"

"Fine," lied Paul Ellery. "I'm getting along fine."

"Mighty good," said Mayor Cartwright. "I'm happy to hear that. By the way, Paul—"

"Yes?"

"I wonder if you'd drop around to my office tomorrow—you know where it is, over in the Court House. I'd like to talk to you a bit."

"What about?"

"Oh, a few plans for your future, and things like that. It's important that you be there, Paul. You know."

"I know," said Paul Ellery, his heart sinking. "I'll be there."

"Fine," said Mayor Cartwright. "I'm sure our talk will be satisfactory."

Cynthia smiled.

17

The Jefferson Springs Court House stood alone, its brick arms outstretched to try to cover a city block. It was a relatively modern-looking structure, and it had an air of distinct surprise about it, as though it still had not recovered from the shock of finding itself in Jefferson Springs. It stood on a side street, just across from the water tower. It was surrounded by elderly gentlemen engaged in an endless contest to determine the best and most consistent expectorator in Jefferson Springs.

Mayor Cartwright perched in haughty aloofness in an office on the second floor. To prove with crushing conclusiveness that he was a politician not to be ignored, he had both a water cooler and an open box of cigars in his office.

Paul Ellery waited until almost ten to give the great man plenty of time to settle himself in his sanctum, and then knocked on his door.

"Come in, come in!" urged the Mayor, in his best never-too-busy-for-my-constituents voice.

Ellery went in.

Samuel Cartwright shook his hand and offered him a cigar. Ellery took it, out of politeness, although he was not overly fond of cigars.

"Close the door, Paul. That's the spirit. Now sit down, take a load off your feet. There. Nice day, mighty nice."

"Powerful nice," Ellery said.

"Yes, sir. Go on Paul—light up that old cigar! I like to see a man comfortable. No airs in *my* office, son. I'm a plain man."

Everybody calls me "son," thought Ellery. *What kind of biology do they have where they come from?*

Mayor Cartwright flicked on a lighter that actually worked, no doubt a product of alien super-science, and set Ellery's cigar on fire.

"Thank you," said Ellery, and blew out a big cloud of smoke to prove that he was enjoying the cigar.

"You're mighty welcome, Paul. Now we can get down to business. I reckon you know why you're here, Paul."

"More or less. I hope I haven't done anything wrong?"

"Not at all, son, not at all. Your conduct, if I may say so, has been exemplary."

True blue, that's me. "Nice of you to say so, Mayor."

"I know it hasn't been easy for you, Paul," the Mayor said slowly, speaking carefully to avoid his lisp. "You've been with us now for almost six months, and you've been in a difficult position. It isn't easy for a man to throw away his old life and start in on a new one. All of us know that, Paul. We've been through it ourselves."

"I guess you have, at that."

"We surely have. We've been watching you, and you've handled yourself very well. However, we have found it advisable not to prolong the adjustment any longer than necessary. A man can't do it all by himself. There comes a time when he needs help. There comes a time when he has to get off the beach and swim in deep water."

"You're right, of course," said Ellery.

Cartwright puffed on his cigar. "That's what the Center is for, Paul. It's to help *you*. We want you to understand that. We ourselves have had to go through Centers, and we send our own children to them. It will take a few years, and there is a certain discipline that you will have to put up with, but in the long view it's all for the best."

"When do I start?"

"As it happens, there will be a convoy ship in this area very early on the first of January—about one o'clock in the morning, I believe. You'll be picked up in a sphere just outside of town, on Jim Walls's ranch. After that, you'll be under Center jurisdiction until they judge that you're ready to come back and take your place in society. I'm fairly sure that you'll be assigned to Earth, since you are already familiar with the customs and the language here, but of course that will be up to them. You'll be leaving on New Year's Day, actually." He smiled proudly. "Rather a nice touch of symbolism, I think."

"Very nice."

"You'll see things and experience things and learn things that are beyond your imagination, Paul. It will be more than a whole new world—it will be a whole new *universe*. And when you come back, you'll be one of us—really one of us. You will have to take my word for the fact that when you come back, Jefferson Springs will seem very different to you. You have barely seen the surface here, Paul. When you return your real life will begin."

"I understand that."

"I'm sure you do. And Paul—"

"Yes?"

"When you come back, you will of course be under our laws—or the laws of some other colony. You may have observed that they can be rather strict under some circumstances. I'm not threatening you, understand; the necessity for our laws will be impressed upon you at the Center. I'm sure that you can see that our position requires diligent law enforcement. This is, you realize, as much for the protection of the natives as for our own safeguarding. Until you leave here, you are legally classed as a native, if you'll excuse my frankness, and you are protected under our laws. We have taken pains to explain your legal position to you previously. If you have any intention of changing your mind about taking advantage of our offer, Paul, now's the time to do it. You can leave now, and still be under Administration protection as a native of Earth. But it will be too late once you board the Center ship, and when you come back you will not, of course, be quite the—same."

"I've made up my mind," said Ellery.

"Fine. Mighty fine. I'm sure everything will go smoothly for you. Until the ship picks you up, just keep right on at your job, and I hope that things will not be unpleasant for you."

"You've all been very kind."

"Well, we *try* to do the decent thing, Paul. We really do. Our position here has its own difficulties, and we take considerable pains, if I may say so, to conduct ourselves like civilized men and women."

"I appreciate it."

"All right, Paul. I'll probably see you again before you leave. The best of luck to you."

He shook Ellery's hand again, and Ellery left the Court House. When Ellery was safely away from both the building and the spitters, he carefully took the cigar from his mouth and ground it under his heel.

Well, now he knew.

He had a little over a month left. Thirty-odd days to be Paul Ellery.

It would be very easy to give up and take what was coming. He could almost do it now. A man could butt his head against a stone wall for only so long, and then he discovered that the wall wasn't going to come down.

He endured some chili and crackers at the Jefferson Springs Cafe, risking a volcanic eruption in his stomach, and then he went to work.

It was one in the afternoon when he checked into his office. Abner Jeremiah Stubbs placed both feet firmly on the plank floor and hauled out his big gold watch. He examined it distastefully, replaced it, and adjusted his green eye shade.

"Official business," Ellery explained. "I had to see the Mayor."

"You had to see the Mayor," Mr. Stubbs repeated, placing each word under a mental microscope. "You—had—to—see—the—Mayor."

"You've got the essence of it, Abner."

"My name, young man is *Mister* Stubbs."

"But your friends call you Abner, isn't that right? Well, am I or am I not your friend? Now I'll get to work and write your front page for you. We can go to press early tomorrow."

"Well," said Mr. Stubbs, pleased. "Getting ink in your veins, eh son? I knew you had the makings of a newspaper man."

"Thank you, Abner," said Ellery.

He proceeded back to his office and heard the creak of the chair which indicated that Mr. Stubbs had resumed his customary tilt and had engaged his attention with the opposite wall. Ellery forced open the window, which seemed to close itself by magic every night. It was getting a little chilly, but the room was too stuffy to work in with all the windows shut.

He sat down before his venerable typewriter, stuck in a yellow sheet, and went to work.

One month to go.

HOME TALENT RODEO PLANNED.

Would Cynthia be waiting for him, if he came back? Did he *want* her to be?

NELLIE FAYE MOSELY WEDS BILLY JOE ADAMS IN CHURCH SERVICE.

Who were the Others? Where were they, what were they like, what did they have to do with all this? Why had he screamed when he had sensed them that night?

LOVELY PARTY IS COMPLIMENT TO CARRIE SUE ROBERTS.

What was John's role in all this? He had more than one, Ellery was certain, but *what were they?*

The phone rang. His phone. It was an ancient instrument in the corner, and he could not reach it from where he sat. It *never* rang. Ellery hadn't even been positive the thing was connected.

He got up and answered it.

"Yes?"

"Mr. Paul Ellery?"

"Speaking."

"We have a long-distance call for you from Austin, Texas. Hold the line please."

Ellery fumbled for a chair and sat down. Austin—

"Hello. Paul? Paul, is that you?"

Anne. His hand began to sweat.

"Yes, Annie. This is me."

"Paul, what on earth are you doing in a newspaper office? I called information and they said that's where you'd be. Paul, what are you doing?"

Mr. Stubbs's chair squeaked in the other room.

"I can't explain just now, Annie. But I'm okay. Don't worry."

"Paul, you sound so far away! Ell, this is Annie."

"I know, hon. It's hard to talk right now."

"Ell, I want to see you. I've got to see you."

"I want to see you, too, Annie. You know I do."

"I don't mean to be nosey, baby, but you haven't written or phoned or anything. Have you gotten my letters?"

"Yes. Yes, I've gotten them."

"Paul, I know it's none of my business. But it's been so long! You know I've tried never to bother you—but—but we've been so close—and I thought—"

"Yes, Annie."

"Ell, could I come down? Just for a little while? I know you must be busy and everything, but I could catch the bus here—I could come Friday and maybe we could drive back together—that isn't asking very much, is it Paul?"

"No, hon. It isn't asking anything at all."

"Can I come? Shall I come? I hate to be so silly—"

"Annie."

"What?"

"Annie, you can't come here."

"Paul, what's *wrong?*"

"I can't explain, I just can't."

"My gosh, you don't have to be so *mysterious* about everything! You talk like you were phoning from Dracula's castle or something. Why *can't* I come down?"

"You just can't, baby. If I could tell you why, I would."

"You—you mean you don't *want* me to come. Is that it, Paul?"

Ellery felt the floor spinning under him. *Go ahead, damn you,* he told himself. *Go ahead and act as if you don't care. Make her hate you. It's the only thing you can do for her now. Be decent for once in your life. Think of somebody else, just once.*

"Is that it, Paul?"

"Yes, Annie," he said. "I'm afraid that's it."

Silence. A silence that rocked the room.

"Paul?"

"Yes, Annie."

"I loved you, Paul. I really loved you."

She hung up. The *click* in his ear sounded like an explosion.

Ellery slowly put the receiver back on the hook. He went over and took the yellow paper out of his typewriter. He gathered up his stories, and handed them to Mr. Stubbs, who was standing in the doorway.

"Easy does it, Paul," Mr. Stubbs said softly.

"Thanks, Abner."

He hurried outside to a pale afternoon sun. He walked fast, away from the office, not going anywhere special.

Just walking.

His eyes were stinging in the chilly air, and it was hard for him to see.

18

For Paul Ellery, time ticked itself out.

The days between Thanksgiving and Christmas had always gone fast for him. He could remember, in school, that the two holidays seemed to come so close together that they almost merged into one. He had never thought much about Christmas coming at the end of the year. It was just a needed break in the routine of classwork, a pleasant time of friendship and relaxation, and then before you knew it New Year's Eve had come again.

New Year's Eve was a party night. It was a night he had spent with Annie for—how long now?

A night of champagne, a night of laughs.

A night of auld lang syne.

A night of fun.

He had never really thought of it as the end of a year. To be sure, he had to remind himself to change a numeral when he was dating letters, but that was about all. He had always religiously skipped the tired editorials and the unfunny radio comedies about New Year's resolutions.

But now it was ending. An ending of his life, and of the Paul Ellery he had known.

It had been a chill, rainy December, and now it was Christmas Eve. Seven days left.

He had worked at his notebooks, half-heartedly, but he wasn't getting anywhere. The secret weapon stayed a secret. More likely, it wasn't even there.

It was seven o'clock in the evening—a nothing hour that was like the phrase someone had coined about the countryside between the cities, an hour that seemed to be designed as a gap between something and something else. It was already dark in Jefferson Springs, and there was little to indicate that it was an evening different from other evenings. Jefferson Springs hadn't even bothered to string up the colored lights and paper bells with which other small Texas towns tried to hide the fact that it almost never snowed in their part of the country.

Ellery had hoped that Cynthia would call, but she was busy somewhere else. He was pretty damned lonesome, and he didn't know what he could do about it.

He didn't have any presents, because they had all been sent to his home. He didn't even think about going home. Somehow, childishly, he missed his presents. He felt forgotten. He knew that it was strictly his own choice, but that didn't help much.

He did have a radio, and he let it play, just for the hell of it. He heard Santa Claus. Santa, it seemed, was spending Christmas Eve in front of the Alamo in San Antonio, and was sponsored this year by a big department store.

Ellery tried another station.

This time he got Christmas carols. They had a sort of melancholy beauty, but they depressed him terribly. He tried again, and suffered through a drama about a mean old man who was just pure gold way down deep, especially when he heard bells and smelled turkey, and whose crusty manner concealed a deep-rooted and decidedly senile sentimentality toward all small children, all homeless dogs, and certain selected cats.

At eight-thirty, there was a knock on his door.

He got up, hoping that it was Cynthia, and swung the door open. It wasn't Cynthia. Instead, like a scene from an old play, it was the two men who had twice escorted him to the great spaceship that hovered over the Earth. The only difference was that this time the perpetual pipesmoker was not smoking.

"Well, gentlemen," Ellery said, glad to see anybody, "won't you come in?"

They hesitated. "We brought you a note," said the one who didn't smoke a pipe.

"Come in anyhow," Ellery insisted. "You know, I must be an awful lot of trouble for you two."

They smiled, almost bashfully. "Not at all," said the pipesmoker. They came in, a bit reluctantly, and sat down on the couch. Ellery took his message, an ordinary white envelope, and tore it open. There was a single sheet of paper inside, with a typed note on it:

"Christmas Eve is no time to be alone. The Scotch is ready. Come on up and we can cuss out Withrow. John."

Ellery felt better. Much better.

"You know," he said to the two men, "I don't even know your names."

The pipesmoker said: "I'm Bob. He's Clark."

Maybe their specialty isn't conversation. "How about some wine, before we go back? Bob? Clark?"

"No thanks," said Clark. "We're on duty, you know."

"Thanks anyway," said Bob. "We're still working our way up, and that sort of thing can lead to trouble."

"Okay," said Ellery. "You know best."

He turned off the radio without regret, and switched on the porch light. After that, the journey was like the others. They got in the big black Buick—did the car stay out in the fields between trips, or what?—and drove out of town. This time the metallic sphere was resting on the Walls Ranch just outside of town. The thing was almost invisible, actually; even when you knew it was there, you could hardly see it until you were almost on top of it. They entered through the panel, and the elevator lifted, buoyantly, up into the night.

Ellery did get one piece of information out of the two men. Bob had fired up his pipe again, with an almost audible sigh of relief. Feeling expansive, he said: "You know, you're quite exceptional, Mr. Ellery."

"How do you mean?"

"I've never seen the old man take such an interest in one of the—in one of the—"

"Natives," supplied Ellery, smiling.

"Yes. Pardon me, I meant no offense."

"Forget it. Facts are facts."

Bob nodded, admiringly. "The old man is—hard to get to know," he said. "He must like you."

Clark nudged his companion, and Bob said nothing more. Ellery gathered that dealing with the natives was apt to be a tricky sort of business. As a general rule, no doubt, it was left to trained contact men like John. Ellery hoped that he wasn't just part of a day's work for John, but it was hard to tell.

Still, there *did* seem to be something more at stake, even though he was unsure as to what it was. John did his job, of course, but that wasn't *all* he did.

Well, if John had something up his sleeve he would have to shake it out this time. Paul Ellery wasn't going to be around much longer.

The globe hummed into the invisible ship and stopped. There was a muffled thump as it locked into place. The sliding panel opened, and the yellowish ship light flowed in.

The two men stood aside and let Ellery find his own way. He walked through the interlocking passage and into the long hallway with the closed panels. He walked down its spotless length, the vast ship throbbing ever so slightly around him, and stepped toward the heavy door set flush with the wall. The door opened without a sound, and Paul Ellery walked into John's sanctum.

The little fat man was seated behind his desk, his feet propped on a spare chair, reading a magazine. He looked up eagerly, and slammed the magazine down with a gesture of supreme irritation.

"Propaganda, that's what it is," he snorted. "Propaganda! Paul, I'm glad you could come. Damn glad!"

"Thanks," said Ellery, warming to the man's bursting personality. He shook his hand, firmly. "It was very kind of you to ask me to come."

"Nonsense, Paul. Nonsense and garbage! Don't you think *I* ever get lonesome up here?"

"Well," said Ellery, sitting down in the chair in front of the desk, "you have your job, your friends, all that."

"My friends are muttonheads," announced John. "I seem to recall that you like Scotch, so I've requisitioned a new supply. It's quite good, really, for a primitive drink. Got a kick to it, a little of the old *sock.* We're getting soft, sophisticated. Ought to get back to fundamentals."

He poured out two drinks, downed his own at once, and poured himself another one.

Ellery felt himself relaxing, forgetting his troubles. *Therapy,* he thought. *John's a pretty fair country doctor.*

"I see you're reading science fiction again," Ellery said, indicating the crushed magazine on John's desk.

John leaped at the bait, eagerly.

"Incredible," muttered the fat man indignantly. "Absolutely fascinating at its best, but so fantastically far off the beam so much of the time."

John polished off his second Scotch. Ellery, knowing John of old, fished out his pipe, lit it, and settled back for the deluge. But even as he settled back, he thought: *He brought me here for a reason. This is his last chance. If he's ever going to do anything, it will have to be now.*

John, however, seemed splendidly unaware of the role he was supposed to play. He was off on his pet peeve. He surged to his feet, bristling, and picked up the science-fiction magazine.

"Look at that," he ordered, holding up the cover. *"Look at that."*

Ellery looked, without much interest, humoring his host. The cover portrayed a bald gentleman with a swollen head. The bald gentleman was staring intently at a wrench, which was hanging in the air, fastening a bolt.

"You *see*?" demanded John.

"Well," said Ellery, "what is it?"

"It's a superman, dammit!" John exclaimed. "I *hate* supermen!"

The fat little man with the red face took another hefty pull at the Scotch and began to pace up and down his office. There was something compelling about the man, something dynamic, something that held your attention riveted to him. He held you, even when he was off on one of his crazy tangents, even when your mind was watching in amazed wonder, asking—

Why?

"You hate supermen," Ellery said. When at a loss for words of your own, he had long ago decided, you could always repeat the other fellow's. He tried to keep his voice matter-of-fact, but as far as he was concerned he might just as well have said, "You hate manhole covers." "Go on from there."

"Yes. Where was I? Ah, yes. Now, I'm a fair-minded man. I would be the last to condemn a craftsman for failing to incorporate in his work data that were unknown at the time he wrote. You wouldn't yell at Shakespeare because he didn't write a story about the hydrogen bomb, would you?"

"No, I wouldn't."

Ellery watched the little man—earnest, red-faced, pot-bellied, a fringe of hair girdling his balding head. John was a bundle of paradoxes. He was a man out of the future, but he resembled nothing so much as a jovial monk or friar from the Earth of long ago. He was frantic and incredible, but he was genuine. He kept out of reach, tossing around ideas that were irrelevant beyond belief, and yet he was communicating something, something that had to be said.

"You look here," John said, waving the magazine. "I don't mind when writers get to yakking about ridiculous mutations that take place without benefit of genetics, that just happen in the 'germ plasm' every time an atom bomb cuts loose. I don't mind when they blithely blow up whole planets filled with intelligent life just to keep the story going. I don't mind racial memories and Atlantis and *psi* factors. I don't mind when they portray everything in outer space as a ghastly monster. I don't object at all when I am depicted as a fiend, damn them. I *do* mind their confounded mutant supermen who take the normal, mixed-up kiddies by the hand and lead them forward to the promised land. Supermen *stink*."

"Oh?"

"A profound observation. Look here, Paul. You're supposed to be a scientist, right?"

"I was, yes."

"You are, yes. Now, if that brain of yours has not atrophied from lack of use, what do you think about a theory that postulates that man progresses because his brain gets bigger and better? Do you think that the next great advance of mankind will come about because of some mutant superman who points the way ahead, like Og, Son of Fire?"

Ellery considered, puffing on his pipe. "I think the theory's wrong," he said.

John sat down in sheer exasperation. "Listen, Paul," he said, "you *know* that theory is wrong. You want some proof?"

"Sure."

John stood up again. "*I'm* proof. Confound it, man, do I have to hit you over the head with it? I represent a civilization as far superior to yours as yours is to the Cro-Magnons'. Here I am, Paul! Am I a superman? Hardly. Am I in any physical way superior to you? Absurd—you could demolish me with one swat. And I *assure* you I cannot read your mind, and have not the slightest desire to do so."

"Okay, John, but what's—"

"Don't rush me." John sat down again, and helped himself to the Scotch. "I'm going to tell you a story. You already know it, but I'll tell it anyhow. On this planet called Earth, a very old but never tiresome story is in progress. Its hero is an animal called man. We'll just dispense with all man's forerunners here—I'm talking about H. Sapiens, Esquire. Call him Cro-Magnon when we first look in on him; it's as good a name as any. There he is, living in caves, existing as a big-game hunter. *His brain is as good as yours, or mine.* Now, let's take a snapshot here and there, at long intervals. Our hero discovers agriculture. He becomes a food producer. His small village expands. A more complex technology develops, and specialists appear, and new kinds of social organization. Man has an Industrial Revolution. He lives in cities, a fact which we have utilized to our own advantage. He splits the atom, a fact which may also be utilized to our advantage. That is the first chapter of the story, Paul. The rest of the book has yet to unfold here on Earth, but elsewhere in the galaxy man has gone on to become a relatively civilized animal. *His brain is still the same.* It doesn't change much, because, as I have attempted to point out to you, *man doesn't change that way.* What *did* change, Paul?"

"His culture, of course," Ellery said, feeling a little foolish. "His way of life."

"*Very* good, Paul. Applause. His brain stayed the same—but it had more to work with as man learned more and more. Now, does man inherit his culture?"

"No. It's historically produced. He learns it." Ellery felt like a singularly dull freshman.

"Fine. Very good. You people are bugs on supermen. It's a very common primitive trait. Have another drink."

Ellery had another.

John put his feet back up on the chair and peered at Ellery intently. "You should think more about man, Paul. Plain old everyday man. He's a remarkable animal."

Ellery waited for John to go on, but John just looked at him, smiling.

"You didn't bring me here tonight just for the hell of it," Ellery said. "I don't know just what your part in all this is, John, but I know there's something that you want me to do. There isn't much time left. You've been talking—"

"That's right," the little fat man said. "I've been doing all the talking, haven't I? And I have accomplished two purposes. The first was to take your mind off yourself. The second was to give you the solution to your problem."

Paul Ellery stared at him, his pipe forgotten in his hand.

19

Christmas Eve had long since turned into Christmas.

The vast bulk of the spaceship floated high in the darkness above the sleeping Earth. It was a shadow, undetected and unseen, slipping through the shifting air currents as a mighty fish might balance itself in a shadowed sea. It moved without sound, wrapped in an envelope of force, proud and aloof over the dark villages it had seeded from the stars.

Alone in one tiny crevice within the leviathan that could swim to the shores of the galaxy, the two men talked.

The talk went on—seemingly trivial in a universe vast beyond understanding, just as the Earth was a trivial thing in a galaxy that had passed her by.

But trivia was slippery stuff to define.

Trivia had an unpleasant habit of turning into something else. Trivia was all art and literature and music and love and science, while all sensible people knew that it was battles and wars and headlines that were really important.

All trivia did was to build civilizations.

Sometimes, though, it seemed a little slow. To Ellery, it didn't seem to be moving at all. "Look here John," he said, "this is one devil of a time to be playing games."

The fat man shrugged. "Depends on what game you're playing," he said.

Ellery helped himself to more Scotch. He was keyed up and tired at the same time, and he had reached that early-morning stage in which a few drinks one way or the other didn't make much difference.

"Let's just pretend that I am a small and rather dull child," he said. "You bring me up here when I have only a few days left before going through a mental meat-grinder, and you tell me why supermen strike you as illogical. You're a good talker, John, and I like to listen to you. But then you tell me that you've just solved my problem for me. Now, unless I'm greatly mistaken, my problem is a simple one. I've got to decide in six days whether or not I'm going to the Center. If I do, I start a new life, with new values. If I don't, I go back to live a life that has become meaningless for me. I can't live like that. You yourself told me, not so very long ago, what I should do. You said: 'If you can't beat 'em, join 'em.' If you've solved that problem, you're going to have to spell it out for me. I haven't got time for riddles."

John frowned, as though disappointed. "I had hopes for you, Paul, or I wouldn't have bothered with all this. I *still* have hopes for you. Let me draw you a small parallel, to help you understand my position. You have been a teacher yourself—I don't know whether you were good, bad, or indifferent, but I suspect that you were indifferent. But let's talk about a *good* teacher. If he's got a student who he thinks has some brains, he can give that student some facts to chew on. He can point out lines of inquiry that may bear fruit. But he can't do *all* the work. The student has got to relate the facts for himself, or else they will never mean anything to him. Most students never do forge a coherent whole out of the information that gets stuffed into them. Sometimes that's the teacher's fault, Paul. And sometimes it's the student's."

"Okay, okay," Ellery said impatiently. "So where are the facts?"

John sighed.

The aborigines are slow, Ellery thought. *You have to lead them step by step.*

"Let's do a little spelling-out then," John said. "We'll start with fundamentals. I am a man." He waved his hand. "No, I'm not making fun of you. You go ahead and get irritated if you wish, but don't let it keep you from thinking a little."

"Sorry," said Ellery. He refilled his pipe and lit it.

John said, "Very well. I am a man. As a man, I was by chance born into the culture in which you find me, and into a society with its customs and laws and policies. As a man, I have a job to do—I am employed, if you wish. Since I have a certain knack for getting along with natives, I am used by my government in contact work when such is needed. In my official capacity, I first met you. I gave you the business, and I flatter myself that I did it rather well. Now, however, I am not in my official capacity. Now I am trying to talk to you as a man."

"I see," said Ellery. "But can't you be more explicit? If you overestimate my abilities, we won't get very far."

John smiled. "If I have overestimated your abilities," he said, "then you are of no use one way or the other."

Ellery absorbed that. He was getting a bit tired of being patronized, but he knew that John was not doing it without a purpose. There were some people you had to sting into giving the best that was in them.

"I'll tell you why I can't be more explicit," John said. "To put it in a convenient nutshell, I am a law-abiding citizen. I *have* to be. I have not the slightest intention of trying to overthrow my government, and couldn't do it if I wanted to."

Ellery waited, almost hopelessly. If he was going to get anything useful, it would have to be soon. *Very* soon.

John drummed his fingers on his desk. "I'm not much of an idealist, son," he said. "My life has not left me starry-eyed and panting about the fate of the downtrodden. I'm not a reformer. I like to think that I'm a practical man, just as you are."

"What do you mean by practical?"

John brightened visibly. "Ah, semantics! A brain cell has stirred into reluctant life!"

"Dammit, John, climb off your high horse." Ellery smiled. "How would you like a swat on the kisser?"

John laughed, delighted. "Wouldn't bother me in the slightest," he assured him. "And it certainly wouldn't help *you*. But I like your attitude. It's a great improvement. Dish it out a little, Paul. You don't progress by just taking it."

"I'll send your sentiments to Edgar Guest."

John suddenly slammed his fist down with a bang on his desk. He stood up, and Ellery changed his mind in a hurry about what a pushover John might be in a fight.

"Practical!" he snorted. "I'll tell you what's practical. It's just one damned thing: being smart enough to survive. Not just you and me—we're nothing. But all of us, everybody! If man survives he's been practical. If he doesn't, he goes down the drain. What do you think of that?"

"Sounds good. What does it mean, specifically?"

"It means, my friend, that the civilization which I have the honor to represent is typical of man in every way. It's a pack of howling jackasses galloping over a cliff! We've made a lot of so-called progress. We've got spaceships and planets and gadgets a million years ahead of anything on that speck of dirt under our feet. And so what, Paul? I repeat: *so what?*"

Ellery smoked his pipe. Invisibly, he crossed his fingers.

John sat down again and folded his hands patiently. "You already have all the facts you need," he said. "You're supposed to be a scientist. Let me ask you a question. What is the one sure thing about colonial policies, in the long run? The one thing you can always count on?"

Paul Ellery said slowly: "They don't work."

"Fine!" John banged his fist down again and helped himself to most of what was left of the Scotch. "You see before you a civilization that covers the galaxy. You see technological triumphs that you can barely understand. And what are you caught up in the big fat middle of, son? A colony! A backward planet taken over as a colony! You see nothing fantastic about that, Paul? Eh? You see nothing fantastic?"

"I guess I've been a little stupid," Ellery said. His brain was churning, trying to digest what it had swallowed.

"Of course you've been stupid! You're a man, aren't you? What other animal could make the same mistake a billion times and still be around to talk about it?"

"You said," Ellery reminded him carefully, "that you were a law-abiding citizen."

"You bet I am. Most human beings are. That doesn't mean that I have to *agree* with all the laws I live under. If everybody had always agreed that current ideas were the ultimate in human wisdom, we would all still be huddled in caves. Indeed, son, we never would have *reached* the caves! Still, as I have pointed out before, I am a non-political person." He smiled. "Practically."

"And now—what?"

"Now," John told him, "I'm going to show you something. I have, in my small way, tried to set you to thinking about the Others. I hope that the problem has interested you?"

"Of course. What are they?"

"That," said John, "is what I'm going to show you."

The tireless little man surged up from behind his messy desk and led the way across the room, like a halfback leading the interference. Paul Ellery followed in his wake, and hoped he could find out where the ball was.

They passed through the sliding door into the corridor, and John set a fast pace through the ship. They passed a number of men and women, none of whom paid much attention to them. The ship was lighted normally; there seemed to be no difference between night and day on it. Or perhaps they hadn't bothered to adjust themselves to the daily cycle of Earth.

They hustled down long, antiseptic passageways, past a confusing multiplicity of doors, panels, and branching tunnels. They rode on elevators and walked up ramps. Finally, when Ellery judged that they were very high in the floating ship—he almost expected the air to be thinner—they came to a stop before a large, closed door.

There was a guard here—the first one that Ellery had noticed anywhere on the ship. The guard nodded to John, but looked a question at Ellery.

"He's with me," John said. "Everything's all right."

The guard said something, not in English, and activated the door. It slid open noiselessly and John led Ellery inside. Behind them, the door closed again.

The room was not large, and looked almost like a standard projection room. There were some twenty rows of comfortable seats, all of which faced one end of the room. At that end, replacing the standard white screen that would have been found on Earth, was a square of cloudy gray. The square was not just a surface, but was rather an area of well-defined substance, like thick, tinted air, gently in motion.

The two men sat down in the front row. John pressed a combination of buttons in the arm of his chair.

"Meet the Others," he said.

All the lights went out.

The gray square turned a milky white and seemed to fill the room.

Involuntarily, Ellery narrowed his eyes to slits against the smokelike stuff, but there was no sensation.

The milky white shifted into a sharp gray-black. Quite suddenly, Ellery caught his breath and felt a distinct sensation of falling. He held on tightly to the arms of his chair, but the chair was falling too. He tried to breathe and there was no air. There was only a vast black tunnel, bigger than the world, and he was falling down it, head first, toward a billion flashlights that picked him out and blinded him as he fell—

Faster and faster—

He saw three sleek spaceships swimming ahead of him. His eyes fastened on them, desperately. Perspective returned. He could breathe.

The spaceships looked like gray minnows, lost in immensity. They edged along the jet black tunnel, toward the staring flashlights that were a huge spray of stars.

The tunnel widened and became deep space itself. The lights flowed together and made an eye-searing splash of frozen flame. Around the edges, there was a scattering of lesser stars.

This was not the galaxy that had given birth to man.

The three ships slipped on through the clinging ink, with tiny white spots of atomic fire bubbling from their tails. Their movement was lost against the Gargantuan scale, but the splash and drops of light came closer.

There was something else.

Ellery could not quite see it. But he hunched back against his chair, and he wished that he could close his eyes.

He almost saw it. He wanted to scream. He remembered that night, a million years ago, that night in the pale blue lights . . .

It was naked in space. Unprotected. Alone

It oozed and undulated in an oily slime.

It came toward the ships and it had eyes.

It did nothing that Ellery could follow, but one of the ships broke in two. Flame licked out into space and dripped away in every direction. Ellery tried not to see.

The two remaining ships started to turn, curving around in a long, agonizing arc. They were tragically slow. It took them forever—

A pale force started to surround the ships. It grew, shimmering. The ships turned—

And then there was one ship. The other disappeared.

The thing with the eyes *flapped*—that was the only word for it. It hung in empty space, coated with slime. It waited.

The last ship got away. It started back up the long black tunnel, away from the splash of light and the thing that rested in nothing. It blurred, and its dimensions changed—

There was milky whiteness again, and then just a square of cloudy gray.

Paul Ellery was back in the projection room.

"Cute, hey?" said John.

Ellery didn't say anything.

The little fat man led the way out of the room and back down the tunnels and ramps and elevators to his office. He poured two glasses of Scotch from a fresh bottle, and this time both men downed them with one long, shuddering drink. John poured two more and sat down.

"That area is known to your astronomers as the Large Magellanic Cloud," John said slowly. "It is an irregular extra-galactic star system. It's where the Others live."

"They live in space? Empty space?"

John shrugged. "They're versatile," he said.

"How much do you know about them?"

"Not too much, but enough. There are other galaxies than this one, Paul, and other life-forms than man. The Others are hostile, if that is the right word. Who could possibly understand their motives, if they have any? They have been sighted within our own galaxy, and they mean trouble. Not now, as far as we can tell, but eventually. One day man will have to face them, Paul. If it came today, man would lose. He wouldn't even be in the fight."

Ellery sat very still. His mind seemed suddenly a tiny, hopelessly inadequate thing. His horizons had been blasted open to include a galaxy, and he had tried to face that problem. And now there were other galaxies—

An ant, lost in the jungle.

"It's getting late now," John said, "and the ship will be moving on. Our time is running out on us, Paul, and I may never see you again. I've almost finished what I had to say to you, and maybe it's been something of a disappointment." He waved at the crumpled magazine on his desk. "I flatter myself that I understand you pretty well. You were looking for a secret weapon of some sort, weren't you? A nice miracle, all wrapped up with a blue ribbon?"

Ellery considered. "I tried to tell myself that there wasn't any secret weapon," he said. "But I guess I was looking for one anyway."

John nodded. "There's only one secret weapon that's worth a damn in the long run, Paul. It's the only one you can't beat by dreaming up a better secret weapon. It's called man."

There it is. Your secret weapon.

"You see," said John, talking slowly and clearly now, with none of the exaggerations that Ellery had come to expect, "you've got to get to know us. You must not think of us as a culture—we're human too, Paul. Culture is an abstraction made up from the lifeways of many different people, all averaged together to get the human element out. A galaxy is a large place, and there are many opinions in it. Sentiment among our people, as among all peoples, is divided. We do the best we can. It's the *situation* that breeds the trouble. Hell, my friend, all of us have a long way to go. No system lasts forever. Someday, all men must stand together, or there will be no men left. You've seen the Others now, and I don't think you'll forget them. Just the same, your problem right now is not wandering around out in space somewhere. Your problem is a gent named Paul Ellery. You should get to know him. I think he's a pretty good Joe."

The silence flowed in and filled the air.

Ellery saw the room around him with a curious, sudden clarity. He saw the books, each one distinct in a brightly etched jacket of color. He saw the tapes, gleaming dully. He saw the desk, the chairs, the comforting walls. He saw the bottle, and the stale, filmy glasses. He saw John, and the words that he wanted to say wouldn't come.

"I guess we're not used to friendship these days," he said slowly. "It embarrasses us. It makes us uncomfortable. We don't know what to do with it."

"I know," John said. "The hell with it, though. If it's there, that's enough."

"Maybe I'll see you again."

"Maybe." John glanced at a clock on his desk. "It's time for you to go."

Ellery stood up, a little shakily. John began to fidget with papers on his desk. Without his solid wall of personality he seemed almost at a loss.

The two men shook hands.

"Hell, boy," John said. "I'll see you around."

"Yeah. Maybe we'll buzz up to heaven and play the same harp."

"Good deal. You'd better roll, Paul, before this crate winds up over Australia somewhere."

"Okay. I know the way. Thanks for everything."

"So long."

Paul Ellery walked toward the door. The door opened.

Behind him, he heard John's voice: "Merry Christmas, son."

The door closed.

He walked down the long passageway, to the globe that would carry him back to Earth. Back to Earth, and back to Jefferson Springs. He looked at his watch.

It was almost noon of Christmas Day.

20

The days that were left to Paul Ellery ticked quickly by.

One, two, three—

Four, five, six—

It seemed only a heartbeat, and then it was late morning on the last day of

December. At midnight it would be a new year on Earth. At one in the morning, the Center ship would leave for deep space.

There was a place for him on that ship.

All he had to do was climb on board. All he had to do was kiss the Earth good-by.

He looked outside from his kitchen window. It was a gray, miserable day. The sun was pale and far away. A cold, biting wind scratched at the old glass in the window.

Kiss the Earth good-by.

Would that be so tough, really? Sure, it was always hard to overcome your own inertia, pull up stakes and leave. It was always hard, but it wouldn't be impossible.

Not now.

There was the diseased, hideous bloom of the hydrogen flower, waiting to flash into sudden growth on every hillside. There were other charming new flora too—the gray-leafed cobalt tree, and the peaceful nerve-gas-weed.

Ellery had seen war, and seen it close. He had been born in a century of war. He had lived with war always on the horizon. The stink of war was in his nostrils.

Hiroshima and Nagasaki had ushered in a whole new technology. They had made warfare obsolete, and the hydrogen-torn holes in the poorly named Pacific had underlined the lesson. The culture of Earth *had* to change, and would change, but would it change in time?

He had heard the voices so often: *"I say bomb the bastards now while we've got a chance. Hit them before they hit us. Maybe we'll get wiped off the map, but let's take them with us."*

War was not practical. War was suicide. But people did not know. They reacted as they had always reacted. No one had told them that times had changed. No one had told them that the solutions of twenty years ago were not the solutions of today.

No one had told them.

"Okay, pal, you tell me a better way."

What was there to tell them?

They didn't trust the United Nations.

They could not believe in faith.

They had learned to be cynical in a tough school.

They did not know what science was. They did not know that science was a method. They thought that science was gadgets and bombs and automobiles and television. Why not? The scientists hadn't bothered.

And the scientists were human, too. They weren't just scientists. They were Frank and Sam and Bob and Heinrich and Luigi. They never agreed on anything. It was a point of honor. They would be debating value judgments when the world went *bang*.

There were the men and the women and the children. Each had his problems, his dreams, his fears. Each was right as he saw it. Each was hurrying, trying, working—

Ants in an anthill.

And then the bucket of scalding water.

Ellery wasn't scared of the Preventers. The Galactic Administration could handle them. He wasn't too worried about the Others, not yet. They were a long way from Earth.

Even Jefferson Springs didn't scare him, not by itself.

He wasn't scared of the Americans or the Russians or the Chinese or the English or the Eskimos.

He was afraid of *all* the people.

He was afraid of Earth.

He ground his cigarette out in a dish on the kitchen table and lit another one. He listened to the icebox humming. He heard water dripping from a faucet over the sink. He got up and punched open a can of beer. Outside the window, the world looked very cold.

So much for Earth.

Suppose he left on the alien ship?

First of all, he would live. That was important to him; he could not pretend he wanted to be a martyr. The civilized people of the galaxy had learned to control their bombs. There was no danger of that kind.

If he went to the Center, he would be different. He would not be the same Paul Ellery. Was that any great loss? Was he so crazy about himself that he could not bear any change in great, big, wonderful Paul?

Different, but not completely so. Maybe he would be changed for the better. Certainly, he would be happy. The Center would see to that. They would give him new values and new goals, and they would equip him to get where he wanted to get.

Wherever that might be.

He would have most of his questions answered—at least the scientific ones. Possibly he could even continue to be an anthropologist, or whatever passed in their culture for an anthropologist. Take the problem of acculturation, for example. Culture change that took place when different cultures came into contact was fascinating stuff. On Earth, scientists were just beginning to get an inkling into the actual nature of the process. At the Center, he could check out a book and get the answers.

The answers to the questions he asked as a man might be more difficult.

He could carve out a life for himself there. A new life, a better life. He could not even imagine the things he might see, the things he might do. He could walk through the future with a notebook. The aliens were people too. He could start over, and face his new life with confidence. He could live in peace, and in safety. He could enjoy himself.

Perhaps, too, he would have an opportunity to help Earth—help her from *inside* the galactic organization. Surely he could do more good there.

Of course, he wouldn't be quite the same, and he might not want to help, and he would be fenced in with laws. But he could still do a lot for Earth. He could be like John.

He tried to believe it.

He looked at his watch. Six o'clock of New Year's Eve. At eight he would be going to Cynthia's to usher in the new year. In seven hours the ship would leave for the Center. He could be on it.

Outside, night had come. He wondered where John was now. He could almost see him here in the kitchen, leaning against the icebox, a glass in his hand. Eyes twinkling, bald pink dome gleaming under the bulb in the ceiling, waving his arms, talking, talking, talking.

John had given him a solution. It was not all tied up in a neat package, but it was there.

The Osage Indians had found oil on their reservation. The oil had been important because it had given them what they needed to amount to something in a commercial culture: money.

John had given him a different kind of oil to deal with a different kind of culture. John had given him information.

Information to bridge the gap.

"It's the *situation* that breeds the trouble," John had said.

The problem posed by the alien colony of Jefferson Springs had no solution because Earth was not far enough advanced to deal with the problem. A problem could not be solved until its existence could be recognized.

"No system lasts forever," John had said.

That was the key. The problem had no solution *at the present time*. That didn't mean that it would *never* have an answer.

The aliens could not legally interfere with Earth, and they enforced their laws. If man could pull himself up the ladder, then the aliens couldn't kick him back down again.

If the Earth could get that far—if there really *was* an Earth and not a patchwork of hostile nations—then the situation would be different. Earth would have found its voice. The alien problem would be understandable, and techniques would have evolved to handle it.

There was more than that. The galactic civilization would *need* a united Earth by then, and need her desperately. The shoe would be on the other foot. Ellery remembered:

"Meet the Others."

"If it came today, man would lose."

The human galactic civilization was not alone in the universe. Already, it had contacted hostile life-forms from another galaxy, the Others who had no name. Men had discovered that the Others were deadly, and one day they would have to be faced. Perhaps by then they would not have to be met with naked force, but man would still have to be united and strong to survive. There were wheels within wheels, always.

Even the Galactic Administration was young. Beyond the Others, who knew what lay in wait for man? He would need his strength.

Ellery could not deal with the colony now. He could not negotiate because Earth had nothing to offer. Applying the right force at the wrong time was worse than applying no force at all. But the right force at the *right* time—that would work. That would always work. The galactic civilization, too, would be interested in survival.

The solution was there. It was centuries away, but it was there.

In the last analysis, Earth's future was up to Earth. It couldn't wish the responsibility off on anyone else. It could pull itself up by its bootstraps until it was a world to reckon with, or it could blast itself to oblivion. At best, the answer was hundreds of years in the future.

Earth might never get there.

Meanwhile, Paul Ellery had a life to live. He looked at his watch. Eight o'clock. He was late. He still had a decision to make, and there was no use kidding himself. There would be no second chance.

There wasn't much time. The old year was almost gone.

He heard the click of a woman's heels come up the wooden steps to his porch. Cynthia would be doing a slow burn. He walked quickly across the living room and opened the door.

A woman stood there. Not Cynthia.

Anne.

21

He looked around for some words and couldn't find any.

"Hello, Ell. May I come in, or are the vampires feeding tonight?"

Anne just looked at him, waiting. Her soft gray-green eyes were shadowed and her dark hair was combed a little too hastily. She had on a blue suit with a white blouse, and the skirt was wrinkled from sitting too long.

"Come on in, Annie," Ellery said. "It's cold out there."

She came in, looked around, smiled faintly at the picture that still hung turned toward the wall. She took off her blue suit jacket, fluffed out her hair, and eyed him uncertainly.

"How did you get here?" Ellery asked inanely.

"I took the bus. The public transportation system is still in operation. I'm happy to report. There weren't many passengers tonight."

"Did you have a good trip?"

"Utterly delightful. I knitted you a ski-suit."

"Sorry, Annie. I'm all fouled up tonight. Want some coffee?"

"Not now. Thanks."

She stood there in his living room, looking for some answers of her own. He wanted to go to her but he did not move.

"Annie, why did you come here?"

"I had to come, Paul. I had to see for myself. We've always spent our New Year's Eves together—I didn't think you could forget them. I wanted to see her, whoever she is. I guess I just couldn't stand it." Her voice was less steady now. "I'm *not* going to cry."

"You shouldn't have come."

"I know that. I'm here, though." She managed a smile. "What are you going to do with me?"

"I'm going to ask you a favor, hon," he said slowly. "Will you do me one more favor?"

"I'll try, Ell. What shall I do—go out to the crossroads and drive a stake through her heart?"

"It's tougher than that. I've got to go out. I want you to wait here and not follow me. I'll leave my car, just in case."

She looked at him, desperately. "What *is* all this, Paul? Are you in some kind of trouble?"

"You might put it that way," Ellery said. "Look, I can't answer your questions. I just can't. You'll have to trust me. I want you to wait here. Will you do that, hon?"

She nodded, not understanding. "How long do I wait, Paul?"

"Wait until one," he said. "I know I'm asking a lot—I would have saved you from this if I could. I tried. If I'm not back by one, take my car and go home and forget me."

"I guess I asked for it, Ell."

"I've got to go."

She was in his arms. He held her tightly, afraid to let her go. He tore himself away.

He grabbed a coat and left.

The night was raw and cold. A chill wind out of the north sighed through the flat streets and whistled nakedly through the bare branches of the trees.

He had less than four hours left.

He walked through the dark streets of the town. The rows of little boxlike houses squatted along the sidewalks, staring at him. Once he saw a glimmer of pale blue light leaking through a crack in a window. His footsteps clicked on the sidewalk. They made a lonely, hollow sound.

Jefferson Springs seemed utterly deserted around him.

He climbed the steps of Cynthia's house and knocked on the door. He walked inside without waiting to be asked.

"Well," said Cynthia, getting to her feet from the couch, "fancy meeting you here."

"Sorry I'm late."

"Sober?"

"Yes."

"This is your big night, lover. Want a drink?"

"Sure."

Cynthia poured him one of her inspired dry Martinis, which he insulted by drinking it at a gulp. She made him another, and kissed him.

"Relax, baby," she said. "Don't you want to get civilized?"

He sat down on the couch. She looked terrific. She always did. Her blond hair was smooth as silk, her blue eyes cool as ice. Her dress was wicked. Cynthia knew how to use clothes.

"I've been lonesome. I'll miss you, Paul."

"Sure you will."

"What's eating you, lover?"

"Cannibals." He laughed, unreasonably.

"You're nervous. I'll fix you another one."

The Martinis warmed him. He could not think. He postponed his thinking and tried to relish what he had come here to do.

Quite suddenly it was eleven o'clock. Time was running out.

"Cyn."

"Yes?"

"I came here to tell you something."

"Say it, then."

The room pressed in around them. A warm room, secure against the outside cold.

He stood up. "I came here to say a lot of things, Cyn. I wanted to call you a bitch and tell you all about yourself. I wanted to tell you I knew what you were after—you wanted to sleep with a caveman, try out one of the natives for kicks. I've known it ever since the dance, maybe before. That's all I was to you, just a savage to play with. I wanted to tell you that I knew all about that. I wanted to say I stayed with you because you were the best I could get. I had it all planned. I was going to walk in here and toss it in your teeth and see how you liked it. It's funny as hell, Cyn. I've been nursing this for a long time—and now it doesn't seem worth doing. So where do we go from here?"

Cynthia sipped her Martini calmly. "I knew you knew, Paul."

He sat down, feeling hollow.

She lit a cigarette. "Baby, we are what we are. Maybe you're just beginning to find that out. I'm a misfit here and so are you. I was lonely, too, if you like. I was *bored*. That was my crime. These people of mine are the supreme bores of all creation, if you want my honest opinion. They're here because they didn't have enough on the ball to stay home. I'm here because I didn't fit in any place. I'm just not a solid citizen, lover. I was alone, and you were something new. You were alone, so I gave myself to you. We had fun, didn't we, Paul? Does that make me evil? Does that make me a bitch?"

"Score one for your team," Ellery said.

She shrugged. "I'll go my way, Paul. I always have. When it's all over I'll have no regrets. When you get back from the Center, if they send you here, come on around and say hello."

"I won't be very interesting then. No more caveman."

She smiled, "We'll see."

"I've got to go, Cyn. Thanks for everything."

"Good luck, lover."

She kissed him, and then he was outside. He put on his coat, shivering in the cold, and looked at his watch.

Midnight. The time was now.

A metallic globe from the Center ship was waiting for him on the Walls Ranch. He would have to get outside the city limits and then pass the Garvin

Berry place. Jim Walls lived in the next house. It was not too far to walk. It might take him half an hour—no more than that.

He stood in the cold wind, fists clenched, eyes closed. He had waited. Waited until the last possible minute. He was caught now. He was forced into it. He had to move one way or the other.

He watched to see what he would do.

The ship was waiting, half an hour away. Peace was waiting, a short walk down the road. A new life was waiting, waiting in a metal sphere.

He had his chance.

He smiled. He started to walk.

His steps clicked on the cold cement. Jefferson Springs was dark and cold around him. He walked through a village of the dead.

He did not walk alone. Memories of Earth walked with him.

Austin. A hot summer day. The lake around the aluminum canoe, still and glassy calm. The sun on his bare shoulders. Hank and Chuck drinking warm beer and munching stale bread. The fish that wouldn't bite. The wonderful, sharp coolness of the water when they had tossed aside the bamboo poles and lowered themselves into the green, green lake . . .

Home. A living room filled with the very special lamps and pictures and chairs that had been his world. Mom humming over the dishes in the kitchen. Dad laughing at some book he was reading. "Pop, can I have a dime for a soda? All the guys are going. Can I Pop?" His street outside, and the dark sunset trees . . .

Los Angeles. A party late at night after a convention. Stale smoke in the air. George and Lois Sage sitting across from him. Everyone talking about what to do if an air-raid alert sounded. Everyone scared of the hydrogen bomb. Lois smiling. "Personally, I'm going to catch a bus for downtown L.A. That way you get vaporized all at once and miss the painful flash-burns . . .

Colorado. A tiny village nestled at the foot of a pass through the snow-capped mountains. Blue sky, clean air, tall pines. A swift river filled with trout. An unshaven old man with his shirttail out. "Sonny, I remember this town when the mines was here and they brung in a hundred whores from Denver . . ."

New York. Bright lights. A little club, a hole in the wall. A Dixieland band. A trumpeter almost completely paralyzed, playing in a wheelchair. Pale face sweating under the white lights. *Aunt Hagar's Blues.* A flushed, excited grin. "You had it then, Johnny, you had it then . . . "

God, it was funny—the things you remembered.

You never knew how much they meant to you.

He walked faster. Down one street, across another. The cold forgotten now.

Hurry, hurry, don't be late—

Don't be late for your new world. Don't be late for your new life!

He had found his place. He had found his people. The odds against him in the only life he could ever know were tremendous. He was a fool—

He didn't give a damn.

Hurry, hurry, don't be late—

Earth had a chance. He had only to believe in it. He had to have only a little faith, a little hope.

Earth was his.

He had a job to do. A little job, a job that paved the way. It was not the business of science to dictate to others. It was not the business of science to force people to its ways. All it could do was make the facts available to all, honestly and without fear.

Science, too, had to have faith in man.

Hurry, hurry, don't be late—

No man could say what might make the difference between chaos and civilization.

It might be a word in a classroom.

It might be one more man who would stand up and be counted.

It might be a faked community study to make men think a little.

There was the high school, frozen under the stars.

He began to run.

Across the street, past his parked car, up the steps of his house. He jerked open the door, ran inside.

And stopped.

Anne wasn't there. But—

He saw her then. In the kitchen, drinking coffee. She looked up, startled. "Paul!"

He kissed her. He kissed her neck and her eyes and her hair. He knocked over the coffee pot. The hell with it!

"Happy New Year, Annie," he whispered. "Happy New Year!"

"Paul!"

"Quick now, Annie! Grab everything of mine you can get your hands on. Throw it in the car. Hurry!"

"But—"

"Are you too proud to marry me, Annie?"

Her mouth made a big round O. She looked at him speechlessly and then pitched in with the energy of a demon. They cleaned the house out in nothing flat. They turned out all the lights and piled into the Ford.

They laughed at nothing, at everything.

He gunned the engine and the tires screeched as he pulled away from the curb. He drove down the street as fast as he dared to drive. Right on Main Street. Past the shadowed square of the ice-house.

Out onto the open road.

Hurry, hurry, don't be late—

Past the Berry place. Past Jim Wall's ranch. The gray sphere was out there in the field, waiting for him. He could feel the prodigious might that hung high above his head, blotting out the stars.

He did not look up. He looked straight ahead.

"If you can't beat 'em, join 'em!"

That had more than one meaning. If you can't beat 'em the way they are now, then catch up with them!

"Hang on, Annie," he grinned. "Here we go!"

They went the back way, across the beautiful and lonely land. Up to Uvalde, over to Kerrville, on through the Hill Country.

There were stars all around them.

Far ahead in the east, where the low, dark hills touched the sky, Ellery could see the first faint rays from the morning sun. Beneath the rising sun, his city waited.

He prayed that this warm, golden sun might be the only one his home would ever know. He prayed that another manmade sun might never sear its shadows across his Earth.

He laughed, exultantly, into the night.

It was good to fight for life.

John was very near and smiling.

Anne was close at his side.

"Paul, it's so good to have you back!"

"It's good to be back," he said. "Annie, Annie, you'll never know how wonderful it is to be back."

Seed of the Gods

by Zach Hughes

1

The flying saucer picked up the Volkswagen that had yellow flowers painted on its dented fenders as it crossed the causeway, rattled the loose boards of the swing bridge over the Intracoastal Waterway and sputtered in acceleration up the narrow asphalt road between the Flying Saucer Camp on the left and the newly cleared pulpwood land on the right.

"Hello, dum-dum," Sooly said to it, but there was a little lifting feeling in her stomach as adrenal activity belied her calm. The flying saucer, in the form of a symmetrical lightglow, posted itself on her port bow and paced her through the pre-dawn dark. She watched it with one wary eye. It was too early in the morning for her to be in the mood to play games with it, but she knew that if she slowed it would slow, and that if she accelerated it would accelerate, and that it would not, if it adhered to the usual pattern, eat her.

"My daughter, Sue Lee," her father would say when introducing her to people. "She sees flying saucers."

It was all a grand joke. Unless you were the one the damned things glommed onto every time you stuck your head out of the house at night.

There were two blinking red lights atop the storage tanks at the Flying Saucer Camp. It was still too dark to count the tanks to see if there were six or seven of them.

The lightglow off the port quarter followed her chugging Volkswagen past the sod-strip airport, the location of which had dictated the installation of one red blinking light on the tallest cylindrical storage tank at the Flying Saucer Camp. It lowered slightly as the car moved through an area of sparse population. Frame houses alongside the road showed lights here and there as someone prepared for an early fishing trip or, more unluckily, for early work. Sooly turned on the radio, pointedly ignoring the flying saucer. She was sick of the whole mess.

Someone had left the radio on the country music station. She was blasted by the gut-bucket voice of Johnny Cash and silenced his tuneless growlings with a quick flip of the dial. The more pleasing sounds of hard rock came from the Big Ape, far to the south. The light of dawn was showing, dimming the glow of the flying saucer.

Ocean City, an early rising town, was waking. It would be a sad day for fish. Everyone in town owned a boat either for making money or for escaping the tensions of making money ashore and the mackerel were running. On Main Street, Ocean County's only stoplight was silent and dead. Sooly shifted down, engine whining, rolled down the window to see if her escort were still around, saw it low

213

and directly above her, and rolled up the window. She turned up the radio and broke the speed limit on Water Street making it down to the small clapboard restaurant on the Yacht Basin. The flying saucer stopped with her, shifted almost uncertainly as she ran from the car to the building, then settled low above the flat roof of the restaurant.

There was the smell of buttered pancakes, coffee, an arrogant early morning cigar, stale fumes of booze from a sad looking party of four fishermen who had spent the night drinking and playing poker instead of resting in preparation for the early departure from the docks. Most of the tables were filled. Sooly paused inside the door, liking the friendly buzz of voices, the clink of forks against plates, the tight, odorous security of the place. The slight shiver which jerked her arms could have been the result of the abrupt change from the early coolness of the outdoors to the moist closeness of the restaurant. She saw Bud. He was sitting with a couple of the charter boat skippers. He had a woolen sock cap pushed back from his forehead, his long hair puffing out around it. He was lifting a coffee cup when she spotted him, and the movement seemed to her to be as full of athletic grace as a Bart Starr pass.

For long moments she stood there melting inside as she looked at him. Then she moved toward him, a solidly built, All-American-girl-type in a warm sweatshirt and cut-off jeans, legs smooth and healthy below the ragged blue, breasts making their presence known even through the bulky shirt, hair cut short for ease of upkeep, no makeup except for a slight flush from the early morning air. She moved with hip-swaying ease through the crowded tables, smiling at Bud with pretty, white teeth, her brown eyes speaking but unable to communicate her fabulously warm feeling.

Bud was an easy smiler with a handsome handlebar mustache, bushy eyebrows. He was better looking, she thought, than Elliot Gould and, although not quite as groovy, even more handsome than George Peppard. As she approached him she felt that vast, surging love sweep through her body with a force which caused her step to falter as her mind overflowed with a confusion of nice thoughts: young puppies and clean babies in blue bassinets and rooms with thick red carpets and cozy fireplaces and the smell of broiled steak and baby formula.

"Hi, Sooly," Bud said. "I tole 'em the usual." He didn't bother to stand. You don't stand up for the girl you've been dating since the tenth grade, the girl who wrote you seven hundred and thirty letters during the two years you were in the service and over in Nam at a cost of seventy-three dollars in airmail postage alone, not counting the perfumed stationery.

"Hi, Bud." She said his name in a way which made the older men, the two charter boat skippers, feel both uncomfortable and envious. He squeezed her hand and looked at her fondly. She felt a great tide well up and capsize all her dikes before it.

Outside, in the growing light of dawn, a marine diesel fired and caught and began to cough out evil-smelling fumes over the smooth, dark water of the Basin. Gulls stopped sleeping or resting on the water and soared, scouting for tidbits. One of the drinking fishermen fell down the three steps of the restaurant and ground his face into the gravel. He lay there embarrassed, bewailing his luck in his befuddled mind, while his three companions shifted their feet. He'd only lost a hundred and six dollars at Acey-Deucey the night before and now this. Low atop the flat roof of the restaurant, hidden behind the upward extension of the walls, the flying saucer flickered and winked out of existence.

Sue Lee Kurt, better known to Bud Moore, her intended, and to other residents of the small coastal fishing village as Sooly, because it was easier to say than Sue Lee and because Southerners tend to slur two-name names, fell to with a healthy gusto as a stack of pancakes with an over-easy egg atop were delivered to the table. She ladled on five pats of butter, poured on half a pitcher of syrup, punctured the eye of the egg and smeared the yellow over the pancakes and, with one contented "M-mmm," filled her mouth.

Bud Moore was taking a busman's holiday. His charter party had canceled out at the last minute, and since he wasn't being paid to take people out into the deep green to catch big, fierce king mackerel, he was taking Sooly and a couple of friends out into the deep green to catch big, fierce king mackerel for fun and, possibly, for enough fish flesh to sell and pay the cost of running his 55-foot Harker's Islander out to the edge of the continental shelf.

Sooly had put together a massive six-course lunch of boiled eggs, tins of Vienna sausage, potato chips, cookies and Schlitz beer, giggling when she bought the latter because Freep Jackson at the market asked to see her I.D. when he knew full well she was over nineteen. Everyone else brought food, too. The ice chest aboard the boat was full, with much of the space given over to cans of beer. There was a tiny hint of a southeast breeze at the mouth of the river. The bar was bouncy with the breeze blowing into a falling tide. Sooly and Bud, knowing that Carl Wooten was prone to seasickness, began to chant, "Up and down. Up and down." Carl obliged by barfing over the stern rail while Melba and Jack Wright laughed, lying side by side on the padded engine cover, arms entwined, causing a flood of pure and happy envy to engulf Sooly. Melba and Jack had been married for over a year and were fabulously happy. Jack wasn't hard-headed like some people Sooly knew. Bud looked at her with a raised eyebrow, asking silently what he'd done to deserve her dirty look.

"You and your damned security," she said, but softly so that no one, not even Bud, could hear over the muted roar of the big G.M. 671 under the engine hatch.

Carl wobbled up from the stern. "Up and down," Sooly said at him, but without real heart. Carl made a weak sound and pretended that he was going to strike her.

At mid-morning, the engine was purring at trolling speed and Carl was forgetting to be seasick for minutes at a time as kings came flashing and squirming aboard, straining arms and slipping drags on the working Penn 6/0 reels. Sooly was at the wheel and Bud acted as mate, taking fish off the lures, untangling lines, handling a gaff hook with one hand and a Schlitz in the other. For a man who got up at four o'clock, mid-morning was the middle of the day and time for a pick-me-up. Sooly thought drinking beer in the morning was delightfully sinful, but there was something about a fishing day which seemed to call for at least one before noon. She liked the taste, but didn't like what alcohol did to her and was known to be a one-drink girl at parties.

The action slowed and Bud stood beside Sooly. She was perched on the stool in front of the wheel. As she brought the boat around to run back through the school of fish, she said, "I saw it again this morning."

"Saw what?" Bud asked, his eyes busy trying to spot the school.

"You know."

"Want another beer?" Bud asked.

"It doesn't bother you at all, does it?"

"Aw—"

"You don't care that every time I go out across the damned marsh at night, no matter what time it is, I'm apt to be carried off or something."

"We oughta get back into 'em soon," Bud called out to the fishermen in the chairs.

"It just doesn't bother you in the slightest, does it?" she asked. "Or is it that you just don't believe me?"

"Sure," Bud said. "I believe you, Sooly. Why shouldn't I?"

Carl was watching the big, green swells overtake the boat from the stern, lifting and then dropping her. He heaved emptily over the rail. Bud giggled and Sooly, feeling sorry for Carl and admiring him for his love of fishing under such terrible conditions, laughed with Bud and forgot all about flying saucers and glowing lights and just let herself revel in the goodness of being alive in the sun with the water clean and deep and the fish cooperating and Melba and Jack sitting in the stern chairs looking at each other so lovingly that it was enough to tear her heart out.

2

Meanwhile, back at the Flying Saucer Camp, Toby and Jay were unloading the new shipment. They worked swiftly and smoothly getting the securely packed cases off the vehicle and into the shed before the day became too far advanced. Toby did the heavy work. Jay had a boss complex. He was newly promoted and in charge of his first independent operation. Responsibility was heavy on his shoulders, so heavy that he neglected his share of work to have time to worry. He panted in his anxiety as he let his worry increase his heart rate, accelerate his pulse and further redden his rodent-like face. His skin was too tight over his cheeks, his large eyes bulged and he looked, all in all, to be hyper-thyroid and coronary prone.

Because Jay was senior and older, and because Toby's young body didn't protest at the extra load of work thrust upon it, Toby did the work with the aid of the machinery, carting the power plants from the vehicle to the shed quickly as the sun melted redly through a silken cloudbank to the east. He paused, the work done, to admire the sunrise. He wished, momentarily, for time to explore the area. It was a nice place, if one liked salt marshes and pine stands and the silty, polluted water of the canal. He'd seen a lot worse places.

The red disc of the sun cleared the clouds and Jay was calling. Toby joined him. There would be no return cargo this trip, so it was only necessary to close the empty vehicle. However, it would be a full day. Wiring had to be run and ducts installed before the power plants could be connected.

In the shed there was an all pervasive smell of long dead and rendered menhaden. The entire facility reeked of it. It was all right out in the air and the wind, but the sheds and storage tanks held the stench and the earth was poisoned sterile-bare by leakage, although the plant had not been operative for years.

From the road the menhaden rendering plant looked, to passing residents of Ocean County, to be as deserted as ever. Long ago, when the local boosters and Jay-Cees announced the "landing" of a new industrial facility, the county had rejoiced because their area had been honored by being picked as the site for the plant, but that was before the plant started melting down thousands of tons of that small, oily fish called pogy, fatback or menhaden. Those who lived downwind from the plant soon began to question the value of industrial progress. At peak operation, the plant employed a half dozen men and brought a hell of a lot more stink than money to poor, isolated Ocean County, and not even the boosters mourned when the plant was closed without explanation and left to smell quietly in the sun. The plant had operated for only one season and the local explanation was that it had been built as a tax dodge.

Only a few people knew that the plant had changed hands recently at a surprisingly low price. The financial problems of the parent company didn't make the weekly paper in Ocean City, but insiders at the courthouse could look at the documentary stamps attached to the legal papers in the files of the Register of Deeds and know within a hundred dollars how much money had been exchanged. The ridiculously low total would make more than one land speculator moan, curse and cry in his beer, for along with the abandoned rendering plant went fifty acres of land bordering the Intracoastal Waterway, a sturdy pier built to hold a hundred and fifty foot pogy boat in winds up to near hurricane force, three large buildings, two small houses, assorted boilers and pipes and other odds and ends of rusting machinery, a loft filled with rotting nets and bags of used net floats, three beached purse boats with gasoline motors still mounted and usable after overhaul and six huge storage tanks which had been erected to store the rendered menhaden oil pending shipment to fertilizer and pet food plants further inland.

The most disgusted of all the land speculators was the Squire. He mumbled into his beer and moaned and cursed because the whole works went for less than a fair acreage price. All that hardware, which could have been sold for scrap; all the buildings, which weren't worth much but would have yielded some good material for resale upon being torn down; the tanks, which would have brought a pretty penny on the scrap market; that beautiful, sturdy dock, which could have been used to tie up the Squire's boat, thus saving thirty dollars a month dockage at the Yacht Basin; all went for less than the Squire had paid for his last housing development site on the Waterway. He was chagrined. He bewailed his stupidity. He cursed the previous owner of the plant as a New

Jersey Yankee and he judged the new owners harshly, especially the new one
with the rat face who came into town in a used Ford pick-up to buy a few dollars worth of lumber from the building supply. Outsiders, all of them.

"Looks like you missed out on that one, Squire," said that smartass, John
Kurt when the word got around. "Fifty acres on the Waterway close to the
beach, the airport and town. Let's see—six lots to the acre at about a thousand
bucks a lot, say three thousand for the waterfront stuff—"

"Haven't you got some oysters to watch?" the Squire asked sourly, sipping
his beer and patting his paunch. Squire was short, somber of mien and perpetu-
ally evil of disposition because he fancied himself to be a problem drinker. Having this problem added a new dimension to his character and got him some
sympathy, but it forced him to drink at least a six-pack a day and he didn't really
like beer. Beer added inches to his paunch, which already sagged softly over his
belt, irritated the lining of his stomach and stimulated the production of acid to
give the Squire a permanent case of heartburn. Add to those troubles the effron-
tery of a mere state employee—a warden with the Commercial Fisheries Division
of the Department of Conservation and Development—and you had a situation
which raised Squire quickly to a simmer.

"As a matter of fact," John Kurt said, pushing his boy scout-type hat back
and grinning, for the conversation was taking place at the shrimp dock with a
few basin characters as audience, "I've been thinking seriously of going out to
the big bend in Big Piney Creek to check on pollution."

The Squire cringed and killed his beer, burping deeply but without much
satisfaction. He knew what Kurt meant. On the inland side of the bend in Big
Piney there was an open garbage dump. The dump grew more rapidly than its
source, which was the Squire's own little town, Big Piney Beach. As the son of
the founder and current and perpetual mayor of Big Piney Beach, Squire knew
that the town could not afford the cost of a sanitary fill, even if the run-off from
the dump did kill a few oysters in the creek. The creek was already ripe with the
results of raw sewage dumpage from the big towns upstream, but the Squire resisted the temptation to put the lowly game warden in his place. In fact, he
smiled. The effort forced his face to bend slightly. The effect was not so
grotesque that it sent the younger members of the audience screaming away, but
it did shock some of the older ones who had known the Squire long enough to
know that he didn't smile except at the closing of a deal where lots of money
changed hands in the Squire's favor or as a ploy while making such a deal. To
see the Squire smile was rare. To see him actually use his most potent weapon
on a lowly game warden was an event.

"I thought you'd be checking on the new owners of the rendering plant,"
the Squire said. "When that old plant was operating it dumped the waste right
into the canal."

"I don't think they're planning to render fish," Kurt said. "At least they've
made no application to dump stuff in the Waterway."

"You don't think?" the Squire asked nastily, seizing on the weak word in
Kurt's statement. "You're so busy worrying about a harmless garbage dump and
trying to raise the taxes of honest citizens that you haven't even checked out a

real threat to the ecology of the area?" *Got you,* the Squire thought. He didn't wait for a rebuttal. He waddled toward his Lincoln, pushing his paunch ahead of him, leaving the loafers to chuckle as John Kurt swung easily into his outboard, backed it deftly away from the dock and went tooling down the Waterway in his never-ending quest for oyster rustlers and shrimp poachers.

3

Garge Cele Mantel knew that she was being capricious and irrational in ordering the two Pronts to two consecutive tours of fatigue duty. Their offense was minor and should have been punished by a tongue lashing. Moreover, they were doing make-work. The outer hull had already been inspected. The tiny meteorite pits sustained while maneuvering at sub-blink speed through a rather impressive asteroid belt had been filled and the ship was conveying perfect mechanical health.

Nevertheless, two young unrated crewmen were outside in the cumbersome suits made necessary by the yellow sun's potent particle spray, crawling slowly over the angles and curves of the hull, checking in dutifully with the watch officer according to Fleet safety procedures and Cele could not find it in herself to be sorry. She was a woman in a woman's world and one of woman's prerogatives is to be capricious in small matters. A delightful unpredictability was one of the small traits which went into making women superior. Men tended toward a plodding seriousness, moving toward a goal relentlessly while overlooking what they considered to be frivolous things which, often, took on importance through sheer neglect.

If it were left up to men, for example, all ships would be cold and barren. She shuddered, remembering the almost deplorable state of the U.A.T. *Entil* when she assumed command. The bulkheads were expanses of drab, bare metal. The crew's quarters were unadorned and utterly ghastly. She was firmly convinced that the monotony of surroundings had been an important factor in the difficulties which arose on past tanker cruises and still, to this day, made fleet tanker crewmen prime candidates for rehabilitation upon return from long blinks. She had, in fact, spent many hours on the outward blink preparing a paper which she would present to the Fleet Board upon return. There was some work left to be done, for the paper would not be complete until she had integrated the statistics regarding crew morale improvement following her renovation of the aging *Entil,* but she was convinced that the final results would be overwhelmingly positive and would result in renovation for the entire tanker force.

It was joyful to watch the changes. The growing incidence of something so simple as a smile was reward for her work. The job was not an easy one. It was a stunning challenge, in fact. A lot of time and energy had been expended on the outward blink in a transferral of certain materials from the cargo wells to their designated places, but as paint was applied to dull walls and bulkheads in pleasing brightness, as soft hangings muted the harsh contours of the quarters,

she could see the improvement. She would have to justify the expense of tossing perfectly good but unattractive hard metal furniture out the jettison hatch to
be replaced by soft-hued, rich woods from the decorator colony on Ankan II,
but she was not concerned. The planet below, hidden from her view by the bulk
of its large satellite, was an example of what could happen when tanker crews
were bored, lonely and far from home without the supervision of a woman. A
happy crew is an orderly crew. By the time she got home, she'd have enough
proof to convince even the penny-pinching senior Garges on the Fleet Board.

A Bakron rating knocked, entered on her signal, laid a report on her free-
form desk. Seeing him, she was once again reminded of Manto Babra Larkton's
magnificient job of uniform design. The crew of the *Entil* would have no reason to be ashamed upon return to the home planet. Thanks to Babra's imagination and talent they would be able to stand proudly beside any ship's crew, even
that of one of the titanic exploration ships. Cele had not seen anything to match
the *Entil's* new colors, not even aboard the *Hursage,* private vessel of Unogarge
Clarke, a ship which was the pride of the system and boasted the latest equipment and luxury and was crewed by handpicked talent from the five home
worlds and all the colonies.

The *Entil's* colors, with the exception of the scarlet capes worn by the officers, were deliciously understated. Yet they were so smart that a full review
inspection with the crew in dress made Cele's eyes sting with pride. She felt that
her pride was justified, not only in the uniform, but in the entire ship. The *Entil*
was, after all, nothing more than a powered cargo hold. The decorating problems were stupefying when one considered the limitations. The quarters, crew
and officer country alike, were wedge-shaped cubbyholes stuck on almost as an
afterthought around the huge central cavity of the holds. The lighting was atro-
cious. Odd shapes and protruding machines defied conventional methods of
decorating. Moreover, Cele had been allowed only two months to specially
order the custom furnishing and she'd been budgeted to such an insignificant
total that she'd been forced to buy some items for her own quarters out of her
own pocket.

Yet, seventy-four long blinks from home, the ship snug in its orbit behind
the screening satellite, the job was complete. She should have been pleased. The
mission was proving to be unexpectedly complicated and there were new, unprecedented demands on her energies and concentration, more than enough to
keep her busy. Still, she was restless. A woman does not rise to the rank of
Garge in the Ankani Fleet without developing the gift of knowing herself, so
she could analyze the reasons. But being a woman, simply knowing the why of
her slight feeling of dissatisfaction did not dispel it. She was simply let down.
Now that the renovation was complete, there was nothing to do to satisfy her
feminine cravings.

She reached out a shapely arm and picked up the report left by the rating. It
was a confirmation of the latest arrival, without detection or incident, at the planetary base. She sighed. Her mature, firm breasts rose and fell under her officer's
green blouse. Once the power plants were installed, a simple procedure rehearsed
a dozen times on the blink out, the slow process of extraction could begin. Mean-

while, survey teams were working in other parts of the planet, sending back a steady stream of reports, some dull, some interesting, some marked "urgent," all of which were beginning to build up a picture which, if she let herself think about it, made her feel a mixture of anger and sadness.

Cele was a mature woman, an outstanding example of Ankani womanhood—born to lead, trained to excel, Garge at forty, a full five years ahead of her classmates, three years in grade and in line for promotion. Her hair was done in the traditional round circlet of burnished bronze around her well-shaped head. Her makeup was applied with a generous hand but was immaculately neat. Her body showed that sensuous maturity which comes only after a woman has borne her two compulsory children. Her genetic configuration was so nearly perfect that she'd been awarded the relatively rare privilege of bearing two girl babies. One was a rising young Larftontwo serving in the home fleet, and the other, less career-minded, was contributing to the esthetic well-being of the race by doing light paintings in the art colony on Ankan II. Two of her second daughter's light paintings formed an eye-pleasing focal point on the long wall of the lounge in Cele's suite. Daughter number one had already been awarded one female-birth, proving that Cele had chosen well when she had opted that nice, quiet Larfton from Computer Center to father the girl.

She was, she knew, a fortunate woman. There was no reason for her depression. It was silly to be sad simply because the interesting work was done and only the duty remained. She would think positively.

Although the *Entil* was just a tired old fleet tanker, being assigned to command was a positive thing. It was standard practice to toss a dull but necessary command to a rising Garge before handing out the split comets, symbol of Larftongarge rank, the magic key to command of one of the expo ships. The Fleet Board knew that it was sometimes a difficult assignment to keep the spirits of a whole ship's crew high in the face of endless months of blinking across empty space to the ore-producing planets of the outer fringes, and during the deadly months of waiting while the extraction team did its work, and then the sluggish, heavily laden blink home. And in view of the disasters involving tanker crewmen in the early days of ore extraction, when Fleet command considered the missions so deadly boring that the ships were manned by male punishment tour crews, tanker command had ceased to be a dead-end for unpromising officers and had taken on the aspects of patriotic duty and high responsibility.

Yes, she was fortunate. She was even fortunate enough to encounter an entirely new situation which gave her an opportunity to exercise the full feminine judgment with which she'd been gifted. If she handled it well, and she had no doubts on that score, her promotion would be assured.

Meanwhile, she had to shake her mood. If the Garge, herself, had morale problems, what about those poor men in the crew? She moved her hand and was in instant contact with the control bridge. The face on the screen was that of a technician, Bakron grade. He was at attention, his eyes showing a sort of wistful respect. He was a fine looking lad on his second deep space blink and Cele had been aware for months that he had developed a passionate attraction for her.

Reminded by his eyes, she studied him carefully, considering the situation. She ran a taut ship, but she was not the standoffish type of Garge. In her previous commands she'd discovered that a bit of compassion on the part of senior officers did wonders for morale. It was not only democratic, it was good policy to opt a tech grade male now and then. Such broadmindedness proved that the Garge was human and didn't consider herself untouchable by lowly tech grades. Of course, she'd already endeared herself to the crew by opting a career Koptol on the blink out, but there was a long period of boredom coming up and showing her warmth to this handsome young Bakron would, at least, be an interesting diversion.

A good officer thinks of business first. "Progress at the base?" she asked, in her no-nonsense voice of command.

"Transportation completed," the Bakron said. "Local reference point moved during the operation, but stayed well within guidable limits."

"I want to be kept informed regarding installation," Cele said.

"Yes, Lady," the Bakron said, still at attention, waiting for her to break the circuit. Cele smiled. A red flush of pleasure crept up the young man's neck to his face. "You've done a good job, Bakron," Cele said.

"Thank you, Lady." His voice was choked with emotion.

"I'm pleased with your success in finding a strong emanation," she said. "It has speeded the mission."

"Lady," the Bakron said, clicking his heels in delight.

"You will find that diligent work does not go unrewarded on my ship," Cele said. "Would you be free during your next off-watch?" One never made an opting request an order. Even a male has some freedom of choice.

"Oh, Lady," the Bakron gasped. "You do me the greatest honor."

Cele shifted to a more comfortable position on the lounge, letting her strong, feminine legs show as she raised one knee. She let him look for a long moment, then closed off with a smile. She knew the word would spread rapidly. Before the end of the current watch every rating on the ship would know that their Garge was, indeed, a very warm and human woman and the reward earned by Bakron John Truto would be an incentive for every man on the ship.

Some Garges were cold and limited their favors to ranking Larftons, putting an unbridgeable void between themselves and the ratings. Cele knew that she was known throughout the fleet as a warm Garge and that her efforts on this blink would reinforce that reputation. Her popularity would soar and, although promotion depended on more important things, a high popularity would certainly not hurt her chances.

Around her the *Entil* lived. A deep spaceship, whether a glamor-wagon exploration vessel or a working tanker, was a complex of interwoven wonders which seemed, at times, to have a life of its own. A deep spaceship was never totally silent, and there was something reassuring about the low level of vitality expressed in the movement of hidden things, the almost inaudible hums, the muted clatter of computers on the bridge, the click of switches and relays acting out the automatic routine of sustaining the life of the crew, the mutter of voices in the quarters, the crisp military precision of the duty watch, the sullen, low roar of power in the engine room. Outside there was a frighteningly hostile nothing. Space. Airless and cold, hateful to all life. The sounds and the feel of the ship made good psychological counter to the mute threat of the great emptiness. To those who chose space as a career, a ship was more than a complex of machinery. Each ship had its own personality. Cele's last ship, an interplanetary passenger liner, was in total contrast to the old *Entil.* A liner was a Lady, sleek and luxurious. A liner's inertial cushions made blinking almost indiscernible, while the poor old *Entil,* prior to blinking, churned and muttered and groaned and shivered as her power banks built the charge and jerked one's eyeballs out as she blinked. A working tanker could well utilize the space given over to inertial cushions on the luxury ships. A liner was a dancer, sweeping smoothly through space. The *Entil* was a laborer in heavy shoes slogging its way from point to point.

Not that the *Entil* wasn't comfortable now that Cele's renovations were finished. Outside she was utilitarian and clumsy, but inside, except in the engine rooms, which were made hopeless by huge mountains of machinery and which had always been and always would be man's country, she was as smart as a ship of the line and only slightly less plush than Cele's former command, the liner. She could not, of course, come close to the oldest and smallest of the exploration ships in style, comfort or equipment, but then the choice *everything* went into the expos.

If Cele had not entertained every expectation of having an expo ship of her own, and not too far in the future, she could have very easily resented the emphasis put on expos. Even when one looked forward to mounting the bridge of an expo, one could still wonder about the wisdom of putting so much emphasis on them. One could wonder if it were actually worthwhile to make expo top priority, as it had been for a thousand years, since the discovery of the Wasted Worlds near Galaxy Center. The best officers, the finest equipment, a surprising percentage of the wealth of the United Ankani Worlds went into those titanic, fantastically beautiful ships which touched down on an Ankani planet only long enough to refit, recrew and reprovision before blinking out again on a computed course into the dense starfields.

Cele, being a good Ankani, did not consider pride to be a vice, and there was a certain pride to be had from the fact that the Ankani were a persistent bunch of bastards. A lesser people would have given up. A thousand years of searching had failed to produce a single additional clue, and still the huge expos lifted, blinked and punched holes in the fabric of space, covering incredible distances, investigating a million stars and a myriad of planets only to send back the report—negative.

"A vast waste," the naysayers cried. "We are alone. Turn the exploratory toys into cargo ships. Concentrate on making our Ankani worlds perfect jewels in this sea of nothing."

In Stellar History IV, at the Academy, Cele read the works of Mari Wellti, Expo Garge, Unogarge of Ankan, intellectual. "The most profound argument against a policy of isolation," Prof. Wellti wrote, "is a tour of the Wasted Worlds."

Cele's graduation trip was to the Planet of Cities. She looked down from a height to see graceful towers, magnificent architecture spreading from ocean to ocean. Then the ship lowered and she smelled the emptiness. She walked through streets and buildings built by something of humanoid form and saw the fused metals and cried because of the total lack of life, the absence of records, the mystery of what happened to what seemed to be so strong and so beautiful a race.

A thousand worlds spun in space: city worlds, factory worlds, farm worlds, pleasure worlds, and all that remained was enduring stone and plastic—no life, no records, no language. Even the inscriptions on stone and plastic had been obliterated, leaving Cele with the conviction that the fate of all the Ankani worlds depended on one word: *why?* For if there was a force in the Galaxy terrible enough to waste a thousand worlds, could not that force, someday, come sweeping down on peaceful Ankan?

"We are alone," said the isolationists, who were still in the minority. And yet there was Orton. Out of a thousand thousand cataloged stars there was one small yellow sun with a nice little family of planets, and on one of them there was life.

"Sub-human life," said the isolationists.

"Life on Orton," wrote Mari Wellti, as she argued for continuation of the exploration program, "proves conclusively that the Ankani planets are not unique in the Galaxy. Our scientific teams have brought back evidence of a definite evolutionary process. The sub-human life on Orton is reaching up, by a process of change which, according to theory, is the result of certain qualities of Orton's sun. There is every reason to believe that Orton life could, at some distant point in the future, achieve all the qualities of humanity."

"The sub-human life on Orton perverted our men," screamed the isolationists. "This hateful sub-life should be exterminated to remove any future temptation from our weaker sex."

Fortunately for the life on Orton, less bloody-minded counsel prevailed and the problem was solved by manning the essential tanker traffic to Orton with picked officers to stand guard over the baser instincts of the Ankani male. Orton ceased to be an issue. The decades passed uneventfully as Orton continued to yield a vital mineral, an element which had always been in short supply on the Ankani worlds, a metal which became more and more important to Ankani technology as the centuries passed and the home supply was used up. Other worlds had the mineral, but Orton had it in more abundance, an incredible 65 parts in one million by weight of the entire planetary mass. For over 4,000 years Ankani ships had blinked out to Orton on regular schedules to mine the mineral directly from the crust. Then more convenient planets were discovered and the small, blue planet with its amazing zoo of life was left to wheel in its lonely orbit undisturbed by Ankani ships for almost two millennia.

Then came the *Entil*. She came with every expectation of being able to lower to the surface and extract her cargo directly and quickly from Orton's crust, but Garge Cele Mantel had not advanced over all her classmates by being rash. Although Orton was well-known and had been scouted hundreds of times in the not-so-distant past, she observed all the rules for approaching an alien world, ordering out a scout party in the space dinghy.

Cele was on the bridge when the first report came back. It was such an astounding report that it took her mind off putting the last pleasurable touches on her redecoration project.

It began informally. "Larkton to Mantel."

"Yes, Babra," Cele answered to her second in command.

"Cele, we're getting something from the satellite." Babra's voice showed a surprising excitement.

"Be specific, Manto," Cele ordered, the use of Babra's title telling her second officer that she considered the situation serious enough to warrant strict military formality.

"Yes, Lady," Babra said, chastized. There was a moment of silence. "Our analyzer says it's high frequency radio waves. They seem to be aimed in a tight beam toward the planet."

"Impossible," Cele said. She moved a hand toward a technician. "Monitor the dinghy's analyzer and feed it into the big computer."

It was done. Within seconds it was established that the signals from the planet's satellite were encoded measurements of the particle spray from the yellow sun. Cele felt weak. For one delirious moment she was sure that she, Cele Mantel, had found them, the people from the Wasted Worlds. At worst, she'd found the people who had destroyed the civilizations there. In one split second she felt the feminine weakness, and then her brain took over and the pitifully inadequate weapons of the poor old *Entil* were readied and the crew was scrambling to full alert and Cele was barking orders and then there was Babra's voice again.

"My God, Cele, the whole planet's alive. All sorts of activity. Long and short waves. Voice transmissions. Good God! Picture transmission!"

"Impossible," repeated Garge Cele Mantel. She still had hopes that *the people* had come to Orton. Anything else was unbelievable, for 2,000 short years ago the sub-humans of Orton had been naked animals sacrificing their fellows on blood altars and killing one another with crude, hand-made projectile weapons.

"They're into atomics," Cele heard Manto Babra Larkton say with ill-concealed awe. "The evil little beggars are trying to poison themselves."

"Impossible," Cele said. But it was true. She'd studied the report of the last expedition to Orton, which described the sub-humans as dark skinned, big nosed, thick haired and having only a rudimentary written language.

"They've been in space," Cele called. "I get launch pads on two continents with vehicles capable of carrying man—I mean—" She paused.

They all paused and wondered and sent out careful scout parties and cursed the bastards down on Orton who had, by making a fantastic leap into the future, added months to their mission. For with an atomic shallow-space culture down there, it would be impossible to lower to the surface and do their extraction.

Fortunately, the Ankani were a thorough race of people. The *Entil* had the

equipment aboard to meet the emergency and the know-how in its Garge and
crew to do the assigned job in spite of the unexpected difficulties.

4

Inqui, the Fierce Saber-Toothed Tiger, and the world's finest New York alley
cat according to John Kurt, bounded on stiff legs from behind an oak tree and
attacked Bem, the panting, fat, ancient Boston dog, as she followed Sooly from
the deck at the back of the house toward the weathered dock on the tidal creek.
Inqui/Tiger (who knew both names because Sooly insisted on using her first-
quarter French and her imagination, and because her father refused to twist his
tongue around the word 'Inqui,' calling the gray-striped kitten Tiger instead)
ruffled his fur in pleasure when his attack caused the old waddling dog to grunt
in displeasure.

Sooly felt as warm as the July sun. She had done everything, helping her
mother put the breakfast dishes into the dishwasher, running the vacuum, scrubbing the grout in the hall bath which represented a never-ending chore, since the
salt-water climate mildewed the damnable stuff as fast as she could clean it with
Clorox and elbow grease. Now, with the day less than half-way gone, she was
a free agent, content with her world and heading for the dock with serious intent. Her goal was to bake herself to a degree of brownness which would cause
oohs and *ahs* of envy when she went back to school in September.

She had to halt halfway to the dock to watch the family's prize pair of cardinals giving their new hatch flying lessons and she spoke harshly to the Tiger,
who took a greedy and unwarranted view of the proceedings. "Beast," she
yelled at the Tiger, flipping at him with her towel to divert his attention from
the excited bird sounds coming from the small tree.

The Tiger made it out of there, tail high, moving so swiftly that Sooly had
to laugh at him. He waited on the dock, his head jerking from the flight of a
white water bird to the cardinals. For a city cat, he was adapting to country life
well.

The Tiger was the only worthwhile thing to come from Sooly's brief stay
in New York. "I think that would be fabulously exciting," Sooly's mother had
said when Aunt Jean asked Sooly to spend the summer in New York working in
Jean's office. So Sooly went as much to please her mother as to satisfy her curiosity about big-city life, and she'd stayed three weeks, just long enough to
miss Bud with a heart-pounding intensity, to rescue the Tiger from unwanted
extinction and discover that New York was not for her.

"The most expensive New York alley cat in the world," her father would
say when he wasn't holding the Tiger in his lap or chasing him out of the
planter, which he seemed to prefer to his kitty litter. For Sooly had spent almost
all her briefly earned salary buying shots, a carrying basket and an airline ticket
to bring the Tiger home.

"No animals," John Kurt was always yelling. "We're not going to have
any more animals. You're good at bringing them home, and then you bug off to

school leaving me and your mother to take care of them." But there was the old Boston dog who was only a few years younger than Sue Lee, and all of John Kurt's grumbling didn't disguise the fact that he liked Bem. "I spend more on that dog than I do on myself," he'd growl, but he always paid the bill for the medication for Bem's heart condition, the pills for Bem's grass fungus, the special salt-free diet dog food which she required. And he'd spend hours playing with the Tiger, who liked sacks and boxes.

"You're nothing but a big fake," Beth would tell her husband when he groused about Sue Lee's animals.

Indeed, animals took to John. When the Tiger finished his first inspection of the Kurt living room, showing by his thorough probing into very small corners that he was aptly named by Sooly, he decided to rest from his rather nerve-racking airplane ride in John Kurt's lap.

"You think he doesn't know who to butter up?" Beth asked, when the kitten leaped up onto John's khaki-clad legs.

When the Tiger, who had never seen dirt before, only the pavement of the city and the interior of Aunt Jean's apartment, made his first trip to the great outdoors, it was John who watched and roared with amusement as the city cat walked gingerly, lifting each foot and shaking it, through the rustling leaves. It was John who retrieved the frightened kitten from under the car, where he'd retreated upon discovering that the country outdoors is a threatening maze of movement—trees, squirrels, blowing grass, flying birds. And it was John who waited anxiously when the developing nerve of the city cat sent him picking his way slowly and with great care into the uncleared bay beside the house. When the Tiger emerged from the jungle thirty minutes later within six inches of the spot where he'd entered, John breathed a sigh of relief and allowed as how the Tiger might just make it.

Sooly liked her parents. She was not in one-hundred-percent agreement with them on everything, but there was none of that communications gap she observed between her friends and their parents. She shared her father's love of the outdoors, would fish with him for speckled trout on the rawest of late fall days and she pleased her very feminine mother constantly with her interest in domestics. Sooly would have been more than content to stay with her mother and practice keeping house and sewing and cooking until Bud saved enough money to get married, but Sooly's abilities extended beyond making a mean pot roast and sewing in invisible zippers. With an ease which she took for granted, she'd graduated with the highest grades in her class, made a valedictorian's speech about the responsibilities of the younger generation and earned a scholarship to a great little girl's school in Virginia where the science faculty was very good. There, during a long, endless school year, she'd added to her total of letters written to Bud Moore, caught rides home for weekends to fish, made-out breathlessly in the back seat of Bud's old Mustang and issued broad hints that Bud could take her away from all that school mess any time he was ready.

As a reward for being a good girl, her father told her not to look for a summer job. She had earned a full scholarship and her school cost him only clothes and spending money so there wasn't a great drain on his just-adequate state salary. She sometimes felt guilty, especially after her failure in New York, because she was, after all, over nineteen and not pulling her weight. But at such times, he would merely hug her and say, "Kid, you'll have your nose to the grindstone the rest of your life. Live it up. Lie in the sun. Go fishing."

Her father was, she thought, one of the world's great men and it was a great world and the sun was just wonderful. She loosened the straps of her halter so that she wouldn't have white stripes on her shoulders, timed her baking to ten minutes per side, sipped Pepsi in which the ice was rapidly melting, and said a friendly word now and then to old Bem, who had found a shady spot under the overhang of the upper dock level, and watched the Tiger practice climbing trees. She was on her third ten-minute turn when a compact ball of energy landed in the small of her back, having sneaked up in dirty tenny-pumps, shushing and grinning at another, smaller ball of energy tagging along behind him. Sooly whooped as the air rushed out of her lungs, rolled over, gathered the small boy in her arms and playfully massaged his scalp with her knuckles through a shock of cotton-white hair.

"Let's go swimming, Sooly," her cousin, Bill, gasped through his laughter.

"Twim, Tooly," said young Anne, coming up to join in the roughhouse.

"In you go," Sooly said, tossing Bill into the creek. He went out of sight, came up blowing and kicking energetically. Sooly lowered Anne by the arms to let her stand on the lower lip of the dock, which was under water on the mid-tide. Hot and sticky with suntan cream, she bailed out, splashing mightily, her hair soon wet and clinging to her head.

On the marsh side of the creek there was a flat of delicious mud. Bill swam over and started taking labored, sucking steps, sinking in to his knees.

"Mud, Tooly, mud," Anne kept repeating, until Sooly swam across with Anne in tow and let the small girl join her brother in the fun. Bill turned out a soft-shell crab which had been hiding in the mud and all three chased the poor creature until it was caught and put into the crab trap by the dock for John Kurt's dinner.

"Hey," Bill screamed in that full-voiced roar which seems to be the common voice of all small boys. "Let's go crabbing."

"You'll have to help clean them," Sooly told him.

"Sure."

The fat, black dog insisted on going, too, although Sooly knew it would be better for the dog to stay at home and sleep in the shade. She hadn't the heart to say no, however, so she lifted Bem into the back of the battered old pick-up which was the family beach buggy and installed Bill and Anne in the back with the dog after severe injunctions to sit still and not move at all. She drove no faster than twenty miles an hour going across the causeway and the bridge, turned left into the little-used dirt road leading up to the Flying Saucer Camp, parked the car in the middle of the road in front of the piece of rusted cable which was stretched across the road to keep vehicles out. Faded signs said PRIVATE PROPERTY—KEEP OUT. She ignored them, as usual. She lifted dog and children out of the bed of the truck, loaded Bill with bucket, crab lines and net, and allowed Anne to carry the rank fish heads which would be used as bait.

The dock at the rendering plant had, for years, been a favorite crabbing spot for people in the immediate area and for summer people, the unlucky ones who worked upstate in the grimy factory cities and looked forward all year to spending two weeks doing what local people did all year round. The absentee owner was never present to enforce the KEEP OUT signs.

There were six tanks. The buildings were closed, walls faded rustic from the original red of the cheap barn paint used on the rough-sawn boards. The two peeling, white houses—windows closed, cheap shades frayed half-way up the panes—looked abandoned. Bem showed an interest as they walked across the bare dirt of the area between buildings, sniffing and grunting in an effort to get both scent and air into her tired old nose. Bill and Anne ran ahead and were busily making the tangles in the crab lines almost foolproof when Sooly arrived at the end of the dock. She hadn't bothered to change, since the Flying Saucer Camp was almost always deserted. She wore a faded blue bathing suit, a size or two too small, selected that morning because it was so far gone that a bit more suntan cream wouldn't hurt it. She finally freed two lines from the tangle, tied fish heads above the lead weights at the end and set her two little cousins to pulling in angry blue crabs which she netted, throwing out the small and medium-sized ones and putting the large ones into the bucket.

John Kurt thought the crop of crabs was good around the rendering plant because of its one season of operation. As the pogy boats were unloaded, fish had been dropped into the Waterway, encouraging the colony of crabs which still peopled the dark water near the dock. Fishing was good.

It was Jay, the worrier, who first heard the loud, childish squeals of delight and looked out a window to see intruders on the dock. His eyes seemed to protrude a fraction of an inch further as he motioned Toby silently to the window. Toby had oil on his hands and smudges on his face and his khaki work costume was wet with perspiration and soiled by contact with the well-lubricated power plants which he was installing.

"Intruders," Jay said. "We'd better get rid of them."

"A female and two young ones," Toby mused, his eyes not missing the flow of girl as Sooly netted a crab and bucketed it. "Our advance studies showed that the people of this area often use the dock to catch various marine species."

"Get rid of them," Jay ordered.

"Me?" Toby felt a flush. "You're senior. You get rid of them." Toby wasn't about to go out there and face a female and tell her to beat it.

"And because I'm senior I'm telling you to do it," Jay said, his voice rising.

"What should I say?" Toby asked nervously, accepting the order as any good man would.

"Tell them it's dangerous. Tell them it's private property," Jay said.

Toby wiped his hands and pushed back his blond hair, leaving a hint of dark oil on it. He braced himself. A man often is called upon to perform distasteful duties. He walked briskly out of the overheated barn, felt the full blast of sun on his face and wondered how much damage its rays were doing. He rounded the corner into a slight sea breeze blowing across the marsh, swallowed as he reached the long dock and let his heels click on the boards to warn the female of his approach. Apparently she didn't hear him, being intent on netting crabs and laughing with the two young ones. He was within ten feet of her back when he stopped, close enough to see the dent in her skin where the upper garment dug in, to see that the lower garment fit snugly and wouldn't zip up all the way, being slightly too small. Her body was as full as a mature woman's, her legs sturdy, her hair nice, slightly mussed as if it had been wet and then hurriedly combed. He waited for her to turn, feeling uncomfortable. After watching her net two more of the vicious blue crabs, he cleared his throat. She didn't hear. He coughed. He caught himself getting a bit panicky. He coughed again and this time she heard and turned her head. She was busy with netting a crab, however, and looked back at her work immediately, using the net expertly, turning to face him only when the job was done.

"Hi," she said. "They're biting good."

"I must tell you," Toby began, his voice weak, "that it is dangerous and this is private property."

"Huh?" Sooly asked.

"What did he say?" Bill piped.

"Oh, it's all right," Sooly said, smiling. "They swim like ducks and I'm a senior lifesaver."

"I have been instructed to tell you," Toby said, his voice growing stronger, "that it is dangerous to be on this facility and that it is private property."

"Pooh," Sooly said, her smile fading. "It's always been private property. Are you the owner?"

"No," Toby answered truthfully.

"Then what's the score?" Sooly asked.

"I am employed here. My superior requests that you leave."

"You've got to be kidding," Sooly said, her face clouding up. "I've been crabbing here since I was a kid."

"Nevertheless—" Toby began.

"No one has ever objected before," Sooly said, interrupting in the way of a woman. "I don't understand why the sudden concern. We're not hurting anything. The old plant is not running, the owner never comes down—"

"There is a new owner," Toby said. "Please leave."

"O.k., kids," Sooly said, thoroughly angered. An outsider was butting in on something that wasn't any of his business, telling her she couldn't do something she'd been doing for years. "The nice man said we have to leave."

"Mean man," Anne said, glaring at the tall, blond man with fire in her eyes.

"I'm sorry," Toby said. "But it's not my choice. I'm only—" he paused, "—an employee."

"I dig," Sooly said. "But who's the C.S. bastard who gave the order? I'd like to talk to him."

"Ah, I'm afraid that would be impossible," Toby said, knowing that there was only one authority and that an order from Jay was, in effect, an order from that authority.

"Well, you'll be hearing from me anyhow," Sooly said irrationally, angry in the way of women. "You can bet on that." She was gathering up the equipment. She swept past Toby with the young ones in tow, eyes flashing. When she was angry, her eyes appeared to be larger and made her so much more attractive that Toby could not help himself. He had to watch her. From the rear she looked very womanly. He tried to wipe such evil thoughts from his mind as he walked back to the shed to resume his work.

"Has somebody bought the old fish plant?" Sooly asked her father over a fine meal of steamed crabs.

"That's the word," John said. "Northern outfit."

"They say we can't crab off the dock anymore," Sooly said.

"Breaks of the game." John cracked a claw and sucked out the meat expertly.

"I think that's terrible," Sooly responded.

"What did he say?" asked John, with only minor interest.

"He said it was dangerous. And he kept talking about how he was ordered to tell us to leave."

"Nice-looking young fellow with blond hair?" John asked.

Sooly thought. "Come to think of it, he was. I was so mad I didn't notice. He was sorta groovy—long blond hair, a wild mustache, big, soft eyes."

"That's Toby. The other one's called Jay."

"There's no reason to make us stop using the dock," Sooly pouted.

"Every reason in the world," John said. "They own it."

"Best crabbing spot around," Sooly said.

"You can always take a boat," he replied.

"Hey, that's right," she said. "We could anchor right off the dock and they couldn't do a thing about it, right?"

"Right," her father agreed. "But can't you find another spot to go crabbing?"

"Sure," Sooly said, "but they've made me mad."

"It couldn't be," her mother asked, "that you're thinking about that groovy blond fellow with his soft eyes and blond mustache?"

"Oh, *mother*," Sooly said.

5

A fresh, new pipe some thirty inches in diameter snaked out of the shed, across the bare earth, down the muddy, sloping bank through the marsh grass to bend down into the Intracoastal Waterway. An identical pipe came out another hole cut into a wall and made its way to the water fifty yards to the west. There were no seams, no visible joints. Toby made a last minute inspection of each pipe, walked through the morning haze to the building, entered, resisting the urge to hold his nose until he could find his mask. Mask in place, he ran down a check list, nodded in satisfaction, gave Jay the go-ahead and nodded again as the three in-line power plants hummed into life. He could hear the rush of water through the intake pipe. Jay, monitoring gauges, nodded. Toby moved around the power plants with a critical ear, listening to the smooth hum. He pushed a button and the extractor whined. He heard the rush of water as it hit the outlet pipe and moved to the extractor to watch the indicators. As he watched, the accumulator gauge moved ever so minutely. He grinned at Jay, opened the access port, dipped up a tiny quantity of material and fed it to the analyzer.

"Ninety-nine point six," he said. Jay frowned. "I know," Toby said, making adjustments. The next small quantity showed 99.88. Optimum. Satisfied, Toby walked to the dock. The intake pipe was sucking hard enough to make a visible current moving into it. The outlet sent swirls of clear water to the surface before it mixed in with the dark water of the canal. Back inside, he checked power consumption. For various reasons it had been decided to use local power. It would have been much easier to use their own power, but the plant was going to be in operation for four months and if they'd put in their own power, sooner or later someone might have asked questions. Using local power posed some problems, of course. For one thing, they had to counterfeit the money to open a bank account so that they could pay their power bills. The way the stuff was being used, their bills would be large. But it was good money—so much a duplicate of the real thing that no detection device could tell the difference. At any rate, that was not Toby's worry. That and many other details of the same nature were handled by another team working in New York. Toby was not a part of that operation, but he knew that the northern team had set up a series of dummy corporations, making it impossible to trace the money back to its source within the time needed to do the job.

Toby's education was limited to language and customs. Although he was prohibited from undue contact, there would be other incidents like the encounter with the female and the two young ones on the dock. He would handle such contacts with as much courtesy as possible and end them as quickly as he could. Meantime; he was in for a long period of boredom. The machinery was automatic and required only a minimum amount of maintenance.

For two days he spent most of his time in the shed, checking and making sure that the initial installation had no flaws. The power plants hummed and the extractor whined and the accumulator gauge clicked steadily now, advancing by minuscule degrees as the material built up in the receptacles. On the third day, Toby requested permission to go into town. This worried Jay. "You know the orders," Jay said.

"I have a special dispensation," Toby said. "I am to be allowed to pursue one of my interest fields while here at the base. To do this, I need access to the library in the town."

"Do you have a card?" the female librarian asked.

"No, I'm sorry," Toby said.

"Do you own your own home?" she asked.

"No."

"Then your card will have to be signed by your employer or by a local property owner," she told him.

All of which necessitated another trip to town with the card signed by Jay who was, technically at least, Toby's employer. It all seemed rather foolish to Toby, for Jay's signature could not possibly mean more to the library than his own, but the rules were to be obeyed. Moreover, the rules worked, for he walked out of the library with an armful of books having a bearing on history. There were also a couple of natural history books, since Toby was fascinated by animal and bird life.

Jay made some remarks about Toby's book selection. Jay spent all of his off-watch time in the lab he'd set up in the second house. Toby didn't mention that Jay's work could have no more relevance than his own. He felt that a man's off time was his own and if a man wanted to while it away repeating experiments that had been performed hundreds, thousands of times in the past, well, that was his business. Toby wasn't very close to Jay. He knew little about the man except that he was well past middle age, was a fleet veteran with an interest field involving medical sciences, a rather barren field since all the mysteries had been solved millennia ago.

Toby developed a horrified interest in war and spent hours going through book after book. His trips to the library were frequent and finally brought a comment from the librarian which he didn't, for the first moment or so, understand.

"What do you do," she asked, "look at the pictures?"

He frowned, trying to find the reason for the comment and then he realized that he wasn't giving enough time to the books, going through two dozen per day. To avoid further suspicion, he limited his reading to a mere four books a day and soon found time hanging heavy on his hands.

For long hours, protected from the harmful effects of the sun by a special preparation which was unpleasantly gooey and which closed his pores so that he could not perspire, he steamed on the dock, making notes and drawings on the astoundingly varied life in the marsh and its environs. He had purchased a book on birds, a paperback edition from the rack in the local drugstore, and he identified two dozen types of waterfowl including a beautiful number called a skimmer gull which fed on minute marine organisms by flying just above the surface of the water with the lower half of its bill skimming up the food. He witnessed a tragedy and was saddened. One beautiful skimmer walked along the mud bank at low tide, weak, feathers muddy and bedraggled, his lower bill broken, starving slowly. He saw death in other forms, too. Squirrels played in the trees next to the plant. One, standing on its hind legs with its forepaws held in front almost in the position of a supplicant, sent out a chirping, bird-like noise, announcing, Toby conjectured, love or territorial claim. Suddenly a hawk swooped down and struggled into the air with the squirrel. The animal's frantic fight for survival ceased before the bird was out of sight as cruel talons sank into soft flesh.

Shrimp boats plied the Waterway before light and near dark, going out toward the sea in the early mists and coming home with a million gulls in attendance as the workers on the boat headed shrimp and tossed the heads over to make a feast for the birds. Pleasure craft sent wake waves crashing against the dock. People waved. Shapely females in skimpy costumes lounged on the sun decks, soaking up the rays of the sun.

The Squire found the younger hairy fellow on the dock the day he tooled down from Ocean City to check out a report that the rendering plant was dumping something into the canal. He was in a sleek ski-boat, for which he had absolutely no use, athletic activity being far in his past. He owned the boat with its hundred-horse outboard engine because, rather shrewdly he thought, he'd insisted on its being a part of a swap.

Seeing that one of the new people was on the dock he went past, turned around a half mile down the Waterway and tooled back up.

Toby saw the boat go past and noted that the operator, unlike most, didn't wave. Then he saw the boat coming back, slower, and he broke off his observation of the sun-worshiping claw-waving of a colony of fiddler crabs to observe. When the boat came in close to the dock he waited for the operator to wave or yell a greeting. The boat moved in close to the outlet pipe and the man aboard it was looking at the clear swirl of water.

The Squire moved his boat to the intake pipe, saw the current moving into the pipe and frowned. Then he remembered that he was being watched and, to live up to his reputation, popped a beer. After this flourish he took off, his mission completed.

"Dear Sir," the Squire, later seated in his study, wrote to the head of the Department of Conservation and Development. "Your man here, a—" here he crossed out the word "smart-ass" and continued "—an impudent fellow named John Kurt, isn't doing his job, since it is my personal knowledge that the old menhaden rendering plant is now engaged in some sort of operation and is dumping stuff into the Intracoastal Waterway. In view of the past persecution of honest taxpayers in such matters, I am sure you will do your duty."

It was that same afternoon when Sooly decided, having done her housework and baked herself to a brown crisp, that it was time to show those newcomers at the Flying Saucer Camp that you can't snow an old-time Ocean County girl. She pushed her father's aluminum boat into the creek, struggled down to the dock with his nine-and-a-half horse fishing motor, loaded in Bill, Anne and the fat, black dog who insisted on going in spite of the heat of the July sun, and ran the creeks to the Waterway and the dock where, as it happened, Toby was still observing the local wildlife. To show the outsider, she anchored only feet away from the pilings and, coldly ignoring him, set the kids to hauling in crabs.

Toby suffered the close proximity of the female and the young ones as long as he could and then beat a strategic retreat to tell Jay that they were back. "Send them away," he said.

"They're not on the dock."

"You said they were back."

"They're in a boat."

"Then they're not back."

"They're just a few feet off the dock and near the intake pipe."

"Maybe you'd better send them away," Jay said.

"You can't do that here," Toby, having returned, told the female as he stood on the dock looking down at her.

"Aha," Sooly said. "Gotcha." She giggled. "This, my friend, is public water and I can do what I damned well please on it as long as I don't come ashore on your property."

"Are you sure?" Toby asked, not knowing what to do.

"You can bet your bippy on it," Sooly said. "Watch out!" This last was to Bill, who, in his excitement over trying to land a barnacle-encrusted grand-daddy of a blue crab, knocked Bem into the water. The dog surfaced, snorting and gasping, and started to swim for the shore. Sooly leaned over and called, but the dog continued to make it for the nearest dry land, swimming directly toward the swirl of current above the intake pipe.

"Watch out!" Toby yelled.

Caught in the current, the dog was drawn to the center of the eddy above the pipe. The suction wasn't strong enough to draw her under, but it was strong enough to prevent her breaking free. She swam in the same place, her eyes frightened, her breath coming in labored gasps. Sooly stood up, dived into the water, leaving the canoe rocking and Bill and Anne squealing and hanging onto the gunwales. Toby, who had seen the sadness of the starving skimmer gull and the quick and violent death of the squirrel, also realized the danger. His splash was only a split second behind that of Sooly.

Sooly reached Bem first, caught her by the scruff of the neck. Toby was there then and he said, "Let me get her."

"She's my dog," Sooly said. She tried to push Toby away and got a mouth-ful of water. She coughed and spit and struggled toward the near bank, since climbing into the canoe from the water was ticklish and she didn't want to have Bill and Anne and the dog in the water with her. Toby, trying to be helpful, laid hands on Sooly, felt her warm softness, flushed with embarrassment, took an elbow in the chin and saw stars. He gave up trying to help and swam along be-hind Sooly. She waded out, sinking into the mud. Bem was gasping and strug-gling in her arms. She was close to the dock. She put the dog on the weathered boards and hoisted herself up. Toby followed, dripping.

"Is it all right?" he asked, as the old dog, exhausted, flopped down onto the boards with her legs stretched out, her fat belly panting.

"She is not an *it*," Sooly said, angered. "What are you trying to do, drown my dog?"

"I did nothing," Toby said defensively.

"You've got that thing out there," Sooly yelled, pointing to the intake pipe. "I think it's illegal and dangerous."

"The intake pipe?" Toby said, flustered by her anger.

"Whatever it is," Sooly said, bending to pat Bem reassuringly. "And she's got heart trouble and the excitement could very well kill her."

"I hope not," Toby said sincerely. "Do you have *troleen?*"

"Of course I have—" She paused. "Do I have what?"

Toby realized his error. "Do you have any medication for her?"

The dog's breath was uneven and panting. "At home," Sooly said.

"Wait." Toby ran to the small house, found the *troleen* in the medical kit, ran back. He was at a loss as to how to get the pill into the animal. He looked at the panting dog helplessly.

"Are you a vet?" Sooly asked.

"A what?"

"An animal doctor, stupid," Sooly said, worried out of her mind about the dog.

"In a way," Toby said.

"Here," Sooly said, taking the pill from his hand. Her fingers touched his. He felt the contact. She thrust the pill far down Bem's throat and forced her mouth closed. Bem gasped and swallowed. The relief was almost instantaneous.

"Hey, great," Sooly cried, as Bem rose, wagged her tail-less rump and sniffed at Toby's feet. "Do you have any more of that stuff? That's the best medicine I've ever seen."

"I'm sorry," Toby said, thinking quickly. "That's all I have."

"Well, thanks, anyhow," Sooly said. "Know where I can get it?"

"It's an experimental drug," Toby said.

"Is that what you're doing here?" Sooly asked, looking at Toby with an approving eye. His wet, blond hair clung to his skull and he looked groovy, like a surfer just in from a wild ride.

"Not exactly," Toby said, wondering how he could get rid of them now.

"Well, listen, thanks a lot for helping." She took her eyes off him. "You kids pull up the anchor," she told Bill and Anne. Bill started working. Sooly yelled instructions and Bill started the motor, put it in gear, banged the boat against the dock. Sooly made it fast and turned to Toby.

"Well, I guess we'd better go."

"Yes," Toby said.

That made her flare up a bit. To punish him, she decided to stay longer. Seeing a pile of books on the dock she bent and checked titles. She thumbed the bird book. "This one isn't complete," she said. "What you need is Goody's *Book of Shore Birds.*"

"I have found it difficult to identify species," Toby admitted.

"They all look alike, huh?"

"But there is an amazing variety," Toby said.

"Look, I'll tell you what." He wasn't a bad guy after all. Any man interested in birds couldn't be all bad. "I've got Goody's. Want to borrow it?"

"I don't want to put you to any bother," Toby said.

"No bother. I'll run it by on the way into town this evening." She frowned. "If it's permissible to come onto your private property."

Toby considered. "That would be nice of you," he said, seeing no harm in borrowing a book. After all, he had permission to pursue his interest while off duty. "If you'll tell me what time you're coming, I'll meet you at the gate."

"I hate being tied to schedules, don't you?" She used her best smile on him. "I'll park at the wire and walk up." She was in the boat before Toby could think of a counteroffer.

Bud was running a charter party to the continental shelf that day. He was due in between 5:30 and 6:00. Sooly started for town at 5:00 with a copy of the bird book on the seat beside her. She parked the car at the cable across the road leading to the buildings at the Flying Saucer Camp and walked the rest of the way. The place looked deserted, as usual. As she passed the largest building she heard the sound of electric motors from inside, but the doors were closed and padlocked. She directed her steps toward the house into which Toby had gone to get the pill for the dog, but once past the building she saw Toby on the dock, lying on his face looking over the edge. She walked to the dock. Hearing her, he turned and put a finger to his lips. She joined him on the edge and looked over. A female marsh hen and her brood were chasing sand fiddlers on the mud. The hen was a long-legged, long-necked, long-billed water bird dressed in dirty black. The chicks were balls of furry feathers, their long little legs adding a touch of comedy to their appearance. They watched in silence until the mother hen led the chicks back into the grass.

"Fascinating," Toby said.

"They're clapper rails," Sooly said. "Are they in your book?"

"I couldn't find them."

"Here," she said, opening the Goody book to the rail section. Toby read in silence for a moment, looked up. "You eat them?" His face showed his distaste.

"Tasty, as a matter of fact," Sooly said.

"How terrible."

"You some kind of vegetarian nut?" Sooly asked.

Toby was silent. He nodded. "No rare steaks cooked on a charcoal grill? Baked flounder? Trout fillets in butter?" She shook her head in pity.

Toby was turning pages rapidly, absorbing the information in the book. Sooly glanced toward the storage tanks. Six of them. The largest one had the light on it. "Very nice," Toby said. "I'd like a while to finish it, if I may."

"Sure."

"If you need it, it'll take just a few minutes."

"You're kidding." It was a big book. Toby saw his mistake. "You can keep it. I'll pick it up in a few days or you can bring it, if you like." Now why did she say that?

"You're very kind," Toby said. "Perhaps I can return the favor. If your dog gets sick again—" He was on dangerous ground. There was something about the woman which made him want to please.

"I thought you didn't have any more of that stuff," Sooly said.

"Perhaps I can get some more."

"Sure," she said. "Well, I've got to run."

He walked with her. She looked up at the tanks, counting. Six. He saw her lips move and her fingers move as she counted. "What are you doing?"

"Nothing," she laughed. She turned her face to him. She was, he thought, very attractive, although her eyes were too small. She laughed again. "If you must know, I was counting the tanks."

"Oh?" Toby dared not say more.

"Sometimes there are seven," Sooly said.

"Oh, no," Toby said quickly.

"They're smart. They park between the two big tanks so you can't tell there's anything there unless you look good."

"They?" Toby asked, his heart pounding.

"The aliens," Sooly said, smiling to show that she was half-joking. "Didn't you know that this is a Flying Saucer Camp?"

"It's just an abandoned fish rendering plant," Toby said, his face flushing. "We're—"

"You think I'm crazy," Sooly said. "Don't mind me. I see flying saucers."

Toby felt as if he wanted to run away and report. He paused, standing near the corner of the big building. Inside the power plants hummed and the extractor whined. "I have to go in now," he said.

"Why?" Sooly asked, annoyed. "Is your mama calling?"

"Thank you for the book," he said. "But I don't think I need it after all." He extended the book.

"Don't be silly," Sooly said. "Keep it." She walked away without looking back. She wanted to look back, because she found Toby to be a very attractive man. She felt guilty about that, and about her secret thoughts, as she drove to Ocean City to admire Bud's catch of fish.

6

The vehicle came in just after midnight and Toby supervised the onloading of the raw material. He was nervous. He'd known there was something wrong when the vehicle landed and Manto Babra Larkton stepped out, dressed in full *Entil* colors. He snapped to attention with Jay and saluted. He was left alone to do the loading while the Manto and Jay held a conference out of his hearing distance. The job done, the vehicle's hold filled with the first products of the extraction process, Toby stood at ease beside the vehicle, waiting.

"Bakron Wellti," the Manto said, striding to him, finished with whatever she'd been saying to Toby's immediate superior, who followed, his eyes bulging, his breathing showing his agitation. "Three times in the past week our instruments have shown the coordinates of the local reference point and the base to coincide. Koptol Gagi can shed no light on this novel situation." Jay shifted on his feet at the mention of his name.

"Lady," Toby said. "Nor can I."

"Yet the Koptol says there have been three incidents of intrusion by native life forms," Babra said.

"Yes, Lady," Toby said. "There have been four incidents, counting the close approach of a native male in a boat."

"And the others?"

"A female, Lady. Twice with two young ones. Once alone. May I ask what this has to do with movement of the local reference point?"

"The local reference point is female," the Manto said. "I know that navigation and shipment is not your field, so I will explain. You're aware that the surprisingly high state of communications science achieved by the Ortonians has made the use of standard navigational and shipping signals impossible?"

"I understand that, Lady," Toby said. "Such signals would be subject to detection by the natives."

"As a result, we selected an alternate method, the monitoring of an individual life emanation," Babra said. "And you know that emanations are subject to change with emotions."

"I've done no work in that field, Lady," Toby said, "but in school I had an indoctrination course. Strong emotions give strong emanations. Pain, anger, fear, love. Yet, as you say, these emotions are subject to rapid and decisive change."

"It was necessary," Babra said, "to find a steady emanation associated with an individual whose day to day activities would not take her beyond useful range. We found that emanation in a local female." She smiled. "You're aware, of course, that female emanations are more powerful?"

"Yes, Lady," Toby said.

"We monitor this emanation constantly. The fact that it moved onto the base, itself, has caused some concern. I am led to believe that you have met the source of this emanation three times. Tell me about her."

"She's quite young," Toby said. "Yet she has a mature body. Except for the smallness of her eyes she is quite attractive. She can be contentious at times, Lady. I had to become quite forceful, in fact, to get her to leave the grounds the first time she appeared."

"And the reasons for her intrusion?"

He told her. He left out nothing. A good man does not try to cover up his mistakes, and he realized now that his having accepted the book from the Orton woman was, indeed, a misjudgment. He stood prepared to take his punishment.

Instead, when he was finished, the Manto smiled. "You have done nothing wrong, Bakron," she said. "I would suggest as little contact as possible in the future. Do not encourage this Orton woman to visit the base, but if she does, be courteous and make her stay as short as possible. Since you're going to be here for some months yet, it will be impossible for you to avoid all contact. Indeed, minimum contact with the local populace should help to divert suspicion. You must convince them that you're human." She smiled again. "You may return the woman's book."

"Thank you, Lady."

"And now there is time," Babra said, the aura of authority suddenly replaced by a softness which caused visceral stirrings in Toby, "for me to spend some time with you in your quarters, if you like." An opting was never an order. Even ratings had freedom of choice.

"Lady," Toby said, pleased and feeling a growing excitement.

"I know it must be lonely for you down here all alone," Babra said, taking

Toby's arm and pressing her warm breast against his shoulder, "and I would welcome an opportunity to talk with you about your work with the Orton animal life. As a descendant of the great Mari Wellti, I'm sure you've reached some interesting conclusions regarding this zoo." She used the Orton word, since there was no comparable word in the Ankani language.

There was talk. It lasted until just before dawn, when Manto Babra Larkton boarded the laden vehicle for the short blink back to the *Entil*. But first, in the darkness of the little room, with Babra's eyes glowing softly—those huge, lovely eyes which took up a full third of her face—there was sweetness and fulfillment and then later talk, and once more before the dawn with Babra soft and clinging and wonderful, a true Ankani woman, beautiful as only an Ankani woman could be, as beautiful as and younger than the Garge herself.

Bakron Toby Wellti was a happy, sleepy man as he watched the seventh storage tank rise slightly and blink out of the space between the two large, odorous fishoil storage tanks. The *Entil* was a good ship with officers who were genuinely concerned with the well-being of its crew. And Babra Larkton was as much woman as he would ever want. He stood in the coolness of the dawn and counted his blessings. Even without the briefing he'd received, even without the stern injunctions against opting with the Orton females, he would never have been tempted to such an animal act. Even if, as in the dim past, the tanker had been crewed by men alone, even after haunting months of loneliness without women, he would never fall victim to such debasement. It was inconceivable to him to think that Ankani men had done such things. For Ortonian life was sub-human. This basic fact was part of every text he'd read in preparation for his first great blink out to the mineral-producing worlds. And in spite of the surprises, in spite of the advanced state of Ortonian technology, in spite of the very human impression given by the Ortonians, especially the males, whose eyes were not really much smaller than those of the average Ankani male, the Ortonians were still sub-human. They ate animal meat. They killed. Their history was only a continuation of the horrors cataloged by the scientists of Ankan from the early days of discovery, when Ortonians fought and killed with rocks, sticks, crude spears, bow and arrow. Even the female of them were using for the emanation had killed. She'd dispatched dozens of blue crabs. He deduced this, since the crabs had been carried away in a bucket, still alive, but it was known that the Ortonians ate the repulsive creatures, and to take them as food required killing, since not even savages could manage to eat scratching, pinching, hissing crabs alive.

Logically, however, it was difficult to dismiss the advances made by the Ortonians. They were in near space in crude, chemical rockets. Their electronic technology was reaching toward some very complicated things. There were, as revealed in the books, scholars among them who had come up with some surprising answers. The emanation female's knowledge of local wildlife proved that even the most ordinary Ortonian had learning capacity. His ancestor, Mari Wellti, a true genius, had postulated a strange concept, a process of natural selection which gradually improved the strains of Ortonian life. He couldn't quite swallow that, for the basic form of Ankani life hadn't changed over a history which reached back 500,000 years. However, he could not completely close his mind to it, for there were strange things in the universe and no one had made a thorough study of Mari Wellti's theory. Take one thing, that furnace of a sun up there, unbelievably close, tossing deadly particles around and through all living things on the planet. Who knew what effects would show in the life forms over the millennia as a result of that particle spray?

"One down," Jay said, coming up behind him. "How many to go?" He answered his own question. "Too many. How I'd like to be off this hell-hole of a planet."

They walked together toward the extraction shed. Toby's mind was on the Orton woman. "Jay," he asked, "what is the nature of the emanation we're using for a blink reference?"

"You wouldn't believe it," Jay said, chuckling. "It's too wild."

"Tell me."

"Suppressed passion," Jay said, with a disbelieving shrug. "The Orton woman has never opted."

7

John Kurt eased his boat atop the roil of water over the discharge pipe and dipped up a jar of the fluid. Holding it up, he squinted and shook his head. He'd never seen anything like it. Obviously, water was being pumped into the old fish plant through one pipe and being discharged in much the same quantity through the other. Unless there were some very large storage tanks inside, the process, whatever it was, was almost instantaneous. And the water coming out into the blackness of the polluted Waterway was as clear and green as any water you'd find forty miles off shore.

He took several samples. He labeled each and put them in a box of straw to protect them from breakage. The fish plant was as deserted-looking as ever. Neither of the two men he knew worked there was visible. He didn't know a lot about machinery, but somewhere up there one damned big pump was working and no one, apparently, was watching it. He didn't dwell on the problem overly long. He was an outdoor man and his knowledge of things modern didn't go far beyond being an avid fan of the moon trips when they were televised. He could do emergency repair on an outboard motor, but he wasn't qualified to speculate on what sort of equipment it would require to pump that much water out of the dirty canal, clean it and pump it back.

John motored back to the Yacht Basin, the wind in his face, at peace with his world. He sent his carefully-packed samples to the laboratory in the state capital by bus that afternoon, and they were tested the next day. Tests showed, in the dark samples of Waterway water, the usual rich mixture of human excreta, lead, industrial solvents, agricultural insecticides and fertilizer, a trace of radiation from the atomic power plant upstream and the usual amount of coliform organisms which, when present in sufficient quantities, indicate the probably sure presence of such goodies as *Salmonella typhosa,* which killed three people and caused 1,497 known cases of gastroenteritis in Riverside, California in 1965. On the other hand, the sample dipped from the clear water coming out of the discharge pipe showed no coliform organisms at all, no organic pollutants in any form, causing a technician to wonder why he couldn't find a hole of water that clean when he went to the beach to pick oysters and dig clams.

Because a local resident of some influence had raised the question, a report on the product of the old rendering plant went to the head of the department and a letter was sent to the mayor of Big Piney Beach to the effect that there would be room in the world for more of the type of pollution put out by the rendering plant. The department head made a mental note to find out what it was they were doing to make water so clean down there in Ocean County, but he was late for a golf date, had a par on the first hole, a bogey on the tough par-five on the back side, a birdie on the seventeenth (on which he won four dollars and fifty cents) and two martinis at the nineteenth.

It was left up to the Squire to ask several days later, "They got a permit to dump that stuff in the canal?"

"Squire," John Kurt said patiently, "they're not dumping anything. They're putting in clean water."

"You put anything into public waters, you gotta have a permit," the Squire insisted, still smarting over the loss of those fifty acres on the waterfront. "How come I have to tell you your job?"

Later that day John found himself confronting the two workers at the plant. "You see," he explained to Jay and Toby, "it's necessary to have a permit from the department before you can dump anything, even clean water, into the Waterway." Being a good citizen, the Squire had insisted on coming with him.

"Tell 'em they'd better shut down," the Squire said.

"I don't think that will be necessary," John explained patiently. "The permit is rather routine and since they're not polluting—"

"I know my rights," the Squire overrode him. "No permit, no dumping. Tell 'em to shut down."

"Come on, Squire," John said.

"It would be impossible to shut down," Jay protested. "We would fall behind schedule."

"You shut 'em down," the Squire repeated, "or I get an injunction against all of you. Man works hard all his life and gets persecuted for paying his taxes like a good citizen, he doesn't take kindly to seeing the law broken."

"Squire," John said, "they'll be able to operate as soon as a permit is issued anyhow. Let's not make trouble for them."

"You don't know what trouble is, boy," the Squire said, turning away.

"All right, dammit," John said to him. Then he turned to the two men. "Look, you see how it is. I'm afraid I'll have to ask you to shut down until we can get this ironed out."

Jay's breathing increased in tempo. "How long will it take?" Toby, who was also anxious, asked.

"I have forms at home," John said. "If you can fill them out today and get them in the mail, it'll take about three days, I'd say." Jay looked as though he might explode.

"How may I get the forms?" Toby asked.

"Well, why don't you run over with me now and pick them up?" John asked. Toby looked at Jay. Jay managed to nod without popping his eyes.

"I hope you're that damned reluctant to help next time some nut complains about my garbage dump," the Squire grumbled.

"I will turn off the power," Toby said. He entered the building. John tried to get a peek, but Toby closed the door quickly. Jay drifted away, looking unhappy.

"I understand my daughter has turned you on to birdwatching," John said, when Toby came out.

"Ah, she's your daughter?"

"Sooly. Yeah. That's her."

"I wonder if you would give me a minute? I've finished with the book she loaned me and this would be a good opportunity to return it."

Sooly was all set to cook dinner when John escorted Toby into the house. "Well, hi," she said gaily. "You're just in time for chow."

"That's kind of you," Toby said, "but it is not yet my meal time."

Sooly grinned. "Quick meal," she said. "We're having crisp fatty animal tissue, unfertilized fowl embryo, liquid mammary gland secretions of an animal, and the congealed fat from that same liquid atop cooked, ground plant seeds."

"Bacon, eggs, milk and buttered toast," John said. "Again?"

"He's a vegetarian," Sooly said, smiling at Toby. "I can whop up a nice salad."

"I have returned your book," Toby said.

"Ignore the teeny-bopper and come on into the den," John said. "I'll get the forms." Sooly followed them in and enjoyed Toby's interested look when he spotted the bookcase. It was six feet wide and the height of the wall and was stuffed with her mother's art books, a set of the Britannica, all of the books of John D. MacDonald, some old goodies handed down from Sooly's grandfather and assorted Book-of-the-Month novels.

"Since you're here," John said, "why don't you help Toby fill in this form?"

"Sure," Sooly said, seating herself at the desk behind the battered old typewriter. She took the forms from her father's hand and inserted the top one in the machine. The form was a simple one. She learned only two things, the name of the company for which Toby worked, uninteresting, and the purpose of the company, rather interesting. "What does your company produce?" she asked.

"We are operating an experimental desalinization process," Toby said.

"D-e-s-a-l-i-n-e-i-z-a-t-i-o-n," Sooly spelled carefully, still spelling it wrong. "What are you producing then, fresh water?"

"Ah, no," Toby said. "We're extracting a certain mineral."

"It says, what does your company produce," Sooly said. "I guess we'll have to put down what you're extracting."

"You call it lithium," Toby said.

"What do you call it?" Sooly asked, looking at him.

"Lithium," Toby said, recovering quickly.

"Sign here as an official company representative," Sooly said. "Like to see the nest of the new baby cardinals in the back yard?"

"I should get back," Toby said.

"Sooly doesn't get a good-looking man cornered often," John said. "You won't get away so easily."

"Right," Sooly said, coming from behind the desk to take Toby's arm in a natural feminine gesture. "Besides, you can't go until I tell Daddy to take you, can you?"

"There is a certain logic there," Toby said, trying to hide the pleasure he felt from her womanly touch.

Beth Kurt stood at the sliding door in the living room and watched Sooly and Toby studying the cardinals as they fed their young. "My, he's a nice-looking boy."

"Now mother," John said. "Just because you don't want your only daughter to marry a poor fisherman, don't start matchmaking. The kid's from up north somewhere. How'd you like for Sooly to marry a damyankee and have to go four hundred miles to visit her?"

"I'd love it," Beth said. "If he's from New York."

8

The last mail truck of the day left Ocean City at 4:00. John had to stand on the back deck and yell at Sooly to remind her that Toby's letter was important. John enclosed a note explaining the need for an immediate ruling. He recommended a permit without further investigation. He had no way of knowing that the Squire was also writing a letter, protesting what he called a biased attitude on the part of the local representative of the department. Both letters arrived at the desk of the department director in the morning mail and resulted in a call to John with instructions to make a more thorough investigation.

"All they're putting into the canal is clean water, chief," John protested.

"What are they doing with the crud they remove from it?" the director wanted to know. "The canal water you sent has a bacteria count just slightly lower than Lake Erie's with a couple of lumps of raw sewage not even broken down yet. If they're moving as much water as you say they are, they're building up a pile of stuff."

"Chief," John said, "would it be pollution if they're doing nothing more than putting back into the Waterway what they took out?"

"We're not concerned with what they take out," the director said, "although we're getting into a question of water usage from a federal waterway without official permission, but once they take it out it becomes their responsibility. Find out what they're doing with the crud."

But before that happened, before the letters arrived and before John got his instructions via telephone, Sooly and Toby went into Ocean City to mail a letter. Bem begged and was allowed to go, taking her favorite place in the luggage space behind the seat. Sooly, sensitive to the gossipy tendency of the locals, stopped up the road and loaded Bill and Anne into the back seat to act as chaperones. She was, after all, an engaged girl and she didn't think it wise to be seen riding around alone with a good-looking cat like Toby.

The ride into town was noisy. Conversation consisted mostly of Sooly's answers to a million questions. Toby came in for a few questions, himself. He was asked, for example, if he used curlers on his hair. He found the young ones to be interesting and rather delightful. It was an entirely new experience to be exposed to the frantically jumping minds of children. He had one bad moment as the yellow-flowered Volks passed the base and Bill began to count, "One, two, three," ending at six. "Only six, Sooly," Bill said.

"They only come at night," Sooly said.

Toby was reminded of the ticklish fact that the Orton woman knew about the transport vehicle. He risked a question of his own. "Have you seen the flying saucers, too?"

"Oh, sure," Bill said.

"True," Anne seconded.

"We seen 'em two times with Sooly comin' home from the show," Bill said.

Toby made a mental note to do something about making his long overdue report about the Orton woman's knowledge. But he wasn't sure. Sooly treated the whole thing as if it were a huge joke. He was sure that others, hearing Sooly and the two young ones talk about flying saucers, would think it a game.

With the letter deposited in the outgoing slot at the P.O., Sooly took the scenic drive along the river to the Basin. "The charter boats will be in soon," she said. "If you're not in a hurry we'll stay and see what they caught."

"I have nothing to do," Toby said. It was true. With the power shut down there was nothing to do but report to Jay and, in truth, he was a bit pleased to delay his return to the lonely base. It wouldn't hurt Jay to stew and worry a bit.

Sooly had two motives—well, maybe three—in staying until Bud's boat rounded the point of Blue Water Beach, slipped inside the markers on a high tide to make the trip between the point and the Basin a bit quicker and backed and bounced off pilings into its slip. She was, as always, genuinely interested in Bud's catch. The more fish his charter parties caught, the quicker the word of his fish-finding ability would spread, the more charters he'd get, the more money he'd make and the sooner they could get married. Of course, she wanted to see Bud himself and, with an inward grin, she admitted to herself that she was not totally unaware of the nice picture she made standing beside blond, tall, powerfully-built Toby. She made it a point to look up into Toby's large, sensitive eyes just as Bud finished the docking process and looked at the reception committee. Toby, unaware of the female's intricate little ploy, smiled back at her. The effect was not lost on Bud.

"Who's the dude?" he asked, when he had a chance to speak to Sooly alone.

"A handsome stranger who is going to take me away," Sooly said. "Are you jealous?"

"I don't think my party would mind if you took your folks a fish," Bud said, lifting a 15-pound king mackerel and holding it in front of Sooly's eyes.

"That war movie is on at the show," Sooly said.

"Look, Sooly," Bud said, with a trace of irritation. "I was up at four o'clock. I've been bouncing around on the ocean for twelve hours." He realized that he was being harsh. He put a fishy hand on her arm. "Why don't you come by the house for awhile? We can pop some popcorn and watch t.v."

"Big deal," Sooly said. But she knew he was a tired fellow and he'd done a fine day's work. The fishbox was overflowing with fish and the fishermen were in good spirits. They would spread the word in their upstate home town about that young skipper who could find the mackerel down in Ocean City.

"That dude with you?" Bud asked, his eyes turning sideways to examine Toby.

"I was just helping him mail a letter," Sooly said, grabbing Anne with one hand on the fly as she almost fell into the Basin.

The director's call to John Kurt came next day and John announced that he was going over to the fish oil plant. "I'll ride with you," Sooly said. Beth Kurt looked at her husband with a tiny smile.

Jay had been locked up all day in his lab. Toby had finished his daily ration of books and was lying on his stomach on the ground observing a colony of small ants. He'd performed one chore. As junior rating he was handed all of the chicken stuff. His head was packed full of enough knowledge to give a small computer a run for its money on most problems, but he didn't have a computer at the base and balancing the checkbook had drained him. There'd been a surprising number of checks, most of them involving Jay's interest, the lab. Toby had seen the items coming in in small and large packages, but he hadn't realized that Jay had made such a variety of purchases. They ranged from pure chemicals to white rats. The latter interested him slightly, but Jay was very possessive and would not allow him into his lab to see the animals. He knew, by the increased supply of food being purchased, that the small animals were multiplying rapidly and he thought it rather selfish of Jay to keep them all to himself. He also thought it rather reckless of Jay to spend so much money on expensive items of equipment such as centrifuges and X-ray machines and an electron microscope. Some of the equipment could have been requested down from the ship, but it was no big matter. The relatively small amount of duplicated money put into circulation by the Ankani base would not affect the topsy-turvy economy of Orton, American division. In fact, from a shallow study of economics he'd undertaken, Toby judged that Jay was merely helping the government by spending the duplicated. When the economy slowed, the government manufactured money and put it into circulation by such artificial means as paying renegade street gangs to teach their skills to younger hoodlums, and by inflating the cost of a single primitive jet aircraft to 13.5 million units of American currency. So Jay was merely helping out by spending a few thousand artificial dollars. What he was doing in the lab was another question. Toby often wondered about that, but his hinted inquiries were ignored.

Ants were more interesting. In many ways they were like the Ortonians, coming in astronomical numbers, running around in every direction with a vast waste of energy and, in spite of their apparent aimlessness, accomplishing something. He was so engrossed in watching one small individual struggle with the amputated leg of a grasshopper that he didn't see Sooly and her father walk up the road.

Sooly thought it was nice to see a man so interested in important things like nature. She stood in the background while John explained the difficulty and saw Toby's worried look. "I'll have to consult the boss," he said.

He was back in a few minutes. Jay had not opened the door to the lab when he knocked, carrying on the conversation through the door. "They want to see the equipment," he told the Koptol.

"Show them then," Jay yelled.

"I think you'd better talk to them," Toby said.

"Tell them only what you've been told to tell them," Jay yelled. "You know that the equipment is made to seem to be of Ortonian origin. I'm busy."

"What we do," Toby said, inside the big shed, his nose full of the stench of long dead and rendered fish memory, but unable to don his mask because it was not of Ortonian design, "is pump water in here and pump it out there. This machine extracts lithium from the water. As you may know, lithium is one of the more plentiful elements dissolved in sea water, making up roughly seventeen parts in one million."

"What do you do with the crud?" John asked, following his instructions.

"The impurities?"

"You're taking out more than lithium," John said. "The lab said your discharge water is as pure as—" he started to say angel's piss, but remembered that Sooly was poking around nearby, "—as the cleanest water in the Antarctic Ocean."

"Well," Toby said, "the impurities get in the way. We merely filter them out here." The filter was a tiny machine mounted in line ahead of the extractor.

"Must be a very new process," John said.

"Quite new. Experimental, in fact." Toby had his cover story down pat. "Once we've proved the effectiveness of this technique, we'll market it."

He could not tell the rather pleasant Ortonian that, once the *Entil* was packed full of lithium, the parent corporation would report that the extraction method tried out on the Intracoastal Waterway in Ocean County was prohibitively expensive and the company would be dissolved.

"Once you filter out the crud, what do you do with it?" John asked.

"We burn it in this small hydrogen furnace," Toby said, indicating another small box.

"Hydrogen?" John frowned.

"Another innovation," Toby said. Actually, there was a small fury of hydrogen fusion going on inside the box.

"You're not making any radiation or anything?" John asked.

"Oh, no. Merely great heat. The crud, as you call it, is reduced to individual atoms and dispersed harmlessly into the atmosphere."

"Sounds like we could use one of those gadgets over at the Squire's garbage dump," John said.

"When will we be able to resume operation?" Toby asked. "It's quite important that we not fall behind schedule."

"I'll call the director tonight," John said.

"Daddy, couldn't you let them start again on your own authority?" Sooly asked. "You can see they're doing nothing wrong."

"Don't see why not," John said. "But if anything comes of it, I'll swear I told you to hold off until the permit comes from the state capital."

Toby threw switches and pushed buttons and looked at gauges and nodded in satisfaction as the accumulator gauge moved minutely. Outside, John shook his hand. Leaving, he turned. "My wife said invite you over for dinner since you're stuck out here without a woman's cooking."

"That's kind of you," Toby said non-committingly.

"I'll do an all-vegetable meal," Sooly said. "How about tomorrow night?"

"I—" He paused. "Yes, thank you." He was thinking of John Kurt's well-stuffed bookcase. He was, however, looking at Sooly in shorts, subconsciously comparing her with Manto Babra Larkton. He would not think such thoughts openly, but it was not unscientific to wonder about the intimate habits of these Ortonians who, on the surface, seemed so much like human beings.

9

"What do you do?" Sooly asked, "just look at the pictures?"

Toby looked up from the book guiltily and lied with what he hoped was a straight face. "I'll confess," he said. "I have a photographic memory."

"Hey, neat," Sooly said. "Can you teach me? Talk about groovy, I could do my homework in minutes and spend the rest of the time doing what I wanted to do."

"I think it's an inherited characteristic," Toby said.

"It would be."

John and Beth Kurt were in the living room watching t.v. Beth had herded Toby and Sooly into the den with a matchmaking obviousness which made Sooly snicker. Beth wanted Sooly to marry a rich man who could afford an apartment in New York where Beth could visit, or at least use the home of her daughter as headquarters while shopping in all the strange little stores in that fascinating flea market of a city. Toby had zoomed in on the bookcase immediately, but he was able to carry on a small-talk conversation with Sooly while reading. By chance, he started on a shelf of novels and was through *Gone With The Wind* and had started *War and Peace*.

"I feel sorry for you," Sooly said. "You'll never know the joy of being a sixteen-year-old girl reading *War and Peace* for the first time. Oh, God, the anger you feel when it seems that Natasha is going to run off with that horrible Anatole."

Toby, who was encountering the romantic idealism of Orton for the first time, had no answer. He was both fascinated and frightened by the premise that the abstract idea, love, could be confined to a one-on-one relationship. He was intrigued, in a visceral way, by the fantastic idea of having one woman for one man, of actually owning a woman. But there wasn't a woman he knew that he would like to spend a lifetime with. For one thing, he was always a bit intimidated by women. It wasn't a matter of questioning the innate superiority of women, no one did that. It was just that women were so different. Manto Babra Larkton, in charge of the education program on the blink out, had understood the complexities of alien contact thoroughly and, when it was discovered that Orton had leaped into the future, she'd been able to organize a new education program quickly, not even hesitating over the absolutely irrational aspects of Ortonian society. Deficit finance, complex moral codes, the ambiguity of the Ortonians in all matters—nothing surprised the Manto, and she could quickly explain why, for example, a crowded world which threatened to over-breed its food supply would spend much time and effort reversing nature's population-control methods by curing disease while killing in wars. The Manto had even explained why a nation such as the United States, engaged in a massive birth-control program, would give government grants to scientists who were trying to make babies in test tubes. She could also show great anger when the research team on the surface sent up reports that the Orton scientists were even making primitive efforts to penetrate to the very heart of life by experimenting with molecular surgery at the DNA level. Toby, who had learned earlier of the atomic experiments which were slowly poisoning the atmosphere and environment of the planet, was merely further saddened by this terrible revelation, and the additional knowledge of the perversions practiced by the Ortonians reinforced his feeling that the Ortonians were, indeed, sub-human.

And yet, there was a certain puzzling beauty in the stories. Was it because his orientation had pounded the language and the thinking of the Ortonians so deeply into his head? Was he being influenced by simply being among them?

He found himself being saddened when Scarlett blew her chance for happiness with Rhett and pleased when Natasha didn't run off with Anatole. And when he dipped into Beth Kurt's art books, he was moved almost to tears by the efforts of Orton's primitive artists. Some of the impressionists gave indication of discovering some of the techniques of the light artists on Ankan II and Paul Klee's amusing work pleased him, even if it was shown to him in a one-dimensional format.

He discovered a treasure trove of archeological books on the bottom shelf and thumbed through them rapidly, truly looking at the pictures, while Sooly talked about the joys of living in Ocean County as if she were a one-woman chamber of commerce. Toby knew, from previous study of the works of Ankani scientists, that the age-old Ankan technique of rock cutting had been used in various Orton civilizations, and he was very interested to note that the last Ankani expedition to Orton, although under the control of officers, had left its mark on the Mayans. Evidently there had been no forbidden activity, but someone had taught the Mayan rock masons how to fit stone with amazing precision. So there had been, at the very least, a bit of culture bleed-through from the Ankani presence. Not, however, enough to make the Mayan culture a long-lived one. It began to flower, Orton date, about 300 A.D., less than two centuries after the last Ankani visit, and died only a few hundred years later.

Sooly, getting restless and a bit put out by having to share Toby's attention with the books, stood, walked to look over his shoulder as he was enraptured by a two-page color photograph of the Mayan city of Uxmal, rising real and ruined from the green of the surrounding jungle with the soft gold of a late sun on its stone. After thumbing through three or four fine volumes which pictured the art, artifacts and ruins of past Ortonian civilizations, he was bemused by the inevitable comparison with the Wasted Worlds near the Center of the Galaxy.

"But what happened to them?" he asked softly.

"Someone zapped them," Sooly said. "They got fat and careless and someone hungrier came along."

"And where are they?" Toby asked, thinking of the people who wasted the thousand worlds of the old empire.

Sooly shrugged. "Who knows? Poor *Indios,* maybe. No one really knows."

Toby came out of his reverie. She, he realized, was speaking of the Mayans.

"They saw flying saucers too," Sooly said. "Sometimes I think I may be a Mayan reincarnated."

Toby was disturbed. He tried to pass it off. "Your nose isn't big enough," he said, pointing to a terra-cotta head of a Mayan woman.

"I don't ask you to believe that I see them," she said, "but why don't you keep your eyes open?"

"When do you see them?" Toby asked, slightly uncomfortable because of the sensitive subject.

"At night. Almost any time I go out."

"What do they look like?"

"Oh, it's usually just a light. It follows me. The other morning it followed me all the way to town."

"But I understand that you people—I mean that people have been seeing unexplained flying objects for years," Toby said.

"Sure. They saw them." She went to the bookcase and came back with a copy of Daniken's *Chariots of the Gods?* "Every primitive culture has its myths about white gods who came from the sky on wings of fire. The Mayans even drew a picture of a man in a spaceship." She showed him. The drawing was from a wall at the temple at Copan. It showed a Mayan in a small space capsule surrounded by fanciful whorls and kinks which could easily have been a primitive representation of machinery not understood by the artist. "And look," Sooly said, showing him pictures of unexplained concrete roads in Bolivia and strange, huge markings in the earth at Nazca, in Peru.

Toby's pulse increased. "May I read it?" he asked.

"Sure, take it with you."

He had himself transported aboard the next vehicle, which arrived to load the extracted lithium two days later. During the period of waiting he had read and reread Daniken's book and did some hurried research at the local library. He also had seen a white rat with teeth like an extinct saber-toothed tiger in the poisoned dirt of the base. The rat was attacking a rabbit with a ferocity which amazed Toby. He made a mental note to check his books, thinking, perhaps, that the rat was not a rat but a large species of shrew. Aboard the ship, he was escorted into Garge Cele Mantel's suite.

"Lady," he said, "I thought you should know that there is a small but surprisingly accurate body of knowledge on Orton about past Ankani expeditions." He proceeded to recite the pertinent facts. The most evident scars had been left by the last ship which extracted minerals on the continent called South America. Large markings remained, markings used to land mineral-carrying vehicles visually. There was evidence to indicate that Ankani aerial maps had fallen into the hands of Ortonians. Eighteenth century (Orton Time) maps showed features of the continents which would have been unknown with the state of the technology at that time. The Mayans and others had possessed knowledge of the stars which could have come only from a space traveler. The Baghdad Museum displayed the actual fragments of an Ankani electrical battery from some piece of field equipment, fragments left on Orton by one of the early expeditions. Even ancient cave drawings showed men in protective suits.

"The original research team reported such items," Cele said. "However, the team determined that reports of flying saucers and other phenomena came from a lunatic fringe and were largely discounted by those in authority."

"True, Lady," Toby said. "The Daniken book seems to have been accepted in the same spirit as earlier works, such as those of Charles Fort. However, I thought it worth note that the Ortonian had stumbled onto such convincing evidence."

"It was all taken into account," Cele said, telling the rating with her tone of voice that he was presuming to think that matters of such import could have been overlooked by officers. "In fact, because of the advances made on Orton since we were here last, we thought, at first, to find and make use of a deserted island in the western ocean. This was not done because of the irrational, warlike posture of the two major powers. Our scout teams learned that both powers keep all oceans patrolled. After much study, we decided that the safest course would be to locate our extraction plant inside the territory of the less paranoid of the two major countries." Paranoid was an Orton word, of course, there being no counterpart in Ankani. "Do you have reason to doubt the security of the base?"

"Lady," Toby said, suddenly ill at ease, "as you know, I have been extended permission to continue my studies in Orton history as influenced by Ankani expeditions."

"We tend to be lenient with crewmen in hardship posts," the Garge said.

"In my limited contact with the Ortonians, I have, as you know, met the source of the emanation used to guide the cargo vehicle."

"Yes, yes, make your point," Cele said impatiently.

"Our beam makes a visible glow while it is in use," Toby said. "The Orton female has seen it repeatedly. She calls it a flying saucer."

"She has talked with you about this?"

"She mentions it as if she, herself, does not quite believe it, but I have reason to believe that she has noticed our vehicle in place on the surface."

"Humm," Cele said. Toby stood patiently as she thought. "Does she tell others?"

"Her father treats it as a joke," Toby said.

"You may go," Cele said abruptly.

As Toby saluted and turned, she stopped him with a soft voice. "Since you're here, Bakron, an opting can be arranged if you like." She had, after all, done her duty with the bridge technician. It was not yet time to demonstrate her democracy again. Another officer would serve in this situation. "It must be lonely down there."

"Yes, Lady," Toby said. "Thank you for your consideration."

"Are you refusing, then?"

"I have not been opted, Lady," Toby said stiffly.

"It is because none of the officers know of your visit to the *Entil*."

"Still," Toby said stubbornly, "I have not been opted, Lady."

She let him leave. They had their pride, those men. So stiff and stubborn in their little minds. Any officer on the ship would have gladly done her duty, but he had to stand on tradition. Merely informing a few willing officers of his presence would, to him, have violated the opting code, making it seem that he was requesting. She sighed. That would mean a special trip to the base for some officer, when the necessary therapeutic kindness could have been performed in comfort abroad the *Entil*. There was just no explaining male logic.

10

"Filth," Cele Mantel said with tight lips.

"Isn't it terrible?" Babra Larkton agreed.

The Manto's full report was on Cele's desk and reading it had given Cele a sick feeling in the pit of her stomach. Those who had thought that war, violence and the killing of life forms, including their own, was the ultimate in Orton's sub-human degradation had a new experience coming.

"I hate to put you through this, Babra," Cele said, bending back as far from the offensive material as she could, "but I must, in all conscience, call a Board to consider this evidence."

"I understand, Lady," Babra said. "My reaction was the same. However, in going over it," she pointed a delicate hand toward the spread of report sheets and supporting material in the form of popular and scientific journals from

Orton, "I have developed a certain immunity to it. It's almost as if my mind has developed protective barriers against the filth."

"Then you won't mind handling the briefing?"

"Speaking of such things is always distasteful," Babra admitted, "but I agree that it is necessary."

The officers of the *Entil* were assembled in the conference room, made comfortable with the Ankani equivalent of tea and tasty cakes. "Ladies," Cele said, after everyone was seated and served by her personal service rating. "Please enjoy your tea, for once we've begun, I'm sure you won't be able to stomach anything." She waited until the rating had bowed and retreated through the soundproof door. The officers, enjoying the rare gathering, nibbled and sipped and laughed and passed friendly small talk.

Cele decided to use shock treatment. She projected the filmstrip which Babra's research team had obtained. On the screen there appeared a surprisingly human-like ovum under assault by sperm. A gasp went up from the gathered officers as the ovum was attacked by hundreds of thousands of sperm. The ovum glowed with the forces of life, a small sun which was soon tailed with sperm as the outer shell was penetrated. The sperm writhed furiously as a shocked silence fell in the room.

"The elapsed time is measured in Ortonian hours," Babra explained as numbers appeared on the lower left-hand corner of the screen. "We have left off the sound, because we see no reason to expose ladies to the crude comments of the so-called scientist doing the narration."

A sperm found access to the heart of the ovum. The heartless film rolled on to the end as the unsuccessful sperm died.

Lights went on. The officers shuffled their feet, did not look at each other.

"The title of this film," Babra said in her tight voice, "is *The Dance of Love*." She let this obscenity sink in. "And, of course, the fertilization took place on a microscope slide."

"Poor thing," someone breathed sadly.

"This is only the beginning," Babra went on. "Our studies have told us that the monsters engaged in this filth have already violated the basic law of life to the extent of growing embryos to an advanced stage outside a mother's womb. Other obscene experiments have been attempted. For example, one doctor has implanted a fertilized egg inside the womb of a subject."

"Don't they know?" asked a pale, young Larftontwo in a subdued voice.

"We will have a question and answer period after the Manto has concluded," Cele admonished.

"We have observed a total lack of sensible genetic practice on Orton," Babra said, "in spite of the surprisingly advanced state of their knowledge. For centuries they have possessed the ability to sterilize obviously faulty genetic sources and yet they have not developed the humanity needed to prevent the birth of damaged individuals. This simple solution, when it has been suggested, is met with rabid opposition. The simplest methods of birth control still face stiff opposition from organized culture groups and deluded individuals who pay lip service to the sanctity of what they call human life. And yet these same groups and individuals do nothing more than make mouthing noises when mad-men tamper with the sacred foundation of life. In addition to producing test tube babies, these Ortonians aspire to changing the very form of life by doing what they call molecular surgery on the molecules which direct the manufacture of proteins, the building blocks of life."

There were uneasy coughs, shufflings.

"One so-called scientist has suggested that through such genetic control, they breed men without legs to man their spaceships." Babra paused to let it sink in. "There is talk of creating a race of supermen by genetic engineering."

"We must kill them," said a motherly Larftonfour.

"Please," Cele said.

"We must not judge the Ortonians without taking all the circumstances into account," Babra said. "Remember that our earlier expeditions, all male ex-peditions, naturally, had quite serious impact on the native lifemode. You have all made a study of the reports by the ship's behavioral scientist on the occasion of the last ore-gathering trip to this planet. At that time it was concluded that, although there were definite cultural crossovers caused by the ill-considered ac-tions of Ankani crewmen, the effects were not overly serious. Then we come, a mere two thousand years later, and discover some rather amazing things. I think there will be some revision in social theory after we get home. The theory that a complex technological culture cannot be passed along to sub-humans, for ex-ample, is in great doubt in my mind. How else do we explain such a quick leap to atomics, a rapidly developing sub-space technology and the even more sur-prising advances into forbidden fields in medicine?"

Babra paused and sipped at her tea. "The Ortonians moved into immuniza-tion theory over a hundred years ago and are, at present, making great strides into viral immunology. This work has led them to the threshold of a complete knowl-edge of the forbidden science of molecular biology, as they call it. Without know-ing the dangers, they are moving ahead, creating primitive protein strands in test tubes. They have the hardware available at this moment to begin the experiments in creating artificial life, growing monsters outside of the womb, making alter-ations in the basic form of life itself. One scientist has, while performing brain surgery, discovered a crude method of stimulating chemically stored memory. This discovery has led to great excitement and some men are talking about being able to implant stored knowledge into a new brain. Because a certain species of worm can pass chemically stored memory to other worms through the simple process of being eaten, these Ortonians joke about saving the stored knowledge of a brilliant man by allowing his students to eat him." She laughed bitterly. "They don't know how close they are to the truth. And, I assure you, our studies have shown that these sub-humans would, if and when they are allowed to discover the techniques, enter into even this unthinkable perversion."

She had her audience spellbound. The faces of the officers were uniformly grim and disbelieving. A few of the younger officers were pale. One had her hand in front of her mouth as if to hold in her sick revulsion.

"It is a recognized maxim that advances in one field of knowledge lead to advances in another. Thus, their approach to forbidden fields is matched by advances in hard technology. They are so close to blink theory that our team would not, at first, credit its findings."

"I think I can illustrate that point," Cele Mantel said. "Ortonian man has existed much in his present form, with certain recognizable outside influences," she smiled wryly, "for some five hundred thousand years. If we compress this into a more easily grasped period of fifty years, the Ortonians were nomadic hunters for forty-nine years. It took him forty-nine years to learn how to plant crops and settle into small villages. This date, incidentally, coincides roughly with discovery of Orton and the first extraction expeditions, leading us to believe that it was Ankani influence which triggered the basic change in the Ortonian nature. After forty-nine and a half years, he discovered writing. He practiced this art in a small area of his world, the area in which our extraction teams worked. Carrying on this analogy, the first great civilization was built up only months ago. For example, the civilization which seems to impress the Ortonians most, the people called the Greeks, flowered three months ago. Their Christian God, Jesus Christ, was on the cross two months ago. Two weeks ago the first Ortonian book was printed. A week ago, they began to use the steam power. And at 11:59 p.m. on December 31st of the fiftieth year their present age of technology began. Consider this. Their knowledge is increasing at an ever-increasing rate. They've gone from animal transportation to primitive space rockets in one week of our relative time, or in less than two hundred of their years. We can only assume that their fumbling approach to blink theory will put them into sub-space within fifty to a hundred years, at about the same time they develop the knowledge which will enable them to re-engineer their life form through genetic meddling." She paused for emphasis. "We could be facing a race of supermonsters within a hundred years, a race with a history of incredible violence."

"And if they fail to learn the dangers of their so-called molecular biology, our peaceful Ankani worlds would be subjected to the tender ministrations of a superrace of madmen," Babra said.

"We are now open to discussion," Cele said.

"It is written," said the motherly Larftonfour who had given vent to a previous impetuous suggestion to kill the Ortonians. "The penalty is death."

"For whom?" Cele asked. "Those who are working in the forbidden field? The governments who permit it? The people who condone it?"

"We cannot ignore the foundations upon which the Ankani race has built," the Larftonfour said. "Whatever it takes, we must do it."

"Could we contact them?" asked a young officer. "Couldn't we warn them of their danger and persuade them to stop their work in the forbidden fields?"

"We are prohibited from contact," Cele said. "The penalty for contact and the passing of knowledge is not quite as severe as that for genetic meddling, but I, for one, have no desire to spend the rest of my life in the dark mines of Asmari."

"The Larftonfour is right," said a senior officer in the nutrition section, "even if it means wiping the planet clean of life."

"True," Cele said, "the easiest solution would be to kill the planet. This, however, seems rather drastic to me. Orton is unique. Many of you have served

on the expos. You know the emptiness of the Galaxy. You know the disappointment of approaching a likely planet to find that life consists of vegetable
matters and primitive organisms. In all the explored Galaxy, Orton is the only
planet which shares that strange and beautiful wonder which we call life. Can
we destroy this so lightly?"

"No," Babra said. There were other negative answers.

"We have limited choices," Cele said. "We can do nothing, complete our
mission and file a complete report with Fleet Board upon our return. Or, we can
take matters into our own hands and sterilize the planet. We do not have the
power to weed out the offenders selectively. This would be a work of years and
would entail not only punishing the active offenders, but cleaning away all
traces of knowledge pertaining to the forbidden field. Even if we could accomplish this task, it would be useless, for the state of Orton technology would lead
them inevitably back to the same point so that we would be faced with having
to perform a distasteful purge every few decades. The third choice is to send a
blink message home, giving as many details as possible, leaving the decision to
the Fleet Board and the Council under Unogarge Clarke. This choice, too, has
its drawbacks. Many of the people in the political arena have not seen Orton and
are unfamiliar with its unique and beautiful position in the scheme of things.
What would you do if you were sitting in the council chamber and were told
that sub-humans on a distant planet were committing the ultimate sin and in
doing it posing a definite threat to the home worlds?"

"I'd probably say kill them," Babra answered.

"Exactly," Cele said. "And that is distasteful to me."

"So we wait, then?" Babra asked.

"I don't know," Cele said. "If we wait and present our views before the
Board and the Council, that will take time. What if the Ortonians made an unexpected breakthrough and upon our return to carry out the decision of the
Council we found them in sub-space? A mastery of blink theory produces an
ability to make the very weapons with which we arm our expo ships. We arm
our ships for the sole purpose of self-defense. Our knowledge of the Ortonians
tells us that they would arm their ships. In fact, my guess would be that the first
blink ship launched would be a ship of the line, armed to the teeth and capable
of inflicting casualties on any ship we might send."

"A disturbing possibility," Babra agreed.

Cele stood. Her large, soft eyes glowed with life. "As you know, the purpose of a Ship's Board is merely advisory. The Garge bears the responsibility
for the final decision. Your views will be taken into account. We will vote now.
For the first solution, sterilization of the planet."

There was one hand.

"For waiting and presenting the facts to the Fleet Board in person, taking
the risks such a course would entail."

Two hands.

"I will inform you of my decision," Cele said, leaving the room quickly.
She was composing the message to Fleet in her mind. There had never been any
question, really. She had merely gone through the formalities. Most junior offi-

cers never had an opportunity to sit on a Ship's Board and she had not wanted to deprive her officers of the opportunity.

11

The saber-toothed rat attacked Toby as he stepped out of his quarters at the base and before he could dispatch it with a handy short length of pipe he was bitten severely on the left calf and ankle. He left the dead rat on the bare earth and hurried to the medical kit to sterilize the wounds and apply the healing rays from the compact little gun-like mechanism which drew its power from the batteries of the kit. The process took over an hour. When he went outside, the dead rat was gone, carried off, he presumed, by some carrion-eating animal or bird.

He spent a long afternoon hour looking through his books in an effort to identify the vicious little animal. That he was unsuccessful did not puzzle him. His library was incomplete. Often the descriptions and drawings of Orton life forms seemed so unlike the actual living animals and birds that identification was, at best, tentative.

The extractor was working steadily and the quantity of stored lithium was sufficient to warrant a blink down by the transport vehicle. Toby made ready for the nighttime visit. Jay was taking less and less interest in the mission, leaving the work to Toby. This suited Toby. Jay had never been a pleasant companion and his absorption with his lab projects seemed to make him even more surly and withdrawn.

Toby had been on the surface for two months. He had an even longer period ahead of him. On any other ore-producing planet he would have been bored stiff. Orton was another matter. He had his engrossing interest in observing the planet's wildlife. He had his books and the ever more fascinating study of Ankani influence on Orton. When the transport vehicle grew into the space between the two large tanks and disgorged two females, he had something else— a gnawing guilt. For reasons hidden in his secret mind, he was not enthusiastic; and he could never admit to the pretty, blond young Larfton that he was not suffering from missing his regular rotation in shipboard opting. However, he was a healthy young male and he soon regained his interest. Jay disappeared into his quarters with a motherly Larftonfour near his own age and Toby buried his guilt and committed himself with abandon to the enthusiastic blond Larfton who was making her first trip to the surface. Opting, as a universal Ankani art form, was raised to new heights as the pumps loaded the transport vehicle. It was a giggling, sated Larfton who boarded the vehicle in the early morning hours, leaning on the supporting arm of the motherly senior officer.

Toby yawned. Life was, indeed, good. His performance left no reason for suspicion in the mind of the officer. She had indicated that she would ask for the duty of the next visit to the base, a sincere compliment. Toby was reassured. For a few silly moments he had felt that she could not help but realize. The vehicle blinked. So far the new procedure had not been detected by the Ortonians. The ship sent a brief burst of communication on a tight beam and in that one instant the instruments in the vehicle locked on and blinked. The technicians on-board the *Entil* were looking for a new emanation, but pending its finding Toby had sent a brief burst for guidance. A quick study had revealed that the particular section of the coast in which the base was located was not under constant monitoring from the defense forces of the United States. In fact, quite often a jet aircraft would practice a sneak approach, flying low up the Intracoastal Waterway to see how near it could get to military installation up the coast before detection, so evidently the base was located in a blind spot. And if another local emanation was not found, the system of brief bursts of guidance beams could be used with impunity.

Jay went tiredly off to bed leaving Toby gazing up at the sky. He had studied the Ortonian star books and could identify the constellations by local name. He mused, as he let his eyes rove over the blinking stars, about those first Ankani crewmen who visited Orton. If anything, Ankani influence on Orton had been underestimated, for Ortonian mythology, as related to their fanciful namings of the stars, showed many links with the Ankani language and Ankan's own history. He felt a warm kinship with those old tankermen who plied the starways alone, without the comfort of women.

He fell into his bed numb with a pleasant fatigue and awoke with difficulty when he heard the screams of agony coming from the building which housed Jay's lab.

What he heard was the death screams of the Squire.

What he discovered when he pushed into the lab behind Jay, ignoring Jay's protests, outraged his moral sensibilities, posed a problem larger and more difficult than anything he'd ever faced, and left him helpless.

The Squire came to the base by a series of coincidences based on the fact that a stationary front was sitting along the coast bringing a night of hushed stillness. The position of the moon also contributed to the Squire's demise by making a low and rising tide match the windless night to create ideal conditions for flounder gigging. Being a sensible man with a dollar, the Squire did little sports fishing. If a man ran a boat out to the shoals and burned eighteen gallons of gas, he paid dearly for the few pounds of fish fillets he gathered—if his luck ran good. The Squire figured that every pound of fish he'd ever caught sports fishing cost him roughly five dollars. On the other hand, flounder gigging from a small skiff cost nothing except the pennies it took to burn a Coleman lantern. It was also good exercise to pole a skiff along the banks of the Waterway and into the creeks of the marsh; and the Squire, while wanting to maintain his reputation as a problem drinker, was secretly concerned with his growing paunch. So a windless night and the right tide sent the Squire, a loner who didn't want to have to split his flounder with anyone, poling on through the night chortling with glee as he stuck a rusty tri-barbed gig into the eyeballs of flat, foolish flounder lying in the mud waiting for minnows. Gigging was so successful he was sure he was going to have enough fish not only to stock his freezer, but to sell a few pounds and make a dollar in addition to getting all that free fish.

He poled until the water had run in so deep the good banks were overrun by the rising tide and then he started home, tired, happy and smug with his success. As it happened, he was on the side of the Waterway next to the old rendering plant and the place was dark, although the pumps were working and his skiff danced as he poled it over the uprushing water coming out of the outlet pipe. He rested holding the skiff alongside the dock and thought about that smart-ass, John Kurt, and the fact that a citizen who paid his taxes didn't have a chance against the big boys like the Yankee owner of the rendering plant and its prime fifty acres of waterfront land. He'd been informed by letter that the Department of Conservation and Development saw no reason not to give the new owners a permit to run their experimental desalinization plant, but he smelled a rat in the woodwork somewhere. It didn't seem reasonable to think that some rich Yankee would go to a lot of trouble just to put clean water back into the Waterway.

It didn't take the Squire long to decide that it was the duty of a good citizen to look into the matter and with everyone asleep he had an opportunity. He carried a pocket flashlight, having tied the skiff securely, up to the big shed and tried the door. It was locked. He could hear the machinery running inside and this seemed nefarious to him. Why were the Yankee bastards running night and day if they weren't up to no good? He prowled and heard a snore coming from the first house, steered away from it lest he wake the two bastards.

Standing with his ear to the window of the second house, he decided that it was his duty to investigate the noises coming from inside. They were not human noises.

"Now look," he told himself, forming the words silently. "If those bastards are just taking salt out of the water why are they dumping the water back in the Waterway?

"Maybe they're taking valuable minerals out," he told himself. "Like gold."

And if some outfit had found a way to take gold out of the ocean he wanted a piece of it. He played around with the market a bit.

But it was not for personal gain that the Squire tried window after window and finally found one with a broken latch at the back of the old house. The noises from inside were suspicious as hell, like a zoo. Bunch of vivisectionists, maybe?

He was inside and he felt something run across his foot and shined his light down and saw the disappearing tail of a white rat and then he was sure that the damned Yankees were breeding rats to spread the plague. A rotten Commie plot?

Cage after cage was lined up along the walls of a room. The Squire was about to shine his light inside one when he saw an astounding thing. He heard movement and turned his light away from the cage. There, lined up in formation facing him, were what seemed a million white rats with pink eyes and teeth as long as daggers. He stifled a scream. He heard a movement near his side and turned with his light and saw a rat scale the wire front of a cage. Hanging by his rear feet, the rat used his forepaws and his teeth to pull the wooden plug out of a simple lock-latch. The Squire was frozen with astonishment. The rat finished pulling the plug and then he flipped the latch and from inside a dozen rats pushed and the cage door flung open and rats poured out, squeaking and click-ing their teeth and then the Squire felt fear. He turned to go. His way was blocked by another million rats lined up three-deep standing on their hind legs looking at him, eyes flashing pinkly in the beam of light. The Squire ran, kick-ing. He felt the rats on his feet and then their teeth were digging into his legs and he screamed and fell and they were on him like schools of four-legged, air-breathing piranha. The Squire beat at them with his light and rolled on top of them, crushing dozens of them. He kicked and struck out and the teeth were rip-ping, and when one dug into his cheek near his eye and stayed there as he beat at it with his empty hand his screams reached a crescendo of pain and horror.

"Get back!" Jay yelled. Bumping into Toby as he fell out the door, kick-ing at the rats which latched onto his feet and legs. The screams were fading away. Toby danced, dislodging clinging rats. Jay had a weapon in his hand, for-bidden for him to have here. Toby, at that stage of the game, with rats trying to climb his legs and succeeding in getting painful mouthfuls of tender flesh, was more than happy to see the blaster, even if it was forbidden. He danced and kicked and yelped as teeth got him and then the sizzling beam of the blaster began to fry the rats into little, steaming globs. The tenacity of the rats kept them close, so that none escaped as Jay sprayed the beam around in a continu-ous fury, picking off singles as Toby kicked them off his legs, then moving into the house to continue the slaughter.

It took a few minutes to clean out the front room, making sure that no an-imals escaped. In the back room, the fiery beam interrupted a grisly meal. When the last rat was beaten off the Squire's mutilated body and melted in the blaster beam, Jay pocketed his weapon, leaned over the body and cursed in a low voice. Toby was leaving bloody tracks as he walked. Jay faced him, his breathing spo-radic, his eyes bulging. "There will be no report," he said.

"I cite the Ratings Code of Ethics," Toby said.

"I cite this," Jay said, waving a tri-dee ecto-model camera in Toby's face.

"Koptol Gagi," Toby said, standing at attention with his own blood wet-ting his shoes. "I have reason to suspect that you have been engaging in for-bidden experiments. It is my duty—"

"And this?" Jay screamed. "Is this, too, duty?"

The ecto-model was embarrassingly intimate. Toby pictured Jay snaking through the bushes to snap it. "I must think."

Behind him, there was a movement. Jay moved quickly, pointing the blaster almost directly at Toby. Toby, thinking the Koptol had gone mad, leaped to one side in time to see, before it was dissolved in the blaster beam, a rat try-ing to free a group of its fellows from a cage by lifting the plug from a catch-latch on the last full cage.

"Their intelligent behavior is astounding," Jay gasped, having difficulty, still, with his breathing.

"Genetic engineering?" Toby asked.

"What harm, here on this sub-human planet?" the Koptol asked. "The re-strictions against it are unthinking and foolish."

"I suggest," Toby said, "that we neglect blasphemy and attend to our wounds. I think you could use a dose of *troleen*."

"In a moment," Jay said, turning the blaster on the Squire's body.

"Don't!" Toby yelled, but the body was shriveling and melting and soon there was only a blob, only slightly larger than the scattered remains of the rats. "You will clear the remains away," Jay ordered.

"Not on your life," Toby said firmly.

"That is an order."

"Insist on it, Koptol Gagi, and I will place an emergency call to the Garge even before I use the medical kit."

"Very well," Jay grumbled, leading the way to the other house.

While ministering to his wounds, Toby considered the situation. A man's sins do have a way of catching up with him. But, oh, sweet winds of Ankan, what a sin! And the event flashed back to him.

"There is a family of otters in the marsh below the Flying Saucer Camp," she'd said. "We can probably sneak up on them in the canoe."

They had—on a beautiful August day with the sun burning her bare shoulders into a more attractive shade of brown, with a soft southeast wind cooling them and a salt spray kicked up from the plowing prow of the canoe. She, knowing the intricate bends of the multiple creeks cutting the marsh, was at the stern, guiding the boat. Well into the marsh she killed the motor, elevated it out of the water and began to move the canoe silently and expertly with a paddle. He sat facing her. Her breasts moved with the motion of her arms, threatening to come out of the skimpy halter of her bathing suit. He'd known her for a few short weeks and she was not his equal. And yet, with the sun on her hair and the spray wet on her face, she was beautiful.

They found the otters and observed them from a safe distance with John Kurt's binoculars. They were lovely animals, antic, sleekly graceful. Then, after the otters had winded them and darted away into the protective marsh, there was a lazy boatride through the maze of creeks to a sandy beach on the rendering plant property. Toby didn't realize how close he was to the base, since the view was blocked by tall trees. There was a picnic lunch. Toby ate fowl eggs and cheese. He'd fallen victim to natural curiosity over the past days and the food of Orton, while barbaric, was good to his palate. She sat on a large beach towel, sharing it with him. They drank Pepsi and talked and she said, after all eternity had passed with a pleasant slowness, after having moved close to him and after having looked up into his large, gentle eyes, "Toby, what does it take to get you to kiss a girl?"

Toby had no idea how much agonized thought went into that simple question. He was beginning to understand a little bit of the Ortonian way of life. When John Kurt patted his wife on the fanny in a friendly, possessive way, he mused about it. No Ankani male would indulge in such a spontaneous gesture without invitation, but it was merely a small part of the rather interesting relationship between Ortonian males and females. Toby could not know the worry he'd caused Sooly, the nights of wakefulness, the feeling of painful sadness which came when she realized that she was no longer spending all her waking moments thinking of Bud. He would not, at that point, have been able to understand her tears and then her fear, for all the time she was falling out of love with Bud and falling in love with Toby he did nothing to indicate that his blue eyes even saw her as a girl. It was in an agony of unrequited love that she took him to the secluded, sandy beach, posed fetchingly for him all through the picnic lunch, made a special effort to put herself within reach of his arms. And it was in sheer desperation—she was on the verge of throwing away long years of her life and a lot of dreams by falling out of love with her childhood sweetheart—that she asked: "Toby, what does it take to get you to kiss a girl?"

She, on her part, had no way of knowing that it took a simple, unmistakable invitation. She had no way of knowing that such an invitation meant more than a kiss to Toby and that by issuing the invitation she unleashed the surprised, pleased and totally uninhibited talent of an expert who had 500,000 years of erotic knowledge at his disposal.

It was the most complete mismatch since David and Goliath. It was a complete rout. Nineteen years of proud morality sizzled into white heat. He had had an Ortonian sub-human.

"If I tell them why the emanation flicked out," Jay said, reading his thoughts and waking him from his reverie, "there'll be one more worker in the mines of Asmari." Jay lay under the healing rays.

"The penalty for genetic meddling is death," Toby countered.

"We both have much to lose," Jay said, fully recovered from his breathlessness after a dose of *troleen.*

"So it seems," Toby agreed.

"A pact of silence?" Jay offered.

"Let me see that ecto," Toby said, reaching out a hand. He studied it. She was there in miniature—round, almost warm to the touch, in a pose which, he found, came naturally when demonstrated by an expert. He remembered her cries of pain, her sobs of regret, her happy smile when he kissed away the tears. *He had owned a woman.* He could understand them fully now, those old tankermen. He could even understand why some of them jumped ship and stayed on Orton.

"Koptol Gagi," he said at last, "I can't accept blasphemy, not even to escape the mines of Asmari. If I am to remain silent, you must give up your experiments."

"You're in no position to dictate terms," Jay said.

"I mean it," Toby said. "No more monsters. No more meddling with the sacred secrets of life."

"The Ortonians themselves are doing it," Jay said. "I learned of it through their publications. I have merely advanced the work they are doing."

"It's a dark sin."

"So is opting with Ortonian females."

"No. That is human." Toby, his wounds closed and healing rapidly, sat up. "And the mines of Asmari are not death."

"I'm in the last quarter of my life," Jay said, his voice soft. "These Ortonians have delved into the secrets of life to an extent which gives me hope. Through my experiments, I can, using the knowledge gained in forbidden work here on Orton, retard further maturation. By breaking down cross linkages and preventing further cross linkages, the connecting rods which join and immobilize the molecules essential to life, I can prevent the rapid aging process which comes to the Ankani male in the last quarter of his life."

"I don't understand what you're saying," Toby said. "I know only that what you've been doing carries the only death penalty left in the Ankani Code. I will turn myself over to the Garge and go to the mines unless you stop." He put his hand on Jay's shoulder. "Is death so horrible? It comes to all. These poor Ortonians, living in their furnace of a sun, die at an age when an Ankani is finishing his primary schooling. They would give their souls to be able to live as long as we."

"The life span of a sub-human means nothing to me," Jay said. "What matters to me is that I can almost feel my brain cells dying. In ten years, I'll be forced to retire. In twenty, I'll be feeble. Then I face thirty years, if I'm lucky, of being almost helpless." He looked at Toby with inspiration in his eyes. "I'll treat you, Toby. You can live to be a thousand."

"No," Toby said. "I'm sorry." He began to put on fresh clothing.

"I will stop," Jay said.

"No more forbidden work?"

"None."

"A pact of silence, then." He reconsidered. "And I will see the Ortonian female as I please."

"For you, permission. For me, nothing?"

"The degree of severity is not the same," Toby said.

"The Ortonians have a saying. It depends on whose ox is being gored."

"No genetic meddling," Toby said.

"There is another way to approach my problem," Jay said. "Not understanding the problem, since we have been under the taboo, our superiors would also think it forbidden. However, you have my word that my experiments are, if one drew a line between black and white, on the white side."

"Not even a bit gray?" Toby asked.

"Only to those who don't understand," Jay said. "You have your Ortonian animal. I have my work."

"May I ask why the saber-toothed rats?" Toby asked, rubbing his scars ruefully.

"Merely to expand my knowledge," Jay said. "To gain competence in molecular manipulation. I know all I must know, and there is no further need for animal experiments. Are we agreed?"

"May you live forever if that's your bag," Toby shrugged.

12

"Darling," Sooly said, "do you know that your eyes glow in the dark?"

Toby closed his eyes quickly, but it was difficult to keep them closed. With his head turned he said, "The glow of love."

"Ummm," she said. "That I believe."

The room was dark. The full moon which had led to the Squire's demise by pulling a low tide in the early part of a windless night had waned and was down, leaving the base in a dark gloom which was even darker inside Toby's quarters.

Sooly, a woman of the world, over a week having passed since that fateful afternoon in the August sun on a small, secluded, sandy beach, suffered merely agonies of guilt instead of the untold agonies which had befuddled her very reason immediately after her fall from grace. She was rather cynical about the fact that the agonies of guilt came afterward, not before.

Here she was, deliciously nude and languid with the satiety of love, alone with her lover in his bedroom, the cool ocean breeze carrying the lovely odd smell of the salt marsh into the open window, unashamed, loving the feel of his hand on her thigh.

"I know," she said sleepily, "that you're really not human and that your fantastic abilities to melt me into a little puddle of purple passion are alien."

Toby looked at her guiltily, seeing her clearly even in the dimness of the room. Her eyes were closed and her lips had been cleaned, in a pleasant, passionate way, of lipstick. He never knew when she was joking.

"And you're going to carry me away to a far star and I'll find that you already have six wives and eighteen kids," Sooly said. "Where did you learn all that?"

"Oh, it just comes naturally," Toby said with a gulp.

"God, I'm jealous," she said, sitting up and wrapping herself around him, pressing her soft breasts against his chest. "Don't ever tell me who taught you." She giggled. "But I'm dying to know."

"You know boys," Toby said. "We talked a lot when I was a kid."

"And read feelthy books?" she teased.

"Oh, yes," Toby said. "That's where I got all my ideas. Actually, I've never tried them on anyone before."

"Liar." She sighed. "You have the most fantastic eyes." She traced a soft finger around one of his eyes. "They get bigger now, in the dark."

They did. There was nothing he could do about that. But there was something he could do about her overall soft warm goodness and he did and she responded once more and clung to him and then, in the sweet after touches, whispered, "I belong to you, darling. I've never belonged to a man before. You know that, don't you? Not Bud, not anybody. Just you."

Yes, he knew that. And it was more astounding to him than the mystery of a dark star. At first he had been a little concerned. It was difficult for him to understand the concept of virginity. Ankani women, he suspected, were born not virgin. But the largest, most beautiful mystery was her complete attachment to him. He'd never known such a lovely joy. It made him feel frightfully evil, for such—you couldn't call it anything else but ownership—of a woman was a totally new experience for him. The concept of exclusive love was alien, but he was astounded by the ease with which he accepted it. The closest thing to it was the comradeship between Ankani roommates in the lower levels of school. But his closeness to his childhood friend paled to insignificance beside the feeling he got with this Ortonian woman. He could touch her as he pleased! It was pure luxury to be able to take her hand during one of the long walks through the pine woods, a delight to be able, when the urge struck him, to pause in his walk and take her into his arms. He could talk with her, look at her with hungry eyes, even make the first advance. It had taken him some time to get over his feeling of degradation when he let his instincts impel him into making the first move toward opting. No, with this woman it was not opting. He preferred the Ortonian word, love. It was different and it was so natural that he spent many sleepless hours examining his concept of morality, which had been severely mauled during the first few days of his—she called it an affair—with the Ortonian.

Once, in the first bloom of the thing, he'd remembered how John Kurt playfully patted his wife on the fanny and he'd tried it. Sooly jumped, smiled, said, "Beast." But the smile was warm and he could tell that his touch had been welcome. With an Ankani female such a gesture would have been unthinkable.

"Why are there more women than men in your country?" he had asked her one day in a moment of unguarded puzzlement.

"There are more women than men everywhere," she said, "except perhaps in some countries where female children are unwelcome. I don't think they still kill unwanted girl babies, but it hasn't been long since they did. And in the Orient, girl babies are still sold, given away, put into prostitution."

That had to be explained and it was something he hadn't encountered in his reading. He was bemused. There was some sort of significance in the related facts of girl babies being undesirable in certain countries of Orton and in girl babies being kept to a ratio of five to one on the Ankani worlds, but he couldn't explain it, since Ankani women were superior to the male and were kept to smaller numbers because it took five Ankani men to do the work and provide for one Ankani woman. By the end of the first week he was so degraded that he had had the blasphemous urge to ask why Ankani women were superior. And why it was necessary to limit the number of women and why an Ankani man had to wait to be asked before indulging in one of man's most pleasant experiences.

Was it because a man, with unlimited opting, or love, available, lost interest in everything but? His work didn't suffer, because the machinery was almost totally automatic, but he found himself thinking night and day about the wonder of Sooly in his arms.

Meanwhile, Sooly had a big worry. She was, she told herself, a stupid goose and if she got caught it would be her own fault, because she'd taken no precautions at all. Of course, she hadn't *planned* to expose herself to the most fearful fate a single girl faces in a situation of sin, but after that first time she could have done something, and she didn't. She couldn't go into the local drug store and say, "Hey, baby, gimme a bottle of pills, huh?" She'd *die* if *anyone* knew. But there in the warm night with her body melting with love she decided that it wasn't fair to Toby. She was *not* going to get a husband *that* way. She'd kill herself first.

Her voice was low and pained. "Darling, I don't know how to say this—"

"Well," Toby joked, "you form the words in your mind, push air through your larynx and move your lips."

"I'm serious," she whispered.

He held her close. "In this most perfect of all perfect worlds nothing is serious."

"It would be if I got caught," she said. There, it was out. "Shouldn't we do something?"

He chuckled. "You are a greedy broad." He liked the Orton word.

"No, damn it, you know what I mean."

"Do I?"

"I'm not protected," she said, having to force the words out.

"Against what?" he asked innocently.

"Oh, Christ, Toby," she said. "I can get pregnant."

"Huh?" It was a grunt of surprise. She couldn't know. And he couldn't tell her. "Well, don't worry about it."

"You want me to be pregnant?"

He hadn't even thought about it. He reviewed all he knew about Ortonian mores and came up with the answer. "I'm protected," he said.

"Oh, God," she said. Her mind raced, wondering if she could love him enough to marry him, to face a childless life. She felt tears ooze out of her eyes.

"What's wrong?" he asked.

"You haven't, Toby. Tell me you haven't."

"Haven't what?"

"You haven't had an operation, not at your age. How could you?" She was so sure she'd guessed right that she turned her back to him, sobbing.

"An operation? No." He tried to pull her back over to him. "Look, there's nothing to cry about. I could give you a baby."

She raised herself up on one arm, trying to see his face. His eyes were wide, glowing. She had an eerie feeling and there was a bit of fright in her which made the sobs harder and the tears wetter.

"Please," Toby begged, distressed beyond his understanding. He'd never seen a woman cry. It was painful. "All I'd have to do is skip my next pill at the end of the month."

His glowing eyes. The lights in the sky above her, which she hadn't seen in days. The fun thing she'd had with the Flying Saucer Camp, seeing a shadowy shape between the two tanks, counting six, seven. "Toby," she whispered, "who are you?"

"A man who loves you," Toby said, his heart pounding.

"There's no pill for men, Toby." She sniffed. Her nose was runny from crying.

"Well," Toby said lamely, "it's new, experimental."

"Like your equipment?" she asked. "Like the furnace which burns up the pollution you take out of the water and leaves no ashes? Like the machine which takes lithium out of the water in pure, huge amounts?" She pushed him away. "I've seen something out there, Toby. I've seen seven tanks. I know I have."

"Shadows," Toby said. "The night plays tricks."

Sooly lay back, her mind in a turmoil. With her shoulder to him, she loosened the small pearl earring from her pierced ear. She tossed it onto the floor. "Oh, darn, I dropped my earring."

"I'll get it," Toby said. He leaned over her, reached down and without fumbling or feeling around retrieved the tiny earring. Sooly, looking down at the floor, saw only blackness.

"How are you able to see in the dark?" she asked.

He had reached out to place the earring in her hand. She took it, then seized his hand in hers. He could not speak. "You're not answering my question, Toby," she said, sadness in her voice. He pulled his hand out of hers and swung his feet off the bed to sit up. "I don't care what you are," Sooly said. "I love you, Toby, but I must know." He remained silent. "Because I don't know what I am to you, don't you see? Can't you see that?"

"You are the best thing in my life," he said softly. "Isn't that enough?"

"For how long, Toby?" she asked.

He resented it. He had been avoiding that thought. It was painful of him to think of leaving her. Yet, not leaving her was also unthinkable. Others had done it in the past, deserted their posts, jumped ship. He, however, was a son of the line of Mari Wellti. Love of Ankan was inbred in him. He was lonely for Ankan even on the outlying Ankani worlds. This alien place with its furnace of a sun shooting killing particles through human flesh? Not to see the black wonder of space again? The slow march of the stars in their glory?

"So I'm just here," Sooly said. "A momentary pleasure. Like a sailor's woman. When will you be in port again, Toby?" She forced a bitter laugh. "Or am I just an animal to you, something of a lower order? You can read a book at a glance. What else can you do?" She seized his shoulder and jerked him to face her. "Look at me. What am I, Toby? Am I just a handy piece of ass?" The harsh words sounded stilted on her lips.

He wanted to tell her. There was no reason for not telling her, since she'd guessed most of it. But he'd disobeyed one order. He was an Ankani male, there lay his loyalties. What other choice was there? Then, too, telling her would merely make her more unhappy and he didn't want to see her suffer any more. Silence, he decided, was best.

"Please don't go," he said, as she dressed.

She didn't speak again. He held the door open, watching her as she ran to her little automobile, heard the motor start, saw the lights come on, sweep as she turned, blink redly as she braked before gunning onto the highway.

13

Sooly moped around with a cloud over her head like the little man in the comic strip, lashing herself with recriminations, hating herself. She told herself that she was acting the part of the betrayed Victorian lass in an age of permissive-ness, but cold logic was worthless. In many ways she was an old-fashioned girl. She was a loner and proud of it, different by choice. Although Ocean City was somewhat of a quiet backwater, the protest generation had been represented while she was in high school by long-haired boys and girls who used pill pre-scriptions. She had not been a part of it in high school and, as a result, was often left out of some of the things which her contemporaries considered exciting. Often, during her senior year, Bud would deliver her to her door at eleven o'clock on weeknights and twelve o'clock on weekends and, after a few thor-oughly enjoyable kisses, motor off in his Mustang to join an after-hours party on the beach where there was beer and booze and a few joints. Bud swore that his dissipation consisted merely of a few beers and professed to disapprove of the drug scene, but his hair gradually grew into a long, unkempt mass and Sooly found herself disapproving of his companions.

On one thing Bud agreed. Since it was an accepted fact that they would be married as soon as he established himself as a charter fisherman, Sooly would "save herself." Many nights, alone with Bud in the coolness of an ocean breeze, they talked and kissed and burned and discussed the universal question of "why wait?" But since marriage and motherhood was Sooly's chosen career, she and Bud agreed that they should start with everything pos-sible in their favor. Waiting was sometimes very frustrating, but Sooly valued her love, did not want to dilute the passion she would take to her marriage bed by pre-marital experimentation. She was, perhaps, not the only nineteen-year-old virgin in Ocean County, but she was, at best, among a select few and she was known in circles of high school society as a prude who not only scorned the new morality but refused to drink, smoke or take a friendly toke from a joint when it was being passed around at a party one night on the strand. In fact, she reacted indignantly when she discovered that some of the members of the group were smoking marijuana and gave an angry lecture on how they were putting her in peril; for if the fuzz had arrived while the joint was being passed, she would have been hauled into the local lock-up and charged along with the guilty.

She was labeled square by progressive elements, the long hairs and their stringy-haired female followers, had few friends, not because she was an un-friendly girl but because she was selective. Her one year in the girl's school in Virginia was much the same. Girls spoke openly about their chosen method of birth control, sneaked pot into the dorm rooms and looked on Sooly as some-thing out of the antediluvian past. As long as she had life with Bud to look for-ward to, this situation didn't bother her.

But now she'd severed her ties with Bud, although he was not fully aware of the startling change, in a way which would, forever, make it impossible to re-pair the damage. This was a sadness to her, but not the overwhelming sadness which she would have once thought it to be. It was not even her fall from grace which sent her moping around the house in a suicidal mood. It was Toby. She was a warm, passionate, idealistic girl with enough love in her shapely body to make heaven on earth for a man and she'd given all that love to some kind of weirdo who could read a book at a glance, see in the dark and who knew so much about the art of love that it was definitely supernatural.

She tried to tell herself that she was imagining all of it and that what had happened was that she had been skillfully seduced by a man of the world, of *this* world. That was pure crap. For she was not crazy. She hadn't imagined the flying saucers and she hadn't been seeing shadows when she could, on more than one occasion, count more than six tanks at the Flying Saucer Camp. And he could see in the dark and he said funny things.

Actually, it was frightfully romantic. Earth girl meets and falls in love with man from outer space. Whee.

She relived that last evening a million times, trying to convince herself that she was wrong. She was always looking out the window the minute she heard a car and hoping that it would be Toby to tell her that he loved her and that the reason for his queer behavior was that he had a rare tropical disease which was not contagious but which had eerie effects, like making his eyes so large and glowing in the dark and making him sterile. She very definitely, flowingly, was not pregnant. Then she could make the grand sacrifice, forego her dream of children and love him selflessly her whole life long.

The cars passed by the house or turned out to be Beth's bridge-playing buddies stopping by for coffee and that made her so very angry, after suffering for two whole days, that she determined to find out once and for all what the hell was going on over there at that damned Flying Saucer Camp.

With luck or with unerring feminine intuition, she chose a night when the transport vehicle was making its regular run. She parked her car beside the bridge, noting that the bridge-keeper was asleep, as usual, and crept up the road dressed in a spysuit, a pair of blue jeans and a dark sweater, so that she couldn't be seen easily. She was peeking around the corner of the large building when the vehicle blinked into the empty space between the two largest storage tanks. It was dark and tall and roughly cylindrical. It scared her so badly that she felt weak and had to sit down flat on the damp ground to catch her breath, but then Toby came out and connected a long, flexible pipe to the vehicle and went into the extractor building to do something which caused the pipe to pulse and make gurgling sounds.

She watched, her own eyes large and frightened, as Toby leaned on the vehicle humming a little tune which was unlike anything she'd ever heard. He didn't look her way and she was thankful for that, knowing his ability to see in the dark. She kept all but the top of her head and her startled eyes hidden. Toby lazily opened a port on the vehicle, climbed in, and came out moving less lazily, walking purposefully toward the second peeling white house where lights showed through the windows. He pounded on the door and the other one came out. They talked in low voices in a language unlike any Sooly had ever heard, and language was her meat. When she was a child, the family lived in Florida and a very progressive school there started third grade students on Spanish. Sooly took to it easily, unable to understand why the other kids had trouble. She took French, Latin and more Spanish in high school and tutored herself in Italian, Portuguese, German, Greek and Arabic. At the girl's school she was deep into Russian and was picking up Hebrew from an Israeli exchange student. She was, she felt, no wing-ding scholar, but somehow language came effortlessly to her once she'd dug her teeth into the basic sound, lettering and grammar of the beast. So when she could not recognize the language being used by Jay and Toby she had one more nail to drive into the lid on the coffin of her love, one more piece of evidence that Toby was something else.

She'd seen and heard enough to convince her and still she could not make herself sneak quietly away. There was a dim moon and Toby looked grand in moonlight and her dreams could not die because she was a girl who had to have something, even a hopeless dream. So she stayed there, tears oozing from her eyes, until she saw Toby unhook the flexible pipe and go into his house to come out with a small package of some sort in his hand. The port was still open on the vehicle and she could see comfortable-looking seats inside. Toby put a foot up and started to board the vehicle. Her reason told her that he was not going to leave for good. The plant was still operating and the other one, Jay, was in his house. But her heart cried out in panic. He was going to leave her without even so much as saying goodbye. That she couldn't stand. She was on her feet and running toward him before she had a chance to reason it out and he was leaping down, turning, crouched in surprise before he realized who it was running across the bare earth crying his name.

She threw herself into his arms. "You shouldn't be here," he said, not in reprimand but in cold fear. He looked quickly up to see if Jay were watching. "Get out of here fast, Sooly."

"Not before—you're leaving—not even goodbye—" Her voice was thick with sobs.

"Get out of here now," he ordered, trying to push her away, but she was clinging to him sobbing heartbrokenly.

"What's going on out there?" Jay called out, standing on the porch of his lab building. He saw that Toby was not alone and ran across, panting with his excitement. "The Ortonian woman!" he gasped.

"She knows nothing," Toby said, in Ankani.

"Not even an Ortonian is that stupid," Jay said.

"A pact of silence," Toby said.

"Impossible," Jay said. And Toby knew that it was true. The situation was definitely out of hand and he could almost feel the cold, clammy air of the mines of Asmari. He patted Sooly on the back and said, "Easy, easy." She sobbed harder. "It will be all right," he told her. "I'm not leaving. I was merely going up to the ship to present a report."

"Oh, Toby," she wailed. "What are you really like? Are you a giant spider or something? Did you kill the human whose form you took?"

He had to laugh. "No, you see me as I am."

Her sobs stopped suddenly. "Well, that's something, anyhow." Her eyes were sparkling in excitement. "Which star are you from? Can you point it out to me? Do you live to be a thousand years old? Are all the flying saucers your spaceships?"

"Whoa," Toby said, seeing that Jay was on the verge of an attack. "All in good time, honey. Right now we've got to decide what to do with you."

She sobered. "I won't tell anyone about you," she said.

"That won't do," Jay broke in, panting. "We can't just let her run around knowing—"

"What do you want to do, kill her and burn her body, as you did to the man?"

"Oh, Toby," Sooly said. "Have you killed someone?"

"He broke into Jay's lab and was killed by experimental animals," Toby said. "It was an accident."

"A funny little man with a pot belly?" Sooly asked.

"Yes," Toby said, still thinking furiously.

"The Squire," Sooly breathed. "And they've been dragging the bay for his body for days."

"We can send her up to the *Entil*," Jay said in Ankani, his voice even now, since he'd popped a dose of *troleen* to make his heart behave.

"And what?" Toby asked.

"Have the doctor excise the part of her memory dealing with us," Jay said.

"And, in the process, read other memories?" Toby frowned in negation. "We have to trust her."

"I can do it, then," Jay said.

"Not on your life," Toby told him. "You are not a surgeon."

"I have the equipment," Jay said. "And it is in my interest field. You can help. It's really a simple process. There is no room for error, it is painless and you, yourself, can monitor the memories we're excising."

"No," Toby said.

"The other choice is liquidation," Jay said. "Look, we're flirting with the mines or worse. You know that."

"I wish you two would speak English," Sooly said, "you're making me very nervous."

Toby looked at her thoughtfully and was melted inside by the softness, the very femaleness of her. "I would never allow anything to hurt you," he told her, "but we do have problems."

"I'm good at problems," she said. "Why don't we sit down somewhere and discuss them?"

Both Jay and Toby were accustomed to taking the smallest suggestion of a female as an order. It was natural that they nod in agreement and, before either could think it over, they were seated in Toby's quarters over coffee with Toby giving Sooly the picture.

"They'll send you to Siberia because of me?" she asked.

"And send me spiraling down into a hot star," Jay said.

"But it's so simple," Sooly said. "I won't tell."

"Jay is frightened," Toby said. "His offense is more serious."

"All right, if you won't trust me," Sooly said to Jay, "what's your suggestion?"

"We can simply erase your memories concerning our origin, the vehicle, the man who broke into the lab."

"That simple, huh?" Sooly said. "Just how do you go about this erasing process?"

"It's a simple machine used in our educational process," Jay said. "We locate the particular brain cells involved in the memory—"

"Whoa," Sooly said. "No one's going to go mucking around in my brain."

The more Toby thought about it the more he liked the idea of simply erasing the incriminating memories. "There's no surgery involved," he said. "And I'll be monitoring the process. We simply find the particular cells involved in memory—"

"And destroy them?" Sooly asked, with a wry face.

"Oh, no. We simply wipe them clean, so to speak."

"Fine," Sooly said. "I've very carefully limited my intake of alcohol all my life because if there's one thing I hate it's the thought of little parts of me, my brain, dying off by the hundreds of thousands. It'll be bad enough when I'm thirty and they start ending it all from natural causes." She looked at Toby and the trust in her eyes made him wince. "Do you want me to do this thing, Toby?"

"Sooner or later, Sooly, I must leave," he said. "And it would be against my orders and my conscience to leave you with the knowledge that we Ankanis were here."

"You could take me with you," she said, unashamed.

"No," Toby said sadly.

She accepted it, "I see. But while you're here? Are you going to make me forget you, too?"

"It would be best," Toby said gently.

"Then I won't do it. Look, if it means so much to you, take my memories of the flying saucers. Wipe out the knowledge of your spaceship, but leave me you."

"Are you sure?"

"Very, very sure."

"Then you're willing?" Jay asked.

"Only to protect Toby," she said.

To prove to himself that Jay knew his work, in the lab Toby allowed the headgear to be fitted and told Jay to seek out a particularly irritating little memory involving a childhood prank. The process was quick. The tiny current went out through Toby's brain, stimulated certain chemical changes and the memory was gone. It was as if it had never happened, and Jay's questioning showed that Toby didn't even know he was missing anything.

Sooly, knuckles white on the arms of the chair, felt the cap-like gear slip over her head. Toby's presence helped her. Jay began to operate intricate dials and Toby, monitoring, got swift glimpses and flashes of the most serene, happy mind imaginable and then Jay was locked in on the flying saucers and ready to erase.

"Make a general survey first," Toby said. "See if we're going to be able to get all of it before we start erasing piecemeal."

The result brought a frown to Toby's face. It would be possible to erase the saucers and the early, game-like suspicions that there was something between the two tanks which counted up to seven instead of six tanks, but after that it became hopelessly complicated. "I don't understand," Jay said in Ankani. "There's an incredible muddle in there."

"She is, after all, alien," Toby said. "Her molecules hold more than a single concept."

"But still we can do the job," Jay said.

But not, Toby realized, without wiping all memory of him from the brain of the girl who sat there quietly, waiting, trusting him implicitly. Astounding as it was, the Ortonian brain, at least as represented by the brain of Sooly, seemed to possess the ability to back-file, to add relevant information to memories already stored. Every memory of Toby was tinged by the knowledge which began to build the night in his quarters when she realized that he could see in the dark. Somehow, Sooly's brain had gone back and planted the nature of Toby, his alien origin, even on the earliest memories, the memories of that first day when he'd told her to leave the dock.

"We must do it," Jay said, preparing to press the proper button.

There was no other person in the entire universe, Toby realized, his temperature rising, his heart pounding, who thought of him as Sooly did. Nowhere in the entire, vast emptiness of the cosmos was there another person who loved him. His reaction was instinctive and faster than the approach of Jay's finger to the button. "No," he shouted, for in erasing those memories of him, Jay would be killing a part of himself, a part which had become, so suddenly and so completely, vital to his very existence. Hands met over the complicated keyboard of an instrument which should not have been on the surface of Orton, an instrument which was, in Jay's hand, as illegal as his experiments on the DNA molecules of the white rats. A jury-rigged instrument, it was built by Jay from available Orton electronic parts with some vital elements pirated from Ankani gadgets. Usually used only in the event of emergencies, Jay's instrument was programmed to do more than the allowable forced education and was capable of more than wiping away traumatic experiences that contributed to mental ill health.

Toby's hand caught Jay's and there was a brief struggle. Jay's knuckle hit a button which sent a tiny beam of energy lancing down into the mysterious portion of Sooly's brain over her right ear, and as the momentary contact was broken she slumped.

"You miserable *nanna*," Toby gasped, pushing Jay away. "What did you do?"

"I didn't mean to," Jay said, gasping for breath and reaching for his second *troleen* tablet of the night. "You made me do it."

"What happened?" Toby demanded, bending over the unconscious Sooly.

"A surgical beam," Jay said. "I think I hit the beam."

"Get out," Toby said, tears forming. "Get out."

Jay left, clutching his heart. Toby, finding it difficult to see, tuned the reader.

Nipari squatted on a brown rock, high, pushing her long lank hair out of her face to see the men in the valley below. They had surrounded a grazing herd and were closing in, using cover expertly. Her pink tongue flicked out, gathering the saliva which flowed at the thought of succulent meat roasting over a fire. She had not eaten, save roots and berries, for three days. Far away, across the valley below, she could see the great waters where brown leviathans reared out of the depths and beyond to the bottomless bogs. But her attention returned quickly to the men as Jar, the leader, rose with a hoarse yell and buried his spear into the heaving side of a frightened animal. Others found targets, also, and Nipari danced in joy, her feet bare and brown on the hot, brown rock.

Mouth-watering aromas rose from the camp. Her lips were smeared with blood as she tore at half-raw meat, growling contentedly. Hunger satisfied, she danced. Gri, the young male, danced with her. Her blood, hot, pulsed through her veins like fire. At the height of the dance Gri, growling, seized her, into the low cave, struggling, fighting, feeling the fire in her, reluctant to enter into the mystery but urged on by forces so powerful—with the yelps and laughter of the elders, watching from the entrance. A stab of pain and a growling, panting acceptance and outside the raucous laughs changing to screams and mutterings of awe and Gri, his long hair stiffening on his neck, running to meet the threat and up above a fiery beast lowering as the people screamed and ran and Jar, the leader, standing steadfast.

A white god came from the bird of fire and spoke to the people. He was tall, pale, had a mane of golden hair and a voice of softness. Finding her fair, he claimed her, after walking the earth like a man for two moons, and she bore him a daughter, writhing in the wholesome pain, a daughter with eyes like moons and skin of lightness and—

"Holy shit," Sooly said, using a word she didn't like, because such words should be saved for extreme emergencies, but she was there, in a chair with the strange thing on her head and there, too, with—

"Are you all right?"

"I remember everything," she said. "What went wrong?" She turned her head and went dizzy as her brain swirled.

Tigri, woman of the square, dependent of the merchant, Tepe, smiled with pride on the two daughters and four sons she'd given Tepe. Her house of sun-dried mud bricks was not luxurious, but according to the law Tepe provided her with grain, oil and clothing and, since Tepe's wife was barren, Tigri's own offspring would fall heir. She was pleased with her lot. Other women of the square had not been so favored by the gods.

Her house stood near the wall of the city. She made her way to the square, her lithe hips swaying, issuing an invitation. The visit of her issue ended, there was business to attend. Atop the ziggurat, the fiery bird of the white gods sat in metallic splendor. One was in the square, waiting. He smiled when he saw her. She arranged the neckline of her garment to show the uplift of her generous breasts, met his smile with invitation. Her eyes, large as the desert moon, seemed to please the god who took her hand and carried her on magic wings to the bitter sea where she lay with him. Her son had pale skin and large eyes and was treated with the respect due to a half-god.

"Toby, what's happening to me?" she asked.

"There was an accident."

"Am I going mad?"

"No," He could not believe the reading of the machine. The patterns were strange.

"Wait, listen," she closed her eyes. "And God said, let there be a firmament in the midst of the waters, and let it divide the waters from the waters. And God made the firmament, and divided the waters which were under the firmament from the waters which were above the firmament: and it was so. And God said, let the waters under the heaven be gathered unto one place, and let dry land appear: and it was so."

"It sounds much like your Bible," Toby said.

"I wrote that," she said, her eyes wide with awe. She shook her head wonderingly. A roaring wave of sickness caused her to swallow deeply, close her eyes.

Larsa, wife of Shurup, sat by his side in honor, smiling shyly at the white god who stood tall and blond before them. He spoke their tongue and it was a language she'd never heard, neither Semitic nor Indo-European nor Romance nor Slavic.

"The two great rivers," the god said, "can be your life. The land between is very rich and will grow your grain."

"The gods have made that land poison and deadly," said Shurup. "The people cannot live there."

"We will help. We will separate the waters, we will make dry land where there is now bottomless mire." The white god spread his hands. "The riches of that land will make you strong. No longer will your villages be prey to the barbarians of the hills."

"Toby, Toby, I'm scared."

"There seems to be little damage," Toby said, feverishly examining, making recordings of Sooly's brain waves. "A few cells, that's all. But I don't understand."

Laga of the moon-like eyes and skin of purest alabaster took the tall, blond god to her and bore him two daughters and flew high over the city in the bird of fire to look down on the two rivers and the bitter sea where the gods dwelt and sent their huge birds to the heavens bearing the salt of the sea. Priestess of Anu, god of the heavens, she kept vigil atop the temple, where the gods came to earth. Her tears dried as the years wrinkled her alabaster skin and the troops of Sargon the Conqueror found her there, faithful, awaiting the second coming of her god. She went to her death with her head high and her body joined others in the trench beside the tombs of the nobles killed in the battle, human sacrifices so that the warriors would not lack servants and the comforts of women. And though she was dead she lived and saw the tall walls of Ur rise and knew the joy of seeing the favor of the gods expand her city to rule all of Sumer, for it was the duty and the privilege of the people to serve the gods, to minister to their comfort and it was the duty of the fairest of the nubile women to lie with them and bear their godlike children, the women of the moon-like eyes and the men of tawny skin and great strength. Priestess of the Moon Temple, she blessed the soldiers who guarded the gates to the land of the gods beside the bitter waters, for man could kill but gods shunned violence. Atop the temple sat the sky bird of the god, Entil, who taught them and spoke with their tongue. The gods smiled upon the city and it prospered and merchants went out to the hinterlands and across the waters and brought back sweet-smelling cedar and soft, wondrous gold. She knew the odd, sweet love of the god and was fruitful and then, on a day of sadness, the gods blessed them and went away into the distant heavens and the city, left without inspiration, fought endlessly against the encroaching, hungry, envious people of the brown hills until the bricks of the temple were stained with blood and she was carried away screaming into slavery, her children slain before her eyes, her city destroyed, her love burning away into a hidden ember as the years passed and she grew old and bent and still he did not come back as he had promised.

"Toby, how old are you?" She found that by holding very still and concentrating, she could stop the vivid images.

"Sixty of your years," Toby said.

Then it couldn't have been him. She was there, she knew it, but it couldn't have been him. "Have you heard of a place called Ur?"

"I am familiar with it in my studies," he said. "Are you feeling better?"

"I'm fine. Something weird is going on, though. Did your people—" and suddenly she was speaking the tongue of the people, a strange, harsh language unlike anything she'd ever heard and he was cocking his head and nodding in wonder "—gather minerals from the bitter waters into which flow the two great rivers, mothers of life?"

It was a strangely accented Ankani. Toby could pick it out, although the phrasing was awkward. "It began seven thousand years ago," he said, "when you Ortonians were savage hunters."

"And you created the land between the rivers, draining the swamps, teaching the people to build cities." Her eyes flashed. "Of all the low things. You did it only to have a barrier, a protection between your extraction camps and the barbarian tribes of the hills."

"No, they wanted to help."

"You left them. You pulled them up out of barbarism and deserted them." She could remember the sadness, the despair, the pain. "You let them carry me off into slavery!"

"Not you, Sooly. Not me." He took her hand. "I don't understand what's happened, but apparently you Ortonians are different, more different than we ever thought. You seem to be able to remember things which happened centuries before you were born."

"You've tampered with us, played with us, seduced our women, stolen our resources," her voice was not her own; it was fuller, more authoritative, a combination of things.

"Our men were lonely and without women," Toby said. "They wanted only to help. Haven't they helped?" He reached behind him, picked up an Ankani technical manual. "Can you read this?"

It was, at first, alien, but she found something, some dark area of her brain and the marks and lines and angles sprang into language. The words were technical and she could not get the meaning, but she recognized it as the cuneiform writing of the city, her city, Ur of the Chaldees.

"We would have done it without you," she spat.

"Perhaps," Toby said, "but not as quickly."

"She was happy," Sooly said, remembering Nipari, the woman of the hunters. "And she was of Earth."

"And you, evidently, are part Ankani," Toby said.

"Does my being a mongrel make me more acceptable to you?" She reconsidered. "I didn't mean that, Toby. I don't know what to think. This is a little too much for me."

"I love you," Toby said, remembering his utter horror when he thought that she'd been damaged. "I understand the word now."

"I've loved you for thousands of years," Sooly said, a happy smile lighting her face.

He was removing the gear from her head to take her into his arms when Manto Babra Larkton, having been sent to investigate the sudden emanation of an education machine from the base, stepped forward, having heard the last half of the exchange from the shadows outside the open door.

"Bakron Wellti," she ordered, her voice showing her anger and outrage. "You will take this Ortonian to the vehicle."

"You don't understand, Manto," Toby said, his voice going servile and pleading. "She's—"

"I understand perfectly," the Manto said. "You have disobeyed a prime directive. You are familiar with the punishment."

"What will you do with her?" Toby asked.

"She will make a most interesting study," the Manto said, "before we erase her memory."

"But extremely large areas of the brain are involved," Toby protested. "I don't think it's possible—"

"It is not for you to think, Bakron," the Manto said haughtily. "Obey the order."

"You don't have to, Toby," Sooly said. "You don't have to do what she says."

"Move, Bakron," Babra said, a blaster appearing in her hand. Toby helped Sooly from the chair. Her knees were weak.

"Toby, I don't want to go. I don't want to be made to forget," she said.

"We have no choice," Toby said, knowing that the blaster was on his back.

Jay waited beside the scout ship which was resting in the bare area between buildings. He trembled as the group approached. "Inside," Babra said, waving her weapon. "You first, Koptol Gagi."

Jay's legs wouldn't work properly. The Manto had seen his illegal equipment. He knew that, under questioning, he'd be forced to tell of his other forbidden experiments. He didn't want to die in the fire of a huge sun. He gathered his strength, took a deep breath, whirled, knocked the weapon from Babra's hand and followed through with a strong right to the Manto's chin. Toby was shocked into a rigid stiffness. Never in his life had he heard of a rating striking a woman and an officer.

"Quick," Jay gasped. "Let's get out of here."

It was crowded in the small scout ship. Toby punched in a random short blink and hoped he didn't blink into an Ortonian mountain or an aircraft. Just before he lost sight of the base as the scout ship faded, he saw the blur of an incoming vehicle. They had made it just in time.

14

Few men had seen such a sight. The Americans and the Russians in their rocket-borne capsules had looked down and watched the march of dawn across the mottled surface of the planet, and, of course, millions had seen it via television, but Sooly was the first woman—no, not the first, for there was in her that other, large-eyed Laga, who flew with her god-lover high above the earth to see two rivers and the sea—but she was the first in thousands of years, the first woman. She flew high above the broad Atlantic and it was narrowed by height to melt into the far shape of her own country and, nearer, the outline of the great mass of Europe and Africa.

From that far point, she could not see the mountains of garbage, the discolored rivers, the dead lakes, the cancerous automobile junkyards, the belching smoke of the factories. Instead, she saw the whorl of a tropical depression in the South Atlantic, the billows of clouds, the dark hue of the continents and it was not the good, green Earth, but the beautiful, blue Earth. The strain of *The Theme From Exodus* kept repeating in her head and the phrase, "This land is mine," took on a significance which caused tears of beauty-inspired joy to glisten on her lashes.

Down there, far off, was Ocean City, so tiny that she could place it only generally on the outline of the continent. Down there was home, the brackish creeks, the white beaches, the glistening white boats plying the waters just off shore, her family, Bem, the fat, tired old dog. A sudden wave of homesickness swept through her. But there was more now. Across the continent of Africa was another home, the parched, arid lands with the ruins of towers which once reached to the sky to bring the people closer to the gods. The gods. She looked at Toby. He was anything but godlike. He was chewing his lower lip in thought. His mane of blond hair was tousled. His eyes were sad. She felt a vast sympathy. Somewhere out there, in the blackness of the space above them, was his home.

"Oh, Toby," she said, taking his hand. "Oh, Toby."

Jay was resting in one of the two rearward seats in the cabin of the scout. His eyes were closed, his breathing labored.

The instruments were lettered in cuneiform. She could not get over her astonishment at being able to make out most of it. For a moment she was tempted to probe once again into that newly opened area of her brain and a flash of hot sun and warm wind swept over her and names came to her tongue, Urnammu, first king of the dynasty, Lord of Sumer and Akkad. She shook her head. There would be time for that.

"Toby," she said, "you're in trouble, aren't you?"

"Trouble?" he asked, with a bitter laugh. "There's a word in your English. Mutiny. There isn't even a word for it in Ankani."

"Who was she?" Sooly asked. "That beautiful woman. She had eyes like Laga." The women of Ur. In one of her mother's books was a grouping of votive statues, small figures, male and female, in an attitude of supplication, right hand clasped over left in front of their breasts. One, a tall, mature woman with her hair rounded tightly about her head, had those lovely, large eyes. She had been, most certainly, the daughter of one of the "gods," one of the tall, fair Ankani men.

"She is the Manto, second in command," Toby said.

"Toby, couldn't we explain? Wouldn't they listen?"

"They don't know you, Sooly." He wondered how to tell her. He didn't want to hurt her. "We Ankanis have been in sub-space for three hundred millennia."

"I think I understand," she said. "We're sort of barbarians?"

"The last time an Ankani ship came to Orton it landed on the continent you call South America. The people there were hunting wild beasts with spears and arrows."

"But we've changed," Sooly said. "We've come a long way."

"Ankan doesn't change," Toby said. "And Ankani opinions change rarely."

"But your men mixed with our people," she said. "The astounding thing was that there was not a distance of thousands of years, not in her mind. It was almost as if the ships of the Ankani had landed atop the towers built to honor them only yesterday."

"In those days tankers were crewed by men. Men without women—" He paused.

"I see. It was something like an English colonist going native in old Africa, huh?"

"Aboard the *Entil*, studies are being made of the surprising advances you Ortonians have made," Toby said. "The first opinion seems to be that these advances are the result of an infusion of, pardon the expression, superior Ankani blood."

"Do you feel that way, Toby?" she asked. "Do you think I'm not good enough you?"

He looked at her quickly. "No. I know you."

"I could talk to them."

"You don't know Ankani women," he said.

"You're ruled by women?"

He nodded.

"Humm," she teased, trying to lift his spirits. "Maybe I was born on the wrong planet." He managed a weak smile. "But, honestly, Toby, I wouldn't want to rule anyone. We have minor examples of that here. We say a dominant woman wears the pants in the family. I don't want that, Toby. I want a man I can respect, a man who can tolerate my feminine weaknesses and love me and protect me and—"

"You can't know how alien that is to me," he said. He smiled. "And you can't imagine how beautiful it is to know the meaning of your word love."

Jay moved behind them. He straightened up in his seat. "You both make me sick," he said. "And you, Bakron, have you forgotten? Doesn't it mean anything to you that we're stranded here on this blasted zoo planet?"

"I haven't forgotten," Toby said.

"You're sure you couldn't go back, explain it all?" Sooly asked.

"I would be explaining all the way down into the heart of a star," Jay said.

"We can find a place," Sooly said. "Some small town somewhere. It wouldn't be so bad. You both know enough to do wonderful things. You could work toward them slowly—"

"And be fried by a furnace of a sun, if your politicians don't fry us with atomics first," Jay said. "I wish I'd never seen this *girnin*-begotten place." He fell back in his seat.

"I'm so sorry, Toby," Sooly said.

Toby shrugged. "It's worse for him. He's old. He has no one."

On the far edge of the world darkness came, a line of shadow moving across. When they were in the shadow the stars gleamed with a brittle sharpness.

"We have to find a place to land," Toby said. "As long as the ship is under power their instruments can track us." He was studying aerial maps of the surface. "Any suggestions?"

A new wave of homesickness swept Sooly. "There are tremendous swamps near Ocean City," she said.

"And advanced means of detecting flying objects just up the coast," Toby said. "No, I think one of the less developed countries."

"Could we go there?" Sooly asked, feeling strangely unable to voice the idea.

He understood. He flew low in the light of a moon. His Ankani eyes saw, apart from cities such as Baghdad, clusters of Bedouin tents, a dam, a pipeline. The rest was wasteland through which ran deep waddies. He lowered the ship into a depression so that it would be hidden from all eyes.

For long, awesome moments, Sooly gave herself to the sweep of 7,000 years, knowing scattered glimpses of human life and achievement and heartbreak, then she controlled it. Her first concern was Toby. For her, he was giving up his country, his birthright, everything.

Into the chill hours of morning, while Jay slept fitfully, they talked. He told her of his childhood on a distant, dim planet warmed by a distant sun and its own internal fires, a planet called home where his night-seeing eyes cut naturally through the darkness. He told her of the achievements of his race.

Sooly had one question which made his brow furrow in thought. "If you've been in sub-space, as you call it, for thirty centuries, and if all those achievements you speak of were accomplished so very, very long ago, what are the advances of the past few hundred years?" She smiled. "I'd have guessed that you would have developed goodies like matter transmission or telepathy or eternal life."

"Blinking is somewhat like matter transmission," he said. "But I see your point. Considering the fantastic progress you people have made in the past two thousand years, we seem rather static, don't we?"

"Maybe you've gone as far as man needs to go," she said.

"There are many things we don't know," Toby said, an entirely new avenue of thinking opened to him. "Our theories of the age and creation of the universe are amazingly like those developed by your scientists and not much more advanced. You know almost as much about the structure of the atom as we, but you've made a tragic detour into the destructive aspects of the science. In some fields you're even more advanced."

"Score one for our side," Sooly teased. "Tell me so I can feel superior."

"I'm not sure it's an achievement," Toby said, "but your scientists have done work in the field of what they call molecular biology which has never been duplicated on Ankan or any of the Ankani worlds." He grinned. "Of course, I must admit that the reason is an ancient and severe taboo against such work, a taboo which is one of the foundation stones of Ankani morality. I was shocked, at first, when I learned of the experiments being conducted, but I admit that you have reason. Do you know that your lifespan is shortened drastically because of the harmful rays of your sun?"

"No," Sooly said, thinking of all the sun baths she'd taken.

"If I were faced with such an early death," Toby said, forgetting for the moment that he was, being an exile on Orton, "I suppose I would try everything to remedy the situation, down to and including messing around with the very foundations of life, sacred as they are." He mused for a moment. "Then there's the theory, first proposed by my ancestor, Mari Wellti, that your sun's rays also contribute to what, apparently, is unique to Orton, evolution of species."

"If evolution is unique to us, how did your race get started?"

He laughed. "In the old records there is a fable much like your Adam and Eve. That's another of the things we don't know. We Akanis can be stubborn people. We've been looking for the mystery of the Wasted Worlds for centuries, for example, but when we run into a problem which has no answer, even our stubbornness wears thin. I think people gave up speculating on the origin of the race thirty millennia ago. It's like you trying to answer the question who created God?" An amusing thought came to him. "And speaking of God, do you know who lit the burning bush in your Bible?"

"Don't tell me," Sooly said, slightly shocked.

"And the pillar of smoke by day and the pillar of fire by night?"

"Bastard," Sooly said, only half-joking.

"Abraham came out of Ur," Toby said. "When his people ended up enslaved by the Egyptians a few of the old tankermen didn't like it. After all, they were our people, in a way. They did something about it."

"The Egyptians were a native people?" Sooly asked.

"I suppose there was some bleed-through from Sumer," Toby said. "We haven't documented it. I'd say that the Egyptian civilization was largely Ortonian."

"Now who's so damned superior?" Sooly said. "You see, we'd have made it on our own."

"You might have, at that," Toby admitted. "And that pleases me."

Sooly had drifted away from him, trying to find memories in that unexplored mystery. She wanted to see the pyramids under construction, to see the legends of Mentuhotep II rebuilding the lost grandeur of the old kingdom, to see if Nefertiti were as beautiful in life as in her statues. Once, as Jay and Toby slept, she brushed past the young man later called Abraham, but she could not follow him. She seemed bound to the area between the rivers and there was ample cause for staying there for the land was good and life, or lives, were filled with joy and sadness and she, half dozing, let her memories live in her. She was *there*. She lived in the walled cities and watched men fight and die and love and was a part of it, sometimes exalted, sometimes a woman of the villages. In a thousand years she could not hope to relive all of it and there seemed to be a barrier beyond which she could not go, the fall of Ur, the last, sad days, the slavery which followed. After that was blankness and before it was a dark tunnel which led back into time past the girl, Nipari, who ate half-raw meat with her hands and saw the first Ankani ore-gathering ship settle to the earth. The dark tunnel narrowed into frightening impressions of savagery and violence and cold and hunger and dimly-seen vistas of animal-studded plains and icy hills. It was more pleasant, for the moment, to see proud Ur rising, extending its influence over the land between the rivers. She lived as a servant girl and died, after thirteen summers, in childbirth. She wept in sadness and, exhausted, slept.

15

Cele Mantel's face went white when she saw the bruise on Babra's chin. Her fury, upon hearing the details, resounded throughout the entire ship and sent timid ratings scurrying to the safety of hiding places to avoid her wrath. Never before in the history of the Ankani Fleet had an officer been struck by a male. There wasn't even a punishment for the offense, it was so unthinkable. That left the punishment up to the Garge and she entertained gory scenes of lungs rupturing in the emptiness of space or a slow broil on a spiraling orbit down into a sun.

To ease her anger, she sent half a dozen ratings on punishment tours in steamy suits outside the ship on the angles and projections of the hull, demoted a Koptol who was one minute late for a change of watch and threw a cup and saucer smashing against a painted bulkhead. This last helped more than any of the others and she calmed long enough to discuss the situation with the Manto, who was still shaken by her unbelievable experience. Ankani women had faced the dangers of space and the pain of childbirth and other such inconveniences, but no Ankani woman had ever been called upon to endure being struck by a man. The Ortonian blink of the U.A.T. *Entil* would make history, but not the sort of history Cele had had in mind. She'd been determined to revolutionize tanker design and her statistics regarding incidence of smiles, completion quotient in optings and general morale had almost assured her success, and now those misbegotten men had spoiled it all. Since the Garge is ultimately responsible for all the actions of her crew, she was the bearer of the guilt, as much so as the Koptol with the bulging eyes and the handsome young Bakron. The offenses involved were as terrible as possible. Opting with an Ortonian female in spite of stern directives to the contrary, and, she thought with complete revulsion, forbidden experiments involving the life forces. Add to that desertion and the unheard of crime of striking an officer and her promotion became a remote possibility.

But Cele Mantel, above all, was an officer of the Fleet. As such, personal considerations took second place to duty and her sense of responsibility. Her first impulse, to begin to sterilize the planet immediately, doing in the two rebels along with a few billion Ortonians, soon on lost its appeal. Her blink message to Fleet was still outgoing, making the tortuous, zig-zag journey along the 7,000-year-old route, pausing at the anchor stations waiting for the small power capsules to build for the next stage of the journey. The message would make the trip in less than half the time it would take the *Entil,* since the *Entil's* bulk made longer waits necessary while the engines built power.

She was not concerned with the possibility of escape for the two culprits. The small scout ship was not equipped with exploratory gear. Its blinking ability was, therefore, limited to anchor station routes, and the only anchor station route from Orton led directly to Ankan, a place where the two ratings would not dare go. On the other hand, it would be next to impossible to capture the criminals, since, by using the planetary bulk as an anchor, a known point, they could blink endlessly around the area of space within half a light-year of Orton. They would be there when the directive came from Ankan. Cele almost hoped that the order would read, "Proceed with sterilization." Above all, the two ratings were not to be allowed to go relatively unpunished for their crime. In a society as old as the Ankani, new ideas were rare and the pure novelty of a male striking a female was so revolutionary that it would, possibly, appeal to that personality fault in men which had proved so troublesome in the distant past, the longing for what the males thought of as adventure. Women were the stabilizing influence in Ankani life. If it were left up to the males, change for the sake of change would be the order of the day.

Of course, being left to die an early death under Orton's killer sun would be a certain kind of punishment, but there was, still, a sort of romantic feeling among certain types about the old tanker crewmen who had learned to like Orton and its women so well that they chose to stay. Some would not consider a footloose life with a nubile Orton woman a punishment. And there was, too, the demonstrated fact that Koptol Gagi had allowed his advancing age to distort his reason. His notes on his experiments with animals and genetic manipulation were downright frightening. Even on Orton he would have a few more years in which to do damage.

Meanwhile, a back-up crew had been sent to the base, for Cele was determined to return to Ankan with a full cargo hold. The transport rating had come up with a mild emanation which was being used as a guide point for blinking down. The mother of the Ortonian woman with whom the young Bakron had become involved was wakeful and concerned.

Calmed slightly, Cele considered all possibilities and decided on one futile gesture. She swept into the communications room with her head regally high, her huge, soft eyes striking sparks. When she spoke on the emergency channel, a signal activated a receiver in the scout ship hidden in a waddi in the wastes of Iraq and Jay snorted in terror, while Toby and Sooly jerked awake, wide-eyed.

"Bakron Toby Wellti. Koptol Jay Gagi. You will be given one opportunity to surrender. For five minutes, the *Entil* will broadcast a periodic blink beacon. If you approach with power off, you will be allowed to board. The Ortonian woman will be treated with kindness and her memories eradicated. As for you, Koptol, and you, Bakron, your crimes are serious, as you well know. I can promise only that your rights will be respected and that you will be accorded a hearing before a Fleet Board."

Toby looked at Jay. The older man was frightened. He opened his pill case and popped a *troleen*. His face was a study in desperation as he looked at the nearly empty case. He fumbled hurriedly into the emergency kit of the scout vehicle and found a supply of a half dozen *troleen* tablets.

"We'll have to go back," he said, his voice almost inaudible.

"You know what they'll do to you," Toby said.

"What's the difference?" Jay asked, holding out his meager supply of life-preserving *troleen*.

"I won't go," Sooly said. "Let him go alone, Toby. Let him put us down somewhere in the United States."

"In five minutes?" Toby asked.

"Then we'll stay here," Sooly said.

"Yes," Toby said, with sudden decision. "It would be only fitting." He put his hand on Jay's arm. "Are you sure? It's certain death."

"On an Ankani sun," Jay said. "Not here on this miserable world."

They watched the scout blink away. It was early morning. The chill made Sooly huddle close, a mixture of fear and a warm glow of being at home causing her emotions to well up into her eyes. At a distance across the flat plain she could see the mound of a ruined city.

"We'll have some explaining to do," Toby said.

"We can say we're survivors of an aircraft crash," Sooly said.

"Without passports or identification?"

"Lost in the crash," Sooly said.

"It might work," Toby said doubtfully.

But it was not necessary to try. As the red sun lifted a swollen rim over the horizon, the scout vehicle lowered on visual control and settled into the waddi. Jay's face was red, his eyes wild. "They tried to kill me," he gasped, "without warning. I blinked out within sight of the *Entil* and they fired two blasters."

"And missed?" Toby asked, although that was evident. He was stunned.

"Thanks to the winds of Ankan, our Garge isn't one to believe in weapons practice," Jay said.

"So she'd decided on summary execution," Toby mused. "That course was last followed forty millennia ago."

"What now?" Jay asked, on the verge of collapse. "What can we do now?"

Toby frowned in worry. "Stay here during the day. We shouldn't be moving about when people can see."

"I don't care about these Ortonians," Jay said. He slumped. "But it doesn't matter. Nothing matters now."

The scout was not constructed for comfort. And, with power off, the sun soon made them feel as if they were, indeed, being spiraled down into a star doing a slow broil. Toby and Sooly went outside, in spite of Toby's distaste for Orton's sun, and lay on the ground in the shadow formed by the vehicle. For the first time, Sooly had time to consider all the implications of the events of the past few hours. She thought of her parents, who would, most certainly, be frantic by now. She hadn't even told them where she was going, walking out of the house while her mother was helping her father write his weekly report. She wondered if they'd have the fuzz looking for her by now. They'd find her Volkswagen at the bridge. Would they drag the Waterway for her body? Here she was on the other side of the world, an incredible distance when one considered the usual forms of communications. Where, in this wasted land, would she find a mailbox? A telephone?

She loved her parents and it pained her to think that they were worrying about her and would have to continue to worry until she found a means to contact them. And poor old Bem, lovingly named because of her most prominent feature, her eyes, Bug-Eyed Monster. It was that way on the registration papers, Sue Lee's Bug-Eyed Monster. Bem had refused to eat for days when she went away to school and had had to be taken to the vet for treatment when Sooly left once more, after being home only days, to spend her abortive short weeks in New York. Poor Bem.

But wasn't it silly to be worried about the fat old dog when Toby faced permanent exile and poor Jay faced an early death without his life-giving medicine?

"Toby," she said, "if this is growing up, to hell with it."

"Hummm?" Toby asked sleepily.

"Cool it," Sooly said, not wanting to burden him with her petty problems.

However, there was one good thing about the whole mess. Her love for Toby. At least they'd be together. It sounded inane to say that she'd make it up to him, but, God, wouldn't she try? But what if he came to resent her? What fantastic ego she had to think that her love, her body, would make up for everything, his losing his whole life to live for a terribly short time, among what to him must seem to be primitive people.

It was all very confusing and she hadn't been able, as yet, to absorb all of it. Her entire concept of herself and of the world had been changed in a few short hours. All the old questions remained, but the answers were different as could be and just as inaccessible. However, looking at the big picture took her mind off her parents and poor Bem and even, although it stayed in the back of her mind, the larger problems. The nature of God and the universe was still too much for her, but she knew a bit about the history of mankind, thanks to the freaky thing which had happened in her brain under Jay's infernal machine. It was a bit belittling to think that her people had been savages living from hand to mouth when the first Ankani ship came to the land between the rivers. And yet, thinking of the girl, Nipari, she could feel a fierce pride, for alone in a land of terrible elements and great beasts, the people had survived and conquered the beasts. And even if they had been given a hand up by Ankani knowledge and an infusion of Ankani blood, she could not quite accept the premise that all of man's achievements were to be attributed to Ankani influence. No. There was that feeling of, something, humanness, earthliness, something.

Curious, wanting to know more, she let her mind go as blank as possible and searched for the memories. She was bemused, at first, by the young Nipari and was tempted to reexperience the first coming of the "gods," to know the fear and awe and the joy of knowing that the gods had noticed and were coming to earth to aid the people. But she wanted to know more and pushed herself back, back, dying at the hands of a raiding band of hunters, being clawed by a huge cat, living, loving in different bodies but always a woman, never able to penetrate the minds of the males around her.

She went back through pain and lust and hunger and the joys of gluttony when the hunt was good, through winds and sand and ice and splashing in clean, clear water, with the memories becoming dim and misty and only areas of high emotional content coming through. Back into the slow, plodding, changing minds of heavy-limbed females, with her spirit sinking and her entire body being drained by the fierce emotions of the beds of natural lust, the killings, the birthings. Only the peaks now, never the quiet moments or the everyday life, and the land changing as the eons rolled back, back. Tortuous treks following changing climate, centuries compressed into moments, and the sun redder, more fierce, winds wet and torrential falls of rain and fierce beasts and it was all becoming so dim, so dim. Rudimentary language. Grunts of pain and anger and lust. Hulking, hairy males with huge, ugly heads and jutting jaws and the crunch of bone as a flint ax crushed her skull and she was so distant, so far that she despaired of ever coming back. Brutal, savage, bloody, dim-witted. Man. Roaring his challenge, taking his women with the strength of his hairy, massive arms. Knowing only the elemental flow of storm and sun and food and lust. Animals. Oh, God. Had she come from this? And yet so far, so far, such a vast sea of change and time and wonder from those upright apes and the joyful youth of the young Nipari.

Nothing. A misty sea of nothing. Aware of being, but in a dull cloud with only hints of pain and hunger and, always, that force, that lust, that urge to perpetuate the race. And just before exhaustion made it necessary to stop the sad, humiliating probe, just before, tears flowing in sympathy for those first men, those animals who stood on their feet, a blinding, brilliant revelation of such force that it was engraved on the memory of the race, a point of light in the darkness.

Shaken, experiencing the wonder through the eyes of a squat, powerful, hairy female, she could, at the same time, relate. It continued for days, weeks. Around her the people gaped, grunted, rolled their eyes in fear. And she could stand it no longer as it continued.

Another answer but an incomplete one. Back once again to the basic question, who created God? Lying there, weak, full of questions, the hot sun baking the dry land around them, Toby dozing. It was utterly freaky. But she knew that they had been alone. Then came—

She looked quickly at Toby to see if he had spoken. He was asleep. Jay was huddled miserably in the scout, ports open, his eyes closed.

Again.

Children

"Toby! Toby!" She was shaking him, frantic. He sat up rubbing his eyes. "You weren't the first, Toby."

"Huh?"

"They put it there. We, I, saw them. It was small and gleaming and they used machines and put it there—"

"Are you all right?" Toby asked. "The sun—"

"You weren't the first. They came long before you. So very long. And I saw them and—"

Children

"Toby, we've got to go there."

"Where?" Toby asked, thinking she must, surely, be suffering from the sun.

"There," she said, pointing. "Now."

"We can't move in daylight."

"Yes we can. We must. Now." She was up, pulling on him. "Because I know, Toby. I know a lot now and I can hear them and I've *got* to go, because they left it there until we could hear it and—"

It was difficult, almost impossible, for Toby to resist the will of a woman. Obeying was ingrained. And it would, at least, get them out of the infernal heat. What did it matter if the movement of the ship led to a few more flying saucer reports?

A family of wandering Bedouins saw the ship rise and disappear and murmured in fear before the wise patriarch dismissed the sights as another mirage of the flat land. Flying high, avoiding the air space of the warring Middle Eastern powers, Toby followed Sooly's pointing hand across the Persian Gulf, over the brown hills of Africa, questioning her.

"They came in huge ships from the sky," Sooly explained, as the small voice repeated itself in her head, guiding her, leading her. "Thousands of them, herded out onto the floor of the valley and forced to disperse by a mere handful of tall beings in space suits. We watched from the shelter of the ridges and we saw them use the machinery to put it there and I think that's what I'm hearing. It's saying, *children,* that's all. Just *children.* But I can feel it drawing me."

Jay was skeptical, but morose enough not to care. Toby was, himself, a bit doubtful, but he'd seen the first racial memories back there while monitoring

Jay's machine and he knew that there was something very different about this
Ortonian girl.

An anthropological expedition was camped in tents in the midst of a vast
wasteland through which ran deep ruts of erosion, exposing the age-old remains
of primitive man. "It doesn't matter," Sooly said forcefully, hearing the voice
very loudly now. "They'll know soon."

Dusty, sweating workers and tired, aging scientists, concerned at that moment with digging at the bones of the earth, itself, stopped their work, staring at
the scout as it lowered, settled to raise puffs of dust.

"We're here," Sooly said to the voice. She waited. There was nothing.
Around them the bare rocks were exposed and a white man in khaki was moving hesitantly toward them, several hundred yards off.

"We're here, damn it," Sooly said desperately. "We're here."

It was not in words. It flowed into her brain in a quick burst and she knew.
"Did you hear it?" she asked. Toby shook his head. She listened. The message
was repeated. There was no more. It was cryptic and she was furious with disappointment. Was that all? The message was repeated.

"We can go now, Toby," she said sadly. The scout blinked up, fading before the startled eyes of the scientists and the black workers.

"They put them here because they were going away," Sooly said. "And
they left the thing there under the earth and I don't think they ever, really, expected anyone to hear it."

"I think it's time you explained," Toby said.

"Toby, on the Wasted Worlds is there a huge city?"

"The Planet of Cities," Toby said, wondering where it was all going to
lead.

"They want us to go there," Sooly said. "To a high tower on a mountain
top, a tower built in the shape of a five pointed star."

"There's nothing there," Jay said. "It's deserted, all clues to the identity of
those who built it erased."

"Tell me the whole message," Toby said.

"It wasn't in words," she admitted. "It was a feeling. They called us children and there was a hint of sadness and then this picture of the tower in the
shape of a star and I knew that they wouldn't be there, because I saw it empty
and deserted, but they want us to go there. I had a feeling that it was part of
some kind of test."

"The Ortonian girl has lost her reason," Jay said.

"Toby, can this ship get us there?"

"Oh, yes." He nodded. "We have synthetic rations for six months. We
draw power from the stars. We can go anywhere in the Galaxy where expo ships
have put out beacons."

"Let's go, then," Sooly begged. "What have we got to lose?"

"Our lives if we get on a beacon with an Ankani ship," Jay said.

"This feeling you had," Toby asked. "Did you have the impression that
those who left the message also built the Planet of Cities?"

"Yes."

Toby looked at Jay. "If we could crack that nut, we'd be home free."

Home. Sooly felt as if something had torn loose inside her. Her parents would be frantic by now. It was purely incredible to think that she was about to embark on a trip into the stars, at distances which were unthinkable to her. It was even more incredible to think that she, Sooly, was to be the instrument in a vast change in the miserable history of mankind. For there was an implied promise in that feeling, that unspoken message sent into her brain from a shining, small object buried far under the earth by someone, someone who had helped people the earth, bringing a sea of humanoid beings to the old plains and valleys at a time when the people were not much more than animals. There was a promise and it was not meant for her alone but for all, for all of them. But in spite of it, of all the vast importance which she knew to be attached to that command, that invitation, she could not bring herself to go bugging off into the stars without telling her parents.

Mom and Dad. I'm going off to a distant solar system with Toby. Don't worry. Jeeeeeeesus. Flip? They'd die. They'd be sure she'd fallen into the hands of pimps and dope addicts and was strung out on some wild drug scene.

It was a time for crazy, almost comical happenings. Like an alien spaceship slowly easing down into the cleared space in the lot next to the darkened Kurt house.

Hey, Mom and Dad, there's a spaceship on the lot next door. How about that?

Toby, who didn't share Sooly's complete confidence that a blink to the Planet of Cities would solve all problems, was not hard to convince that Sooly should leave some kind of message for her parents. He was more than willing to postpone the nerve-racking trip to the heart of the Galaxy, because all the odds were against them. So he put her down on the vacant lot in a small clearing among big oak trees and she stepped out.

Bem was sleeping outside. She always did when Sooly was out, waiting up for her on the coolness of the cement stoop to greet her with wagging rump and snorting breaths. Bem was a silent type. A bark from her was an event and was not inspired by ordinary events such as the passage of a cat, a coon or a fox through the yard. The last time she had barked was when the bobcat got on the roof after a field mouse and so it was out of complete surprise that she gave one strained yap as she saw the ship come down. She was undecided, at first, but she caught Sooly's scent and came lumbering out to meet her, her whole backside wagging with happiness.

"Hi, old fatty," Sooly said, bending to pat the dog. "Old black dog."

The house was quiet. It was late. She imagined her mother inside, wakeful, perhaps. At best sleeping fitfully. How wonderful it would be to use her key, go in, wake them. But she couldn't. There would be hours of explaining and her father would yell. He was the type of father who had to be told everything and she'd never objected to that. It gave her a feeling of being valued and having to give information about where she was going and when she'd be in was a small price to pay for the place she had in that household.

She left the note pinned to the inside of the rear screen with a bobby pin.

Luvs

    Please don't worry. I'm fine and in no danger and I love you both very much. I'll be back soon and when you hear about it you'll forgive me for causing you this concern.

Sooly

Bem followed her back to the scout, snorting her disapproval of Sooly's behavior. "You can't go, baby," Sooly said. "You have to stay." The dog trembled and snorted. Sooly was crying. It was bad enough to worry her parents, but this poor, dumb old dog would never understand why she'd been deserted once more. "She won't eat when I'm away," she sniffed to Toby.

"Bring her if you like," Toby said. "If you think she can eat concentrated rations."

"She'll eat anything when I'm around," Sooly said, with a burst of silly happiness. Bem curled up in the seat beside her and went to sleep, snoring loudly. It was going to be a long, fantastic trip, but Sooly had something, at least. With Bem along, she would not feel that she was leaving everything behind on the world which grew small and disappeared as the scout blinked.

16

Seldom in the fine history of the Ankani Fleet had a blink been made in more discomfort. The scout, built for short missions, had no sleeping facilities, only four seats and a space just wide enough to accommodate a body between the banks of engines. As always on a blink, it was the long periods of waiting at the blink beacons which were the most deadly. To the pure tedium was added the tensions of uncertainty. As the stars grew more dense and the blinks became shorter, the Ortonian route merged with other starways. If an Ankani ship had blinked out while the power banks were gathering energy, the explanations would have been, to say the least, sticky. Curious officers would have wanted to know why a scout was at such a distance from the mother ship, and both Jay and Toby knew the impossibility of hiding the truth long from an officer.

The long blink was difficult for Toby in another way. He could see and touch the most fascinating woman he'd ever known, a woman for whom he'd given up so much, and yet common decency prevented him from opting with her. This tension added to all the other considerations made him, at times, moody.

The redeeming feature was that the long periods of waiting could be used for talk, for speculation about the nature of things, for personal confidences. By the time three-quarters of the distance between Orton and Ankan had been covered, Toby knew everything there was to know about his woman. His woman! The very words made him grin with a fierce joy. He was the first Ankani man in thousands of years to have his own woman and that wondrous fact made it all worthwhile.

As for Sooly, she asked thousands of questions and expressed loud and indignant surprise at each new revelation of the Ankani way of life, a life which had been controlled by women for fifty millennia. During a discussion of opting customs, she realized with a feeling of sadness that Toby had known many beautiful Ankani women, but she did not ask him specific details. He, sensing her hurt, kissed her, ignoring the scornful snort from Jay. "All that is past," he said. "I have made my final opting." And that satisfied her.

The message from Fleet Board was intercepted one short blink from the nearest Ankani world, with the communications gear monitoring all frequencies and both Jay and Toby on the alert for Ankani ships. It came in a one-minute burst and was extended by the repeater.

"Sterilize?" Sooly asked, upon hearing the message. "What do they mean, sterilize?" But she was deathly afraid that she knew. She'd been told of the Ankani taboo against genetic meddling and her stand was that such a taboo was fine for Ankanis if that was the way they felt, but that they had no right to impose their taboo on the people of the Earth.

"It means wipe off all traces of animate life," Toby said sadly.

"We have to go back," she shouted. "We have to stop them."

"How?" Toby asked.

"I don't know. We can go to Ankan. We can talk to this Fleet Board of yours."

"They wouldn't listen," Toby said. "Our only chance is to go on to the Planet of Cities. If we can provide the Board with the secret of the Wasted Worlds, perhaps they'll listen." He sighed. "We're two blinks away. It will take the message approximately four of your weeks to reach the *Entil,* about another week for the ship to prepare the sterilizer. We have time to get to the Planet of Cities and back to a point where our message might just get there before they carry out the orders."

"But if we don't learn anything?" Sooly asked.

"We can only try," Toby said. He was thinking of the small birds and animals around the base, back there on Orton. They would feel nothing. But for a long time the stink of carrion would pollute the atmosphere of the planet while a few surviving micro-organisms toiled away to decay unthinkable mountains of flesh. For the first time in his life he was not proud of being Ankani.

In spite of Sooly's desperation, there was no way to hurry the two remaining blinks. But then, with the sense of urgency that had an almost tangible force in the cabin of the scout, the Planet of Cities was below, magnificent in ruins, lit by a mild sun whose benevolent rays glowed golden on the enduring age-old buildings. Jay, who had made two trips to the planet as a youthful crewman on scientific ships, found the star tower by trial and error, with only a few wasted hours.

There was a gentle breeze. It made its way through the deep canyons between buildings to caress them, to belie the grim message of death which was flashing and resting, flashing and resting, through the stars behind them. The entranceway penetrated to the center of the square and led them into a tremendous, domed hall. The walls were niched, but all the recesses were empty, save for a fine, ancient dust. Sooly paused in the center of the hall, looked around, listening. Not even the sigh of the wind could be heard inside the huge building. Her feet left tracks in the fine layer of dust on the floor. She had never felt so lonely. She'd seen the extent of the empty cities and the vastness of the planet. On that entire world four entities breathed. A woman, two men and a fat, black dog. Dust got in Bem's nose and made her sneeze.

"Anything?" Toby asked.

"No," she said, her brow furrowed in concern.

She walked slowly around the great hall. Doorways led off at angles into the points of the star. The wall niches were irregularly shaped. She completed the circuit of the hall and stood with Toby, feeling despair. "This is the place," she said. "I know it is."

"It's estimated that this planet was deserted as long as five hundred thousand years ago," Toby said.

"But they told me to come here," she said. "This has to be it."

"There are other deserted cities on other planets," Jay said.

"The planet I saw was this one," Sooly said. "I saw it in my mind. It was one vast city from horizon to horizon. No oceans. No mountains. Are there others like that?"

"We know of none," Toby said. "But—"

"Oh, goddamn," Sooly said. She raised her head. "Speak to me, you bastards. We've come all this way. Now you speak to me."

The only sound was Bem's troubled breathing.

"We can search the other rooms. The other floors." Toby's voice contained little optimism.

"We have to hurry," Sooly said, remembering that deadly message winging its way to the Ankani ship in orbit around her home. "Let's separate." Toby frowned. "If this damned place is as deserted as you say, there's no danger."

"Some of the buildings are in an advanced state of decay," Toby said. "And we'll have to get power belts to reach the upper stories. The elevators don't work, of course, and there are no stairways."

"We have to do something," Sooly said desperately. "I'll start on the ground floor while you two get your belts or whatever and begin on the upper floors."

It took two days to search the building. After Toby and Jay went to the scout for power belts, Toby suggested that a separate search would be useless, since Sooly had been the only one able to hear the message back on Orton. None of them knew exactly what they were looking for, but judging from the way the message was received by Sooly on her own planet, there would not be, perhaps, any external sign of the hidden communications device. So having to guide Sooly through every room of the huge building took time and energy. Bem was left outside, snorting and worrying when Sooly was lifted by the power belt to the upper stories, but she soon grew calm when she realized that Sooly wasn't going far away and would come back at intervals.

Level after level yielded nothing, only empty rooms, odd-shaped rooms, surprisingly conventional rooms, long tunnels, unexplained shafts. Toby, able to find good in most everything, applied his brain to a detailed and complete study of the architecture of one Wasted Worlds building, but it was an exercise in futility with no reward in view, for he was resigned now to being an exile. He was angry about, but also broodingly resigned to, the destruction of Orton. He was powerless to stop it.

Late in the evening of the second day, dusty, tired, despairing, they reached the topmost level. The tips of the star were much the same as on other floors, but at the center of the star, circled by a wide hall, was a solid core of the enduring plastic used for much of the building on the Planet of Cities. The enclosed space was large, but there were no entrances.

"It could have contained a sealed power unit of some sort," Toby guessed.

"Such a large space would not have been wasted," Jay agreed.

"If we had a weapon, we could blast out a section," Toby said.

Jay produced a small hand blaster. Toby had forgotten that his former superior rating had carried an illegal weapon back on Orton. Jay stepped back as far as possible, put the weapon on narrow beam, and aimed it. The force was absorbed by the material of the circular wall of the inner core. Jay frowned, increased power. The energy would have cut through five feet of stainless steel. The wall, however, did not change in the slightest. Jay walked a few paces, tried another spot. The result was the same.

"We must be onto something," Toby said. "There is no material known which can withstand a sustained blaster force."

As if to confirm that statement, Jay pointed the blaster at the outer wall and a section of material smoked and disintegrated. "It would seem to me," Toby said, "that the entire thing is a sort of test. That object which you say was buried on Orton had been there for a long time and no one heard it before you. To get to this planet, we had to have certain advanced knowledge. Perhaps we don't, as yet, possess the knowledge required to break through this wall."

"We have to," Sooly said.

They started walking around the circular core of the building again, examining the wall carefully. It was solid and continuous. Not one crack or blemish marred its white expanse. At intervals Jay tried the blaster with negative results. Sooly was becoming increasingly desperate and irrationally angry. They'd been led this far and she was not going to be put off by trickery.

After circling the unbroken wall twice, Toby was stumped. "Look," he said. "Let's go back to the ship, have some food, think it over."

"No," Sooly said emotionally. "This is it. I know it is. We can't give up." She faced the wall and hated it with a fury which sent color into her face, increased her heartbeat, set her glands working furiously. "You, in there," she said, her voice low, intense. "You've got to help us. You can't just lead us on and then stop us cold."

Directly in front of them the wall changed color. The unbroken white turned dim blue and deepened in the shape of an arched doorway. They waited. The color change was complete and still the wall was intact. Toby pushed against the blue outline of the doorway and it was firm, solid. He stepped back. Jay used the blaster. The blue doorway melted, leaving an opening into a large, circular room. It, like the other rooms of the building, was empty, but in the center was a round column which extended from floor to ceiling and, upon approaching it, they saw two niches in the shape of the human form, one obviously female, the other male. With a wild excitement, Sooly approached the column. She touched it, waiting. Nothing.

"I think we're supposed to stand inside, in the niches," Toby said.

Sooly moved quickly into the niche which was cut into the shape of a female. She fit snugly. Toby stood in the other. She heard, felt, sensed it immediately. But it was merely a meaningless series of numbers. She opened her mind and waited. The series of numbers was repeated. Disappointment was a vile taste in her mouth. After hearing the series of numbers three times, she stepped out. Toby was standing in his niche, frowning.

"Did you hear anything?" he asked.

"Didn't you?"

"No," he said.

"It was just numbers," she said. She repeated the first few as best she could remember. Toby looked at Jay.

"Blink coordinates?" Toby asked. Jay nodded, interest on his face for the first time in weeks.

"Go in again," Toby said. "Write them down carefully. Be sure you don't miss a single digit."

She listened four times through to be sure. Satisfied, she handed Toby the paper upon which she'd written the series of numbers which were meaningless to her.

"Let's get down to the ship and check the charts," Toby said. "The first one is the coordinate for this planet. But I think the second and third must be wrong."

Back in the scout, hunger forgotten in the excitement, Toby checked and rechecked. "Meaningless," he said sadly. He showed his calculations to Jay. Jay's face fell. Toby tried to think how he could tell Sooly that the blink coordinates she'd heard in the room there atop the ancient building were meaningless.

"Right out into inter-Galactic space," Jay said. "Right into limbo."

"What does he mean, Toby?" Sooly asked worriedly.

"Blinking is tied to the known mass of a particular star," Toby explained. "When a ship blinks, it ceases to exist, for all practical purposes. It goes out of the fabric of time and space and is in—" he thought of something she'd understand, "—whatever it is, but you might call it another dimension, but it's a dimension with no dimension. It just doesn't exist. It happens so fast that you don't know it. It seems almost instantaneous. But when a ship blinks, it and everything in it literally ceases to exist and the only way it comes back into existence is to use the mass of a large star to pull it back from this nowhere. To blink, you have to know in advance the exact location and the exact mass of the anchor star. We've been traveling a route which was mapped out laboriously, going from star to star to set up known beacons and coordinates. But this first blink in your series of numbers would put us completely outside the Galaxy, out in space where there would be no anchor. We'd have nothing to pull us back. We'd just cease to exist."

"No," Sooly said, remembering the sadness, the kindness she felt when she first heard the call of the small object beneath the African plain. "They wouldn't do that. They must have known."

"Perhaps the mechanical object which delivered the message has lost some of its effectiveness," Jay said. "It could have given her the wrong coordinates."

"Yes," Toby said.

"Check again," Sooly told him. "It's right. I know it's right."

Toby checked again. This time he checked the entire blink through. From the plane of the Galaxy, the first blink went out toward the vast emptiness on a line perpendicular to the flattened spiral. The second extended outward, coming back toward the plane of the spiral at an angle, to end near a giant, outlying star. That one made sense. It ended near an anchor. The third blink disappeared into the thin stars of the periphery opposite the planet of Orton, all the way across the huge, central bulge of stars from Ankan.

"Could they have calculated the mass of the entire Galaxy?" Toby asked, with sudden inspiration. "I know it sounds impossible, but could they have done it?"

Jay was interested. "The first blink is far enough out," he said. "It's a fantastic idea. It would open us to inter-Galactic exploration."

"They built this planet," Toby said. "They put people on Orton, according to Sooly's memories." He made his decision. "I'm willing to try."

"What the hell?" Jay shrugged, using an Ortonian phrase.

17

The Galaxy was spread before them like an illustration in an astronomy book. The flattened central disc was a brightness which seemed to draw the eye from the whorls of the spiral arms. Huge globular clusters appeared as single stars. Other, more distant galaxies were pinpoints in the blackness. There was time to admire and for a long time none spoke and when they did it was in awed whispers. Meanwhile, the power banks were drawing on that vast panorama of stars, using the entire Galaxy instead of a single star and the process was accelerated, the second blink programmed and executed before they had time to enjoy, to drink in the incredible beauty of a spiral galaxy seen from a distance just great enough to allow an appreciation of the symmetry of the system. Jerked out of nothingness by a huge fellow on the Sagittarius periphery, they were still awed by the last vista which had sent light patterns into their eyes before blinking. The nearness of scattered stars was a letdown. But now only one short blink was ahead.

They came out near a kind of dim star without a family of planets. Alone, it wandered an emptiness on the fringe of the Galaxy, their destination—and an evident disappointment until Toby activated the sensors and found, at a respectable distance from the sun, a tiny mass too small to be called planet, too large to be called asteroid. They moved close enough to measure its mass, blinked in close. And they knew that they had reached the end of the search, for the planetoid was artificial, a circular mass of white material with the same readings as the unbreachable wall back in the Tower of the Star. Expecting another test, Toby lowered the scout to the surface and was preparing to set down when a force seized them, moved them across the surface, lowered them, power banks dead, through an opening which appeared at the last second.

Blank white walls surrounded them with an unbroken expanse. A quick test proved the atmosphere to be breathable. With a growing eagerness and some fear, Sooly followed Toby outside the scout. A section of wall opened. An unseen force urged them forward into a chamber which was so luxuriously furnished that it took Sooly's breath. The carpet underfoot had the feel of thick, closely-mowed grass. Furnishings were strangely shaped, but blended into the overall contrast of color and texture in an alien but delightful way. And the walls, while giving the impression of being at a distance, were not walls but shouting, heart-stopping works of art which seemed to change and alter while speaking directly to the mind, giving an impression of beauty which made Sooly's heart forget, for the moment, the urgency of the situation.

Children, you have come so far

The voice was unheard, inside them. It was feminine.

"Please," Sooly said. "Please talk with us."

So far we are pleased

"Are you the people of the Wasted Worlds?" Toby asked.

You call them that you will be seated while we———you

There was no understanding of the concept. However, they sat on soft, yielding cushions which, while yielding, supported them in comfort.

Pleased, excited laughter. But you have combined forces marvelous. Puzzlement? The native life form? Unforeseen—a male voice—pleasure, surprise. The large-eyed ones and the hairy animals of———III. Delightful.

Children you may go

"Go?" Sooly asked. "We can't. Not yet. You must help us. They're going to kill everyone—"

Regret. Indifference. A trace of resentment and boredom and impatience and then a leak-through of pleasure so keen that the infinitesimal amount which filtered through

Stop you'll burn them out

Random punchings.

Wait can't you see

No matter

Yes put them back

Long, long journeys into ecstasy with three frail children lying, stunned, on the grass-like floor

Put them back

Feminine weakness if you want them back you put them back

I went out it is the rule a small part of you

Simpler to eject them

No put them back we all agreed to see them

A glow over the fallen bodies touching, entering, erasing. An unseen force lifting, moving. A small, black animal giving one startled bark before she, too, was limp. A glow hovering and time which wasn't time passing as the scout blinked and lowered to a dead Planet of Cities and then movement in the recesses of the ship's instruments as time turned backward to leave no record of the

Late in the evening of the second day, dusty, tired, despairing, they reached the topmost level. The tips of the star were much the same as on other floors, but at the center of the star, circled by a wide hall, was a solid core of the enduring plastic used for much of the building on the Planet of Cities. The enclosed space was large, but there were no entrances.

"It could have contained a sealed power unit of some sort," Toby guessed.

"Such a large space would not have been wasted," Jay agreed.

"If we had a weapon, we could blast out a section," Toby said.

Jay produced a small hand blaster. Toby had forgotten that Jay had carried an illegal weapon on Orton. Jay stepped back, put the weapon on narrow beam and cut a hole in the wall. Toby led the way into the large, circular room. He'd seen photographs of others like it. Although all of the equipment which had once filled it had been removed in those dim, dark days of the distant past when the worlds were divested of any clue as to the form or achievements of their inhabitants, such rooms did give Ankani scientists reason to suspect that they were once repositories for advanced machinery probably used to develop some type of energy. It was empty. The floor was devoid of the layer of fine dust which was present in other, unsealed, rooms, but it was totally empty. Nothing marred the smoothness of floor, walls and ceiling. And, although she tried and vented all her anger on the unfeeling things which had led them so far on a fruitless mission, Sooly heard nothing. Nor did a repeated search of the starshaped tower yield anything.

"We have time to get to Ankan," Toby said.

"For what? Our executions?" Jay asked in a surly voice. He was hoarding his last *troleen,* and his heart was reminding him of his age with irregular sharp pains.

"It may be too late already," Toby said, "but maybe they'll believe that Sooly heard something on Orton. Maybe they'll send a message canceling the sterilization order. If the *Entil* hasn't started—"

"We have to try," Sooly said. God, she felt old. She was nineteen years old and she'd found the man she loved and she lived so long, so very long, all those thousands of years back to Nipari and beyond and now it was all going to end and they'd kill Toby and Jay and it was so damned unfair. But then what had ever been fair about being human? She knew the pain of death and the horror of seeing a city overrun by the barbarians of the hills and the crunch of teeth on bone and the momentary burst of brilliant sun when the skull is crushed and through it all man had lived and died as hopelessly as even the most depraved maniac could ever have imagined and what did it all mean? Nothing, goddamn, nothing.

The little scout lifted, blinked. Four short blinks away was Ankan.

18

*O*nce every four-thousand pairings she was allowed by mutual consent to play a certain combination of six keys of a certain sequence against just over seven thousand of his keys in a complicated action which brought a surprisingly simple pleasure, happy nostalgia. She never became bored with it, although he preferred more sophisticated pairings made by random, experimental punches. However, with eternity ahead and eons behind and the punching combinations infinite, he indulged her and wallowed in her teary nostalgia, rather enjoying it, as a matter of fact. Actually, no combination was unenjoyable, some were just more lasting and exciting.

Around them the gleaming white asteroid pulsed silently with mechanical activity as undying, self-renewing servos drew needed atoms from the distant sun and remolded them into the necessary elements. Immediately after the departure of the children, the force fields had crackled into place, distorting light to make the asteroid disappear and enclosing it in a cocoon which would have defied almost any force, up to the energies released by a supernova. After a brief, only mildly amusing interlude, pleasure flowed without interruption once again. The interruption was only the second in five hundred thousand years, the first being necessitated by a normal change in a particular star which required a move to the kind, pale sun at a respectable distance from the planetoid.

They were so cute

She had not, he decided, recovered from the novelty of communication other than through pleasure. Since it did not interfere, being carried on with only a small, insignificant portion of the entity, he did not object.

And the small black animal

Nine-eight-five-two-oh-six-two paired four-four-one. She had a thing about low numbers and in his random punches he humored her. The massive jolt of pure pleasure existed for an eternity and dimmed not and communication was not worth the effort for it was a happy combination reinforced by the nature of the combined entities massed into two and submerged in the sea of something above sex, above life, above the pleasures of food and drink.

But she remembered and, on her combination, she allowed a small part of her to visit the knowledge banks and seek out an unremembered figure.

On————, she told him, evolution produced two hundred million species of plants and animals and it is estimated that the planet of the dark ones, being younger, has still produced one hundred million species

It disturbs you

The word has no meaning

A new combination. He was fantastically lucky with his random punches. It shattered her with new sensation.

Remember the Techcals

Of course

We could call up their shades

To what purpose

She chose a known combination, less adventurous than he, reveled in its familiarity.

We had never expected them to follow the trail, she told him, and were it not for the vitality of the native species they would not have been able to hear would it not be interesting to watch to see if they can achieve more for we are responsible

Meaningless

For creating them, the big eyes and the dark ones and the others, in our stumbling way moving toward

This, a combination which blasted with pleasure.

Once we were like them

Laughter. A long time ago

When I——— them I saw the beautiful, large-eyed women. They have managed to continue their numerical superiority. Laughter, feminine, delightful, teasing. An achievement. And the young female was moving into a primitive stage of awareness

———III which they called Earth or Orton contains the age-lasting concept of animal force and violence

But we, too, went through that stage I know long ago and just two thousand of their years from barbarism to a shallow-space culture

Because of the influence of the large-eyed ones, which were more successful

The girl's development was mostly evolutionary. Don't you see—the experiments were not so unsuccessful

Even the large-eyed ones are hopelessly primitive. Are they not going to exterminate an entire planet

Remember the Techcals, how we———ed their colonization fleet of two thousand ships and then———ed a few hundred stars on the rim of their Galaxy as a further warning. We had remnants of barbarism

Self-protection. We could not co-exist with the Techcals. We were mutually destructive

The large-eyed children see themselves threatened by the primitive attempts of the scientists of———III. And did we not implant the repugnance in the large eyes

It was decided long ago that we should allow them to develop naturally

And there were those among us even then who said that we were responsible

Females

They were our children not of our flesh but of our eggs. We had our arrogance. Creating them engineering them for special purposes. The large eyes for the dim planets and the dark ones for the fiery suns

You were sad when we left them, I know. But we felt we were right not only in altering them to spread life through a sterile Galaxy

Not sterile there was———III, a planet much like the home world with the same sun the same slow process of change. And you were not content to leave it to develop but peopled it with our children the special purpose ones

A wrong guess. We should have allowed more time for testing

You admit you were wrong

Do you realize this is the first time you've exercised the old feminine technique of I-told-you-so in forty millennia

In all the Galaxy two, just two, and because our sun was older and was developing life while the sun of———III was still being formed we are going to allow the large-eyed ones to destroy all life. They are ending the experiment and that ends our last influence on that mixture of native life, our children from the fiery suns and the blood of the large-eyed men. We made them and we were fumbling in fields which we did not fully understand. Not even our great knowledge of life could make them perfect outside the mother's womb with the building blocks of life manipulated to make them suitable for the marginal planets. And now we are given a second chance through the happy accidents which have produced that young girl. What will be left if we do not act once more. The large-eyed children will live and continue to make their minute advances but they will never reach

He saw and laughed. Fickle woman, are you so bored with me that you want another to play your console

And you radiant one with random punches and your lust for the novel, would you not view with pleasure the opportunity to share pleasure with an entirely new entity

I would have to go out once more

This time I will go. The eggs which produced them were taken from me. It will take but a moment

A multi-digit punch and a lucky one left her momentarily weak with joy and then she was gone. To amuse himself he broke into his billions of component minds and reviewed the history of the race for he would not punch his own console

That small, detached part of her found them preparing to leave. She——— through the solid walls of the scout's cabin, a vibrant glow which caused the small, dark animal to bristle and bark warningly. For a moment she looked directly into the child's eyes and she found them to be beautiful, almost as beautiful as the orbs of the large-eyed ones. She sent a momentary message of reassurance and then entered, causing their bodies to go limp and sink back into the seats. It took but a moment. Then the ship's clock went wild, speeding backward, other instruments adjusting.

As she waited, she tried forms. This caused some minor discussion among the individual parts of her entity, but it was decided, in plenty of time, that she would take the form of a primitive. It was novel. Of course, the flesh and blood form could not appreciate the pleasures of breathing the old air of the home world, but in the absence of true pleasure it passed the time. She traced their passage through lower levels. They were, of course, empty.

19

Level after level yielded nothing, only empty rooms. On the evening of the second day, dusty, tired, despairing, they reached the topmost level. There were only empty rooms in the arms of the star, but at the center, encircled by a wide hall, was a solid core of the enduring plastic used for much of the buildings on the Planet of Cities. The enclosed space was large, but there were no entrances.

"It could have contained a sealed power unit of some sort," Toby guessed.

"Such a large space would not have been wasted," Jay agreed.

"If we had a weapon, we could blast out a section," Toby said.

Jay produced a small hand blaster, the same illegal weapon he'd used against the rats on Orton. He stepped back. The wall absorbed the energy of the blaster. Puzzled, since no known material could resist the energy of a blaster, Jay advanced the power and tried again. The wall didn't even heat. They walked the circular hall, Jay trying the blaster at intervals without success. There was no crack, no blemish, in the whiteness of the wall.

Sooly's world was ending. With a mixture of anger and despair, she faced the wall. "You in there," she said, her voice low, emotional, her glands working, her face flushed, her tears forming. "You must help us. You can't lead us all this way and leave us with nothing."

A section of the wall in the shape of an arched doorway changed to a pleasing blue shade. Toby pushed against it. It was unyielding. But when Jay trained his blaster it melted away, giving them access. The room was huge, windowless, empty. But it was lit by a source which Toby could not discover. Sooly ran forward, paused.

"Empty," she said desolately. She listened. There was nothing. Toby took her hand, trying to console her.

The woman materialized in the exact center of the circular room. The first impression was one of a blazing beauty which made one want to close one's eyes. Her hair was the blackness of space and her eyes were the blue of a summer sea and her hair was arranged in a style which none of them had ever seen. She wore a shimmering gown cut below firm, outthrust breasts but the effect was one of naturalness because of her regal bearing. She stood motionless, smiling out at them.

"Yes, Lady," Jay said, moving as he spoke, running out of the room with an agility which belied his years and the precarious state of his health. He returned with a wide angle tricorder and in the interim, Toby and Sooly tried not to stare, but their staring seemed not to bother the woman. She was as still as a statue, her expression not changing, the pleased smile frozen on her face.

"Children," she said. "Having come this far, you have shown certain traits of development for which we have been waiting." Her words were natural, soft, without pomposity. None of them noticed, so closely was their attention riveted to her beauty, that her words were being engraved deeply into the impervious material of the walls, but the tricorder was filming the formation of the words as it recorded the sound of her voice, the engraved words being additional, eternal proof of the miracle.

"Our own development dictated our actions. To achieve our destiny, we left you, for you could not accompany us. Yet, we prayed that you would follow us in achievement and would, someday, join us in—" They felt a feeling of eternal peace and joy. "Now you have made the first, tentative steps and although you do not need to know all, you may know our nature, as we were." And they saw the Planet of Cities living. It was an administrative and scientific center and the people were tall and fair and happy. "This state of Galaxy-wide peace and plenty is within your reach. What follows is largely dependent on your own ambitions and abilities."

She paused. Sooly was deathly afraid of what was going to happen then, expecting her to disappear and leave the problems unresolved. She moved forward, and in moving saw the wall clearly through the form of the beautiful woman. In the period of silence, she gathered her courage and walked to the woman. Her hand went through the image without disturbing the smile on her beautiful face.

"We erred," the woman said, the smile fading for the first time, "in making you." Jay and Toby gasped as fifty millennia of Ankani pride was blasted. "To prevent a repetition of such error, we implanted in you the abhorrence of genetic meddling which limited you."

"You didn't make me!" Sooly said, before she could stop herself.

"No, child." The woman looked directly at Sooly with a particular fondness. "And you are the hope. Nature—" she smiled sadly. "You see, in spite of our great advances, we do not have all the answers, either. So let us call that force nature and say that she, as the millennia crawled past, worked to rectify our mistakes. She took what we gave her, you, the large-eyed ones, the others which were placed on your Earth, child, and combined them to put life back on the track, to lead upward once again. Together, you can achieve." Once again they felt that unearthly joy and wonder, bliss, pleasure, fulfillment.

"The men of Ankan, outnumbering women five to one, find the daughters of the Earth to be fair and the women of Earth outnumber men. You must take up the surpluses by intermingling, for the seeds of both are necessary. The vitality of Earth. The knowledge of Ankan. Continue your abhorrence of altering the building blocks of life which nature has provided you, but moderate your position, men of Ankan, to work with the scientists of Earth to understand the mind. You have far to go, because it is the nature of man to be rigid. Your women of Ankan will protest and the men of Earth will resent the strangers who take their women, but," her face grew serious, "you are not alone and there is the danger." Images of alien life, strange, menacing, utterly different, came to them. The tricorder took the emotions and implanted them. They saw the ancient war, the aliens coming from inter-Galactic space in their strange ships. Confrontation. Mutual destruction. "They are crowded." In their distant Galaxy they saw the aliens, teeming, expanding. "People first the outlying worlds, for the Techcals have seen the ability of the people of this Galaxy and your mere presence on the outlying worlds, which they would have to colonize first, will be your first defense."

She faded. "Wait," Sooly cired. "Please wait." But she was gone. And the order to sterilize her Earth was speeding across the wastes, leaping from star anchor to star anchor faster than any ship could travel, at the same speed, with an impossible head start, that a following message would travel.

Jay, having discovered the engraved copy of the beautiful woman's words, was recording it head-on, so that it would be distinct and readable.

Sooly sat on the floor and wept. They had come so near and the only hope was that they could get to Ankan, show the proof to the powers there and dispatch an order canceling the sterilization message and hope that the ship had delayed long enough in executing the order. It was, as Toby had explained, a remote possibility. Garge Cele Mantel was an efficient woman. It would take her only a matter of days to prepare the ship for the sterilization.

Sooly tried to get hold of herself, rose. "Toby," she said, "let's go."

The scout blinked out from the Planet of Cities and held at the first anchor point, building power. The wait seemed endless. Time ticked past and the death of a planet came ever closer.

Jay, who had taken his last *troleen* in the aftermath of the appearance of the beautiful woman, felt fine and bemused himself by playing back the tricording of the event. Toby was gnawing his lips in concern and Sooly felt as if she were going to have Jay's heart attack, so great was her fear and horror.

"If there were only a way to blink directly to Orton," Toby said, knowing that he was repeating himself, for he'd made that futile wish many times. But they were in the dense star fields, near the central bulge of the Galaxy. Between them and Orton, on any straight line, were hundreds of stars, and blinking was a straight line process. The immense fields of the stars distorted, had to be bypassed.

He studied his charts, hoping desperately to discover a route overlooked by the expo ships, but he knew that he could not possibly hope to discern, with one human mind, what banks of computers and hundreds of years of expo work had failed to find. He felt anger toward the beautiful woman. She had known, even if she were merely some sort of image. She'd known of the developments which brought them to the Planet of Cities, so she should have known about the crisis on Orton. She could have helped. If she had the abilities she had to possess in order to achieve the things she'd intimated, she could have helped them.

"Stars of Ankan," Jay exploded, the portable triviewer still in place before his eyes. "Copy this." He read a series of numbers. Toby recognized them immediately as blink coordinates. He checked his charts. "At the very end of the written message," Jay said. "She didn't speak them, but they were there."

"From the Planet of Cities into space outside the Galaxy," Toby said excitedly. "They computed the mass of the Galaxy and used it as an anchor point!"

Power was nearly total. The blink back to the Planet of Cities was a short one. Once there, there was time to check and recheck. The blink coordinates led, indeed, to Orton, and in three short blinks. The first went vertically out of the plane of the Galaxy and the second anchored to a star near Orton and the third would put them in sight of Orton's sun. Power built, they blinked and stared out in awe at the ponderous wheel of the Galaxy, used the power of the

entire Galaxy to build the banks and blinked in an amazingly short time. The
rest was elementary.

20

Cele Mantel nodded grimly when the message was received. She approved. It
was a terrible thing to contemplate erasing all animal life on the planet, but
there was no other choice. Five hundred thousand years of civilization was in
the balance and there were no other choices. The evil scientists of Orton had
chosen their own destiny. Her only regret was that the deserters would not be
on the planet when she unloosed the killing rays. Ship's instruments had
recorded the departure of the scout, blinking out toward Ankan weeks past. But
they would not escape. Their travel would be limited to known starways and
sooner or later they'd blink into a beacon station with an Ankani ship. At best,
if they had incredible luck, they would find sanctuary on some empty planet and
go into a permanent exile until some Ankani ship revisited, because the scout
was incapable of traveling to uncharted planets. It might be a slow process, but
they'd be caught. The alert had been given and soon all Ankani ships would be
on the lookout for the scout.

The conversion to sterilization power occupied the crew for days, while
Cele fretted with impatience and Babra Larkton examined her face in the mirror to see if the bruise on her face had really faded, at last. There was an atmosphere of gloom aboard the *Entil,* for, although she'd told the entire ship the
vital reasoning behind sterilization, it was a serious, unprecedented action. She
sympathized with the younger officers who repeatedly asked if there weren't
some way to do it differently, just punish the offenders and leave, at least, the
amazing variety of lower animal and bird life. Cele tried to console them by
saying that the rays would not penetrate into the depths of the oceans and that,
therefore, the seeds of life might survive to crawl out of the ocean again, if, indeed, the theories of evolution on Orton were correct. It was small comfort.

When, at last, the engineering section reported that the weapons had been
altered and were ready, Cele set the hour. It would begin on the western continents, radiating in hundreds-of-miles-wide bands sweeping from pole to pole
and overlapping to prevent any survivors.

At the appointed hour, she positioned herself at control. She would not
merely give a cold command. She would push the button herself, for it would
be, at best, a traumatizing experience and she was not a Garge who would ask
her subordinates to do something she would not do herself.

"We are prepared, Lady," said a glum-faced rating standing before the
power switch.

"Five minutes and counting," Cele said, going through the countdown procedure to emphasize the seriousness of the operation. "Four and counting."

Time crawled. Chronometers crawled, oozing out the last minutes of a
world. "One minute and counting," Cele said, "Fifty-nine, fifty-eight—"

Her heart was pounding surprisingly. For a panic-filled moment she took her eyes off the clock and looked at the viewer to see the blue planet swimming in space below them. She felt tearful regret, but her determination was as hard as steel. She was going to insure the continued survival and supremacy of her race. "Thirty seconds and counting," she said, her voice choked with emotion.

"Lady—" A rating on the censors.

"Twenty seconds," Cele said.

"A vehicle," said the rating. "Approaching under power."

"Ten, nine, eight," Cele counted, her finger on the button.

"He's coming on a collision course," the rating yelled. "He's going to ram us."

"Hold!" Cele cried, leaping from her command chair to see the small scout brake, ran its nose into the orifice of the main battery with a jar which was felt even through the vast bulk of the partially loaded *Entil*. "Use the grapples and get them inside." This part she was going to enjoy. For she knew her own scout when she saw it and providence had delivered the rebels to her. They'd come in a vain attempt to stop the sterilization. She should have known they'd try. They'd gone native, adopted the ways of Orton. Naturally they'd make some dramatic, manlike gesture to stop the destruction of life on their chosen world.

Toby felt the grapples engage. "They'll wait now," he said. "She'll want us down there before she begins."

The scout was drawn into the *Entil*. A reception committee of officers and ratings were waiting outside. "Follow me out," Toby said, Jay's blaster in his hand. He popped the port and leaped out to confront the startled officers. Unaccustomed to the ways of mutineers, they were not expecting an armed and determined man, but a cringing, begging, rating seeking mercy. Manto Babra Larkton reached uncertainly for her weapon and looked, for the first time in her life, into the orifice of a blaster.

"I'll fire," Toby told her and she believed him. She'd never seen such a look of determination on the face of a rating. "I want to see the Garge, quickly."

Unthinkable! A mere rating giving orders to females. "Now," Toby said, as Jay and Sooly arranged themselves behind him and Bem, in strange surroundings, gave one short, hoarse bark from the open port.

"You can't hope to stand against an entire ship," Babra said with a cold fury.

"Move," Toby said, surprised at himself. He added, "Move, please, Lady," to calm the sense of guilt.

The passage to the bridge was uneventful, although surprised, white-faced ratings watched as the little group moved swiftly through the corridors, winding around the central cargo hold to the Orton-oriented command room where Cele Mantel waited with impatience.

"What?" she gasped, when Babra entered first, Toby holding his blaster at her back.

"He's mad, Cele," Babra cried tearfully. "Blast him. Don't concern yourself with me."

"Lady," Toby said. "There is no need for blasting. If you will only listen."

"Take him," Cele said, her voice shrill with shock. "Seize them."

"Lady," Toby said. "I've never killed a man, but then no one has ever tried to kill a planet, either. I believe that I could kill anyone, even you, to prevent such a disaster. Please don't make me decide before you listen."

"Hold," Cele said, to the ratings who were edging nervously toward Toby as he stood with his blaster in Babra's back. "And if we listen, then what?"

"I can't answer that," Toby said. "I ask only that you see and hear a tricording made on the Planet of Cities."

"Impossible," Cele said, quickly calculating the time which had elapsed since the scout blinked out of the Orton system. "Are you telling me you've been to the Planet of Cities?"

"We have," Toby said. "And we have here a tricording which will change the course of history." He lowered his blaster. "Will you see it, Lady?"

"Your trickery will avail you nothing," Cele said. "However, I am a reasonable woman. I will see your tricording if you first yield your weapon."

"Don't do it," Jay said. "Remember that she promised a fair hearing and yet she trained the ship's blasters on me when I approached."

Toby felt a cold sweat of indecisiveness break out on his forehead. Babra turned, held out her hand grimly.

"Give it to her, Toby," Sooly said. "I don't think your Lady will forget your honor twice."

The decision was made for him, Toby handed the weapon to the Manto.

"We will view your nonsense," Cele said. Jay, his *troleen* losing its effectiveness, weakly handed the tricording to a rating, who inserted it in the projector.

"As I thought," Cele said, when the image of the beautiful woman appeared on the ship's screens, "look at the small eyes. An Orton woman."

"Wait," Toby begged.

"Children," said the image, and, as she viewed it through, Cele Mantel's pride began to shatter.

It was a different woman who called the Ship's Board of Officers into session, with Jay, Toby and Sooly present, to show the tricording again. Babra Larkton was furious with hate. She could not contain it, breaking out before the second showing was finished.

"Trickery," she shouted, "a cheap trick, filmed on the planet below, to save their own necks and postpone the inevitable justice which the demons on Orton deserve."

"Can you be sure?" Cele asked sadly. "Can we continue with the plan of sterilization as long as there is the slightest doubt?"

"No, Lady," Toby said, feeling sympathy for the Garge. He, too, had known the painful, humiliating agony she was enduring.

"I don't think you realize what this means, Cele," Babra said. "It means that we not only call these Ortonian barbarians equals and allow our men to opt with them, but we actually acknowledge them as our superiors in some ways."

"Not superiors," Sooly said. "Equals, yes. But not in knowledge. You have knowledge we can't imagine. But she, the woman on the Planet of Cities, wants us to work together. We go into the future together, side by side. We both have something to contribute."

"If it is true," Cele said, "then we are both imperfect creations and, although I would like to believe that Ankani life sprang into being fully formed and the masters of the Galaxy, we have not been able to solve the riddle of the Wasted Worlds. We have not advanced as rapidly as the Ortonians. On a relative scale, the achievements of the Ortonians in the past two thousand years make us look like backward people."

"No, Cele," Babra cried.

"Babra, didn't you feel it? Didn't you experience the emotions of the woman as she showed what she and her race considered the ultimate in human achievement? Have you ever experienced pleasure in that degree? That alone is enough to convince me that the matter must have further investigation." She sighed. "And we dare not ignore the threat of the aliens. If it is true, they've had half a million years to arm themselves, to prepare. It is a risk we cannot take."

The *Entil,* not yet fully loaded, blinked sluggishly through the stars. Even with her beliefs crumbling around her, Cele could not bring herself to believe the story told by the ratings of blinking out into inter-Galactic space. She would not risk her ship and her crew on untried experiments. And there was another advantage to the slow, eye-popping blink home, the multiple layovers while the huge tanker's power banks charged. It gave her time to talk with the Ortonian woman, to analyze her, to see for herself, with the aid of the educator, the memories buried deep in the girl's brain. It was astounding to think that any brain could hold more than the million-billion impressions which were accumulated in an average Ortonian brain during a lifetime, but this brain could and did and when she saw, after a long, awesome session, the ships unloading the hordes of people on the green valley floor of the Ortonian continent called Africa, she was, at last, fully convinced.

Alone in her quarters, she looked at herself in the mirror. Those eyes, age-old symbols of the beauty of Ankani women, were artificial things engineered to see on dim planets—an imperfect creation—product of the very techniques which were the most odious concept in Ankani thinking. They were weak, incomplete, unable to follow the parent race into eternal bliss. She wept with her shame. She looked ahead and saw the inevitable changes, for she was certain that investigation of the circular room in the star tower on the Planet of Cities would find the engraved words there on the indestructible walls. Yes, her entire world was changing, even as the *Entil* shivered and jerked into another blink. It would never be the same and she mourned the passing of ideas which had been perfected, a meaningless word, over fifty millennia. Ankani men, always tainted with that puzzling hunger for newness, would flock to do the bidding of that woman in white with her breasts shamelessly exposed. And the planets of the distant stars would be peopled with their sons and daughters, not with pure Ankani blood. The fair skin of the Ankanis would be darkened by alien suns, browned by the mixture of bloods.

"Oh, winds of Ankan," she whispered aloud.

For the first time in her life she allowed her brain to become befuddled with stimulant, tossing down good Ankan brew, equivalent to wine, until she slept. She awoke to the realization that her bloodshot Ankani eyes had to be indicative of the Galaxy's most infernal hangover, but even though thinking was painful, she was more ready to accept. After all, past experience had proven that Ankani genes were dominant in some matters. Ankani-Ortonian girls would have large eyes and if, in exchange, they received the almost frightening vitality of the Ortonians, well, it would be a fair trade. And the outward movement toward the rim of the Galaxy would require huge new ships. Expo ships.

By the time the *Entil* startled port officers by blinking in months ahead of schedule, Cele was fully recovered. She entered the emergency meeting of Fleet Board dressed in the gorgeously understated colors of the *Entil* and enjoyed the envious glances of the shore-duty officers in their shabby uniforms. Her head high, eyes blazing with excitement, she mounted the hearing platform.

"Ladies," she said, her voice proud, unflappable, "I, Garge Cele Mantel, commanding the U.A.T. *Entil,* report respectfully that with the aid of my crew I have solved the mystery of the Wasted Worlds."

The gasps which came from the gathered ladies of the Fleet Board made the whole thing worthwhile.

21

"Toby Wellti," Sooly said in a teasing voice, as Toby primped before the mirror, "you look great as it is. If you make yourself any prettier I'll have to fight off all the young Larftons."

"A father should look his best when meeting old shipmates," Toby grinned. "And about those young Larftons—"

"Not a chance, boy," Sooly said grimly.

"What? And offend our guests?" He was grinning happily as he adjusted his sash.

"You takes your choice and you sticks by it," Sooly said, "and you done taken yours, old buddy." But in spite of her teasing tones, she felt a little pang of something. She approached him, pressed her swollen stomach against him and hugged him. "Oh, Toby, am I so ugly? Would you like to opt with one of the pretty young Larftons?"

He turned, held her at arms' length. "Little mother, no one could be half as beautiful."

The tender moment was shattered by a wail from the nursery. "The call of the wild," Sooly sighed, pulling away. Bem, five pounds lighter and frisky on a regular dosage of *troleen* and a couple of other wonderful drugs from the settlement hospital, panted into the bathroom, gave one sharp yip and waddled back toward the nursery, looking over her shoulder to see if Sooly were following.

While Sooly administered to the messy young Mari Kurt Wellti, Beth Kurt entered the front door without knocking, reporting for her babysitting job. Bem wagged her backside in greeting and returned to supervise the changing.

"She's inbound," Beth said. "If you want to see her land you'll have to hurry."

"Gee, Mother, can you finish Mari? I haven't even combed my hair." Sooly darted for the bath without waiting for an answer and Grandmother Beth finished the pin-up job and then proceeded to thoroughly spoil Mari by lifting her from her crib to bounce her on a shapely but grandmotherly knee.

Outside, the sunlight was late evening, or at least it seemed that way. She could never get used to it, she thought, but it had its compensations. None of those killer particles put out by good old Sol, just a gentle warmth and enough light, really. And the trees were close enough to being real trees and so beautiful. The mocking bird carried from Earth in the settlement ship was happily feeding a nest of young in a fruit tree and the almost grass of the lawn was doing nicely, now that the boys down at Agricenter had found the combination.

They walked the short distance to the Village Green and she was up there, a growing dot which expanded to be the size of a small mountain and made Sooly use all her will power to keep from running out from under it, for it seemed that the silently descending ship would have to fall and crush all the life out of the entire population of the village.

It didn't. The United Planets exploration ship *Earthlight* nestled as light as a feather on the large, cleared area and the Boy Scout band struck up the Ankani anthem, following it with the *Star Spangled Banner* as crewmen snapped smartly to attention in their gorgeously understated but colorful uniforms. Mantogarge Cele Mantel stepped out to stand in salute of the tiny population of the world of Sumer—outpost, bastion, planet on the edge of nowhere, home.

Cele stepped down when the band finished and approached the official welcoming stand.

"Our hearts and our homes are open to you, Lady," said Governor Toby Wellti of the planet Sumer. "And to your officers and crew."

"I bring greetings from the United Council," Cele intoned formally. "And the congratulations of both peoples for the success of your settlement."

There was more formality, a tight, impressive little ceremony which warmed the hearts of the villagers. After that there was the official banquet, at which many young crewmen, Ortonians and Ankani alike, found the fruit of Sumer to be to their liking. Toby was pleased, because, for the first time, the planet had provided all the delicacies a laden table can offer. It was late evening and the three moons of Sumer were making night into day when Cele was escorted into Sooly's cozy house.

"Christ," Cele said, taking off her hat, sitting down and kicking off her shoes. "I'm glad that's over." She smiled at Sooly. "How are the offspring?"

"This one's restive," Sooly said, patting her big stomach. "Mari is full of beans."

John Kurt entered from the kitchen, a drink in his hands, dressed in work clothing. "Hi, Cele," he said. "Have a snort?"

"I'll take one, too," Toby said, as Sooly started for the kitchen.

Cele was still not used to seeing women do the bidding of men, but the Galaxy was changing. "Jay sends his regards," she said. "We stopped on Ankan

II for minor repair. He's fit and the labs are doing marvelous work. You're not the only one," she said to Sooly, as she entered with a tray, "with that trick memory. Other Ortonians have developed it, and they're working now to narrow it down to specific areas. One day soon we'll have a mind which contains all the knowledge of your world."

"Golly," Sooly said. "I don't know if I'm ready for that. I have trouble organizing what I know now." She served drinks. "To be frank, things are moving just a bit too fast for me."

"I think I'll take a look at the offspring," Cele said, to keep from laughing. She stood over the cradle and looked at the closed, large, baby eyes, which were Ankani and beautiful. Her mind idled. Single pairings aboard the *Earthlight,* men and women forming alliances. Scattered settlements all along the rim. Ankani and Earth scientists pooling resources to make fantastic discoveries. Things were moving too fast for the girl who had set them in motion?

"God," she sighed, not noticing that she had picked up still another Ortonian word. "You should look at it from these eyes." Her lids closed slowly, covering the huge, pretty orbs. Soon she rejoined the little party.

Author Notes

Joe Haldeman's most famous work is the short story "Hero," regarded by many as one of the first stories to examine the more taboo aspects of the Vietnam Conflict in a science-fiction setting. A recipient of both the Hugo and Nebula awards, his latest book is *1968*, a non-science fiction novel drawing on his experiences in Vietnam. His short stories are sometimes lighter in tone, such as this one, which examines the different agendas of humans and aliens.

Algis Budrys has held editorial positions at *Galaxy, Fantasy and Science Fiction,* and *Ellery Queen's Mystery Magazine*. He has also been a science fiction reviewer, columnist, and worked in public relations. His novels, most notably *Rogue Moon* and *Michaelmas*, explore one man's struggle to maintain a situation that threatens to spiral out of control at any moment. He has received both the Science Fiction Writers of America Hall of Fame award, and the Mystery Writers of America award.

Theodore Sturgeon (1918-1985) combined penetrating insight into the human mind with fantasy and magic to create stories that are still relevant today. He was awarded the World Fantasy Life Achievement Award in 1985, and won both the Nebula and the Hugo awards as well. His most famous story is "Killdozer," which was made into a comic book as well as a television script. He also wrote for television, and worked as a literary agent, advertising copy editor, and a bulldozer operator.

Gene Wolfe first gained a reputation in the science fiction community with his Sevrian series, about a torturer in a society where he is deemed necessary who renounces his career, and the consequences thereof. His later novels, *Free Live Free, Soldier of the Mist,* and *Castleview,* are no less noteworthy. He has also written over one hundred short stories, many of which examine the character of mankind in both science fiction and fantasy settings. A recipient of the World Fantasy Award, he lives in Illinois.

C.M. Kornbluth (1923-1958) primarily collaborated with Frederik Pohl on novels of social science fiction, but it is his shorter works that are considered his more excellent stories. Often combining a humorous look at social mistakes with a strange sense of piercing the veils of common perception, many of his stories straddle the boundary between fantasy and science-fiction. "The Silly Season" continues this tradition.

Henry Kuttner (1915-1958) wrote many stories under pseudonyms, even going so far as to create fictional autobiographies for two of his aliases. Whatever the name his work was written under, however, the stories and novels produced are still popular today. After marrying Catherine Moore in 1940, the majority of his work was produced with her, resulting in novels like *Valley of the Flame, Fury,* and *Well of the Worlds*. The message of resisting authority is an underlying theme in many of his pieces, and this story is no exception.

J.G. Ballard is best known for his novels examining how man lives in the world he has created and what happens when that world breaks down. His novels *Crash, Concrete Island* and *High-Rise* best illustrate these ideas. Preferring to concentrate on the psyche of the human mind, he has also written what has been termed "psychological horror stories." While there has been debate as to whether his stories count as science-fiction or as speculative fiction, their power cannot be denied.

Eric Frank Russell (1905-1978) first achieved recognition in the science-fiction world with the publication of *Sinister Barrier*, the novel that launched John W. Campbells' *Unknown* magazine in 1939. Usually at the forefront of the science fiction scene during the next two decades, he was adept at tackling such humanistic issues as race relations and transposing them to the science fictional realms. His story "Allamagoosa" won the Hugo award in 1955.

Isaac Asimov (1920-1992) is probably the most well-known science fiction writer in the world. His Foundation trilogy is considered a classic of sociopolitical science fiction, examining the decline and fall of a galactic empire set thousands of years in the future. He also wrote many nonfiction articles on the theories of science itself, as well as hundreds of short stories, both science fiction and mysteries. His most famous short story, "Nightfall," about a planet's civilization which descends into anarchy when they experience the setting of their suns for the first time, was adapted into a novel with fellow author Robert Silverberg.

Chad Oliver (1928-1993) used his background as an anthropologist to form the basis for his science fiction, thereby strengthening the idea of social science as a platform for science fiction. His novels and stories of alien contact with humans realistically illustrates the differences between mankind and extraterrestrials in a fundamental way that goes far beyond physical reactions. He was born in Texas, and worked at the University of Texas as a professor of anthropology.

Zach Hughes has been freelance writing since 1962 and has had over thirty of his novels published in the last thirty years. The setting for several of his books is the United Planets Confederation, which appears in *The Book of Rack the Healer, Gold Star, Closed System* and *The Dark Side*. In "Seed of the Gods," he brings his talents to the idea of mankind's first contact with aliens. He lives in North Carolina, is married, and has two daughters.